SHARI'A AND LIFE

Authority, Compromise, and Mission in European Mosques

Drawing on five years of field studies in pragmatic- and dogmatic-inclined mosques across Europe, *Shari'a and Life* explores how Muslims engage with shari'a norms in general, and specifically with the challenges they face as Muslims living in majority non-Muslim societies.

The book examines how fatwas (advice on shari'a-related matters) are quested, negotiated, paraphrased, contested, or ignored in mosques, on the internet, and elsewhere. It also analyses individual strategies, external to religio-legal discourse, through which Muslims mitigate conflicts between interpretations of shari'a and everyday life.

Among the issues discussed in the book are financial transactions, education, the workplace, sports, electoral participation, Christmas greetings, proselytizing, and the legitimacy of choosing to live in a non-Muslim country. Shifting the focus from the authors and texts of fatwas to their recipients, *Shari'a and Life* gives voice to those often left voiceless and demonstrates the great discretion and flexibility with which tensions between shari'a and life are resolved.

URIYA SHAVIT is a professor of Islamic, Democracy, and Migration Studies at Tel Aviv University.

FABIAN SPENGLER earned a PhD from Tel Aviv University. His main research areas are Muslim minorities in the West and the discourse about Islam, education, and integration in Germany.

Shariʿa and Life

Authority, Compromise, and Mission in European Mosques

URIYA SHAVIT AND FABIAN SPENGLER

UNIVERSITY OF TORONTO PRESS
Toronto Buffalo London

© University of Toronto Press 2023
Toronto Buffalo London
utorontopress.com

ISBN 978-1-4875-5227-5 (cloth)   ISBN 978-1-4875-5504-7 (EPUB)
ISBN 978-1-4875-5437-8 (paper)   ISBN 978-1-4875-5575-7 (PDF)

Library and Archives Canada Cataloguing in Publication
Title: Shariʿa and life : authority, compromise, and mission in European mosques / Uriya Shavit and Fabian Spengler.
Names: Shavit, Uriya, author. | Spengler, Fabian, author.
Description: Includes bibliographical references and index.
Identifiers: Canadiana (print) 20230198910 | Canadiana (ebook) 20230198945 | ISBN 9781487552275 (cloth) | ISBN 9781487554378 (paper) | ISBN 9781487555047 (EPUB) | ISBN 9781487555757 (PDF)
Subjects: LCSH: Muslims – Religious life – Europe. | LCSH: Islamic law – Europe – Interpretation and construction. | LCSH: Fatwas – Europe. | LCSH: Muftis (Muslim officials) – Europe. | LCSH: Conflict of laws (Islamic law) – Europe.
Classification: LCC D1056.2.M87 S53 2023 | DDC 305.6/97094 – dc23

Cover design: EmDash Design
Cover image: Husby Mosque Stockholm, July 2018 by Uriya Shavit

We wish to acknowledge the land on which the University of Toronto Press operates. This land is the traditional territory of the Wendat, the Anishnaabeg, the Haudenosaunee, the Métis, and the Mississaugas of the Credit First Nation.

University of Toronto Press acknowledges the financial support of the Government of Canada, the Canada Council for the Arts, and the Ontario Arts Council, an agency of the Government of Ontario, for its publishing activities.

 Canada Council for the Arts   Conseil des Arts du Canada

 ONTARIO ARTS COUNCIL
CONSEIL DES ARTS DE L'ONTARIO
an Ontario government agency
un organisme du gouvernement de l'Ontario

 Funded by the Government of Canada   Financé par le gouvernement du Canada

To the beloved memory of
Pnina Shavit
Hildegard Spengler

Contents

List of Illustrations and Tables ix

Acknowledgments xi

Note on Transliteration xiii

Introduction 3

1 The Religious Law of Muslim Minorities 21

2 Across a Wasati-Salafi European Spectrum 65

3 The Mustafti Is the Mufti 107

4 There's Shariʿa, and There's Life 144

5 A Mission with Few Missionaries 185

Conclusion 216

Notes 225

Bibliography 247

Index 269

Illustrations and Tables

Illustrations

2.1   The Stockholm Mosque   67
2.2   'Umar Ibn al-Khattab Mosque, Dortmund   76
2.3   The Grand Mosque of Iceland, Reykjavik   83
2.4   The Salafi Mosque, Birmingham   93
2.5   The Salafi Bookstore, Birmingham   102
2.6   Hassan Blidi Mosque, Marseille   106

Tables

3.1   Knowledge about the existence of the European Council for Fatwa and Research   110
3.2   Opinions regarding gathering knowledge about Islamic law on the internet   127
3.3   Opinions about the European Council for Fatwa and Research and the Saudi Council of Senior Scholars   128
3.4   Views on controversial religio-legal issues   131
4.1   The role of shari'a in everyday life   148

Acknowledgments

We are thankful to Dr. Carl Yonker, Tel Aviv University, for helping us improve the manuscript, and to Hakan Yar, MSc, a long-time friend and insightful observer of European realities, for his instruction and advice regarding the statistical methods applied in the study and the analysis of the data. The late Prof. Yechiel Klar directed us to indispensable studies in social psychology. He is badly missed.

We are also thankful to al-Hasan Badar, Amir Oneli, and Tamar Lidar for their assistance in different stages of this study. Research for this book was supported by the Israel Science Foundation (grant number 1434/17). We are thankful to Mali Zur of Tel Aviv University's Research Authority for her patient and generous cooperation.

We thank the three anonymous reviewers for comments and corrections that helped us improve an earlier version of the study. We are greatly indebted to Stephen Shapiro, acquisition editor, University of Toronto Press, for his wise advice that made the finalization of the project and publication of this book possible. We are also thankful to Mary Lui, managing editor, for her insightful comments, and to Dr. Melanie Magidow for her meticulous copyediting.

Our deepest gratitude goes to hundreds of mosque attendees, imams, and members of mosque boards who participated in this study. They shared with us personal thoughts and daily practices and generously gave us their trust and their time, while we could offer them in return nothing but our curiosity. Any contribution this book may have to the understanding of the relation between shariʿa and life belongs first and foremost to them.

Note on Transliteration

We have generally relied on IJMES guidelines. However, we did not include diacritics, which are of little use for readers who are not proficient in Arabic, and, given the limited Arabic vocabulary in this book, are not essential for those who are. Names of imams and other public activists were transliterated to English as they transliterate them. The names of some muftis, as well as their transliterations, in particular those who are *salafi*, appear in different publications in different forms, and in some cases appear in different forms even in the same publication, resulting in some bibliographical variations.

SHARI'A AND LIFE

Introduction

In the introduction to his masterful *Magellan: Der Mann und seine Tat*, Stefan Zweig, a skilled soul surgeon, commented that books are born of quite different sentiments. Some books are authored out of excitement. Others out of gratitude. Still others out of embitterment, rage, and anger. Curiosity, the desire of writers to make sense for themselves of people and events, is a motivation, but so are impure drives such as arrogance, greed, and narcissism. Zweig urged authors to self-reflect, upon entering a new project, on what their inner motivation really is.[1]

In the case of the work before you, figuring out the motivation was an easy task. We pursued it in order to learn more about a crucial question that previous studies, including studies by these authors, left open: What impact has the religio-legal discourse of *fiqh al-aqalliyyat al-Muslima* (the religious law of Muslim minorities) had on its primary target audience, European Muslims?

Fiqh al-aqalliyyat al-Muslima is a field of Islamic jurisprudence that deals with religio-legal challenges resulting from the massive migration to and permanent settlement of millions of Muslims in Western countries since the Second World War – starting with whether such settlement is religiously legitimate. It has developed intensively since the 1980s through the issuance of fatwas on issues ranging from the permissibility of receiving Christmas bonuses to the permissibility of serving in Western military forces, as well as through treatises that developed theoretical guidelines as to how the field should be engaged with.

The most prolific and systematic contributions to *fiqh al-aqalliyyat al-Muslima* represented two coherent and contesting approaches developed mainly (but not only) in Arabic by experts based in the Arab world or descending from it. One, the *wasati*, pragmatic and integration-inclined, championed by the Egyptian-born and Qatar-based Yusuf al-Qaradawi and the Dublin-based European Council for Fatwa and

4 Shari'a and Life

Research, and another, the *salafi*, dogmatic and introverted, associated with the Saudi religious establishment.[2]

Academic studies on *fiqh al-aqalliyyat al-Muslima* discourse have focused either on textual analysis of fatwas and treatises or on the political motivations and organizational structures of their main producers and disseminators.[3] On the other hand, the reception of the discourse or of elements within it by its intended audience was primarily given anecdotal attention. Thus, we know very little about the extent to which European Muslims engaged with *fiqh al-aqalliyyat al-Muslima* and what they made of what it offers.

The response of recipients is a worthy issue to investigate with regard to any corpus of publicized texts. It is of particular interest in studying shari'a discourses because the scope of public responsiveness, and interpretive loyalty to the texts such discourses introduce, is fundamental to their evaluation.

In a normative sense, the shari'a comprises the instructions presented by God and His final Prophet, Muhammad, to humanity through the Quran and the examples set by the Prophet through his speech and conduct, recorded and passed on. It is oriented to an idealized past, which contemporaries repeatedly interpret.

A core notion of the Muslim faith is that following the shari'a is the way to find peace and balance in this life and heavenly rewards in the afterlife. This notion involves a moral warning that breaching boundaries set by the shari'a constitutes defiance of God, while allowing space for negotiations of what those boundaries are.

To find out expert opinion about what the shari'a requires, Muslims may act as *mustafti*s (inquirers on shari'a-related matters) and engage in *istifta'* (the act of inquiring, either through explorations of existing responses or initiation of independent new queries). The Islamic tradition encourages Muslims to do so when they are unsure what the shari'a instructs about a certain situation; or hesitate over which of several interpretations contained in it is correct; or are certain about what it requires but wonder if their particular circumstances could justify concessions. Then muftis provide *mustafti*s with opinions in the form of fatwas (advice on shari'a-related matters) that draw on their general approach to the shari'a.[4] It may also be the case that muftis address a matter they consider of social importance without being specifically approached by individuals or groups.

The raison d'être of muftis is to impact the actual world in line with their specific understandings of religious norms. Some people compose poems and conceal them in drawers (though few do not entertain secret hopes for the ultimate discovery and public praise of their lines). But

Introduction   5

there is no evidence for the existence of muftis or wannabe muftis who author fatwas without the intention of making them public.

Because fatwas are responses to the realities of life, produced through communications between non-experts and experts who aim to shape those realities, they have the potential to inform us about the social contexts in which they appear. They can expose issues that concerned Muslims in different times and places, how Muslims presented their concerns, and what were the more and the less dominant religio-legal norms of their time.

However, analyses restricted to the textual content of fatwas have considerable limitations as small or large mirrors of social practices and norms and risk privileging and distorting certain realities while ignoring others. Talal Asad pointed to the modern tendency to consider the ability to articulate religious knowledge as a prerequisite for religious practice.[5] It is obvious why fatwas can tell us nothing about Muslims who do not consider themselves committed to the shari'a at all. Yet they can also tell us very little about Muslims who do but practice religion without inquiring about religio-legal issues, or about those who are confident that their own judgments are as good as anyone else's.

Another limitation is that it is difficult to verify the authenticity of such texts: that *mustaftis* are who they claim to be; that the mufti did not make up a query for didactic or other purposes; and that the text, printed in a compilation or another form, is loyal to the original fatwa.[6] Yet another is that when not accompanied by anthropological inquiries, an investigation focused on the texts of fatwas will inevitably leave us guessing what *mustaftis* actually understood from the advice they were given, how they chose between different opinions when faced with such a choice, and what of their choices they actually applied to everyday life situations and to what extent. Even if we can somehow authenticate that a certain *mustafti* presented a certain query to a mufti and establish that the *mustafti* loyally understood and applied the terms of the fatwa issued, we would still not know how representative the inquirer's conduct was of society at large.

It makes particular sense, therefore, to study fatwa discourses, not only textually but also anthropologically. Giving due attention to their diffusion and to the effects they have on their recipients, we aim to go beyond the three layers of analysis allowed by the study of the texts of fatwas, as noted by Larsen – the question, the answer, and the justification.[7] We explore an additional layer, the reception, examining not only what muftis were asked and what they said about different realities, but also what, if at all, Muslims made of and applied of what muftis said.

6 Shari'a and Life

Studies of Muslim societies offer a distinctly small number of anthropologically or psychologically oriented works that focus on the engagements and responses of the intended audiences of fatwas (the same applies to Jewish studies, regarding the recipients of rabbinical edicts). While prolific literature analyses the contents of fatwas and the power structures and ideologies that produced them (as is the case in the study of rabbinical edicts), we know almost nothing about the intensity with which *mustaftis* approach experts, who those *mustaftis* are, how they understand the advice they receive, how they determine whether to accept, reject, or mitigate advice given, how they choose between conflicting advice, and to what extent their choices reflect broader trends.

Obviously, when studying *istifta'* of the past, only printed texts have a voice. Analyzing how they were understood and the extent to which they were applied borders, in most cases (albeit not in all), on the impossible. Anthropological studies of present-day *istifta'* are, on the other hand, possible to conduct, just as any other studies on the reception of texts. Yet, they present particular challenges.

To begin with, mufti-*mustafti* communications are, in large part, transmitted orally, in different forms, including private conversations. As a result, establishing the scope and impact of their totalities on the lives of individuals requires engagement with texts that are difficult to observe and record.[8] Then, understanding what *mustaftis* made of fatwas, and the extent to which they are guided by experts in everyday life decisions, if at all, requires presenting people of faith with intimate questions about beliefs and conduct. This includes pressing them to reflect on their innermost thoughts about their beliefs, reveal practices and compromises they are possibly less than proud of, betray the limitations of their religious knowledge, and express criticism about eminent scholars.

Indeed, while considerable academic attention has been oriented to the anthropological study of Islam as a lived experience, *mustafti*-mufti relations and the social impacts of fatwas have largely been overlooked. This has also been the case in the anthropological study of social manifestations of Islam in Europe.[9]

The lacuna in anthropological analyses of fatwas counters the broader trend in the study of texts. Over the past four decades, in particular, the recipients of texts – be they novels, medical bulletins, juicy gossip, jokes, political speeches, scenes in feature films and sitcoms, or famous last words – have gained intense scholarly attention, providing nuanced theoretical and rich descriptive literature about the reception and contextualization of diverse kinds of content. Studies have introduced recipients of texts as active and independent participants in the continuous creation of functions and interpretations. They have celebrated the human capacity to imagine, innovate, and distort; to make of the text something that was possibly not intended by its original producer.

"People read the same text differently for the same reason they have different preferences in religions or in noses: themselves." So explained Holland in 1975, laying the foundations for Reader Response Theory in his study of readers' diverse engagements with William Faulkner's "A Rose for Emily."[10] He offered a model of four principles of the literary experience, the first suggesting that if a reader responded positively to a literary work, he has been able to put elements of the work together so they act out of his lifestyle.[11]

Another classic study published around that time, Ginzburg's *Il formaggio e i vermi* (The Cheese and the Worms), became a model for how a single text (in this case, legal documents) can inform about the cultural world of a single forgotten individual. It speculated what books were read by a sixteenth-century stubborn and imaginative Italian miller and how, in part through his distortion of the meanings of the ideas contained in them, those books may have shaped the blasphemous views for which he was interrogated, and ultimately burned, by the Roman Inquisition.[12]

Subsequent studies similarly demonstrated that texts are understood in ways defined by recipients' age, education, ethnicity, socio-economic status, ideological convictions, tendencies, and psychological conditions, resulting in their assuming of different and even conflicting interpretations. One particularly appealing example is a demonstration of how Israelis understood episodes of the American soap opera Dallas, which captured the nation's attention in the early 1980s, when Israel had only one, and public, television channel. Liebes and Katz showed that ethnic backgrounds determine how individuals retell and interpret storylines. Arab Israelis and Israeli Jews of Moroccan extraction retold the plots linearly and related the plots from a sociological perspective that focused on the protagonists' status in the family. In contrast, Israeli Jews of Russian extraction retold the same plots schematically and interpreted them as American capitalist propaganda.[13]

The shift in scholarly focus from authors to the recipients of their works also demonstrated that people may approach the same texts to serve different and multiple emotional, educational, and social functions. Just as any other product competing in a market, texts find customers by responding to their specific, diverse, and potentially changing needs and expectations. Their ability to do so determines their popularity.

8   Shariʿa and Life

Studies in this area tended to focus on non-canonical works, whose existence and popularity depend on their responsiveness to the demands of the market. One of the pioneering and classic examples, Radway's study of women's reasons for reading romantic novels, found that different primary motivations, which are not mutually exclusive, encourage the purchase of books from this genre of easy reads, including escaping daily problems, learning about faraway places, and relishing in the knowledge that the plots would always have a happy ending.[14] Other studies similarly demonstrated the diverse motivations for consuming different genres of popular print and visual texts, from pulp fiction[15] to porn movies,[16] from softcover thrillers and spy fiction[17] to soap operas.[18]

Another instructive contribution of studying recipients rather than authors was enriching the understanding of how and why texts change through lines of transmission in ways that, in some cases, alter their original meaning. The process of transmission was described as a process of paraphrasing, in which diverse versions of an original text are born.

Studies suggested that the content of texts, and the context of their telling, impact how they are engaged with and retold. One example is the work of Stubbersfield, Tehrani, and Flynn, who explored the changing contents of urban legends, tales whose original authors are hard to identify. They argued, controversially, that because humans are more dispositioned to handle social situations than survivalist ones, they tend to retell information of the former kind contained in urban legends more accurately than information related to health and security.[19]

The minimal supply of similar anthropological and psychological studies on the reception of fatwas at large, and in the field of the religious law of Muslim minorities, in particular, created a challenge for us in pursuing this project because there was little comparative empirical data to guide us. But it was also a source of encouragement. While our initial objectives were limited to descriptive documentation and analysis of how certain European Muslims engage with a discourse focused on their particular situations, as our work progressed, we began to think of our case studies as a potential contribution to a broad theoretical understanding of aspects of mufti-*mustafti* relations and the processes through which fatwas are approached, understood, accepted, rejected, negotiated or ignored in modern times.

This book, therefore, presents a twofold ambition. First, to inform about the specific impact *fiqh al-aqalliyyat al-Muslima* discourse has had in certain European Muslim publics. Second, to introduce patterns and typologies that, if supported by future comparative studies in other contexts, would allow for broader theorizing on the sociology of religious law.

Fiqh al-aqalliyyat al-Muslima comprises textual treatments of hundreds of issues, some bearing potential effect on most Muslims who live in the West, and some only on a fraction; some on which broad agreements exist within the discourse, and some on which heated debates surfaced. It involves complicated and nuanced challenges, and relatively trivial ones. While we explored a diversity of social issues discussed in *fiqh al-aqalliyyat al-Muslima*, our anthropological investigations focused on the reception of three groundbreaking options contained in this discourse at large.

One option the discourse offers was opened by the ambitious statement of mission presented by the *wasati* European Council for Fatwa and Research that sought to become an exclusive or at least primary authority for all Muslims in Europe on issues pertinent to the shari'a. In a European Muslim reality characterized by organizational divisions, ideological polemics, and contesting fatwas on crucial and trivial issues alike, the idea that communities and individuals should embrace uniformed *ifta'* produced by a trans-ethnic, transnational panel had transformative cohesive potential.

A second option opened by *fiqh al-aqalliyyat al-Muslima* discourse was applying shari'a-grounded pragmatic facilitations to resolve conflicts between shari'a norms and the realities of living in Western societies. The *wasati* approach suggested that a correct interpretation of the shari'a calls for granting Muslim minorities special concessions and controversially applied long-established fiqh mechanisms to that end. The implication was that certain shari'a norms could be transgressed within the confines of shari'a interpretations and through the authority of experts on fiqh. Accepting this position had the potential to bring relief to Muslims navigating between religious norms and the norms of Western societies. Rejecting *wasati* pragmatism could also be meaningful, endowing those who do so consciously with a sense of enhanced religiosity and devotion.

A third option the discourse opened was the infusion of a theological meaning and a spiritual task to movements of migration that were encouraged predominantly by financial considerations. Almost all participants in the discourse, including *wasatis* and *salafis* alike – the former generously and the latter grudgingly – advanced the notion that Muslim presence in the West was legitimate (and even desired) if Muslim migrants become a proselytizing vanguard working to make Islam the universally hegemonic religion it was promised to be. The missionary ideology had the potential to reconcile migrants' concerns that they

10   Shari'a and Life

favoured material gains over faith by moving to the West, assuage any sense of alienation and marginalization felt by migrants, and establish an enhanced, prouder religious identity.

Our field studies in European mosques collected data regarding what, if at all, certain leaderships and attendees know about the core groundbreaking options introduced in *fiqh al-aqalliyyat al-Muslima* discourse and their chief disseminators, when and why they attend to these options, and how they select between conflicting opinions about these options. The data we assembled resulted in several broader observations about the dynamics of *istifta'* by the individuals studied, which are at the heart of this book:

- Fatwas are sought out and then accepted, rejected, or mitigated in non-structured and non-committed ways. With few exceptions, and regardless of their orientations and levels of education, *mustafti*s refrain from aligning with one specific mufti or panel of muftis and insist on their right and duty to serve as the ultimate arbiters regarding the validity of fatwas.
- Fatwas rarely directly impact major life decisions in a hierarchical manner of a query presented and advice subsequently heeded. Contemplating existential matters, *mustafti*s tend to seek out fatwas and invoke them to justify inclinations they already have or actions already taken.
- Fatwas, and their conclusions, including those that received much publicity and scholarly attention, have different existences: as what their texts actually say, a form in which they are familiar to few, if at all; and as shadows-outside-the-cave, what paraphrases, re-interpretations, and contextualizations make of them through lines of transmission influenced by the personal situations, inclinations of the heart, and the intellectual capacity of their recipients.
- Although direct and comparative readings by mosque leaderships and attendees of the actual texts of fatwas issued by qualified muftis are minimal, public opinions about controversial issues correlate with the scope of the discursive agreement. Across the spectrum of orientations, the more discursively controversial the legitimization of a prohibition is, the less support it gains among mosque attendees.
- Some *mustafti*s comfortably shift between shari'a-grounded pragmatism where the issue at hand affects them personally and shari'a-grounded dogmatism where it does not. This transitioning allows them to preserve an image of strict religiosity while accommodating where it matters most.
- The internet is a significant resource for instruction on shari'a-norms, yet it is also widely suspected as unreliable and shunned.

The pluralistic and highly competitive development of Islamic online operations encourages a lack of commitment to a particular platform by users who do trust it.

- *Istifta'* and the attainment of fatwa-based pragmatic concessions is only one of the means through which conflicts between shari'a norms and the pressures of life are resolved within a religious context. Other strategies include: (a) confession of sin – acknowledging that an unlawful act was committed and that the potential consequence could be a heavenly punishment; (b) minimization of sin – explaining that while the prohibited was committed, the scope of the transgression was minimized to the best ability of the transgressor; (c) universalization of sin – stating that the prohibited could not have been avoided in a different environment; (d) separation of spheres – arguing that while the shari'a should be respected in all aspects of life as a matter of principle, it is impossible to abide by it concerning particular aspects of life.
- Pragmatic strategies external to *istifta'* are also applied by Muslims who are ideologically dogmatic. That is one reason why adherence to dogmatic *salafi* ideology carries fewer injuries than what its texts imply. Other reasons are the localized and mitigated versions of this approach that *salafi* leaderships in Europe advance, as well as the lack of relevancy of several dogmatic constraints to the actual lives of some *salafis*. Thus, as categories of practice, 'pragmatism' and 'dogmatism' are less coherently distinguishable than as notional textually-constructed categories.
- Ideological embrace of a legitimizing narrative does not necessarily lead to practicing demands for action presented in the narrative, while practicing such demands does not necessarily involve notional acceptance of the narrative's terms.

Fiqh and Ifta'

A few introductory notes about fiqh and *ifta'* are in order. Fiqh is the science of ascertaining what the instructions of the divine Lawgiver are. It is turned to especially when the Quran and the Prophetic traditions offer no explicit instructions or when pertinent instructions appear to conflict with other instructions. To decide on such situations, experts invoke hierarchies between the Quran and the traditions, as well as between Quranic verses, and apply analogies of various kinds.

Fiqh investigations apply different points of view and methodologies that yield contesting results. The Sunni tradition developed as inherently pluralistic with the emergence of four schools of law (*madhahib*)

12   Shari'a and Life

in the ninth century, which established distinct corpora of *ifta'*. Specialists in fiqh did not consider competing *madhahib* as beyond the pale of legitimate Islam.

The function of the mufti is almost as old as Islam itself. It has rested on the principle that all Muslims are obligated to act in accordance with God's laws, but not all are equally skilled and experienced in the science of fiqh. When uncertain about an issue of shari'a, Muslims should voluntarily seek the advice of experts with profound knowledge.[20]

There developed in Sunni Islam agreed upon criteria as to who is an eligible mufti. These include being of mature age, sound mind, moral and just character, and having a good command of the Arabic language, the Quran, the Prophetic traditions, *tafsir* (Quranic exegesis), and the science of fiqh. Until modern times, establishing a reputation as a mufti involved studying in a madrasa, a school for the instruction of Islam, being mentored by an experienced mufti or muftis, the ultimate accreditation of a pupil as qualified to issue religio-legal opinions, and then the establishment of a reputation within a community through the issuance of fatwas and other religious studies. The prestige of the mentor had a potential impact on the status of his student.[21]

In modern times, the process of becoming a mufti has been academically institutionalized, as has been the case with other fields of specialization. While even in today's Islamic world a state-regulated academic certificate is not a legal condition for holding the title of mufti and being respected as such, it borders on being a prerequisite. Muftis in our time are usually people who have university-level education in the study of fiqh and related topics, attained in institutions where the curricula are not taught or adjusted individually. Holding a doctoral degree, or at least an MA, in fiqh from a prestigious university and publishing treatises that gain the approval of eminent scholars is the safe path to becoming a respected mufti, similar to how reputation is established in other academic fields.

The combination of openness to a plethora of external influences and the production of knowledge by academic elites have, in and of themselves, the potential to create substantial gaps between expert articulations of what the shari'a dictates and broader social inclinations and interpretations. The advice muftis give is a human effort (even from a religious point of view), and as such, it springs from society. But not all of society is involved in its production, and thus it cannot be taken for granted that it mirrors more than the efforts of those involved.[22]

Unlike *qadis*, state-appointed judges who rule in accordance with shari'a and whose decisions may be enforced through the police power of the state, the advice muftis issue in response to individual queries carries only moral weight. This weakness is also a potential source of strength. As demonstrated by Agrama, the voluntary nature of engaging with muftis, their personalized case-based treatment, which allows for mutual interactions and empathy, the non-adversarial nature of approaching them, and their freedom to issue decisions independently of political institutions and laws perceived as human-made, can endow them with more public esteem than that acquired by religious courts appointed by the state and operating strictly within its confines.[23]

Muftis do not always function without the power of the state behind them. Some Muslim regimes made the decisions of a state-appointed mufti or panel of muftis binding on some issues. The religious obligation to abide by those decisions could then be legitimized, even if they are deemed erroneous, based on the religio-juristic notion of avoiding *fitna*, civil strife that could result in anarchy.[24] However, compelled obedience is different from an assertion of truth or correctness.

In the post-Ottoman Muslim world, nation-states created hierarchical structures of muftis to assert governmental control over society and enhance social cohesion. They established fatwa panels to advise the government and the judiciary and scrutinize and legitimize the compatibility of their actions with the shari'a, as well as issue fatwas in response to queries of individual *mustafti*s. Such panels include, for example, the offices of grand muftis in Egypt and Saudi Arabia and their higher offices for *ifta'*, the Egyptian Dar al-Ifta',[25] and the Saudi Hay'at Kibar al-'Ulama' (Council of Senior Scholars).[26] While the bureaucratic premise of state-regulated *ifta'* panels is confined to the nation-state, these panels also address queries by citizens of other states. Pan-Islamic transnational panels, for example, the Islamic Fiqh Council of the Muslim World League, are, by the nature of their organization, composition, and statement of mission, transnational bodies that aim to serve Muslims wherever they live.

Muslims who are not qualified muftis (and do not claim to be) can still earn recognition in their communities and beyond them as reliable sources for the instruction of the shari'a. Such "lesser authorities" include Muslims who demonstrate a convincing enough proficiency in the sources of jurisprudence to offer valuable advice.

Imams, the religious heads of mosques who lead the prayers and guide the community, are a primary example. They do not always hold academic-level education in fiqh and are usually not qualified muftis. Even so, they may be recognized by attendees of their mosques as people with greater knowledge of the requirements of Islam, as well as more resourceful in locating correct advice. It helps if they manifest certain exceptional skills, such as having memorized the entire Quran

14   Shari'a and Life

by heart. The more they gain the respect of attendees as sources for religious guidance, the more their position vis-à-vis the board or organization that pays their salary improves.[27] *Mustafti*s may also seek the advice of trusted teachers, proselytizers, family members, and friends and independently search for answers in archives and compilations of existing fatwas.

Technological developments have lessened the dependency of *mustafti*s on local experts and resources. In pre-modern times, other than conferring with a mufti, or with another expert, who could be approached in person, there were few options for a person who wanted to consult with a distant expert on a pressing matter that was not sufficiently answered in books. The most sensible way was to write a letter.[28] But doing so required that the *mustafti* was literate, or could find someone who would write and read for him; that the *mustafti* had the financial means to send the letter; that the matter at hand was not urgent, and that it was not trivial, or else there would be no point in going through the trouble; and that there was a reason for the *mustafti* to believe that an authority on fiqh that is not easily accessible is more likely to provide sound advice than one that is readily available.

The existence of all these conditions was exceptional, and as a result, sending such letters was not commonplace. Much of what we know about the presence of religious concepts in the daily lives of Muslims in medieval times is based on various correspondences of *ifta'* that have been preserved. However, those correspondence reflect the more challenging, paramount, and principal dilemmas that engrossed communities, rather than the totality of issues that concerned people and were most likely asked and addressed orally between *mustafti*s and the most respected of the accessible authorities in their vicinity.

The relative increase in literacy rates and the introduction of printing presses and mass media to the Muslim world in the nineteenth and twentieth centuries broadened the possibilities available to *mustafti*s. But, in practical terms, they remained limited because the means for searching for opinions beyond those delivered by local experts who could be accessed in person continued to require considerably more time, effort, and, in some cases, also money. For example, presenting a query to a mufti writing in a newspaper or journal still involved the cost and effort of sending a letter, and the waiting period of the time it took the letter to arrive, the expert to write his response, and the newspaper to print it – and it was far from guaranteed the query would be answered at all. Seeking advice in this manner on a pressing matter was inefficient and doing so on a trivial matter made no sense. To browse for relevant advice on a specific issue in books, a person had to either have a decent library or have the time to visit a library or a bookstore – and it was possible that the search would end in frustration.

Internet websites, social media, and satellite channels have offered radical solutions to these limitations with the proliferation since the late 1990s of platforms that present archives of fatwas and muftis who could be consulted online. The effort involved in presenting queries to distant experts was minimized. For people with internet connections, it required no additional costs. Reaching out to experts from any place to any place around the globe was as easy as reaching out to a person living in the neighbourhood. Thanks to search engines, browsing through already existing fatwas was far more effective than any of the previous means of locating relevant opinions.[29]

The core requirement of the shari'a is that people avoid impermissible acts (haram) and engage only in permissible acts (halal). Acts that are not impermissible can fall under the categories of mandatory (*wajib*), recommended (*mustahab*), neutral (*mubah*), and disliked (*makruh*). An important part of the work of muftis and other authorities consulted is to help *mustafti*s recognize to which category acts they have already performed or are considering performing belong.

The most sensitive decision a mufti or expert can make is to declare that an act that is unequivocally recognized as impermissible is conditionally legitimized because of specific circumstances. Deciding this to be the case does not transform the haram into halal; rather, it recognizes that exceptional conditions justify the temporary suspension of prohibitions. The debate as to which circumstances justify such suspensions, particularly regarding Muslims living in majority non-Muslim societies, has potential existential implications. This debate is at the heart of the *wasati-salafi* polemic in *fiqh al-aqalliyyat al-Muslima* discourse.

An introduction to that polemic is the subject of the first chapter that explores *wasati* and *salafi* ideologies, methodologies, and organizations that participate in *fiqh al-aqalliyyat al-Muslima* discourse. The second chapter explores the spectrum of mosques in which field research for this study was conducted. The third examines the impact the *wasati* European Council for Fatwa and Research has had on mosque attendees from different orientations and how they view its ambition for exclusive authority. The fourth focuses on strategies applied by mosque attendees to pragmatically resolve conflicts between their interpretations of shari'a norms and the pressures of life in the West. The fifth explores approaches to the concept of the Muslim migrant as a missionary, whose presence in Europe is legitimized through contributions to spreading Islam.

Research Methodology

The book is based on two levels of field studies conducted in 2016–19, the fundamental one in four European mosques, whose leaderships were found in preliminary research to reflect different positions on a spectrum of approaches to the *wasati-salafi* polemic. These are the ethnically diverse Stockholm Mosque (also known as the Stockholm Grand Mosque, the Stockholm Central Mosque, and, officially, the Zayd b. Nahyan Mosque), whose leadership affiliates with and commits to the decisions of the *wasati* European Council for Fatwa and Research; the predominantly ethnically Moroccan Dortmund-based ʿUmar Ibn al-Khattab Mosque, whose leadership is pragmatic-inclined and where Moroccan experts are privileged; The Grand Mosque of Reykjavik, whose leadership is pragmatic-inclined, does not privilege any authority, and endeavours to distance itself from past *salafi* influences; and Birmingham's Salafi Mosque, a hub of British and European *salafiyya*, that aligns with the agenda of the leading contemporary Saudi muftis and *iftaʾ* panels and is one of its chief disseminators in the West.

The populations surveyed do not represent European Muslims at large. Rather, the study deliberately focused on Muslim populations hypothesized to have the greatest likelihood of engaging with *fiqh al-aqalliyyat al-Muslima* discourse.

First, the study involved only Muslims approached in mosques. Yet not all Muslims in Europe attend mosques, and while it is difficult to assess the number of those who do not, they are not a negligible minority. Islamic identity is manifested through different world views and approaches, including secularism which denies or is sceptical about the revealed authority of religious norms and practices and does not privilege the shariʿa as a source of guidance. Adherence to that option does not necessarily mean that a person will never frequent a mosque (a practice that may be encouraged for traditionalist, cultural, social, or other reasons). Still, a study focused exclusively on mosque attendees is likely to under-represent Muslims who are alienated, indifferent, or care little about the notion of revealed law.

Second, not all the mosques in Europe are predominantly attended by Muslims originating from Arabic-speaking countries or are led by Arab imams or by imams affiliated with authorities in the Arabic-speaking world (or all the above), whereas at least one of these criteria applies to each of the mosques we surveyed. Given that *fiqh al-aqalliyyat al-Muslima* has primarily developed in the Arabic-speaking world and is authored mainly in Arabic, the sample involved European Muslims with a greater potential to be knowledgeable about the discourse.

Third, in the mosques we surveyed, the leaderships are opinionated about *fiqh al-aqalliyyat al-Muslima* discourse, the options contained in it, and the pragmatism/dogmatism chasm that underlines it. In two of them, the leaderships openly and adamantly affiliate with the *wasati* or the *salafi* approach (which does not mean that the attendees do, as the book will show). This is not reflective of the situation in all European mosques; our visits to several ethnic-Turkish mosques, for example, suggested that chasm is largely unfamiliar there.

The study of the four mosques involved a mixed method of semi-structured interviews and written questionnaires. The 78 interviewees at the four mosques included imams, administrative leaders, and mosque attendees. We approached attendees inside the prayer halls of the mosques, on their way in and out of them, or in attached book-stores, introduced ourselves, and explained our study's objectives. Most of the interviews were conducted on the premises of the mosques or on nearby benches and in cafes.[30]

The interviews involved similar sets of questions. These included the biographies of interviewees; their knowledge of fiqh concepts and terminologies as well as of muftis and *ifta'* panels; the conditions that encourage or discourage their engagement in *istifta'*; the authorities they chose to consult with and the means and frequency of doing so; how they decide whether to accept, reject, or mitigate fatwas; what the last religio-legal issue they searched for was; their opinions on debated issues in *fiqh al-aqalliyyat al-Muslima* discourse; how and when they developed those opinions, and the practical implications they had on their lives; and their notions about the legitimacy of living in a non-Muslim country and of their roles as Muslims living in Europe.

We often had the impression that interviewees were happy about the opportunity to discuss their relation to the shari'a and the challenges of living in a non-Muslim country. In part, it was because it helped them make sense for themselves of how they understand issues that matter a great deal ideologically but are often neglected in the feverishness and noise of life.

While our research focus was clear and unconcealed, we welcomed being led astray from the designed structure to any theme interviewees wished to broach. In hindsight, the flexibility helped us better assess the actual importance the issues and concepts highlighted in our hypotheses have in the interviewees' experiences.

Interviews were conducted in Arabic, English, French, and German, based on the choice of the interviewees. We recorded only interviewees who gave permission to do so; otherwise, we relied on notes. Most interviews ended in one session, but we met several interviewees more

18   Shari'a and Life

than once and also outside the mosque or its proximity. We mention only the first name of interviewees and changed them for those who requested this.

The written questionnaires were distributed randomly among mosque attendees outside the entrances of the mosques before and after a Friday congregational prayer. Respondents were handed a pen and a candy and were given a brief explanation about the study.[31]

The main purpose of the questionnaires was to provide a control for the semi-structured interviews. For the interviews, we approached attendees at the entrances of mosques throughout the week, when the population present is sparse relative to Friday congregational prayers. As a result, the interviews give an outsized voice to the exceptionally devout, volunteers, retirees, unemployed, and people who live or work close to the mosque. Randomly surveying the attendees going in and out of mosques when at their fullest capacity offered indications that the opinions expressed by interviewees do not radically differ from those of these mosques' general populations.

The questionnaires inquired about similar issues to those discussed in the interviews, only without the depth allowed by conversations. Participants were asked for their age, occupation, family status, and country of origin. They were asked whether they knew the main *wasati* and *salafi* panels of *ifta'* and, if they did, they were asked to rank their approval of these panels on a scale of one (most negative) to ten (most positive). They were also asked to note whether they regulate all, some, or no aspects of their lives in accordance with the shari'a and their primary sources of education on shari'a in their childhoods. They were asked to rank the reliability of the internet as a source for knowledge about the shari'a and whether they searched for fatwas online and sent queries to online sources over the past year. They were requested to state their views on some of the central issues debated in *fiqh al-aqalliyyat al-Muslima* discourse, including whether they accepted or rejected the conditional legitimacy of mortgages for Muslims in Europe who have no alternative, extending Christmas greetings, and electoral participation.

The manner in which the surveys were conducted made it possible to verify that only people who attended the mosques studied participated and that they answered the questionnaires independently. The downside of basing surveys on reaching out to populations of dozens or hundreds of attendees entering or leaving mosques almost at the same time was relatively small samples, resulting in high margins of error.

An alternative or complementary method could have been conducting online surveys with respondents affiliated with mosques or Muslim organizations.[32] However, not all mosques have email lists of registered members, and those with such lists would not necessarily share them with us.

We found that, in any case, in the context of this study, the disadvantages of this method would outweigh its advantages. First, even if mosques had such lists and shared them, it would have been impossible to verify whether respondents actually still associate with those mosques and whether they still reside in the town or the country. Second, online surveys allow for quick Google searches while responding, and, therefore, the credibility of responses to knowledge-based questions could be damaged. Third, it is likely that people who are not technologically inclined or reluctant to provide personal information online would not participate in online surveys. For a study seeking to establish data on attitudes towards authority, including the usage of online sources for *istifta'*, a gross misrepresentation of these groups would be damaging.

To better understand the sociological and intellectual environments in which attendees of the four mosques surveyed engage with religious identity and norms, we visited in the course of the study dozens of additional mosques that are in geographical proximity or in ideological agreement or rivalry with them. In these mosques, we interviewed imams and members of the administration, as well as some attendees, and surveyed the libraries or attached bookstores. In four of these mosques, we conducted written surveys identical to those undertaken in the four mosques that were the focus of the study, providing a richer and more nuanced spectrum for the quantitative part of the study.

The four are the Husby Mosque, Stockholm, where the leadership are open competitors of The Stockholm Mosque and have leaned toward *salafiyya* but present a nuanced approach towards the *wasati* European Council for Fatwa and Research; Dortmund's Markaz Imam Malik Mosque, which is ethnically Moroccan and where the leadership privileges Moroccan authorities as in 'Umar Ibn al-Khattab Mosque, but where the imam has significantly greater seniority; Reykjavik's Al-Nur Mosque, a multi-ethnic mosque from which the leadership of Reykjavik's Grand Mosque split, which advances a more pragmatic approach than its rival, and is hostile to the European Council for Fatwa and Research; and the Hassan Blidi Mosque in Marseille, which manifests an independent-styled *Salafism* and distances itself from the Saudi-affiliated propagation advanced by Birmingham's Salafi Mosque. (Several major mosques in England meet this definition. However, each presented limitations that made conducting a written survey difficult; thus, we ventured to France).

The study was also informed by hundreds of interviews with European imams and mosque attendees before its commencement, including at the headquarters of the European Council for Fatwa and Research. Analyses were also supported by field observations and interviews in Morocco, Turkey, and Egypt.

Women participants were not included in the study. The primary reason for their exclusion was the grounding of the methodology in samples of attendees at the time mosques are most crowded – Friday congregational prayers. Attendance of this prayer is obligatory for men, but not for women. In some of the mosques studied, it appeared that only a handful of women were present on Friday at noon.

There is little point in speculating whether interviews and questionnaires with women would have yielded different results. While some of the more groundbreaking fatwas debated in *fiqh al-aqalliyyat al-Muslima* are not gender-related, general adherence to *salafi* dogmatism does involve considerable limitations that Muslim men may not experience. One way or another, to learn whether gender impacts the responses and practices presented in this study, additional research focused on women will be required.

Chapter One

The Religious Law of Muslim Minorities

Post-Second World War migration to Western countries was the first time in history in which masses of Muslims voluntarily and individually left predominantly Muslim lands and settled in non-Muslim lands, in most cases for the purpose of improving their economic situation. Their choice created an unprecedented theological and religio-juristic challenge. The shari'a already offered a spectrum of responses to different conditions of Muslims living as a minority, but theologians and muftis (two capacities that in some cases mix) had never before dealt with a reality of millions of Muslims who make countries with Christian pasts and secular presents their permanent homes.

Adding to this fundamental difficulty were apparent conflicts between shari'a norms and Western norms and practices. As Muslims became an integral part of job markets, schools, civil society organizations, and leisure facilities in Western countries, numerous dilemmas emerged.

These included whether it is legitimate to take a mortgage or a student loan where Islamic banks are not an option; naturalize; vote in local and national elections in the West; serve in non-Muslim military forces fighting in Muslim countries; work in jobs that involve the selling of alcohol and pork; allow children to participate in mixed-gender gym and swimming lessons and girls to remove their headscarves in schools that ban the practice; congratulate Christian neighbors on their festive occasions; and accept Christmas bonuses. Some of these dilemmas were aggravated by two simultaneous processes: the institutionalization of Islamic life in the West and the revival of religiosity among some migrants on the one hand and the rise of anti-multicultural sentiments on the other.

The field of religious jurisprudence that developed in response to these questions and comprises the totality of fatwas and treatises that

22   Shari'a and Life

address them is called *fiqh al-aqalliyyat al-Muslima*, the religious law of Muslim minorities (referred to by some just as *fiqh al-aqalliyyat*, a term that also denotes the field of jurisprudence pertaining to non-Muslims living in Muslim lands). The religious law of Muslim minorities draws from the religio-juristic heritage that developed concerning previous minority conditions while aiming to resolve dilemmas that muftis have not treated in the past.

The development of *fiqh al-aqalliyyat al-Muslima* saw, by the late 1990s, the emergence of two distinct and competing approaches, the pragmatic-leaning *wasati*, associated with Yusuf al-Qaradawi and the Dublin-based European Council for Fatwa and Research, and the dogmatic-inclined *salafi*, associated with the Saudi religious establishment and its disciples outside the Kingdom. Both constitute extensions of the competing ideologies and methodologies that *wasatis* and *salafis* promote in contemporary majority Muslim societies and reflect, in a dialectic manner in some cases, the general disagreements and disputes between these approaches.

Wasatiyya and *salafiyya* share many fundamental assumptions about the crisis of religion and the modern world: Islam has been attacked by external and internal forces and, as a result, much of the Muslim world has deviated from following God's final revelation; Islam must be reformed and re-established as a comprehensive system governing all aspects of life; to reform Islam, false understandings of Islam must be rejected, and Muslims must return to the Quran, the Prophetic traditions, and the example set by the first three righteous generations, the *salaf*. It is at this point that the two approaches sharply diverge. While for *salafis* the latter contention serves to promote an agenda that largely rejects an accommodation of shari'a norms to the challenges of modernity, for *wasatis* it serves as grounds to promote facilitations.

In their quest to convince others that their approach to fiqh is the only legitimate one, *wasatis* and *salafis* ironically demonstrate that a coherent, essentialist, and universal "truth" cannot be derived from the revelation. Their efforts make a claim for "authenticity" at the core of revivalist projects but expose that the past means different things to different people. While *wasatis* and *salafis* alike describe their projects as a return to religion in its "true" manifestations, their approaches lead to conflicting results. To paraphrase Talal Asad on frictions within contemporary Saudi religious discourse,[1] *wasatis* and *salafis* disagree profoundly over what authentic Islam is, but as Muslims, their differences are challenged on the grounds of that very concept.

This chapter provides a brief description of the contours of the ideologies and methodologies of *wasatiyya* and *salafiyya*; their approaches to *fiqh al-aqalliyyat al-Muslima* and specific controversies within the field, as reflected in fatwas; and the institutions that advance the two approaches in Europe.[2]

The Wasati Approach

In contemporary religious Arab discourses, various groups and associations champion the idea of Islam as a *wasati* religion. One reason is that Islam is described as *wasati* in the Quran. Another is the universal preference of ideologues to present their views as centrist and mainstream rather than extremist. However, only one complete set of modern ideas about Islam has been labelled by its formulators with the title *wasatiyya* and gained wide recognition as such. Thus, this study's definition of *wasatiyya* is empirical-descriptive rather than normative. It does not aim to judge which ideas best represent the *wasati* ideal in Islam.

Wasatiyya is not a political party, nor is it a social movement, and there exists no foundational canonical text that represents it. Rather, it is an approach to shariʿa and, more broadly, a call to reform Muslim societies. This approach was led, systemized, institutionalized, and popularized by the Egyptian-born Yusuf al-Qaradawi (d. 2022), a graduate of al-Azhar and a former member of the Muslim Brothers who, from 1961, found intellectual shelter in Qatar and severed his official ties with the movement. Other contemporary muftis and theologians of formidable stature have endorsed the approach's central themes, including one of al-Qaradawi's primary sources of inspiration, Muhammad al-Ghazali (d. 1996).

Viewed from a historical perspective, *wasatiyya* is a continuation of the modernist-apologetic school established by Jamal al-Din al-Afghani (d. 1897), Muhammad ʿAbduh (d. 1905), and Muhammad Rashid Rida (d. 1935), particularly in its quest to provide an Islamic context to modern concepts and institutions and allow their conditional, mitigated integration into Muslim societies, as well as in its firm belief that a revived Islam is the ideal solution to the problems of humanity in modern times.[3] It is also a continuation of the Islamist project led by Hasan al-Banna (d. 1949), himself an expounder of the modernist-apologetic legacy, in its emphasis on intense yet cautious and gradual grassroots political and social activism as a means to transform Islam into a system that governs all aspects of life. However, al-Qaradawi's scholarship is characterized by an attempt to cross the factionalism of the Brothers and appeal to wider audiences.

Al-Qaradawi argued that the concept of *wasatiyya* was already present in his first book, *The Permissible and the Prohibited in Islam* (*Al-Halal*

24   Shari'a and Life

wa-l-Haram fi l-Islam), published in August 1960.[4] The book expressed several ideas that would later become signatures of *wasati* thought. However, it did not ascribe these ideas to a particular self-defined and systemized *wasati* agenda.

During the 1970s and 1980s, al-Qaradawi described Islam as a *wasati* religion but did so still without systemizing *wasatiyya* as a distinct approach. An effort to this end was undertaken in a book he published in 1988, in which he elaborated the reasons for the "Islamic awakening" experienced in the Arab world and its characteristics. He described the trend of Islamic *wasatiyya* (*tayyar al-wasatiyya al-Islamiyya*) as the most significant, the strongest, and the deepest-rooted among the various trends of the "awakening" and the one that best reflects the essence of Islam. In systemizing *wasatiyya*, al-Qaradawi stressed the balance between renewal and the ways of the *salaf* and between the eternal and the temporary. He also pointed to the potential of Islamic law to be adapted to the times and different locales in matters on which no unequivocal revelation-based evidence (*dalil*) exists.[5]

Since the mid-1990s, as al-Qaradawi's approach to fiqh became more audacious, he systemized, popularized, and institutionalized *wasatiyya*, consciously striving to be recognized as the leader of a distinct socio-juristic approach that was inseparable from his public figure and stretched outside the Egyptian context to all Muslims.[6] Friends and foes alike acknowledged him as the leader of this approach.[7] His views were spread through the extensive use of satellite television (the call-in program *Al-Shari'a wa-l-Hayat*, or *Shari'a and Life*, on Al Jazeera) and a popular internet portal (Islamonline.net). Two organizations that he headed, the European Council for Fatwa and Research (established 1997) and the International Union of Muslim Scholars (established 2004), provided him with an organizational platform and accorded his understanding of *wasatiyya* with an aura of broad legitimization.

*Wasati*s take their name from Q. 2:143: "We have made you a temperate people that you act as witnesses over man, and the Prophet as witness over you."[8] Along with temperate, median, and middle-way, *wasat* can mean balanced, just, and good. These words have different connotations, but *wasati* thought suggests that they are synonymous, in the sense that the middle way is the best way and the just way.

Al-Qaradawi and other *wasati*s argue that Islam provides a harmonic balance between several contrasts, including the permanent and the temporary, revelation and rationality, liberties and duties, permissiveness and rigidness, materialism and spiritualism, and individualism and communalism.[9] *Wasati*s do not call for an understanding of God's religion as the middle ground between conflicting views. Instead, they argue that God, who knows His creation best, provided humanity with guidance that harmonizes views that in other civilizations conflict.[10]

An obvious conclusion to be drawn from describing Islam's essence as a harmonizing middle ground is that other approaches to God's final revelation, specifically those that fail to capture this essence, are misguided. *Wasatiyya* has been presented as an alternative to two kinds of ideological extremes. One extreme is Muslims who blindly embrace Western "imported," "man-made" ideologies and reject Islam and Muslims who have not fallen into that trap. The other is Muslims who champion Islamic approaches that are not *wasati* and, in doing so, injure the potential of Islam to be renewed and prevail against its rivals. The latter groups comprise jihadis and dogmatists. The jihadis reject al-Banna's legacy of massive, grassroots peaceful mobilization as a means to promote an Islamic revolution; adhere to the later preaching of Sayyid Qutb (1906–66); excommunicate Muslims who do not apply Islam as they understand it; and act violently against them. The dogmatists fail to understand the necessity of facing and pragmatically accommodating the challenges of our times.

According to *wasati* theorizing, for the *wasati* alternative to prevail, that is, for Islam to regain its *wasati* essence, a process of *tajdid*, or renewal of Islam, must occur. *Tajdid* involves *ijtihad*, the practice of interpreting and contextualizing the revelation in a way that does not blindly imitate previous explanations. *Wasati* rejection of *taqlid* (imitation) relates to the two connotations this concept has, as elaborated by Hallaq: accepting another religio-juristic authority without doubt or evaluation of the evidence, as well as strict adherence to a school of religious law.[11]

The process of *tajdid* that *wasati*s call for involves the promotion of two ideological objectives: *taysir*, or facilitation, and *tabshir*, or spreading Islam (*da'wa*) through pleasant and gradualist means. The two are identified with a slogan that has reflected, since the late 1990s, the essence of *wasati* jurisprudence as systemized by al-Qaradawi: *al-taysir fi l-fatwa wa-l-tabshir fi l-da'wa*.[12]

The objective of *taysir* was dominant in al-Qaradawi's writings already in *The Permissible and Prohibited in Islam* from 1960,[13] but was clarified and dealt with systematically only in a comprehensive book he struggled to write over a number of years[14] and finally completed in July 1996 (according to the introduction of the book published in 2000), when his ascendance as the leader of *wasatiyya* began to take shape.

Al-Qaradawi opened *Taysir al-Fiqh* by arguing, in an apologetic tone typical of *wasatiyya*, that facilitation in decisions is not a response to the pressures of modern times or to the spirit of the time. Rather, it is a religious duty because Islam is fundamentally a religion that makes things easier rather than harder, one that spreads through pleasant and gradualist means (*tabshir*), not by generating animosity and rejection (*tanfir*).[15] Al-Qaradawi supported this statement with Q. 5:6, 2:185, and 4:28, which, he argued, testify that the basis of God's laws is making things easier; Q. 22:78 and Q. 21:107, which testify that God's laws aim to relieve believers of hardship (*haraj*); and several Prophetic traditions in which the Prophet Muhammad commanded that the easier of two or more paths of action be taken.

Al-Qaradawi described *taysir* as tasking muftis with two missions. The first mission is to issue decisions in clear, simple language that considers how busy people are and uses modern terminology.[16] (This indeed characterizes the style of some, even if not all, of his contributions). The second mission is to issue fatwas that make it easier for people to abide by the shari'a and be committed to it. Al-Qaradawi cautioned that *taysir* does not mean that a new shari'a should be invented, that the impermissible can be made permissible, or that one can endorse *tajdid* of a kind that God forbids (all allegations directed against him).[17] Rather, it means that (a) when more than one decision is permissible, the easy option should be preferred to a difficult one;[18] (b) necessity permits the prohibited (however, only to the extent needed to address it; see below, *maslaha*);[19] (c) prohibitions must be tied to Quranic verses, credible Prophetic traditions, and sound analogies;[20] (d) religio-juristic decisions must accommodate different individual hardships: the law for the strong is not similar to that for the weak, and for the young is not similar to that for the old;[21] and (e) change of places, times, habits, and circumstances must be given consideration in issuing decisions, especially in difficult times.[22]

While *taysir* is required at all times, al-Qaradawi believed that it was all the more necessary in modern, corrupted times because people's faith had weakened.[23] *Tabshir fi l-da 'wa* follows from it and complements it; where people are not overburdened (that is, subject to *ta 'sir*), they do not find Islam objectionable (that is, they do not experience *tanfir*). In advocating *tabshir fi l-da 'wa*, al-Qaradawi demanded that Islam be presented to Muslims who are weak in faith, or are still learning about it, as well as to non-Muslims, in a way that is compassionate and loving rather than threatening; that teaches them about God's mercifulness rather than about His punishments; that allows them to abide by His laws in a gradualist manner; and that ultimately brings them closer to pleasing their Creator.[24]

Tajdid through *ijtihad*, which promotes *taysir* and *tabshir*, demands that *wasati* muftis exercise great discretion and produce creative solutions. Yet, to maintain legitimacy, they must do so within the established confines of fiqh. To that end, al-Qaradawi championed from the late 1990s the application of firmly rooted religio-juristic mechanisms in a broad, flexible, and dynamic manner. First, he advocated for a hierarchic distinction between the Quran as a constitution and the Prophetic traditions as instructions that should be read in light of that constitution. Similarly, he distinguished between universal Quran verses and verses that apply only to certain situations. That distinction greatly expands the discretion of a mufti to limit the application of certain restrictions.

Second, drawing on a concept that was hotly contested in classic jurisprudence and adopting the more radical view, he stated that *maslaha mursala* (safeguarding of one of the primary objectives, or *maqasid*, of the divine Lawgiver in a context that is not explicitly attested to in the Quran) does not have to rank at the highest rank of necessity and apply to all Muslims in order to justify the accommodation of a revealed law. Rather, and differing from his original view in the 1960s, he stated that the lifting of *haraj* suffices for the determination of *maslaha mursala* and that needs (the second-highest category of *maslaha*) may qualify as necessities in suspending prohibitions.[25] Also, he added honour, security, justice, solidarity, personal rights and liberties, and the creation of a *wasati* nation to the classic list of five primary objectives that the shari'a aims to safeguard, as introduced by Muhammad al-Ghazali (d. 1111).[26] With these positions, he greatly expanded the discretion of muftis to suspend prohibitions and accommodate fatwas to different situations.

Third, al-Qaradawi emphasized the utility of cross-*madhhab* search. He explained that it was a mufti's duty to detect and accept the view that rests on the strongest evidence provided by revelation, even if his *madhhab* did not endorse that view, and that exclusive reliance on one *madhhab* may unnecessarily over-burden the believers. The shari'a in its entirety is vast and rich enough to provide a remedy for any problem or hardship, but the four schools of law are not.[27] This opinion can be interpreted as an encouragement to "fish" for the most lenient solution in the schools of law and beyond them. However, the *wasati* emphasis on *taysir* as being an essence of Islam suggests not only that there is nothing wrong with an effort directed to that end but that it is, in fact, required.

Al-Qaradawi and other *wasatis* promoted a number of social and cultural reforms that they believe Muslim societies direly need. One priority is advancing empirical sciences and advanced technologies in Muslim societies. Another is the democratization of Muslim societies. *Wasatis* maintain that the Islamic concept of *shura* (consultation), as articulated in the Quran and several traditions, requires, rather than

28   Shari'a and Life

simply allows, Muslims to live under elected, transparent regimes that respect human rights and that any form of political tyranny breaches God's command.[28] As with their approach to the sciences, they are careful to emphasize that while Western societies have been doing a far better job at maintaining Islamic political values than Muslim societies do, they do so in a godless and, therefore, distorted and corrupted way. The *shura* regime they promote differs from liberal democracies in several ways. Most importantly, the authorities of its legislative organs are restricted to areas in which God has not already legislated.[29]

Another fraught socio-political issue treated by *wasatiyya* is gender roles and relations. *Wasatis'* general attitude toward the role of women, both within the family and within society, is traditionalist. They believe that the husband is the leader of the household, that the wife must obey him (and that he may beat her lightly as a last resort if she does not), and that a woman's primary duty is to attend to her husband's needs and take care of the children.[30] They also believe that women who freely intermingle with men other than their husbands or immediate family and who do not dress modestly are a potential source of *fitna* (in this context, temptation) that risks fornication and undermines a primary objective of the divine Lawgiver – the preservation of lineage.[31]

However, *wasati* writings suggest that it is women's right, and in some cases, even a necessity, to be granted access to higher education and the job market. *Wasatis* also believe women can serve as members of parliament.[32] They went as far as suggesting that women could serve as heads of state.[33] While, according to *wasatis*, women must dress modestly and cover their body (except their hands) and hair, they are not obliged to wear a niqab, or a garment that covers their faces.[34]

Wasati pragmatism and moderation are also evident in the realm of leisure activities. *Wasatis* believe that it is permissible and, in fact, ordained by the Prophet for Muslims to seek pleasure so long as religious norms are maintained. In their view, striking a balance between duties and pleasures is part of Islam's harmonizing, middle-ground nature. For example, *wasatis* take a permissive stance on singing and music, hotly debated issues in Islamic jurisprudence.[35] *Wasatis* also legitimize watching and practicing sports, not only to maintain a healthy body, but also for pure enjoyment. However, they caution against excessive indulgence in sports and loss of modesty.[36]

Another issue emphasized by *wasatis* is the importance of good relations with non-Muslims. They argue that terms that cause non-Muslims to misunderstand Islam, particularly *dhimma* (the status of protection, under restrictions, of Jews and Christians in a Muslim state), must be expressed differently to clarify Islam's real intentions.[37] They hold that

Muslims must interact with non-Muslims in a tolerant, just, and kind manner. Thus, interfaith dialogue should be encouraged, provided that it does not undermine Islam.

The importance of maintaining good relations between Muslims and non-Muslims was championed by al-Qaradawi in his first book in 1960 and reiterated in later publications. He suggested that Muslim relations with non-Muslims should be governed by Q. 60:8–9: "God does not forbid you from being kind and acting justly towards those who did not fight over faith with you, nor expelled you from your homes. God indeed loves those who are just. He only forbids you from making friends with those who fought over faith with you and banished you from your homes and aided in your exile. Whoever makes friends with them is a transgressor."[38] His interpretation of Q. 60:8 emphasized that God commanded the believers to be just to non-Muslims who do not attack them and to be kind to them and do good to them. Al-Qaradawi stressed that this command, while also applicable to idol-worshippers, is all the more valid in the case of Jews and Christians, or "the People of the Book."[39]

The Salafi Approach

King ʿAbd al-ʿAziz ʿAbd al-Rahman Ibn Saʿud (d. 1953), the founder of the third Saudi Kingdom, rejected the definition of his state as *wahhabi* and declared himself a *salafi*.[40] During his reign, however, the association of the approach to Islam endorsed by the religious and political establishments of Saudi Arabia with the term *salafiyya* was not prevalent. Rather, as Ibn Saʿud himself noted, the Saudis of his time were commonly described as *wahhabis*, that is, followers of the Najdi revivalist theologian Muhammad Ibn ʿAbd al-Wahhab (d. 1792), who played a vital role in the formation of the first Saudi state.

It is not clear exactly when the term *salafiyya* became almost monopolized in popular Arabic and academic discourses by an approach to Islam that is synonymous with both the teachings of the mainstream of the contemporary Saudi religious establishment and movements and individuals that identify with some crucial aspects of those teachings while challenging others. It is likely that the vastness of Saudi resources, and their control of several international media outlets, played a role in the process.

In line with the warning of Ibn Saʿud, contemporary *salafi* authors emphasize that the word *wahhabiyya* is "not a legitimate title," neither for describing Ibn ʿAbd al-Wahhab's project nor for describing those "following in his steps."[41] They suggest that those who prefer the name

30   Shari'a and Life

*wahhabi*s to *salafi*s do so "either out of ignorance, blind imitation of others, jealousy, stubbornness or following their own whims and desires, or adherence to traditions, *bid'a* (unlawful innovation) and evil actions that go against the evidence [of shari'a]."[42] Their insistence on the label *salafiyya* (and of *salafi*s as *Ahl al-Sunna wa-l-Jama'a*, "the people who follow the Prophet's example and are united") is for a reason. According to a tradition narrated by 'Abdallah b. 'Umar, the Prophet Muhammad said: "The best people are those living in my generation, and then those who will follow them, and then those who will follow the latter. Then there will come some people who will bear witness before taking oaths, and take oaths before bearing witness." The tradition implies that the closer Muslims were to the days of the Prophet, the better their conduct was. It is a basis for the consensus among Sunni muftis that the first three generations of Islam – the Prophet's Companions (*sahaba*), the following generation (*al-tabi'in*), and the generation after that (*tabi' al-tabi'in*), known collectively as the pious ancestors (*salaf*) – provide the example that Muslims should follow and, thus, are the ultimate reference. Whereas the name *wahhabi* depicts followers of a religious reformer who was controversial even in his own homeland, the term *salafi*s describes standard-bearers of the only true and legitimate understanding of Islam.

Salafiyya, as a contemporary crystalized approach to the shari'a and Islam in general, relies predominantly on the legacies of Ahmad b. Hanbal (d. 855), Taqi al-Din Ibn Taymiyya (d. 1328), his student Ibn al-Qayyim al-Jawziyya (d. 1350), and the above-mentioned Ibn 'Abd al-Wahhab. Its construction is associated primarily with the efforts of two individuals: the Kingdom's highest religious authority since the early 1970s (and its grand mufti since 1993), 'Abd al-'Aziz b. 'Abdallah b. Baz (d. 1999) and his second-in-command, Muhammad b. Salih al-'Uthaymin (d. 2001). *Salafiyya* is represented in individual works and the studies and fatwas issued by Saudi Arabia's two main religio-juristic institutions: its highest religious authority, the Council of Senior Scholars (Hay'at Kibar al-'Ulama'), established in 1971 and responsible for advising the king, and its subsidiary, The Permanent Committee for Scholarly Research and Ifta' (Al-Lajna al-Da'ima lil-Buhuth al-'Ilmiyya wa-l-Ifta'). Most, but not all, prominent contemporary *salafi*s are Saudi-born. The Albanian-born Muhammad Nasr al-Din al-Albani (d. 1999), who taught for three years at the Islamic University of al-Madina (established 1961), is the only non-Saudi almost on par with Ibn Baz and al-'Uthaymin in his impact on the contemporary *salafi* approach.[43]

In Saudi Arabia and outside the Kingdom, individuals and movements who reject one or more of the core principles represented by the contemporary mainstream of Saudi Arabia's religious establishment also present themselves and are identified as *salafi*. Wiktorowicz's anatomy of the *salafi* movement pointed to two offspring of the Saudi mainstream *salafiyya*: the jihadis and the politicos.[44] The former include al-Qaeda and ISIS.

Hegghammer, who characterized jihadi-*salafism* as an extremist blending of the *wahhabi* religious tradition and the Qutbist Islamist trend and pointed to its internationalist orientation, traced the earliest origins of the term to an interview given in 1994 to the London-based jihadi magazine *Al-Ansar* by Ayman al-Zawahiri, al-Qaeda's leader (2011-2022) and formerly a member of the Egyptian Qutbist Islamic Jihad.[45] While *salafis* and jihadi-*salafis* agree on some doctrinal issues, the fundamental difference in their respective approaches to violent dissent against Muslim regimes that do not apply God's laws (as they interpret them) to the letter makes the two sworn enemies.

A less pronounced dispute is between the mainstream *salafiyya*, represented by the contemporary Saudi religious leadership, and what Wiktorowicz terms "politico-*salafis*" in Saudi Arabia and outside the Kingdom. According to Wiktorowicz, the latter engage with the political reality, and some reluctantly and conditionally participate in electoral processes as a means of changing it.[46] Notwithstanding the utility of this definition, mainstream Saudi *salafis*' abstention from engaging with political realities and their rejection of electoral politics has been undermined since the 1980s. Thus, the two trends do not represent categorically conflicting agendas.

At the heart of the *salafi* approach, as articulated by Ibn Baz, al-ʿUthaymin, and their followers, are the affirmation of *tawhid* (the oneness of God) and the rejection of *shirk* (associating partners with the attributes of God). *Salafi* writings on *tawhid* continue the legacies of Ibn Taymiyya, Ibn al-Qayyim, and particularly, Muhammad ibn ʿAbd al-Wahhab, who centred his call for reform on the conviction that the Muslims of his time had betrayed true monotheism and associated others with God. The specific betrayals al-Wahhab pointed to included believing that particularly righteous people might intercede with God on behalf of believers, wearing talismans, making pictures of living creatures, seeking the advice of fortune-tellers, prohibiting what God has permitted or permitting what God has prohibited, and mocking God, His book, or His Prophet.[47]

Salafis stress that *tawhid* is the essence of Islam. Ibn Baz explained the centrality of *tawhid* as follows: "[Islam's] reality is recognizing the oneness of Allah in His ownership, His control of affairs, and His actions. It is also signalling Him out for worship and recognizing His uniqueness

32   Shari'a and Life

in His names and attributes. It is complying with His commands and accepting His law."[48] 'Abdallah b. Salih al-Fawzan (b. 1935), a member of the Saudi Council of Senior Scholars and the Permanent Committee, is one of the more prolific contemporary *salafi* muftis. Relying on Ibn al-Qayyim, he explained that the entire Quran is about *tawhid* and the rejection of *shirk* and that Islam's religious obligations were not revealed (in the Medinan *suras*) until *tawhid* was presented and established within the souls of the people.[49]

Breaching *tawhid* involves two types of *shirk*: (a) major, such as ascribing to something other than God an attribute that belongs only to Him (like the belief that there is someone else who gives life), and (b) minor, constituting anything that may lead to major *shirk* (like venerating people or objects but without attributing to them attributes of God).[50]

The *salafi* emphasis on *tawhid* is not unique, as testifying that there is no God but God is the first pillar of faith for all Muslims. The uniqueness of *tawhid* in *salafi* writings lies in its utilization as a means to describe *salafi* interpretations of Islam as the only ones that are genuinely loyal to monotheism, while chastising other interpretations as either *shirk* or sins that risk leading to *shirk*. Thus, *tawhid* enhances the quest of contemporary *salafis* to monopolize *salafi* truths. The centrality of the concept also supports the mainstream *salafi* reluctance to participate in politics. Mainstream *salafis* argue that because *tawhid* is so crucial, there is no point in attending to topical issues unless the oneness of God is established in the minds of Muslims.

Also central to *salafi* writings is their conception of *al-wala' wa-l-bara'* (loyalty and disavowal). Expanding on a rich tradition of engagement with these terms, *salafis* have integrated "loyalty" and "disavowal" into one coherent concept that divides humanity into two profoundly hostile camps: Muslims who accept God's truth and non-Muslims who reject it.

The proliferation of deliberations on the subject in recent decades has elevated the concept to a signature of the *salafi* doctrine and was instrumental in the efforts of *salafi* muftis to limit the interactions of Saudi society with other societies and to minimize its integration of modern practices. *Salafis* have invoked "loyalty and disavowal" to argue that friendly personal relations between Muslims and non-Muslims are prohibited. Their writings suggest that the principle of "loyalty" demands only those actions that please God, including reserving love exclusively for God, His Prophet, and the believers, and reserving friendship (or alliances) exclusively for the Muslim believers. The principle of "disavowal," on the other hand, demands despising and spurning the infidels and their religions.[51] *Salafis* also emphasize that God's demand for total submission requires the believers to be uncompromising in their

The Religious Law of Muslim Minorities 33

enmity toward those who reject their Creator and His true religion. "Disavowal" is as essential as "loyalty"; the two are parts of a whole, without which devotion cannot be complete.[52]

Along with objecting to loyalty to and friendly relations with non-Muslims, another main limitation that the *salafi* interpretation of "loyalty and disavowal" places on Muslims concerns the strong prohibition of perceived imitations of and resemblance to infidels. *Salafis* stress the need to differ from the infidels, citing Q. 3:100, 45:18, 9:69, 59:19; the Prophet's warning, narrated by Abu Dawud, that "whoever imitates a people is one of them"; and several other traditions. They identify three categories in which it is impermissible to imitate infidels: worship, customs, and the conduct of worldly affairs.

First, imitating infidels in their beliefs, rituals, or holidays is prohibited. According to al-Fawzan, this type of imitation, when intentional, constitutes *kufr* (infidelity),[53] while according to al-'Uthaymin, whoever imitates infidels in their acts of worship "puts himself at great risk and that may lead to him becoming an infidel who is beyond the pale of Islam."[54]

The second type of imitation is infidel customs, prohibiting, for example, shaving or dressing in a way similar to them. Al-Fawzan quoted the Prophet Muhammad: "These are the garments of the infidels; do not wear them."[55] He cautioned against differentiating between "important" and "unimportant" in imitating the social patterns of infidels. Possibly influenced by Ibn Taymiyya's understanding of the issue,[56] he explained that garments should not be considered purely external because they reflect a person's consciousness and tendencies. Thus, in wearing European clothes, a Muslim subconsciously fuses his tendencies with those of the European, an act that will eventually lead to a fusion of their views.[57]

A third category of imitation, comprising worldly affairs such as science and technology, is less conclusive. If *maslaha* is served by learning from the infidels in these fields, then there is no harm in doing so, providing what is learned does not exist in Muslim societies, does not breach the teachings of the shari'a, and does not humiliate Muslims in the process.

Contemporary *salafis* share an elitist mindset. They believe that other approaches to Islam reflect not simply errors of judgment but rather absolute deviations for which the punishment will be hellfire. This warning is based on the tradition – narrated by 'Abdallah b. 'Umar, invoked by 'Abd al-Wahhab and referenced by contemporary *salafis* – according to which the Prophet said: "This *umma* will divide into seventy-three sects. All of them will be in the fire except for one." When the Companions asked the Prophet which is the one group to be saved, he answered that it would be the group that is based upon the values and traditions that he and his companions hold dear. *Salafis* believe that they are the group that follows the example of the Prophet and the Companions and thus will be saved.[58]

This elitist belief is coupled with *salafiyya*'s demand for total devotion, which draws from another division within the *umma* (the Muslim community), which Ibn Taymiyya emphasized. He declared that the *awliya*' (loyalists) of God are divided into two categories: the forerunners (*sabiqun*) and the Companions of the Right (*ashab al-yamin*). The Companions of the Right do what God has ordered and refrain from doing the prohibited, but do not perform the recommended acts of worship and do not refrain from unnecessary permissible actions. The forerunners perform optional acts of worship after having performed the obligatory acts. They draw closer to God by doing all that is within their capability. Therefore, they are beloved by God and will drink directly from the fountain of heaven (*tasnim*), as opposed to the Companions of the Right, who will not.[59] Combined, the "saved sect" and the "forerunners" concepts establish *salafiyya* as a call for the most devout and able only.

Contemporary luminaries of *salafiyya* are aware that they are condemned as reactionaries and fanatics. Their defense against these allegations is simple: God has given humanity through His Prophet a set of perfected, comprehensive, clear, and beneficial rules. Happiness, salvation, strength, honour, and security await those who follow those rules.[60] Whatever is in accordance with His laws is moderate; whatever contradicts them is extreme.[61]

Salafis maintain that their version of Islam is *wasati*. Yet unlike *wasatis*, they hold that *taysir* is not the essence of Islam's *wasati* nature and argue that deliberately choosing the easier religio-juristic opinion on a controversial issue may lead to infidelity.[62] Instead, they suggest that to be a *wasati* is to adhere strictly to the Prophet's example without exaggeration or negligence.[63] Al-Fawzan emphasized in a clear, albeit indirect, reference to *wasatis* that violating the shari'a in the name of *wasatiyya* is not the essence of *wasatiyya* at all. Rather, *wasatiyya* is to follow God's laws and abide by His book and the Prophetic example without exaggeration but also without negligence.[64] *Salafis* caution that though there are issues of greater and lesser importance, nothing that God and His Prophet commanded should be taken lightly. The shari'a should be obeyed in all aspects of life and neglecting any part of the shari'a is equal to neglecting all of it.[65] For example, the Prophet ordered the believers to let their beards grow and trim their mustaches. Ibn Baz, in his answer to a query on whether this is a trivial matter, cautioned that there are no trivial matters in Islam because, based on Q. 9:65–6, "there is the fear that the person who says such a thing by way of belittling or mocking may be apostatizing from his religion thereby."[66]

Whereas the *wasati* approach establishes a hierarchy between the Quran and the Prophetic traditions that privileges the former and specific verses in it, *salafis* emphasize that the traditions are an equally valid independent source. The essence of the *salafi* religio-juristic methodology is that the Quran and the traditions, as the *salaf* understood them, should guide Muslims and that nothing revealed should be rejected by the intellect.[67] *Salafi* jurisprudence is more than a straightforward process of referencing the appropriate verse or tradition, leaving no room for *ijtihad*. However, the discretion allowed for muftis is narrower, as indicated by the *salafi* approach to *maslaha*.

Salafi muftis accept the general premises of *maslaha*: the idea that the shariʿa is intended to safeguard particular objectives, that fatwas can change in order to facilitate the safeguarding of these objectives, and that muftis should consider what the results of decisions will be under given conditions and accommodate them accordingly.[68] Though they accept in practice *maslaha mursala* as grounds for suspending otherwise prohibited actions, they do so only in cases of necessity. They are more inclined to legitimize the impermissible based on *maslaha* involving either strategic state interests or an individual's need to obey state organs, reflecting the influence of the *salafi* theory of political authority.[69]

The *salafi* approach to cross-*madhhab* search draws from its foundational principle of strictly adhering to the Quran and the Prophetic traditions. Muftis and *qadis* must not accept an opinion simply because it was stated by one of the four schools of law; rather, they should accept the opinion with the strongest evidence on any given matter.[70] In the words of al-Fawzan: "It is not permissible to blindly follow any one of them. We only take from them if they bring evidence."[71]

When establishing the Shariʿa Court system in 1927, Ibn Saʿud declared that it is "not restricted by any particular *madhhab*; rather, it decides according to what appears to be [applicable] from any of the *madhhabs*, and there is no difference between one and the other."[72] In 1934, Ibn Saʿud reemphasized, "we obey neither Ibn ʿAbd al-Wahhab nor any other person, unless what they say is clearly endorsed by Allah's Book and the Prophet's Sunna. [Wherever] we find strong evidence in any of the four *madhhabs*, we refer and hold to it."[73] However, he also added that where strong evidence is lacking, the opinion of the *Hanbali* school should be adopted. The Saudi religious establishment has continued this norm to this day. Its preference for the *Hanbali* school,

36 Shari'a and Life

as interpreted by Ibn Taymiyya and his disciples, is explained by its greater reliance on the Quran and the Prophetic traditions compared to other schools.[74]

A signature of the *salafi* approach is its marginalization of women. Based on a literalist interpretation of verses and traditions, *salafi* muftis emphasize the physical, mental, and intellectual inferiority of a woman in comparison to a man, a woman's duty to obey her husband or her guardians, and the need for her complete separation from the company of men in order to avoid *fitna*. *Salafi* writings are rich with contempt for women, based on a firm conviction that God created them as lesser than men. Al-'Uthaymin considered apologetics about Islam as a religion of equality to be a lie. Islam, he argued, believes in justice, not equality, and justice is based on treating equally those who are equal and differentiating between those who are different. Women are different from men, who are stronger, tougher, and have a better capacity to understand matters. Therefore, different laws are applied to them.[75]

Salafi muftis describe the sexual desires of men as being so strong that any glimpse of a woman's body risks leading to the gravest of sins: adultery and fornication. Thus, women must seclude themselves from the presence of men outside their family circle and, in those cases that necessitate their presence in the public sphere, totally cover themselves.

This fear of fornication provided the rationale for decisions that established patterns that came to identify Saudi society and *salafi* communities elsewhere. *Salafis* argue (as did Ibn Taymiyya) that women must wear niqab, a veil covering their entire face and not just the hair, not only because adherence to the Prophetic traditions calls on women to do so, but also because the face is where a woman's beauty concentrates and is the main source of temptation.[76] To even ridicule this opinion is, they believe, tantamount to an act of infidelity.[77] The *salafi* objection to the participation of women in the job market is also based on the fear that men would be tempted. Al-Fawzan, for example, suggested that efforts to "remove" women from their homes, where they belong, and place them into professions that serve men, such as nursing or teaching in mixed classrooms, are led by "Muslims who have sickness in their hearts" and "wish to transform the woman into a cheap commodity in the marketplace of the desirous and satanic temptations."[78]

Salafi muftis apply similarly rigid logic when considering the issue of leisure. Their decisions profess aversion for and distrust of many forms of amusement that *wasatis* conditionally legitimize. This position is based on the conviction that most forms of entertainment are vanities that involve deviation from religious norms, as well as from the insistence that the truly devout must dedicate every moment of their lives to God.

The Religious Law of Muslim Minorities   37

Music is one example: while conditionally permitted by *wasatis*, it is strongly prohibited by *salafis*, who draw from Ibn Taymiyya's depiction of it as strengthening satanic states.[79] The prohibition is strict. For example, Ibn Baz stated that it was only permissible to listen to radio programs that contain music if one turns down the volume when music is played.[80] There are no exceptions: music is forbidden for children and adults, and patriotic and religious songs accompanied by music are equally prohibited.[81]

Restrictions on playing sports are another example of the *salafi* approach to leisure. While *wasatis* accept Muslims' having fun for the sake of having fun, *salafis* encourage physical exercise as a means to enhance one's health and readiness for jihad and emphasize that in Islam, sports are never a goal in and of themselves.[82]

Salafis consider any drawing or documentation of facial features as a breach of *tawhid*, gravely limiting photography and drawings of humans (and of animals). A signature of *salafi* books, including children's books, is that humans and animals appear without facial features or with only their backs showing. This is also the approach taken with *salafi* toys.[83]

The *salafi* theory of politics rests on two foundations. One is the rejection of democracy as an infidel, man-made system. *Salafis* utterly deny any compatibility between democracy and Islam or that the former is rooted in the latter. They believe that, in principle, democracy constitutes a form of *shirk* and that its essence denies the sovereignty of the Creator and His absolute right to issue laws. In the eyes of some, this view does not deny electoral participation if a *maslaha* is served.[84] Another foundation of *salafi* political theory is the duty to obey the political leader, or *wali al-amr*, and avoid oppositionist or subversive actions in almost all circumstances. This foundation rests on three historical legacies.

The first historical legacy is the *Hanbali*, particularly Ibn Taymiyya's, concept of authority, which emphasized the essentiality of a stable, even if far from ideal, political regime as a means for safeguarding religion.[85] A second legacy is the eighteenth-century alliance of Ibn ʿAbd al-Wahhab with Muhammad Ibn Saʿud, which created a system in which political decisions were monopolized by the Saʿuds and legitimized by religious scholars. The third legacy is the breakdown of the first and second Saudi Kingdoms during the nineteenth century, which demonstrated the great danger of internal strife. This legacy was reinforced by the trauma of the very short-lived support granted by Ibn Baz to the religious movement opposed to the Saudi invitation of American military forces, which gathered momentum during 1991 and called to transfer the monopoly on strategic decisions from the House of Saʿud

38   Shari'a and Life

to a council of religious scholars. The Saudi religious establishment retracted its support for the dissenters within two months and has been unequivocal ever since in publicizing its resentment of religious scholars' and the general public's involvement in politics.[86]

Wasati Fiqh al-Aqalliyyat al-Muslima

In the late 1990s and early 2000s, when *wasatiyya* was crystalized as a distinct approach associated with Yusuf al-Qaradawi, he guided the systematic composition and institutionalization of a *wasati* approach to *fiqh al-aqalliyyat al-Muslima*. The efforts centred around the European Council for Fatwa and Research, a panel established in London in 1997 through the initiative of the Federation of Islamic Organizations in Europe (FIOE), an umbrella organization of several hundred mosques and Islamic organizations across the continent. Al-Qaradawi, who was appointed the Council's president, was considered the ideal nominee for several reasons: his esteemed albeit controversial position as a religio-juristic authority in the Sunni Arab world, pragmatic social views, Islamist credentials, and long-time, even if occasional, interest in religio-juristic issues pertaining to Muslim minorities. Shortly after the Council's inauguration and following the appointment of the imam of the Islamic Cultural Centre of Ireland, Hussein Halawa, as secretary-general of the Council, its headquarters moved to the Irish capital. Its humble offices have been located at the mosque ever since, where Halawa is helped by only one assistant.

Upon its establishment, al-Qaradawi defined the objectives of the Council in ambitious terms. Along with bringing ease "rather than difficulty and hardship" to Muslims in Europe, the Council was to "promote a uniform fatwa in Europe and to prevent controversy and intellectual conflicts regarding the respective issues wherever possible."[87] In its inaugural meeting, the Council declared as first on its list of objectives "achieving proximity and bringing together the scholars who live in Europe, and attempting to unify the jurisprudence views between them with regard to the main fiqh issues."[88] In his opening speech, Ahmad Rawi, the President of the Federation of Islamic Organizations in Europe, expressed hope that it would become "an essential reference for European Muslims," helping them solve the typical problems they face and promote integration.[89]

Among the 32 Council members listed in the first compilation of fatwas it published, 19 were based in Europe. Halawa said in an interview with one of the authors in 2012 that he believed the Council had established itself as a *marja'iyya* – an authoritative reference – for Muslim minorities at large and that most Muslims in Europe, including those of Turkish descent, accept the Council's religio-juristic approach and its fatwas.[90]

Membership on the Council's board is contingent on the recommendation of a Council member; once approved by the other members, it is for life. Convening every year in June (until 2008, it met twice a year), the Council discusses the most challenging queries that arrive at its offices or at the offices of the committees for fatwa issuance it operates in France, Germany, and England, as well as queries directed from governmental bodies. The queries it addresses are initially deliberated by its head sub-committee for the issuance of fatwas, and some deliberations are based on studies it commissions. An absolute majority establishes the Council's decisions, and the president does not have the power to veto. Along with fatwas, the Council publishes religio-legal treatises and a meticulously edited bi-annual journal, *Al-Majalla al-'Ilmiyya*.

In fatwas and treatises, the Council, as well as individual contributions by al-Qaradawi and other members, have applied the motto of the *wasati* approach – *al-taysir fi l-fatwa wa-l-tabshir fi l-da'wa* – to Muslim minorities in Europe. Highlighting the importance of relieving Muslims in Europe of *haraj*, they suggested that living in majority non-Muslim societies constitutes an inherent condition of weakness. Thus, just as a sick person is entitled to leniency that a healthy person is not, Muslims in Europe are entitled to more leniency than those living in Muslim societies. In this regard, al-Qaradawi noted that all the *madhhab*s agree that a change of geographical location may justify a change of fatwa, and no such change is more fundamental than moving outside of *Dar al-Islam* (Abode of Islam). The reason is that despite all the shortcomings and deviations of Muslim societies, living in those societies nevertheless encourages Muslims to perform religious duties and refrain from the prohibited, while living in non-Muslim societies does not.[91]

Tabshir fi l-da'wa, the second pillar of the *wasati* approach, appeared in two contexts in *wasati fiqh al-aqalliyyat al-Muslima*. The first drew from the general *wasati* theory on *tabshir*. *Wasati*s suggest that Muslims in the West who have deviated from Islam, or face considerable difficulties when practicing it, could not be brought back to Islam at once. Consideration must be given to their situation and, more specifically, to their level of alienation, with the hope that they would commit to God's laws over time.

Al-Qaradawi emphasized that the gradualism required when dealing with Muslim minorities is the gradualism that was applied in revealing the Quran and was the way of the *salaf*.[92] The Council embraced *tabshir* as a means to bring Muslims in the West closer to Islam in its

40   Shari'a and Life

first session, when it addressed the issue of hijab. It advised exercising gentleness rather than harshness when dealing with a new convert who refuses to wear a headscarf because, she claims, it puts her in a state of hardship. The Council explained that while the headscarf is obligatory, it is only a partiality of law; if imposing it may lead the woman to a state of *tanfir* and cause her to forsake Islam altogether, it should not be imposed.[93]

The second context of *tabshir* suggested that Muslims in the West should act as missionaries. *Wasati* writings on *fiqh al-aqalliyyat al-Muslima* legitimized Muslim migration to and settlement in the West with an array of justifications covering almost the totality of motivations for migration, including one's need to provide for one's family, finding political shelter, and pursuing academic studies. The prospect of bringing non-Muslims to Islam served as an additional justification and was fundamental to *wasati* theorizing on Muslim minorities.

This opinion developed a notion introduced on the religio-legal spectrum already in the eleventh century, when the *Shafi'i* Abu al-Hasan b. Habib al-Mawardi (d. 1058) argued that if a Muslim was able to manifest his religion in one of the unbelievers' countries, this country became part of *Dar al-Islam* and, hence, it was better to reside there than migrate because the Muslim living as a minority would potentially convert non-Muslims to Islam.[94] Shams al-Din al-Ramli (d. 1596), the grand mufti of Egypt, cited the example of the group of Muslims the Prophet allowed to remain in non-Muslim Mecca to argue that Muslims who live in Aragon and can manifest their religion are not required to migrate to Muslim lands. Instead, they are required to remain because their residence among infidels might help to propagate Islam.[95]

Proselytizing as a legitimization for remaining in non-Muslim countries entered *wasati* writings in the early 1980s and was fully integrated into some of the more systemized works on minority fiqh in the first decade of the twenty-first century, including al-Qaradawi's broad theorizing about the religious law of Muslim minorities in 2001, *Fi Fiqh al-Aqalliyyat al-Muslima*. Al-Qaradawi went as far as to state that, considering Islam's universal mission on the one hand and the West's current leadership of the world on the other, Muslims must have a presence in the West and spread Islam there. Thus, if there were no Muslim presence in the Western world, such a presence would have had to be created.[96]

Detailing the "duties of Muslims living in the West" in 2006, al-Qaradawi noted that along with protecting their and their families' religious identity, which is the essential condition for continuing to live in non-Muslim countries, Muslims have a missionary role. They "ought to be sincere callers to their religion. They should keep in mind that calling others to Islam is not restricted to scholars and shaykhs, but it goes so far as to encompass every committed Muslim. As we see scholars and shaykhs delivering *khutbas* (sermons) and lectures, authoring books to defend Islam, it is no wonder we find lay Muslims practicing *da'wa* while employing wisdom and fair exhortation."[97]

The notion that migration to the West could be legitimized based on criteria that include proselytizing was not unique to *wasatis*. As will be explored below, it was also advanced by *salafis*, albeit far more narrowly. Moreover, muftis, graduates of Islamic universities, and others who took interest in the state of Muslim minorities, and who were neither *wasati* nor *salafi*, presented similar notions in fatwas, dissertations, and treatises. For example, the mufti of Tunisia, al-Shadhili al-Nayfar, addressed the *Maliki* hostility to Muslim residence in the West by noting that today, unlike in the time of the Reconquista, Muslims living in non-Muslim lands enjoy freedom of religion and some are able to engage in Islamic activity. He added that their residence there may be of merit, for if they manifest Islam's ideals and values, non-Muslims will embrace it.[98]

Wasatis, and the Council in its application of *wasati* doctrine, broadly applied the two mechanisms of fiqh that are central to *wasati* methodology to promote their ideological objectives. One is to search for the most suitable answer among all four Sunni schools of law and beyond them. Al-Qaradawi and others noted crossing *madhhab* boundaries is essential for the fiqh of minorities (as it is for fiqh in general) because it provides muftis with greater discretion; a *madhhab* that is strict on one issue may be lenient on another, and rulings that have been neglected may be revived.[99] Drawing on these assertions, the Council professed that "the four schools of law, as well as all other people of fiqh knowledge, are regarded as a resource of immense wealth" from which muftis should choose whatever is supported by "the correct and best evidence that achieves the best interest."[100] It cautioned against *madhhabi* fanaticism.[101]

The other mechanism central to *wasati fiqh al-aqalliyyat al-Muslima* is the generous application of *maslaha*. In addressing his approach to the religious law of Muslim minorities, al-Qaradawi emphasized the utility of the idea that there are more than five primary objectives to the shari'a and that needs may qualify as necessities in legitimizing the suspension of prohibitions.[102]

These two concepts were applied in the fatwas issued by the Council. The most innovative aspect of those decisions was the elevation of proselytizing to a primary objective that justifies suspensions of the prohibited. This move established cyclical reasoning in which the triumphal

42   Shari'a and Life

conceptualization of Muslim migration as a means of spreading Islam in the West legitimizes pragmatism and integration into Western societies.

While al-Qaradawi and his Council were the most systematic and innovative in presenting a pragmatic *wasati* approach to *fiqh al-aqalliyyat al-Muslima* and the most audacious and prolific in authoring fatwas based upon that approach, they were not alone in advancing integration-inclined and pragmatic solutions to challenges faced by Muslims living in the West. The implication is that on some issues, Muslims living in Europe can find pragmatic, legitimizing fatwas from sources other than the Dublin-based Council, including panels that have longer and more esteemed traditions.

Other formidable actors included Dar al-Ifta', Egypt's supreme state-panel on religious law (whose website includes a section dealing exclusively with queries from Muslims living in the West); the Fatwa Committee of Egypt's al-Azhar University, the alma-mater of the leading *wasatis* (which since 2020 operates a Fatwa Global Center to address questions of Muslims living outside Egypt); and the Fiqh Council of North America, a religio-legal panel established already in 1986 by Taha Jabir al-'Alwani (d. 2016). The Iraq-born, al-Azhar educated, Saudi-employed, and eventually American-based al-'Alwani preceded al-Qaradawi in recognizing the need for a pragmatic religio-legal approach to Muslim minorities. He presented his ideas in a systematic book, *Fi Fiqh al-Aqalliyyat al-Muslima*, a year before the publication of al-Qaradawi's book which bore the same name and contained similar ideas. [103] While he was not a member of the European Council for Fatwa and Research, al-'Alwani served on the advisory board of its journal and recognized al-Qaradawi's seniority.

Examples of Facilitations

Fatwas issued by al-Qaradawi and the Council addressed various issues that are fundamental to the daily lives of Muslims living in Europe and the West at large. A number of these fatwas broke away from confirmed and long-held religio-legal opinions.

Mortgages When No Alternative Is Available

Q. 2:275–7 prohibits usury (*riba*) and warns that God and his Prophet will wage war against those who do not obey this command. In modern economies, in which corporate and individual transactions often rely on interest-based loans, this prohibition creates a challenge. Islamic banking systems have developed several mechanisms that circumvent the prohibition on *riba*. In real estate, the most popular one is *murabaha*: the bank serves as an intermediary that buys a house at the customer's request and then sells the house at a higher price, which the customer pays in instalments.[104] In some Western countries, Islamic banking systems are not available. Since some Muslim migrants in the West are not affluent and cannot afford to buy a house without a mortgage, the issue has become highly relevant.

Responding to this situation, the European Council for Fatwa and Research decided to conditionally legitimize mortgages at its fourth session held in October 1999. The decision, which was front-page news in one of the most distinguished Arabic newspapers, the London-based *Al-Sharq al-Awsat*, reflects the ideology and methodology of *wasati fiqh al-aqalliyyat al-Muslima*, and their potential to legitimize pragmatic decisions. The fatwa began with a reaffirmation of Islam's prohibition on usury. It encouraged Muslims in the West to find religiously permissible alternatives to mortgages, such as the *murabaha* system offered by Islamic banks. It also encouraged Islamic organizations in Europe to ask European banks to adopt Islamic systems in order to attract Muslim customers. Still, the fatwa stated that if there is no alternative, then a Muslim living in Europe who does not own a house and does not have the means to purchase one without a loan is permitted to take a mortgage.

The Council based its argument on two notions. First, it argued that a need (*haja*) can be regarded as a necessity (*darura*), even if the need is individual (i.e., does not apply to all Muslims, a condition placed by some muftis for needs to qualify as necessities). The fatwa explained that a "necessity" is something without which a Muslim cannot live, and a "need" is something without which a Muslim would be put in a state of *haraj*. Q. 22:78 and 5:6 state that Islam will not put Muslims in a state of hardship. Thus, certain needs can be regarded as necessities, and in addressing them, it is possible to legitimize what is prohibited. While having a home (rented or owned) is a necessity for a Muslim family (as indicated in Q. 16:80), for Muslims in Europe, owning a home is a need that can be regarded as a necessity because it is crucial for preserving Islamic identity and for promoting the spread of Islam.

The fatwa explained that a Muslim in Europe who does not take a mortgage may be compelled to pay rent to a non-Muslim landlord for many years without getting any closer to ownership and remaining under the threat of eviction, while a Muslim who is permitted to take a mortgage will be relieved of these concerns and will be able to choose a home that is close to a mosque and an Islamic school. Buying homes

44 Shari'a and Life

may bring together Muslims living in non-Muslim majority countries, strengthen their ties, and enable them to create small Islamic enclaves within the larger society. Furthermore, mortgages advance proselytizing efforts and thus constitute a communal need in two ways: (a) by becoming homeowners, Muslims will present a respectable face to non-Muslims, and (b) relief from the financial burden of renting a house will make it possible for Muslims to pursue their duty to engage in *da 'wa*.

The other argument presented in the fatwa draws on the *wasati* method of cross-*madhhab* search. The fatwa invoked the *Hanafi* opinion (endorsed by some *Hanbalis*) that contracts between Muslims and non-Muslims that are typically prohibited are permitted outside *Dar al-Islam*. This opinion is based on two notions: first, while living among infidels, a Muslim is not obligated to follow the rulings of the shari'a on civil, financial, political, and similar matters because following them is beyond his ability, and God does not require people to do more than their ability. Second, Islam seeks to strengthen its believers in all respects, including the elimination of financial hardships. The fatwa criticized the argument of several *Hanafi* muftis, namely, that Muslims in non-Muslim societies can charge interest, but not pay it, because they do not benefit from paying interest. The Council explained that no consensus was reached on this issue and that by paying interest on a mortgage, the Muslim receives a benefit because he will eventually own a home. The Council emphasized that it regards the *Hanafi* legitimization of mortgages in Europe merely as a supplement to its main argument; to wit, that in the European context, a mortgage may be considered a "need" that qualifies as a "necessity." It noted that muftis of all schools of law can permit mortgages based on its main argument.[105]

Responding to harsh criticism of the fatwa, including by members of the Council, al-Qaradawi reaffirmed the legitimization of mortgages and its broad interpretation of the concept of necessity. More than a quarter of his 2001 book on the *wasati* approach to the religious law of Muslim minorities is dedicated to the Council's 1999 fatwa; clearly, al-Qaradawi felt that he needed to defend it. He conceded that in legitimizing interest-based loans for European Muslims, he adopted a position that he had opposed his entire career.[106] He attributed his change of heart to the softness and confidence that comes with age.[107]

Al-Qaradawi added several elements to the Council's description of home ownership as essential for leading an Islamic life in the West and promoting Islam, including that Muslims who own apartments have access to better education; reside in greater proximity to local mosques, Islamic centres, and other Muslims; enjoy better public services; enable their wives to walk around the house without being watched by neighbors (as is the case in rent-based residential areas), and gain the respect of all walks of society, from school teachers to drivers of garbage trucks. Al-Qaradawi hinted that the lateness of his religio-juristic transformation on the matter had been harmful to the interests of the *umma*, noting that Muslims from the Indian subcontinent, who adhere to the *Hanafi* school and have taken mortgages, are some of the richest people in contemporary London.[108] Other *wasati* muftis have also defended the Council's stand on mortgages.[109]

Student Loans

In its eighteenth session in July 2008, the Council legitimized usurious student loans. The decision pointed to the system's fairness and that it was matched to the rise in the consumer price index. It was based on a study by Salim al-Shaykhi (b. 1964), a Libyan-born, Saudi-educated, and England-based mufti and member of the Council. He noted that Muslims in Britain do not have access to reliable Islamic-regulated, interest-free loans, and suggested that the principle that a need can be regarded as a necessity legitimizes the taking of interest-based student loans.

Al-Shaykhi explained that higher education is required for individuals to find good jobs. Since most Muslims in the United Kingdom work in low-paying occupations, they will be unable to afford higher education if student loans remain prohibited. Furthermore, to facilitate integration, Muslims must establish a presence in the public and private sector, and they can do so only if they have access to higher education.[110]

Service in a Non-Muslim Military Force

Shortly after 9/11, as the United States was preparing to retaliate in Afghanistan, a Muslim chaplain in the American army, Muhammad ʿAbd al-Rashid, presented Taha Jabir al-ʿAlwani with a query on the permissibility of participation in a war against the perpetrators of the attacks. Realizing the gravity of the query, al-ʿAlwani consulted with al-Qaradawi, who joined four *wasati* experts in approving Muslim participation in the prospective war.

Their decision broke a solid religio-juristic taboo against service in non-Muslim forces that fight against Muslims. It was based on two justifications: first, the 9/11 attacks were terrorist acts, and Muslims should be united against those who terrorize innocents. Second, they argued that if Muslim American military personnel were to resign their positions, they would cause harm not only to themselves but also to

46   Shari'a and Life

millions of Muslim Americans, and this harm would be greater than that caused by participating in a war. The muftis advised the *mustafti* to ask to serve in the rear, unless such a request would raise doubts about his allegiance or loyalty.[111]

Following the commencement of the war in Afghanistan in October 2001, al-Qaradawi authorized military participation, provided that the Muslim soldier did his best to avoid direct confrontation, in a fatwa responding to a query from Zaynab, a Canadian, on the permissibility of participation in the war. His fatwa began by stressing that a Muslim who fights another Muslim has committed *kufr*. He invoked the tradition narrated by al-Ahnaf, in which the Prophet reportedly said that if two Muslims fight each other, not only the killer but also the killed is doomed to hell because he was willing to kill his fellow Muslim.

However, al-Qaradawi argued that a Muslim who is recruited to a non-Muslim army to fight against Muslims finds himself in a difficult position that calls for special consideration. This Muslim might be a "helpless" soldier who has "no choice" but to yield to his commanders' orders. If that is the case, the Muslim soldier can join the rear guard to help in military service while avoiding combat confrontation to the extent possible. If he participates in a war against Muslims, the soldier should have an inner feeling of resentment, the "least of faith."

Al-Qaradawi noted that the harm caused by dodging a war would be greater than that caused by participating in it because if a Muslim soldier refused to fight other Muslims, "the Muslim, as well as the Muslim community, may be accused of high treason. Such an accusation may pose a threat to the Muslim minority, and this may also disrupt the course of *da'wa* that has been in full swing since tens of years ago [for decades] and has started to reap fruits."[112]

Continuation of Marriage to a Non-Muslim Husband

Wasati fatwas aimed to make the lives of converts easier. Examples include allowing them, and even encouraging them, to maintain their close relations with non-Muslim relatives and permitting them to inherit from their non-Muslim relatives, as seen later in this chapter. A particularly audacious contribution in this regard was the treatment of marital relations.

In his theorization on his *wasati* approach to *fiqh al-aqalliyyat al-Muslima*, al-Qaradawi brought the matter of female converts married to non-Muslims as one example of how cross-*madhhab* search enhances the implementation of *taysir*, which God wishes for humankind.[113] The shari'a allows men to marry Jewish and Christian women but prohibits

The Religious Law of Muslim Minorities   47

Muslim women from marrying non-Muslim men. The opinion among muftis of all four schools of Sunni law has been that if a woman converts to Islam and her husband does not follow in her footsteps, she must divorce him.

That was also al-Qaradawi's original opinion, but, like his change of heart on mortgages, he revised his view on this matter and made it permissible for female converts not to divorce their non-converted husbands.[114] His detailed deliberation suggested that in reading afresh into the depths of Muslim traditions and interpretations of those traditions, it becomes clear in his mind that while there is unanimity on the impermissibility of a Muslim woman's marriage to a non-Muslim man, there is no consensus regarding the obligation of a convert to terminate her marriage with a non-Muslim.[115]

Al-Qaradawi's opinion was uneasily embraced by the Council in its eighth session in 2001 in a fatwa that followed three lengthy meetings. The Council stated that while the four schools of law call on female converts to divorce their non-Muslim husbands, "some scholars" believe that it is permissible for female converts not to terminate the marriage and to maintain all their marital rights and duties as long as the husband does not limit their ability to profess their religion and as long as they aspire to bring their husbands into the fold of Islam.

The Council justified this opinion by explaining that women should not be deterred from embracing Islam. In stating that female converts who remain with their non-convert husbands can exercise all "duties and rights," the Council was even more lenient than al-Qaradawi, who hinted, drawing on the traditions, that converts need to refrain from sexual relations with their husbands until they are convinced to convert.[116]

Inheritence is another example of a *wasati* effort to protect converts from damage. The four schools of law forbid Muslims to inherit from non-Muslims, and non-Muslims to inherit from Muslims, based on the tradition according to which the Prophet said, "A Muslim does not inherit from the *kafir* (infidel) nor does the infidel from a Muslim." This consensus seriously injures the financial prospects of Western converts to Islam whose parents did not convert.

Al-Qaradawi, relying on Ibn Taymiyya, broke from the consensus. In his 2001 book on *fiqh al-aqalliyyat al-Muslima*, he noted that Islam seeks to benefit the believers, and the fear of losing the right to inherit their families' fortunes is a major concern of people contemplating conversion. Therefore, there is a *maslaha* in permitting inheritance from non-Muslims.[117] The Council adopted this view. It explained, as did al-Qaradawi, that the tradition that forbade inheritance from non-Muslims related only to infidels who were in a state of battle with Muslims.[118]

48   Shari'a and Life

Haram in the Workplace

Q. 5:2 prohibits Muslims from assisting in sins and transgression. The implication is that Muslims are not only prohibited, for example, from drinking alcohol and eating pork, but also from selling them. However, based on the consideration of *maslaha* (in this case, the need to provide for one's family), *wasati* fatwas have legitimized the continuation of employment in workplaces that engage with haram, as long as the employee searches for a permissible alternative.

For example, in its second session, the European Council for Fatwa and Research addressed a query by an employee in a McDonald's that sells pork products who wrote that he finds it "immensely difficult" to leave his job because his wife is about to give birth. The Council advised that the work that the Muslim is performing is prohibited because it is associated with selling an item that is haram. The Council advised the employee that "it is upon you to try your best to find an alternative means of making a living" and that "if you fail in doing so, then you may ask your managers at McDonald's to excuse you from selling pork, or you may coordinate with another worker so that you may work at other matters which do not involve selling pork." However, "if you find difficulty in doing so, or if you realize that this may affect your work at this food vendor, then you may continue to work if you do not have another sufficient source of income. You must, in any case, remain in pursuit of another job which does not involve dealing in any haram."[119]

Electoral Participation

The Council, in its second session in 1998, issued a decision on a query about the permissibility of participating in municipal elections in Europe and about voting for a non-Muslim political party that "may not serve the interests of Muslims." The Council stated that "this matter is to be decided by Islamic organizations and establishments. If these see that the interests of Muslims can only be served by this participation, then it is permissible on the condition that it does not involve the Muslims making more concessions or losses than gains."[120] In its seventeenth session in 2007, the Council stated that political participation is a necessity, i.e., the highest rank of *maslaha*.[121]

Relations with Non-Muslims

Wasatis emphasized that Muslims in the West should be kind and just to non-Muslims, reach out to them and assist them. The theme has been particularly highlighted following the 9/11 attacks. Some *wasati* comments on this theme read as indirect refutations of *salafi* treatises and fatwas on the duty to disavow non-Muslims.

For example, writing in the European Council for Fatwa and Research's journal, Jamal Badawi argued that when correctly read, the following truths are derived from the revelations: Muslims should extend their love and friendship to non-Muslims who do not fight against them and are not hostile to Islam, and act justly and compassionately to those non-Muslims; Islam should not be forced upon non-believers; the punishment for disbelief is not exacted in this life; and while fraternity based on religion is the noblest of fraternities, other kind of bonds between humans, including between Muslims and non-Muslims, are also permissible.[122]

Writing in the same journal, Ahmad Jaballah argued that Muslims living in a non-Muslim country must not betray or cheat it even if is acts unjustly towards others. He noted that nothing should prevent Muslims from seeking the prosperity of the societies in which they live, even if those societies are not Muslim, and stressed that Muslims should prefer interactions with non-Muslims to segregation.[123]

Christmas Greetings

Like several other panels and muftis,[124] the Council reflected favourably on seasonal greetings to Christians. The decision it issued demonstrates the importance *wasati*s attribute to promoting good relations with non-Muslims and their elevation of proselytizing to a principal religio-juristic objective. To a great extent, it reads as a refutation of the *salafi* understanding of "loyalty and disavowal" and previous *salafi* decisions on Christmas greetings (see below), although in a manner typical to these dialectics, the contesting party is not mentioned by name.

The Council noted that it had received numerous queries on this issue from Muslims living in the West. It stated that one may congratulate non-Muslims "either verbally or by sending a card [that] contains no symbols or icons of religious implications [that] may contradict Islamic faith and principles, such as the crucifix."[125] The decision is based on Q. 60:8–9 and additional evidence according to which God commanded Muslims to differentiate between non-Muslims who fight against Muslims and non-Muslims who interact with Muslims in peace. The latter must be treated in a kind manner.

Furthermore, a Muslim must never be less charitable or pleasant than a non-Muslim and should return polite treatment with similar

50 Shari'a and Life

treatment. "Indeed, the permissibility of congratulating non-Muslims on their festive days becomes more of an obligation if they were to offer their greetings on festive Islamic occasions, as we are commanded to return good treatment with similar treatment, and to return the greeting with a better one, or at least with the same greeting (Q. 4:86)."[126]

Invoking proselytizing as an objective, the Council argued that the significance of congratulating non-Muslims on their festive occasions "increases dramatically if we are interested in inviting them to Islam and to liken Muslims to them, which is an obligation upon us all." It is impossible to achieve the goal of converting non-Muslims by mistreating them. Instead, they should be treated in a way that builds trust, as was the way of the Prophet with the polytheists in Mecca despite the animosity directed against him and his companions.[127]

Al-Qaradawi also personally elaborated on the matter in response to a query from a Muslim PhD candidate from Germany. In his reply, al-Qaradawi legitimized Christmas greetings, basing his decision primarily on the permissibility of treating non-Muslims who do not fight against Muslims kindly, citing Q. 60:8–9 and other evidence central to the *wasati* refutation of *salafi* "loyalty and disavowal," as well as the objective of converting non-Muslims.

In reference to *salafi* fatwas on non-Muslim holidays, which invoke Ibn Taymiyya's strong opposition to any form of participation in or endorsement of a non-Muslim holiday (see below), al-Qaradawi argued that had Ibn Taymiyya lived today, he would have adapted his ideas to the changing circumstances, which necessitate congratulations. Among the circumstances he cited are: (a) the world has become a global village, and Muslims need to interact with non-Muslims who, regrettably, have become their mentors in many sciences and industries; (b) Muslims need to be gentle in order to proselytize, engaging in *tabshir* rather than *tanfir*; and (c) Christian holidays today are most commonly celebrated as national traditions. Therefore, if Muslims congratulate Christians, there is no risk that their false religious ideas will be reaffirmed.[128]

Beyond Formation

The development of *wasati fiqh al-aqalliyyat al-Muslima* and the European Council for Fatwa and Research can be divided into three main stages. The first, between 1997 and 2001, saw the publication of the formative *wasati* treatises on the ideology and methodology of *fiqh al-aqalliyyat al-Muslima* and several groundbreaking and controversial decisions, including the aforementioned fatwas on the conditional permissibility of mortgages and the continuation of marriage to a non-Muslim spouse.

The Religious Law of Muslim Minorities   51

In the post-formative second stage, until 2018, and still under the leadership of al-Qaradawi, the Council maintained its pragmatic approach, but did not issue new radical and highly controversial fatwas. One reason is that it had already treated the most crucial and sensitive issues in its first years of operation. Another is, perhaps, that its leaders were pressed to contain their audacity in the face of the controversies they caused during the initiation phase.

In that post-formative stage, responding to the pressures on Muslim populations following the September 11, 7/7, and Madrid attacks, the Council's publications emphasized the duty to be kind and just to non-Muslims and to abide by the laws of states where Muslims live.[129] The missionary rationale that dominated the foundational legitimizations of Muslim presence in Europe all but disappeared (while never textually refuted) from the Council's works, and was not actualized in any on-the-ground initiatives.

One example was offered in interviews in 2012 with the Dublin-based secretary-general of the Council, Hussein Halawa. It was clear that Halawa appreciated the political sensitivity of the missionary ideal or felt it was a theoretical notion irrelevant to its actual operations and impact. Asked what the most significant achievement of the Council was, he answered, succinctly and without hesitation, "that Muslims in Europe can live without *haraj*." Asked about proselytizing, he emphasized that the Council did not seek the Islamization of Europe, nor did it consider *da'wa* as a primary objective of the divine Lawgiver. To support his assertion, he noted that although the Council permitted Muslims to take mortgages when no alternative exists for them to purchase a home, it did not permit doing so to build mosques and enhance proselytizing. Contrary to his depiction, the 1999 mortgages fatwa was unequivocal in its treatment of *da'wa* as a *maslaha* that justifies suspension of the prohibited. It was retrospectively interpreted as such by 'Abd al-Majid al-Najjar, a member of the Council who supported the idea that in some cases, facilitation in decisions is essential in order to promote proselytizing.[130] Browsing through portions of the 1999 fatwa to prove the point, however, Halawa skipped the paragraphs that address the advancement of proselytizing.[131]

In November 2018, a third and new stage in the development of the Council began. During its annual session, held in Istanbul, Dr. 'Abdallah b. Yusuf al-Juday', one of al-Qaradawi's two deputies and a member of the Council since its inception, was elected as al-Qaradawi's successor. Al-Qaradawi simultaneously resigned from the presidency of the International Union of Muslim Scholars. His departures were dictated by the constraints of age. In his mid-90s, he could no longer intensely engage in travels, media events, and religio-juristic deliberations. By overseeing orderly leadership changes, al-Qaradawi could rest assured that his disciples succeeded him and that power struggles would not follow his departure.

The Leeds-based al-Juday', born in 1959 in Basra, Iraq, has lived in Britain since 1993 and is a British subject. He holds a PhD in Islamic economics from the University of Wales Trinity Saint David (2011). His thesis examined contemporary Islamic jurisprudence on banking interest, and he has served as a consultant on Islamic finances for business firms. His two elected deputies, the French-based Ahmad Jaballah and the London-based Suhaib Hasan, have also served on the Council's board since its inception. Hussein Halawa maintained his position as the secretary-general of the Council, and his mosque in Dublin remained its headquarters.

The Council's announcement of the nominations described the election of the new, European-based leadership as a "significant change" in the history of the panel, as it actualized the founding principle that called for queries of Muslims living in Europe to be addressed by experts who reside in the continent and are profoundly familiar with the situation there.[132] The announcement went almost unnoticed in the European and the Arab presses.

The first years of the new leadership, with activities constrained by the COVID-19 pandemic, did not see fundamental changes in the Council's pragmatic and integration-inclined approach nor in its modes of operation.

In its twenty-ninth session, held in Paris in July 2019, the Council stressed the importance of maintaining good relations and cooperating with non-Muslims and avoiding alienation and extremism, instructing Muslims to conduct their congregational and Eid prayers in a way that would not disturb their neighbors. It also asserted the generous approach to *maslaha* that regards needs as potential necessities. In line with past decisions, the Council stated in that session that Muslims should not celebrate non-Muslim religious holidays but may congratulate non-Muslims on their festive occasions and should do their best to leave work in order to attend Friday congregational prayers, but if unable to do so, may nevertheless maintain their jobs as a matter of necessity.[133]

In its thirty-first session, held through Zoom in September 2020, the Council stressed, in line with *wasati* methodology, the importance of *cross-madhhab* search and of protecting the primary objectives of the divine Lawgiver. Loyal to its integration-inclined ideology, it also noted that where a conflict between shari'a norms and the laws of the state exists, Muslims should abide by the latter while aiming to exhaust legal options for appeal.[134]

Salafi Fiqh al-Aqalliyyat al-Muslima

Salafiyya began to spread in Europe in the 1980s through students (and students of students) of Saudi institutions who promoted the ideology and priorities advanced by the late twentieth-century Saudi religious establishment. These included graduates of the Islamic University of al-Madina, which became the Kingdom's hub for international students. As it spread, luminaries of *salafi* thought began giving considerable attention to issues pertaining to living as minorities in non-Muslim lands.

Unlike the *wasati* efforts, *salafi* muftis and *ifta'* panels have not endeavoured to devise a specific religio-juristic approach to Muslim minorities. On the contrary, one of their underlying objectives in writing about Muslim minorities was to clarify that the shariʿa applies universally. Still, a rich and distinct corpus of theoretical *salafi* deliberations and fatwas in that field developed.

The *salafi* approach to the religious law of Muslim minorities is similar to that of the *wasati*s in one crucial aspect. Like the *wasati*s, *salafi*s regard Muslim residence in non-Muslim lands as potentially permissible for those who can practice Islam and stress proselytizing as a justification for migration. Unlike *wasati*s, their legitimization is grudging and minimalist. Based on Q. 4:97 and the tradition according to which the Prophet stated his disavowal of Muslims who live among polytheists, *salafi*s hold that, in general, Muslims must live in *Dar al-Islam*. They consider residence in infidel lands as extremely risky and highly undesirable, conditionally tolerable at best. They characterize *daʿwa* efforts by Muslims who are strong in faith and can practice their religion as an almost exclusive justification for voluntary migration to non-Muslim lands.

The reluctant legitimacy *salafi*s offer for Muslim residence in non-Muslim lands is rooted in the approach of the *Hanbali* school. *Hanbali*s chose a middle ground between the *Maliki* approach that prohibited residence in infidel lands and the *Shafiʿi* approach that, as noted above, legitimized and even encouraged residence that could enhance proselytizing. *Hanbali*s argued that if Muslims can practice Islam in a non-Muslim territory, they may remain, though it is recommended that they ultimately move to Muslim territory. *Wahhabi* jurisprudence in the nineteenth century maintained this line of thought.[135]

Salafi muftis addressed two situations: visits to non-Muslim lands and permanent residence. They strongly prohibited visits, but this

54 Shari'a and Life

prohibition is not without exceptions. The Permanent Committee, headed by Ibn Baz, stated that it was not permissible to go on vacations in Europe for fear of temptation, basing its decision on the tradition according to which the Prophet said he disavowed Muslims who live among the polytheists.[136]Al-'Uthaymin similarly stated that vacations in infidel lands were impermissible, noting that there are plenty of tourist options in Muslim countries.[137]

The tolerance of sojourns in non-Muslim lands for academic study or business was more nuanced. *Salafi* muftis strongly advised against studying in Western institutions but accepted that it is permissible in cases where no Muslim institution provides a parallel program and the Muslim's faith is strong enough to avoid doubts and temptations.[138] Ibn Baz stated that it was impermissible to travel to a non-Muslim country for commerce or personal visits.[139] His deputy on the Permanent Committee, 'Abd al-Raziq 'Afifi, offered a more lenient view (and exceptional, in the *salafi* context). He stated that a Muslim who can find a job in a Muslim country was not permitted to sojourn for the purpose of working, but a Muslim who could not find work was permitted if he was able to avoid imitating the infidels and could maintain his religion there.[140] In this instance, the necessity of providing for one's family was cited as a *maslaha* that legitimizes an otherwise prohibited act.

The only case in which sojourning was not only conditionally legitimate but also potentially desirable is when intended for *da 'wa* activities among Muslim minorities. Al-'Uthaymin approved of knowledgeable Muslims travelling to lands of disbelief "for the sake of Muslim brothers who are living there but have insufficient knowledge to respond to specious arguments." In fact, "it might be imperative" for them to sojourn "in order to help and support them [Muslim minorities] and to show them that they have brothers elsewhere."[141]

The attitude of *salafi* muftis to Muslims who are already settled in non-Muslim lands was uncompromising in tone but left open the possibility for interpretations that legitimize permanent settlement (with few exceptions, most notably al-Albani's, who called for the immediate migration of all Muslims who live in non-Muslim lands to Muslim lands). They argued that it was strictly forbidden for a Muslim to permanently live in an infidel society but offered two particular exceptions: being unable to migrate to a Muslim country or being active in proselytizing.

While this approval appears narrow and circumspect, they avoided detailing what kind of hindrances legitimize continuous residence among a majority infidel society or how active a Muslim should be in *da 'wa* for his efforts to legitimize his choice of staying. They did not

The Religious Law of Muslim Minorities   55

state, for example, that the nature of the hindrance has to be such that it prevents any possibility of moving to a Muslim land or that proselytizing should be the exclusive occupation of the Muslim living in a land of infidels. This vagueness, untypical of *salafi* fatwas, suggests that *salafi* muftis understood the unlikelihood of a massive Muslim return from the West.

Thus, their fatwas aimed to encourage Muslim minorities to consider their religious status as severely endangered, to strengthen their devotion, and enthusiastically engage in proselytizing. To note a few examples, the Permanent Committee, headed by Ibn Baz, answered a query by a seventy-five-year-old Lebanese Muslim who married a non-Muslim and settled in Brazil. His two sons had neglected Islam, and he was concerned that he would not receive an Islamic burial upon his death. Based on Q. 4:97, the Committee advised him to move to a Muslim country. However, it said that if he were unable to do so, he may remain in Brazil, based on Q. 4:98–99, so long as he continued to practice his religion with dedication.[142] The decision was careful not to describe what constitutes legitimate reasons for being unable to move or, for that matter, what constitutes practicing Islam.

Based on Q. 4:97 and the tradition according to which the Prophet disavows Muslims living among polytheists, Ibn Baz stated that "living in a land where *shirk*, Christianity, and other false creeds are prevalent is not permissible," whether the reason was work, business, or study.[143] It is obligatory to migrate, "except for a man who has knowledge and insight" and toils "to call people to Allah."[144] Al-'Uthaymin stated that residence in infidel lands poses a grave danger to one's religion, morals, and practices and was therefore permissible only if the Muslim was strong in faith and could practice his religion. He based the latter decision on Q. 4:97. One's possible activities when residing among the infidels are divided, according to al-'Uthaymin, into only two categories: either he dedicates time to *da'wa*, which is a religious duty and a form of jihad, or to the study of the moral corruption of the infidels, which is also a form of jihad because it helps warn against their corrupting influence.[145]

The Permanent Committee advised a 26-year-old, French-born of Tunisian extraction, father of two, who hesitated to migrate to his ancestral homeland given the limitations on the practice of Islam there, that living in a non-Muslim country is forbidden, except in situations of necessity such as medical treatment not available in the Muslim world or proselytizing. They advised that if returning to Tunisia is not Islamically safe, he should move to another Muslim country.[146]

The editors of a popular *salafi* website advised that Muslims in the West must not remain there, but offered a long and rather flexible list of

56   Shari'a and Life

exceptions that included "those of you who are forced to stay or need to do so, because they have no other place to go, or because they are sick and need treatment, or they are active in da'wa, calling people to Islam; or if you are natives of that land and can practice your religion openly."[147]

As opposed to *wasatis*, *salafi* muftis did not argue that Muslim minorities were entitled to any kind of concessions based on the unique hardships they face or on their duty to proselytize. This position was derived from the foundational *salafi* view that God's laws are universal and should be interpreted and applied literally, and that strictly adhering to these laws constitutes the essence of Islam's *wasati* nature. In the eyes of *salafis*, the grave challenges Muslim minorities face are opportunities for demonstrating strong devotion. Thus, *taysir* – a foundation of *wasati fiqh al-aqalliyyat al-Muslima* and its main practical implication – is absent from *salafi* theorizing on residence among non-Muslim majorities, and some *salafi* fatwas on Muslim minorities read as negations of *wasati* facilitations (although only a few are explicit refutations).

Examples of Dogmatism

Mortgages

Salafi fatwas vehemently opposed *wasati* facilitations on interest-based loans. In addressing the issue, *salafis* rejected the broad *wasati* approach to *maslaha* and applied two foundations of their approach to the jurisprudence of Muslim minorities: God's laws are universal, and only a *maslaha* at the rank of necessity, dire and unquestionable, justifies permitting the prohibited. Lifting a hardship does not qualify as justification, neither does promoting proselytizing. The unlikely situation of a family finding itself without any roof over its head might qualify, though.[148]

Queries directed in the 2000s to *salafi* muftis on the matter suggest that the European Council for Fatwa and Research's decision was known to the *mustaftis* who sent them. Often, *mustaftis* pointed to *maslahas* that could be incurred if a loan is taken in the hope that it would convince the mufti or the panel to offer a lenient decision. In response, they were instructed that with regard to interest-based loans, leniency is not an option, no matter what the personal or communal gains may be. For example, the editors of Islamweb.net were asked, five years after the issuance of the European Council for Fatwa and Research's fatwa, whether a decision had been issued by al-Qaradawi permitting interest-based mortgages for Muslims who were not homeowners. Without repeating al-Qaradawi's name, they replied that they were not aware of such a decision and that mortgages are prohibited based on the Prophet's words that those who charge or pay interest will be cursed.[149]

Student Loans

Salafi fatwas equally rejected student loans, so long as any interest is charged. They did not accept the view that paying back a loan based on the rise in the consumer price index does not constitute usury. In their opinion, any payment that is higher than the loan constitutes unlawful interest, and this matter is not debatable.[150]

The editors of Islam Question & Answer were presented with a more complicated situation of a Muslim student in Norway who was entitled to a loan. If he passes his midterm, it will become a grant, yet if he drops out or his grades do not allow him to pursue his studies further, the loan will be valid and will carry interest. Is it permissible to take a loan? The editors answered that the money is only permissible if it does not carry any interest and the amount paid back is the exact amount given. If there is even a potential for being charged interest, then the loan is impermissible.[151]

Service in a Non-Muslim Military Force

Salafi muftis held service in non-Muslim militaries impermissible. This opinion is based on a foundation of "loyalty and disavowal," that Muslims should not help infidels become stronger. However, they did not dismiss this option altogether, provided that the Muslim soldier is not involved, in any way, in aggressions against Muslims. Their limited legitimization, based on *maslaha*, demonstrates their inclination to apply a measure of flexibility when the relations between individuals and non-Muslim states are at stake. It also demonstrates indifference or ignorance of the potential impact fatwas can have on the actual lives of Muslim individuals and communities in the West.

In this spirit, al-ʿUthaymin stated that service in a non-Muslim military is "problematic" because it has the potential to help the infidels wage war against Muslims or those who have a treaty with Muslims. Even if this is not the case, a Muslim is only permitted to serve in a non-Muslim force in two capacities: as a spy who learns secrets; or as a preacher, imam, or muezzin, serving Muslims and calling non-Muslims to Islam.[152]

Continuation of Marriage to a Non-Muslim Husband

In direct contrast to *wasati* legitimization of such relations, *salafi* luminaries did not encourage the continuation of relations with non-Muslim

58 Shari'a and Life

relatives. They made clear that prospects for bringing non-Muslims to the fold of God's truth constitute no justification for facilitation but, on the contrary, should motivate strict, uncompromising adherence to divine laws.

The issue of continuation of marriage was presented before al-'Uthaymin in words encouraging legitimization of the prohibited. The *mustafti* wrote that some women wish to convert while their husbands do not; pointing to *maslaha*, the query noted that, alas, the fear of losing beloved husbands who also provide financial support, as well as the concern for the children, make these women hesitate. In many cases, the husbands embrace Islam after a year or so, and the wives hope to promote their conversion by remaining with them. Considering that times have changed, and based on *maslaha* and the principle of choosing the lesser of two evils (choosing the act that involves lesser injury to *maslaha*), is there room for *ijtihad* on the matter?

Al-'Uthaymin replied that there is not. He stated that based on the elaborate words in Q. 60:10, the explicit law prohibiting the continuation of marriages between Muslim converts and non-Muslim husbands belongs to the category of laws on which there is no room for *ijtihad*. Even if the *maslaha* of a law belonging to that category is not evident under certain circumstances, and even if abiding by the law is difficult, one must still abide by the law. The *salaf*, he noted, did not hesitate to kill even their own fathers and sons for the sake of God.[153]

Salih al-Fawzan's fatwa on the matter was issued following the European Council for Fatwa and Research's decision. The query addressed to al-Fawzan noted that "a body that is called the European Council for Issuing Fatwas" issued a fatwa that allows an infidel woman who became a Muslim to remain with her infidel husband. Is the fatwa correct? Al-Fawzan answered that the above-mentioned fatwa was invalid based on Q. 60:10. If a woman converted to Islam, she must separate from her infidel husband. If the husband becomes a Muslim during the *'idda* (three monthly periods), she should return to him. If not, based on Q 2:221, she must leave him for good.[154]

Salafis also strongly rejected the facilitation of inheritance of non-Muslims, noting that "The believer does not inherit from a *kafir* and the *kafir* does not inherit from the believer."[155]

Haram in the Workplace

Salafi fatwas recognized that Muslims living in majority non-Muslim countries are often ill-positioned to negotiate the terms of their employment or find another job. Yet, they did not consider this reality as justifying facilitations. Rather, they demanded that Muslims quit jobs that force them to commit haram deeds or assist others in committing such deeds and suggested that Muslims who could not find appropriate alternatives should migrate to a Muslim country.

Al-'Uthaymin was asked which alternative is better for Muslim women who live in Western countries, where there is no gender segregation in schools and workplaces: staying home, resulting in severe economic repercussions, or covering themselves and studying and working in non-segregated environments. Relying on Q. 29:10, he stressed that Muslims must abide by God's laws even in the face of hardships or else they are hypocrites who only claim true devotion. Relying on Q. 4:97, a central element of *salafi* evidence against residence in non-Muslim lands, he stated that if a workplace did not segregate men from women, it was not permissible to work there, and if another means of making a living cannot be found in the West, then a new job should be sought in another country.[156]

Salafi fatwas emphasized that a Muslim whose job requires assisting in transgressions must find another job.[157] They commonly provide reassurance that another job will be found. On rare occasions, facilitations were granted, but in a way that did not provide for even modest financial security. A waiter who works in a restaurant that sells pork was told that he may remain at his job based on necessity while searching for another. However, the waiter was ordered not to possess or save the money he earned and, once he had found another job, to spend whatever was left from the haram earnings on the "general interest of Muslims," like schools.[158] In a way typical of *salafi* deliberations, the authors of the fatwa did not consider the obvious negative implications abiding by their decision could have on a low-paid employee and his family.

Electoral Participation

In contrast to other issues, a majority of *salafi* luminaries joined the *wasati* opinion and legitimized Muslim political participation in the West based on similar justifications. For example, asked whether it is permissible for Muslims to establish Islamic parties in secular states where they are officially subjected to secular laws provided that their objective is to practice *da'wa* secretly, the Permanent Committee replied positively: "It is prescribed for Muslims who live in non-Islamic states to unite, cooperate, and work together, whether in the name of Islamic parties or Islamic societies, for it is cooperating in righteousness and piety."[159]

There is, however, a substantial difference between the two legitimizations. Unlike *wasati*s, the permission some *salafi*s granted did not

60   Shari'a and Life

encourage Muslims to vote and, moreover, did not oblige them to do so. However, the religio-legal result is similar in practical terms, making it possible for Muslims who adhere to the *salafi* approach to vote and compete in general and municipal elections.

This result is explained by the nuances of *salafi* attitudes towards political authority, electoral politics, and Muslim minorities and, specifically, by how *salafis* interpret and apply *maslaha* in the context of these fields. First, *salafis* contextualize political participation as another means to protect and promote the interests of Islam and Muslim communities who are faced with the coercive power of non-Muslim regimes, rather than to ease specific hardships faced by individual Muslims in certain social spheres. Second, *salafis* conditionally approve of voting in unlawful political systems in Muslim countries. Legitimizing voting in non-Muslim states does not constitute a radical break from their views. This is not to suggest that they hold sinful Muslim systems and infidel systems to be the same. Third, the contentious nature of politics reassures *salafis* that by participating in the political arena, Muslims will not breach their concept of "loyalty and disavowal."[160]

Relations with Non-Muslims

Drawing on the concept of *al-wala' wa-l-bara'*, *salafi* fatwas made it clear that Muslims must not befriend or show affection to non-Muslims. These standards are universal, but their potential implications for minorities living in non-Muslim countries are far more significant than for Muslims living in a country like Saudi Arabia.

To note several examples, Ibn Baz stated, based on Q. 49:10 and the Prophet's words, as narrated by 'Abdallah b. 'Umar, according to which "the Muslim is the brother of the Muslim," that Muslims must not take non-Muslims as friends and must disavow and hate them.[161] Al-'Uthaymin, relying on Q. 60:4 (see above) as well as Q. 58:22 (which forbids believers from socializing with infidels), cautioned that it is "impermissible for a Muslim to feel any love in his heart towards the enemies of Allah who are in fact his enemies."[162] Relying on Q.11: 45–6, he wrote that a Muslim should not address a non-Muslim as "my brother" unless the non-Muslim were his biological brother or they shared a wet nurse because, other than these two kinds of brotherly bonding, the only brotherhood is that of the believers. Relying on Q. 58:22, he argued that a Muslim must not address a non-Muslim as a "friend" or a "mate" in a way that signifies affection; it is permissible to do so only in neutral situations, such as when addressing someone whose name is not known.[163] He stressed, citing Q. 60:1 and 5:51–2, that any infidel is an enemy of God and His Prophet and that Muslims must hate him with all their hearts.[164]

While leading *salafis* interpreted "loyalty and disavowal" in a way that promotes enmity towards non-Muslims, they were careful to emphasize that Muslim minorities must respect the laws of their receiving states, avoid cheating and stealing for personal gain, act justly towards the non-Muslims who do not attack them, and shun terrorist activities. Hostility should be confined to the heart rather than outwardly expressed.

These demands were based on four main justifications: God's permission for Muslims to respect and be just with infidels who do not fight against Muslims (Q. 60: 8) and the prohibition of harming the innocent; the concern for the wellbeing of the Muslim community and the safeguarding of its interests (that is, a communal *maslaha*); the religio-legal duty to abide by contracts, and the belief that visas or citizenship constitute forms of contracts; and the *salafi* rejection of individualistic subversive political or violent acts, which they also apply to non-Muslim states.

Ibn Baz, for example, stated that while Muslims must hate non-Muslims and disavow them, the principle of "loyalty and disavowal" in no way means to mistreat them or attack them or avoid being gentle to them, unless they attack Muslims.[165] According to al-Fawzan, while infidels hate, betray and plot against Muslims, Muslims must nevertheless treat with justice and kindness those who do not fight them, hate them, or drive them out of their homes.[166]

Christmas Greetings

Unlike *wasatis*, *salafi* muftis prohibited Muslims from congratulating Christians on Christmas. For example, al-ʿUthaymin explained that congratulations signify approval of the holiday and help Christians propagate their infidel beliefs. His fatwa relies on Ibn al-Qayyim al-Jawziyya, who held that wishing someone "a merry Christmas" is a greater sin than congratulating him on drinking wine, committing murder, or having illicit sex.[167]

Salafi fatwas allowed almost no exception to the prohibition of engaging with non-Muslim religious (and civilian) holidays, even if it results in substantial financial losses. They stated that a Muslim may not accept a Christmas cash bonus "because it is a kind of honoring their festivals and approving of them, and helping them in their falsehood."[168] Neither may he eat food prepared by infidels for their holidays;[169] accept gifts related directly to an infidel holiday;[170] distribute candies on those

62   Shari'a and Life

holidays;[171] hold parties that imitate an infidel celebration;[172] sell the infidels items that they use to celebrate their holidays, such as clothes, perfumes, decorations, and greeting cards;[173] or collect donations for low-income families on the occasion of Christmas.[174]

Based on the principle of *al-wala' wa-l-bara'*, *salafi* luminaries opposed congratulating non-Muslims even on occasions that are unrelated to their holidays. Al-'Uthaymin prohibited congratulating an infidel on his safe arrival home, quoting the tradition narrated by Abu Hurayra, according to which the Prophet forbade initiating greetings to Jews and Christians.[175] The potential implications such discourtesies may have on Muslims living in majority non-Muslim countries were of no concern to al-'Uthaymin.

Beyond Formation

At the turn of the century, when a distinct *wasati* approach to *fiqh al-aqalliyyat al-Muslima* was being formulated, *salafiyya* lost its two contemporary luminaries and main articulators. Ibn Baz died in 1999; al-'Uthaymin died two years later. Nevertheless, by the time of their departure, the two, along with Saudi Arabia's state-run religio-legal panels, had already publicized detailed treatments of the core challenges of living in the West.[176] These became a legacy of dogmatism, suspicion, and introversion-mindedness. The legacy was continued in the next two decades by newer leading authorities and, thus, carried the capacity to respond to new situations.

There developed no pan-European or even national-level organizations and *ifta'* panels speaking for the *salafi* approach. Rather, independent mosques, associations, Islamic centres, and publishers function on local levels. While some *salafi* organizations in Europe affiliated loosely with other *salafi* organizations, the institutionalization of *salafiyya* in Europe has been characterized by conflicts and deep rivalries, as is often the case with small, ideologically fervent, and dogmatically-inclined groups.

In his "beautiful advice" to *salafi*s in Europe, the Saudi 'Abd al-'Aziz al-Rayyis lamented that "many of the *salafi* centres in Europe – after being places of knowledge, learning, and study – change into places of differing, problems, and argumentation among the *salafi*s themselves."[177] Al-Rayyis, an official at the Ministry for Islamic Affairs, Endowments, Da'wa, and Guidance, called on European *salafi*s to change course and to realize that there are issues on which there can be differences of opinion, as well to appreciate that not every person with ties to Saudi Arabia is necessarily correct in what he says.[178]

Some *salafi*-inclined mosques have the label *salafiyya* in their title or affiliate with the approach by bearing the name of one of *salafiyya*'s main protagonists, while others struggle to distance themselves from this banner. One reason for the latter preference is the association of *salafiyya* in the European public mind with radicalization and the common confusion in the media between *salafiyya* and jihadi-*salafiyya*.

In all *salafi* mosques, the luminaries of the Saudi religious establishment, its institutions, and its foremost students are privileged, and their dogmatism is preached as the exclusively legitimate choice for those loyal to Islam. However, those mosques have differed in their levels of direct engagement with and commitment to Saudi-based or other external authorities.

Among the Saudi-based muftis who have been particularly active in the *salafi* European mosque scene is Rabi' b. Hadi al-Madkhali (b. 1932), a professor at the University of Madina and a student of Ibn Baz. While not regarded as one of the Kingdom's greatest religious scholars, since the early 1990s, he has contributed a particularly adamant voice against democratic politics, jihadi-*Salafism*, and Islamic political insubordination at large (especially that led by the Muslim Brothers), to the extent that rivals label mosques that privilege his teachings as Madkhali mosques.[179]

While the signature of the approach is its uncompromising nature, *salafi fiqh al-aqalliyyat al-Muslima* does allow space for priorities and nuances. One crucial example is relations with non-Muslims; a choice can be made to focus preaching on the need to demonstrate disloyalty and despise of Westerners, or on the duty to abide by the laws of the land and to act against violent groups. Some *salafi* groups have tended in recent years to choose the latter option – in part as a defense against their association with violent radicalization, following the September 11, 7/7, and Madrid attacks and the rise of ISIS, and in part to promote the prospects of their proselytizing efforts.

Only a small minority of Muslims in Europe – one per cent would be a generous estimate – have become affiliates of *salafi* groups. However, the *salafi* approach has enjoyed considerable marketing reach, one that is massively disproportionate to the number of its loyalists. The amount of Arabic and translated *salafi* titles on sale is one aspect of this reach. Time and again, we were surprised to notice the quantity of *salafi* works in mosques and Islamic-interest bookstores in Europe that have no particular sympathy for this approach.

The other aspect of *salafi* marketing has been state-of-the-art websites, which include general guidance and vast fatwa archives and allow Muslims worldwide to submit queries. Along with the websites of the Saudi

64   Shari'a and Life

Permanent Committee and individual muftis, among the popular *salafi* platforms are the Riyadh-based ar.Islamway.net (formerly Islamway. com, launched in August 1998), and its English version en.Islamway. net; the multilingual Islamweb.net, sponsored by the Qatari Ministry for Endowments and Religious Affairs; and the multilingual Islam Question & Answer, operated by the Syrian-born (1960) and Saudi-based Salih al-Munajjid. Blind queries on Islamic jurisprudence demonstrate the effectiveness of *salafi* online operations. A European who will learn about Islam only through Google will find it hard to believe that *salafiyya* is not the voice of the majority and the mainstream.

Chapter Two

Across a Wasati-Salafi European Spectrum

The following pages present brief histories and ethnographic information about the mosques focused on in this study. They present the origins
of the mosques, their organizational structures and modes of operation,
their demographic compositions, how their imams and administrations
understand fiqh, and where they are positioned on the *wasati-salafi* spectrum. They also introduce the challenges attendees of these mosques
encounter from their majority non-Muslim societies and from rival
mosques and Muslim organizations in their vicinities and beyond.

Stockholm

The Stockholm Mosque, officially the Zayd b. Sultan al-Nahyan
Mosque (also known as The Grand Mosque of Stockholm or its Central
Mosque), was inaugurated in 2000 in the lively Södermalm district, the
capital's heart of tourism and leisure (figure 2.1). The opening of a large
mosque at the centre of Stockholm followed several years of planning
and public debates.[1]

The mosque is located in an impressive building constructed in the
early twentieth century and inspired by Moorish architecture; it originally served as an electric power plant. It is run by the Islamic Association in Stockholm (*Islamiska Förbundet i Stockholm*), established in 1981.
In 1987, this Association established the Islamic Association in Sweden
(*Islamiska Förbundet i Sverige*), which operates out of the mosque. It runs
and co-runs several religious, instructional, educational, and cultural
Muslim organizations in Sweden, and was one of the architects of the Muslim Council of Sweden (*Sveriges muslimska råd*), an Islamic umbrella
organization established in 1990. The Islamic Association in Sweden is
also a founding member of the Federation of Islamic Organizations in
Europe, the founding organization of the European Council for Fatwa

66 Shari'a and Life

and Research. Twice, in 2003 and 2017, the Stockholm Mosque hosted the ordinary sessions of the Council, headed by al-Qaradawi.

The Swedish government does not provide official figures about the number of Muslims in the country. According to the most generous estimate, some 800,000 Muslims live in Sweden, comprising slightly more than eight per cent of its population and its largest religious minority.[2] Other estimates put their number much lower at some 500,000, 300,000, and 250,000. Stockholm (960,000 residents) has a large and ethnically diverse Muslim population. As of early 2017, it was home to 16,245 Iraq-born, 11,815 Iran-born, 7,827 Somalia-born, 7,356 Turkey-born, 6,357 Syria-born, and 2,559 Morocco-born residents.[3] The Swedish liberal and humanitarian approach to refugee crises is the reason for the dominance of Muslims from several war-torn countries in this demographic breakdown.

Because it is the most prominent publicly visible manifestation of Islam in Sweden, and because of its affiliation with an Islamist-oriented organization, the Stockholm Mosque has been the focus of several public controversies since its inception. Swedish politicians and media, as well as rival Swedish Muslim leaders, have accused the mosque of endorsing radical views and being under the spell of the Muslim Brothers.[4]

In the 2003 ordinary session of the European Council for Fatwa and Research hosted by the mosque, al-Qaradawi was reported to have legitimized suicide attacks against Israeli civilians. He stated that "The martyrdom operations carried out by the Palestinian factions to resist the Zionist occupation are not in any way included in the framework of prohibited terrorism, even if the victims include some civilians."[5] In 2004, an investigative report by one of Sweden's largest newspapers suggested that the mosque watered down the anti-American content of Friday sermons in their English translations.[6] In 2005, the police raided the mosque's bookstore to investigate allegations that it was selling anti-Semitic cassettes (no charges were filed after the investigation).[7] On several occasions, swastikas were painted on the mosque's doors, and threatening letters were sent to its administration.[8]

At Friday's congregational prayers, we observed, during sweltering summer days, approximately 1,200 male attendees (the number of participants in prayers, in this and all other mosques surveyed, was calculated based on counting the number of shoes during the time of the prayers). The written survey and our observations demonstrated an ethnically diverse population, without a dominant ethnicity, with attendees originating from Syria, the Palestinian Authority, Tunisia, Morocco, Iraq, the Gambia, Somalia, Côte d'Ivoire, Pakistan, and Bangladesh.

Figure 2.1. The Stockholm Mosque. Entrance to the mosque, located in a building that originally served as an electric power plant. The gates are closed between prayers, in part to avoid tourists and refugees.

Before and after the prayers, hundreds of men rushed in and out, while others stood in small groups and conversed. Only a few wore traditional attire. Most wore jeans and trainers. Several volunteer security officials walked around to maintain order, but they were not really needed. When the prayers began, the mosque was filled to capacity, and some attendees had to pray outside.

The atmosphere at the gates was somewhat festive, crowded yet relaxed. Some attendees came early to secure a spot to perform a religious duty, meet old friends, and make new ones. Dates and water were offered free of charge. Here, an older man, dressed in a grey suit, carrying a self-made poster, asked for donations for the Palestinians of Gaza. There, another man raised his voice, asking for donations for the victims of the war in Syria. Here, fliers were distributed for a mobile phone service, and there, for a political party. During the other days of the week, only several dozen men attended prayers. Between prayer times, the heavy gates of the mosque were closed. We were told that the reasons are the substantial number of tourists and refugees in the city and the fear of further anti-Muslim vandalism.

Khaled ʿAbd al-Hakim al-Dib, born in 1972, father of four (two boys, at the time of the interview aged 14 and five, and two girls, aged 13

68 Shari'a and Life

and eight, all of whom attend Swedish state schools), has served as the imam of the mosque since 2012. He is an al-Azhar graduate who speaks Arabic with a noticeable Egyptian accent. The mosque employs another imam, Mahmud Khalfi, who serves as its director, whereas imam al-Dib leads the Friday prayers. We attended two of his eloquently delivered *khutbas* (sermons), in which he broached concepts that are core to the *wasati* agenda. In one, he discussed the relationship between democracy and *shura* (consultation). In another, he elaborated on the meaning of *maslaha*.

Al-Dib generously welcomed us for two interviews without prior appointment, in which he pronounced his mosque's affiliation and complete commitment to the European Council for Fatwa and Research as a binding religio-legal authority. He described this affiliation as a continuation of the policy that had guided the mosque since its establishment. He declared that he would accept any decision the Council issues, even if he disagreed with it (to date, he had, however, "never, ever read a single decision" by the Council that he disapproved of). He shrugged off the suggestion that the Council exercised excessive leniency, arguing that *fiqh al-aqalliyyat al-Muslima*, which is different from the fiqh applied in Muslim countries, must be applied lest people fail in observing their religion. If there is criticism against the Council, he said, it is only because some of its fatwas were ahead of their time.

According to al-Dib, the Council should be privileged over individual muftis because it comprises 40 members with different specializations and backgrounds and should be privileged over other panels because it is based in Europe. In line with al-Qaradawi's religio-juristic approach, and the raison d'être of the Council, al-Dib suggested that the issuance of fatwas requires not only a firm command of religious disciplines (including Quran, Hadith, *tafsir*, *'aqida*, and *falsafa*) and the Arabic language, but also of the *mustafti*'s reality. Familiarity with the petitioner's reality is essential because fatwas may change in relation to different people, situations, and environments. Thus, Muslims in Europe should not consult with non-European authorities on issues pertaining to Europe. They should reject what al-Dib termed "imported fatwas."

This principle applies universally. Al-Dib would not consult with his alma-mater al-Azhar when issuing opinions for Muslims in Sweden, and would similarly not give advice to people living in Egypt: "My country of origin is Egypt. I have lived outside it for six years. If you asked me about a fatwa in Egypt, I would be dishonest and unreliable if I answered." To further elaborate on the matter, al-Dib offered a medical metaphor: Just as doctors in a hospital attend only to illnesses in their fields of specialization, so too should muftis attend only to realities with which they are familiar. To this, he added another metaphor: The foundation of driving regulations is the same everywhere, but regulations in Sweden are different from those in Egypt. In Egypt, one follows the driving regulations of Egypt, whereas, in Sweden, one should follow the driving regulations of Sweden.

The imam's admiration of al-Qaradawi reinforced his commitment to the Council. For example, al-Dib related that hundreds of lives could have been saved if only Saudi authorities had heeded al-Qaradawi's warnings about infrastructural deficiencies at the Jamarat Bridge near Mecca.

Al-Dib's concept of *ifta'* is structural and hierarchical also concerning *mustaftis* who approach him. In most cases, he would expect them to accept the *wasati* position he would offer without further deliberations. He explained that if a Muslim without education in Islamic law asks for his opinion on a religio-legal matter, he would not provide evidence for the decision (*dalil*) because that Muslim could not comprehend it. Offering yet another medical metaphor, he compared the lay *mustafti* to a patient diagnosed by a medical doctor; the patient should not expect detailed explanations from the expert about a tumor before undergoing an operation, but rather just accept the expert's authority. Further, the *mustafti* should not consult with more than one mufti because that could encourage "fishing" for the most lenient opinion.

Al-Dib agreed that there had been some loss of trust in religious scholars across the Muslim world. He attributed this phenomenon to the proliferation of unqualified imams and media that amplified the erroneous opinions of some shaykhs. He did not conceal his concerns about *salafi* influences on Swedish Muslims, although he did so only in response to a direct question, and refrained from mentioning them by name. He described *salafiyya* as a "big problem," and noted that in his role as the president of the Swedish Imam Association, he leads efforts to ensure that young Swedes do not travel to Egypt, Saudi Arabia, or Jordan to learn the shariʻa, but instead remain in Sweden to learn from scholars who know well both the shariʻa and the realities of life there. Asked about the *salafi* argument that only *salafis* apply the shariʻa in a way that is loyal to the Quran and the traditions, he turned the argument on its head:

We say: we have the Quran and the Sunna. What is commensurate with the Quran and the Sunna – welcome … Did the European Council for Fatwa and Research [ever] issue any decision that contradicts the Quran and the Sunna? No, it did not.

70   Shari'a and Life

To clarify his point, al-Dib offered a final medical metaphor: if two doctors do not agree, they go to the head of the department for a decision. The Quran, he said, serves as the head of the department for the Muslims. The only question is whether anything in a fatwa contradicts the Quran, which is not the case in those issued by the Council.[9]

In practice, al-Dib's direct communications with the Council are minimal. He stated that he contacts Dublin only three or four times a year on average (the last question he recalled sending was about the legitimacy of bitcoin). He explained that the Council had already provided advice on most of the issues that he encounters.

Al-Dib's criticism of *salafis* was not directed against far-away or fictitious rivals. With only a handful of mosques and Islamic organizations in Stockholm and its suburbs, two rising *salafi* groups pose the most direct challenge to his mosque's dominance and leadership. The Husby Mosque (officially the Husby Islamic Cultural Centre) is led by another Egyptian, Muhammad al-Makkawi. The Ibn Abbas Center is led by a group of graduates and students of the Saudi Madina University, including a Swedish convert and popular proselytizer, Johannes Klominek, who adopted the name Abdullah as-Sueidi following his conversion.

The Husby Mosque is located in the Husby district of the Rinkeby-Kista borough, where 79 per cent of the population have a migration background (two-thirds are from the Middle East and Africa).[10] In May 2013, the district – socio-economically the poorest in Stockholm – was the centre of widespread riots protesting police violence against minorities.[11] The riots raised concerns that Sweden's welfare state and communalist tradition could not accommodate the country's changing demographics. The mosque has been active since the mid-1970s. It opened under its current name and with the administration of a registered association in 1986. On the Friday of our visit, it was packed with some 400 attendees, including dozens who prayed on carpets laid out in its parking lot.

Al-Makkawi, born in 1977, married, and the father of two daughters, grew up in Saudi Arabia, where his parents had relocated. He returned to his hometown of Cairo as an adult, and in 2003, moved to Sweden for his studies. He holds three graduate degrees, including one in Islamic studies he pursued with a Malaysian university while living in Sweden (his thesis was about methods of *da'wa* for youth in Sweden) and two PhDs – in engineering and in information systems – and has worked as a researcher at the Department of Computer and Systems Sciences at Stockholm University. He explained that while his original plan was to return to Egypt after completing his studies, the political situation created by the Arab Spring convinced him to stay in Sweden.

His work at the mosque is voluntary. He said that he was qualified to issue fatwas based on his accumulated knowledge through the years rather than his academic studies. Al-Makkawi takes pride in being a *hafiz*, or a person who has memorized the Quran. He leads prayers with a beautiful voice.

The first meeting with al-Makkawi was accidental, occurring after having knocked on a wrong door in a different neighbourhood where he was coordinating the final registration of a group for the hajj. He was quick to start a conversation and offer an invitation to meet with his mosque's *da'wa* committee. In two interviews, several members, while aware of the academic motivation of the meetings, could not restrain their missionary zeal. They offered Qurans and asked us to consider converting.

Al-Makkawi and his colleagues did not conceal their rivalry with The Stockholm Mosque. Their criticism was ideological: the Husby leadership, while suggesting that Islam does not recognize a division between politics and religion, resents the Muslim Brothers for what they see as their scheming and segregationist ways and for their leniency on religio-legal matters. It alleges that The Stockholm Mosque is affiliated with the Brothers (other than insisting that some 15 years ago, a group of teenagers from The Stockholm Mosque, who visited Egypt, were asked to swear allegiance to the Brothers, the Husby leadership could not provide any evidence for the allegation).[12]

As is often the case, the rivalry between the mosques is not just ideological. The Husby Mosque was part of The Muslim Association of Sweden, from which it withdrew. Swedes have the option to allocate around one per cent of their income to one of the country's recognized religious organizations, which in turn divides the income among member associations. The state also generously funds non-governmental organizations. The Husby leadership said in our interviews that they felt The Stockholm Mosque marginalized their mosque. Their disaffection also reflects their belief that many Muslims in Stockholm attend The Stockholm Mosque only because of its central location, and that the leadership of Stockholm's Mosque enjoys more governmental and public attention because its religio-juristic pragmatism advances the kind of Islam that Swedes want to hear.

Asked for his opinion on the European Council for Fatwa and Research, al-Makkawi emphasized the Council's affiliation with the Muslim Brothers and said he did not seek its advice. However, he offered a nuanced view of the Council's *wasati* approach. He suggested that the facilitating ideology of the Council suits certain Muslims who are weak in faith, but not him and other Muslims who are more devout

72   Shari'a and Life

and desire to engage in *jihad al-nafs* (the jihad against the self, or the greater jihad for purification and self-perfection).

This point of view grants the Council's ideology and methodology a degree of legitimacy, but only as a means of keeping those Muslims whose level of religiosity is such that they cannot endure within the fold of Islam without concessions. It belittles the Council without altogether rejecting its broad approach to *maslaha* and without directly confronting its foundations. As we will see in the next chapter, these nuances allow for creative pragmatic contextualization of audacious decisions issued by the Council.

The alternative al-Makkawi and his associates found when in need of counsel on shari'a are the three luminaries of contemporary *salafiyya*, which they described as "the trusted shaykhs": Nasir al-Din al-Albani, 'Abd al-'Aziz b. 'Abdallah b. Baz, and Muhammad b. Salih al-'Uthaymin. Al-Makkawi and his *da'wa* committee aligned themselves with *salafi* views on all issues debated in *fiqh al-aqalliyyat al-Muslima* discourse and other issues. For example, they opposed Christmas greetings as a form of confirming falsehood and held that listening to music is prohibited. Al-Makkawi explained that the mosque's leadership accepts the three *salafi* luminaries as authorities because "we are closer to their *'aqida*" and because their reliability is recognized by all Muslim groups, including Ikhwanis (Muslim Brothers), Tablighis (members of Jama'at al-Tabligh), and *salafis*. Thus, he presented the leading figures of contemporary *salafiyya*, who speak for a minority of Muslims, as the subject of broad agreement.

We were unable to ascertain whether the identification with *salafiyya* preceded the organizational rift with The Stockholm Mosque or serves as a means of portraying the rift as ideologically motivated. Clearly, it nurtures a self-image of "us," the devout, as an alternative to "them," the lenient and ready to please of The Stockholm Mosque. Still, partly because the Swedish public associates the term *salafiyya* with terrorism, al-Makkawi is uncomfortable with defining his mosque as *salafi*, preferring to characterize it as one that follows the way of "*al-salaf al-salihun*."[13]

The other *salafi* challenger to The Stockholm Mosque, the Ibn Abbas Center, is located in a residential apartment in Stockholm's Rinkeby district, part of the Rinkeby-Kista borough, and a few minutes drive from the Husby Mosque. Its activities are focused on operating a Facebook page with almost 40,000 followers, contributing content to a popular website, Islam.nu, and delivering lectures in mosques across the country. The Center does not have an official, structured leadership.

According to one of the founders, Mustafa Gibril, a Palestinian (b. 1976) who moved to Sweden at the age of fourteen, the origins of *salafi* activities in Stockholm date to the mid-1990s and to the preaching of Abu Bilal, a student of the Yemeni *salafi* scholar Muqbil b. Hadi (d. 2001).[14] When he met Abu Bilal, Gibril suffered a crisis of faith and appreciated what he understood to be an authentic and cross-national expression of Islam.

The Ibn Abbas Center opened in 2005. While cooperation with the Husby Mosque would seem sensible, members of the Center implied that they do not consider its leadership to be "properly-*salafi*," suggesting that the Husby leadership is influenced by the Muslim Brothers more than it is willing to concede.

Johannes Klominek's path to Islam, and then to *salafi* Islam, took place in his teens, and passed through The Stockholm Mosque. Born in 1986, as a child he travelled a lot with his parents, both atheist medical doctors. When he was 16, the family toured India, and he witnessed the plurality of religions there. When he returned home, he began to read about the world's religions. He remembered being impressed with the universal and egalitarian nature of Islam, as well as the direct path to God it offers.

His conversion took place at The Stockholm Mosque, but he soon decided its leadership was focused on politics. He recalled how a few minutes after converting, the leaders of the mosque already discussed with him whom he should vote for in the upcoming Swedish elections. Through Mustafa Gibril, he discovered *salafiyya*. In 2006 he moved to Saudi Arabia to pursue Islamic studies at al-Madina University. When we met, he was close to completing a PhD on atheism in Christian and Jewish thought, spending his summers in Sweden where he proselytized and developed the Center's online media operations.

Charismatic and engaging, already after two meetings, Klominek invited us to his home to meet some of his associates, and discussed his life and thoughts with great openness. However, we did not meet his wife and felt that any questions about her would cross a line.

Klominek's general approach to the concept of a European-based *ifta᾽* panel was positive and consistent with the specific version of *salafiyya* he advanced – one rooted in the teachings and the priorities of the contemporary luminaries of the Saudi religious establishment, but also independent, localized, confident, and inward-oriented.

He emphasized that he was not committed to decisions only because they were issued in Saudi Arabia, and examined every fatwa based on its merits. He argued that panels are more qualified to issue fatwas than individual muftis for two reasons. First, many issues require specific specializations. For example, experts on economics are required when attending to economic issues, and specialists in astronomy are required

74 Shari'a and Life

when determining prayer times. Second, Islam commands the exercising of *shura*. The larger the number of people who discuss a matter, the better the result. Contrary to the universalizing standpoint of *salafiyya* as preached by contemporary *salafi* luminaries, he suggested that it was better that European-based panels issue fatwas on matters pertaining to Muslims living in Europe because "sometimes it is hard to comprehend issues if you live in another country."

Still, Klominek rejected the specific project of the European Council for Fatwa and Research. While he admitted that he knew little about the Council's ideology and methodology, and was determined not to criticize others in the interviews, it was clear that he did not consider it a credible source for instruction and had never taken much interest in its efforts. He rejected the Council's broad approach to *maslaha*, emphasizing that *darura* only applied in life and death situations. A European fatwa panel, he said, is a "good idea, but it is sometimes the wrong people at the wrong place." For such a Council to be meaningful, "you would first have to collect scholars that have studied Islam and don't have the whole broad *maslaha* thing."

His *salafi* yet independent and locally-oriented views also serve as a response to the opposition of The Stockholm Mosque to "imported fatwas" and the *salafis* that advance them in Stockholm:

> Sometimes when they [The Stockholm Mosque] warn against us, or maybe against somebody else, they come up with bad names and even come up with some lies. They say these people [the Ibn Abbas Center] are totally Saudi influenced and so on. We are not Saudi influenced. Ok, I study at al-Madina, but that does not mean that I only listen to Saudi scholars. Most of the books that I read are from before Saudi Arabia came on the map. We are not related in any way to the Saudi government. We never take any funds. You see, this [pointing to the room where we are sitting at the Ibn Abbas Center] is a small place.[15]

Dortmund

Muslim migration to Dortmund began in the early 1960s. It mainly comprised guest workers from Turkey, as well as smaller numbers of migrants from Morocco. The German census does not include religious affiliations that do not have the status of *Körperschaften des öffentlichen Rechts* (i.e., legal recognition as religious communities). As a result, the number of Muslims in the country or different parts of it can only be estimated. One report notes that 29 per cent of the population of Dortmund does not belong to the Catholic Church, the Protestant Church, or the

Jewish community. Still, not all of the unaffiliated are Muslim because this category includes secular Christians, Buddhists, and Hindus as well.[16] Based on data about countries of origin provided by the city, it can be estimated that approximately 15 per cent of Dortmund's population of 600,000 are Muslim, of which around half are ethnic Turks.[17] A report in 2013 noted that one in five schoolchildren was Muslim.[18]

Islamic life in Dortmund is primarily organized through ethnic affiliations. According to an Islamic data source, there are 41 mosques in the city, including 19 ethnic-Turkish mosques, an ethnic-Albanian mosque, an ethnic-Bosnian mosque, and four ethnic-Moroccan mosques.[19] Our visits to the addresses listed revealed that several of the mosques no longer exist. None of the mosques in the city officially affiliates with the European Council for Fatwa and Research, and none subscribes to the *salafi* agenda. The few *salafi* activists we met in the city centre were affiliates of the Cologne-based *salafi* proselytizing organization Die Wahre Religion (The True Religion) and were not affiliated with any of Dortmund's mosques. (The interior ministry of Nordrhein-Westfalen banned the organization in 2017, and 20,000 copies of the Quran it intended to distribute were confiscated.[20]) While state police estimated that a handful of jihadi-*salafi*s originated from Dortmund, it did not consider the city a hotbed of radicalization or violent radicalization.[21]

The roots of the ʿUmar Ibn al-Khattab Mosque are with a registered association (*eingetragener Verein*) by the name of Islamisch Marokkanisches Kulturzentrum – Moschee Omar Ibno Alkhatab e. V., established in 1974 with the emergence of a Moroccan sojourning community in Dortmund (figure 2.2). The mosque was initially located in a small commercial space that could not accommodate the growing demand. As a result, some attendees left and established a new mosque, Abu Bakr, in a converted factory, which became one of the largest mosques in the city and is no longer dominated by Moroccans. The ʿUmar Ibn al-Khattab mosque relocated twice, ultimately landing at its current location on Zimmerstraße in 1992, some ten-minute drive from Abu Bakr. Long-time attendees emphasize that the split between the mosques was due only to space limits and did not involve any ideological disputes.

The current spacious compound that houses the mosque served as a cinema before the Second World War. During the war, it became a church, and after it, a discotheque. The association that bought the compound does not receive public funding, foreign donations, or support from the Moroccan or other governments. The financing of the mosque is based on the 150 members who pay monthly fees of between 10 and 20 Euros, as well as occasional donations.[22]

76   Shariʿa and Life

Figure 2.2. ʿUmar Ibn al-Khattab Mosque, Dortmund. The spacious compound that houses the mosque served as a cinema before the Second World War.

The mosque looks like an ordinary residential building from the street, with a yellow façade and black and grey mosaics on the windows. A small gate leads to a sizeable semi-roofed courtyard around which is a prayer hall decorated with blue and white painted tiles, as well as other facilities. These include a grocery store that sells homeland products such as spices, couscous, olive oil, and dates, as well as a small collection of religious books; a café with satellite television; and rooms for a gender-separate Quran school for children that meets on weekends. Before Friday congregational prayers, grocery products are offered for sale at the centre of the courtyard. There is the scent of a bazaar in the air. The performance of a religious duty mixes with reconnection to and affirmation of Moroccan identity.

On weekdays of our visits, several dozen Muslims at most attended the prayers. On Fridays at noon, the prayer hall, which can accommodate as many as 300 people, was fully packed, and several attendees prayed on carpets laid in the courtyard for that purpose.

The written survey indicated that approximately 80 per cent of the attendees were of Moroccan extraction, while others were from various North African, Sub-Saharan, Middle Eastern, and Balkan countries. Some attendees hurried in and out before and after the prayer from their day jobs. Others, primarily ethnic-Moroccan retirees, sat together in the courtyard for more than an hour before the prayer commenced and stayed long after it ended. The sermons were delivered in Arabic. Allegedly, a volunteer was tasked with translating them to German, but he was not present at any of the sermons we attended.

The administrative board of the mosque finds it difficult to pay the bills. The gas bill alone, we were told, adds up to 500 Euros a month. The carpet of the prayer hall needs replacement, but the cost – thousands of Euros – is beyond its reach. Given that the coffers of other ethnic-Moroccan mosques in the city are not brimming either and that there are no ideological rifts between them, unification with another mosque would seem reasonable. We were informed that, indeed, the matter was negotiated with the Abu Bakr Mosque, but unsuccessfully. Because Abu Bakr is also packed on Fridays, a union necessitated finding a new building or constructing a new mosque. The two administrations could not agree on an existing location, and building a new mosque was beyond their means.

While the ʿUmar Ibn al-Khattab Mosque boasts the finest building of the ethnic-Moroccan mosques in Dortmund, and while the facilities it offers were the most comfortable, it was not blessed in selecting imams to oversee it for an extended period. Over the two years we visited, the person at its helm changed at least three times.

The imams possessed various levels of Islamic education. Ideologically, however, they were of the same mould. The three expressed pragmatic and integration-inclined views. They privileged experts on fiqh from their homeland, a preference they described primarily as a matter of tradition and convenience rather than an ideological persuasion or *madhhabi* affiliation. The ethnic preference did not involve a commitment to any individual mufti or panel. Despite their pragmatism, they were indifferent to or resentful of the European Council for Fatwa and Research.

In August 2016, the imam of the ʿUmar Ibn al-Khattab Mosque was the then newly appointed Yusuf Zahir, born in 1974. He spoke with us following a stirring Friday sermon, in which he discussed Heaven and Hell and what one needs to do to escape from the latter. Zahir split his time with another mosque where he served as imam, in the city of Holzwickede, some 20 minutes drive from Dortmund. After living in Germany for thirteen years, he still found it difficult to converse in German, and asked that we speak Arabic.[23]

78 Shari'a and Life

Zahir emphasized the importance of tolerance, pluralism, and integration into German society. He said that while he was raised as a *Maliki*, as an imam in Germany, he believed it was his duty to search for religio-legal views across the four *madhhabs* and to find the answer that is the most pragmatic. He stressed his opposition to *salafi* positions imported from Saudi Arabia, as represented by individuals like Pierre Vogel (b. 1978, a former boxer who converted to Islam and was active with Die Wahre Religion). He described Vogel as a media phenomenon and a person who, based on limited religious knowledge, dares to excommunicate other Muslims.

Zahir emphasized that his views are the ones that are faithful to the heritage of the first three generations of Muslims. Thus, he is the true *salafi*. For example, whereas *salafis* hold that playing football (as played in Europe) is prohibited, he takes great interest in the game, and his sons play on youth teams. He said he warned his community against using the internet to acquire religious knowledge because he believed the internet sways young Muslims to extremist views.

While his pragmatic tendencies resembled those of the European Council for Fatwa and Research, Zahir said he took little interest in its work. He remembered only one (and recent) occasion on which he relied on a fatwa it had issued – the permissibility of using astronomical calculations to determine the beginning of Ramadan. He was, however, critical of several of the groundbreaking contributions of the Council and explained in detail why it had made grave mistakes. For example, in his opinion, mortgages are impermissible in all circumstances unless the Muslim is a *Hanafi* who legitimizes prohibited transactions outside the Abode of Islam.

Another example is the permission given to female converts to maintain their marriages with husbands who refuse to convert. He said that this decision was based on the invalid notion that in Europe, women are responsible for raising children. Zahir recalled that in 2014 he attended a conference at King Muhammad I University in Morocco, where "many scholars" spoke against the Council. However, he could not provide specific examples of what was said against it.[24]

Zahir was well-liked by attendees but did not last long in the position. When we visited the mosque two years later, a new imam, 'Abdallah, born in 1963, had taken the reins. His academic credentials were modest, and his attitude about sharing personal details, including his family name, was more apprehensive. 'Abdallah, who does not have a high school education, took a few classes that prepared him for the vocation of imam in Morocco, and he worked in that capacity for a while before moving to Spain with a group of other imams in order to provide for his family. When the economic crisis hit the country, he decided to try his luck in Germany. He landed in Frankfurt, and when he learned that a mosque in Dortmund was searching for a new imam, he offered his services.

ʿAbdallah insisted that because of his lack of education in fiqh, his job was restricted to moral guidance, conducting the prayers, instructing attendees about ʿibadat (worship), and advancing good relations with non-Muslims. He neither referred attendees to existing fatwas nor told them which mufti or panel of muftis to consult. When approached with queries, he advised mustaftis to search for answers online and decide for themselves. He declined to share his opinions about controversial issues broached in our interview, such as Christmas greetings, mortgages, or working in places that sell haram products or services, but his answer about the former indicated that he was inclined toward pragmatism and integration.

He said that in inquiring about fiqh matters himself, he would prefer consulting Moroccans, and explained it as a matter of fact rather than an ideological or a madhhabi preference: Moroccans ask other Moroccans, he said. He added that while he identified as a Maliki, should Turks or Pakistanis who are Hanafis approach him and ask whether they may act in accordance with their madhhab, he would approve of that because all the schools of Islamic law are legitimate and because he did not want fitna, or internal divisions in this context, in the mosque.[25]

Around one year after the interview with ʿAbdallah, we learned that he had left his post. We were told that his wife and children were unwilling to move from Frankfurt to Dortmund, and the commute was too difficult for him. The administration quickly found a replacement: twenty-nine-year-old ʿAbd al-ʿAli. The new imam had studied fiqh at the universities of Tangier and Oujda in Morocco, and then moved to Fujairah, one of the seven emirates that comprise the United Arab Emirates, where he worked as an imam, before moving to Germany.

ʿAbd al-ʿAli, who hardly commanded any German, said like his predecessors that should a mustafti approach him with a query beyond the scope of his knowledge, he would turn it over to shaykhs (learned men in Islamic studies) in his native Morocco. He explained the ethnic-national choice by arguing that the environment in which one was raised influences one's way of thinking, in general, and about fiqh, in particular. Just as Germans and French people think differently, so do, for example, Moroccans and Saudis. Throughout history, Moroccans have intensely interacted with other cultures and religions, whereas Saudis did not. That is why, for example, Saudis hold that music is

80   Shari'a and Life

haram, whereas Moroccans do not. Thus, an imam of Moroccans, such as his himself, should seek counsel from Moroccans.[26]

The new imam presented a moderate and tolerant outlook. Asked, for example, about the impermissibility of celebrating birthdays, a *salafi* flagship, he said that he did not celebrate his birthday. Still, if people want to do so, it is legitimate, and if we invited him to our birthdays, he would come. His advice to Muslims would be not to host a large party but rather something smaller, like offering colleagues tea and cookies.

The constant changes of imams at the mosque injured the prestige of that post. Two of the interviewees at the mosque suggested that they would bring their queries to the imam of another ethnic-Moroccan mosque, Markaz Imam Malik Mosque, where that position had been stably occupied by al-Hamdi 'Abd al-Wahad, whose family was in control of the administration.

Markaz Imam Malik was established in 2009 by a group of Moroccan-German and other Arabic-speaking members of an association that promoted Islamic objectives founded in 2002. At the time of our visit in 2016, this small house of prayer was collecting money for an ambitious reconstruction project. An elaborate poster in the hallway detailed the names of individuals who had made contributions, some as large as 5,000 Euros. The mosque had a small library but no bookstore or grocery store. Its website boasted that it brought together three generations of Muslims, from first-generation labour migrants to second- and third-generation academics and youth. It emphasized the sanctity of life and the importance of peace and tolerance.

On the evening of 30 August 2016, some twenty males attended the mosque, including one who travelled more than an hour to ask the imam for advice about his ailing child. During the Friday congregational prayers, the number of attendees rose to almost 100 males, the mosque's capacity. Some prayed in the hallway due to the lack of space in the prayer hall.

Al-Wahad said that "as a Moroccan," when faced with an issue that called for further consultation, he either conferred with colleagues in Germany or sought the advice of panels based in Morocco. He explained that Muslims in Europe were closely linked to their homelands; thus, Moroccans tend to seek the advice of Moroccans, and Turks tend to seek the advice of Turkish panels. While he adhered to the *Maliki* School, he believed it was his duty to present *mustaftis* with the full spectrum of permissible options within the four schools, leaving them to decide.[27]

His approach to the European Council for Fatwa and Research was mixed. He said that he had never consulted the Council or relied on any of its decisions. However, he recognized (in a way reminiscent of the patronizing approach of imam al-Makkawi at the Husby Mosque in Stockholm) the positive role it played in providing direction (*tawjih*) for Muslims who have little knowledge in Islam. He suggested that the Council had issued both strong and weak decisions. For example, contrary to the view of the Council, in his opinion, a need can only be established as a necessity that legitimizes mortgages on a case-by-case basis and not as a universal rule for all Muslim Europeans who are not homeowners.

Like imam Zahir, al-Wahad was concerned about online radicalization. He conveyed that he was advising young people that it is permissible to go online and learn about different opinions (he did not believe that prohibiting them from doing so would be effective). Still, he asked those who did so to consult with him so that he could help them discern between correct and incorrect opinions.[28]

Reykjavik

An old Jewish joke alluding to the tendency of small religious communities to split over trivial matters tells of a Jew rescued from a lonely island after 30 years. To their great surprise, the rescuers observe two synagogues. They ask: "Why did you build two houses of prayer, being one Jew, on a deserted island?" The Jew points to the more distant synagogue and explains: "You see that one? I shall never set foot in there!"

The story of Reykjavik's Grand Mosque suggests there is truth in every joke. In a city with approximately 2,000 Muslims, some of whom are not practicing, the Grand Mosque is at the centre of a bitter rivalry with two other mosques. Animosity developed because of strong personal dislikes and struggles over resources. With an eye on the support of the Icelandic public and its concerns about the impact of Saudi intervention, it involved reciprocal allegations and counter-allegations about advancing anti-integrationist *salafi* dogmatism. Yet, it also involved accusations of excessive pragmatism.

In 1970, only 20 Muslims resided in Iceland.[29] ʿAli al-Muntasir al-Kittani, who between October 1973 and January 1974 led a Muslim World League delegation that surveyed Muslim communities in the Western Hemisphere with great detail, dedicated only a few lines to Iceland in his final report, and stated that only a few Icelanders converted to Islam, and there existed no Muslim organizations in the country.[30]

That changed in 1997 when Salman Tamimi, a Palestinian high-tech professional who had moved to Reykjavik in 1971 at the age of 16, established the Association of Muslims in Iceland (Félag Múslima á Íslandi). Tamimi settled in Iceland almost by accident: on his way to the United

82   Shari'a and Life

States, he stopped in Reykjavik to visit his brother, who was already living there, liked what he saw and decided to stay.[31] He became a public figure in the 1980s after founding the Iceland-Palestine Association and effectively championing the Palestinian national cause in the national media. His efforts to institutionalize Islam were assisted by an Icelandic convert, Ibrahim Sverrir Agnarsson. At the time, the number of Muslims in the country was still in the low dozens.

In 2002, the Association of Muslims in Iceland opened Al-Nur Mosque, Iceland's first. Located on the second floor of a commercial building in the Ármúli district, the relatively small facility befitted the small community it served. Over the next decade, the Icelandic Muslim community rapidly grew. By 2010, it numbered 1,251 people,[32] almost all residents of Reykjavik.

One of the new migrants was Karim 'Askari, a Moroccan from Mahmudiyya who left for Italy in 2000, migrated to Iceland in 2005 to work in the fishing industry, and joined Tamimi's mosque. In 2009, 'Askari and several associates left Al-Nur. 'Askari argued that the split had nothing to do with ideology. He felt Tamimi was unwilling to accommodate the growing community's needs or share his responsibilities with others.[33] Tamimi offered a different explanation. He said that 'Askari and his associates endorsed *salafi* views that countered integration and impeded the prospects of developing Islam in Iceland – for example, that it is impermissible for men to shake the hands of women (more on the controversy about handshakes in chapter 4). He stressed that unlike 'Askari, he thought that Muslims should follow the historical example of the Jews by successfully integrating into European societies.[34]

Following his departure from Al-Nur, 'Askari established the Islamic Foundation of Iceland, which received hundreds of thousands of dollars in donations from the Saudi King 'Abdallah and other Saudi donors. According to 'Askari, the Saudis did not attach any ideological demands to the donation. Their only stipulation was that a mosque must be established.[35]

Presenting himself as the man who chose integration over financial support, Tamimi ridiculed that statement. The Saudis, he argued, never give money without spreading their agenda. He added that while he respected Muhammad Ibn 'Abd al-Wahhab, eighteenth-century agendas were not suitable to our times. With pride, Tamimi shared a comment he made in a newspaper interview against political oppression in Saudi Arabia, which, so he claimed, enraged their government.[36]

Whatever the Saudi motivations actually were, the donation allowed 'Askari to purchase a spacious, hexagon-shaped, two-story building close to the city's centre that had previously served as a wedding hall and as a school for the disabled. In 2012, the upper floor was converted into a state-of-the-art mosque, including a dining area and a seating area, named Al-Rahman and operated by a new association ʿAskari established, The Islamic Cultural Center of Iceland. The lower floor was converted into a hostel run by the association. The surplus from the Saudi donations and the steady income from the hostel allowed ʿAskari to become a full-time paid chair of the Foundation.

The rivalry between Tamimi and ʿAskari was only the beginning of factionalism in Iceland's small Muslim population. Upon the mosque's inauguration, ʿAskari invited an Egyptian, Ahmad Sadiq, a graduate in Islamic Studies from al-Azhar, to Reykjavik to serve as the community's first full-time imam. After three years, relations between the two deteriorated. ʿAskari explained the problem was that Sadiq came to Iceland without prior knowledge of European realities and developed overbearing tendencies.[37] Sadiq responded that ʿAskari did not allow him to implement his *daʿwa* programs and accused the chair of treating him like a ring that "one puts on and takes off."[38] To this, ʿAskari responded disdainfully that Sadiq was invited to lead prayers, not to administer anything.[39]

Figure 2.3. The Grand Mosque of Iceland, Reykjavik. The mosque is located in a hexagon-shaped, two-story building that had previously served as a wedding hall and a school for the disabled.

84   Shari'a and Life

The ensuing power struggle ended up in court. 'Askari maintained control over the Foundation, its funds, and the compound that housed Al-Rahman Mosque. Ever the excellent marketer, he rebranded Al-Rahman Mosque as The Grand Mosque of Iceland (figure 2.3). Sadiq took control over the Islamic Cultural Center, along with its registered members and almost empty coffers. He established a small mosque under that name where the final word is his, located in a converted office space on the upper floor of an office building. It comprises a large room with a small library with Qurans and an eclectic collection of fiqh books, a small prayer room for women, and Sadiq's tiny office.

The bad blood between Tamimi and 'Askari paled in comparison to the bad blood between 'Askari and Sadiq. While we wanted to focus on shari'a-related issues in our interview, Sadiq repeatedly returned to discussing his nemesis, accusing him of corruption and forgery. He admitted that the financial situation of his mosque was dire.

It is, apparently, easier to preach about the unity of the believers than to act upon these words. Unlike in other cities we visited, ethnic and linguistic differences, or capacity limitations, could not explain the plurality of mosques. On the Fridays we visited congregational prayers, we counted up to 100 attendees at the Grand Mosque, some 50 at Al-Nur, and some 60 at the Cultural Center.

The demographic composition at the three mosques was multi-ethnic, reflecting the diversity of Muslim migration to Iceland. The questionnaires at the Grand Mosque informed that it was attended by Somalis, Moroccans, Algerians, Iraqis, Iranians, Macedonians, Kazakhs, Afghanis, and others. The questionnaires at Al-Nur informed that the mosque was attended by Syrians, Albanians, Turks, Senegalese, Pakistanis, Eritreans, Palestinians, Djiboutians, and others. In neither of the two mosques did any ethnic group comprise more than 30 per cent of respondents. In the three mosques, sermons delivered in Arabic were translated to English, which is used as a lingua franca in all of them.

Religious associations in Iceland receive governmental funds based on the number of taxpayers registered with them. We noticed that Sadiq, who has no other means of financial support, made an effort to register as many new members as possible. We were surprised to learn that the Grand Mosque was hardly active in similar efforts. 'Askari was not shy to disclose that he does not encourage registration. He explained that at around four Euros per member a month, government payments are redundant, and people who register "come with all sorts of demands."[40]

Perhaps because it was not dependent on customer satisfaction, the Grand Mosque offered a limited number of activities. It had a negligible library and a handful of free booklets. It did not operate an Islamic bookstore. It did not organize any activities other than a Quran school for children and occasional dinners and competitions. 'Askari preferred to think big: he was considering establishing a small museum on the history of Islam. He was also trying to raise donations to erect a minaret. However, he did not plan to have calls to worship (*adhan*s). He said that since there was no Muslim population in the mosque's vicinity, an *adhan* would merely irritate local neighbourhood residents.

Immediately after Sadiq's departure, 'Askari invited 'Abd al-'Aziz al-Wal'ani, a Moroccan born in 1951 who worked in a cleaning supplies factory in Italy and volunteered in the mosque there, to serve as the imam of the Grand Mosque. Al-Wal'ani was paid USD 2,000 per month. His wife and children remained in Italy.

The change of imam at the Grand Mosque left it without a confirmed authority on shari'a. Al-Wal'ani, a friendly and uninspiring man, earned his BA in Islamic studies from Jama'iyyat Usul al-Din in Tetouan, Morocco, a subsidiary of Al-Qarawiyyin University. He described himself as a *da'i* (proselytizer) with limited knowledge in fiqh.[41] His charisma hardly rose to that of Sadiq's, a disparity highlighted by the exaggerated, unnatural hand gestures he uses when delivering his sermons in Arabic. From 'Askari's point of view, his new imam's modest and rather insecure character was a change for the better. Some attendees also found the new imam's character an improvement from what they interpreted as Sadiq's arrogance, while noting in the same breath that Sadiq is more of an authority on shari'a.

The leadership of the Grand Mosque denied Tamimi's allegations that it is or ever was *salafi*-inclined. 'Askari anxiously distanced himself from that affiliation. He explained that Saudi fatwas were appropriate only in a Saudi context. As an example, he noted that women wear veils on Saudi planes only after crossing into Saudi airspace. In his view, this practice was not appropriate for Moroccans, let alone for Moroccans living in Iceland. He accused *salafis* of being two-faced, telling Western governments one thing and telling Muslims another, and preaching hate and being inward-looking through their concept of "loyalty and disavowal." Stressing the independence of his mosque, he argued further that a mufti must experience the conditions of the country about which he advises, which is why he would also not accept fatwas from Morocco on issues pertaining to the situation in Iceland.

Whereas Tamimi argued that 'Askari invited Ahmad Sadiq to advance his and his associates' pre-existing *salafi* views, 'Askari said they were unaware of Sadiq's ideology when he was asked to come. 'Askari acknowledged that many attendees in his mosque sympathized with *salafi* notions but attributed this to the lingering impact of the ousted

86   Shari'a and Life

Sadiq, which, he said, the Grand Mosque was working to rectify. He argued that Sadiq advocated *salafi* views during his time at the mosque, including that children should not participate in birthday parties and that it was impermissible for men to shake women's hands (an allegation Tamimi directed against 'Askari himself). He further charged that Sadiq wanted his wife to wear a full-face veil.[42]

Sadiq, in response, insisted that he was not a *salafi*. He said it was a mistake to think that the Saudis give money only to those who propagate *salafi* views. Rather, they finance European Muslims of different persuasions as a way of showing that they accept everyone. Emphasizing his independence from Saudi influences, he said he usually offered advice on fiqh-oriented matters by himself.

On the rare occasions that he needs advice, he communicates with individuals from his alma mater, al-Azhar. While he appreciates the Saudi Council of Senior Scholars, he did not consider himself bound by or committed to its decisions. Sadiq admitted that his wife liked wearing the niqab back in Egypt but assured us that she had never done so in Iceland. He implied that 'Askari was throwing stones in a glass house, noting that when 'Askari's mother visited Iceland, she wore a niqab.[43] 'Askari was shocked upon hearing the counter-accusation but did not respond.[44]

While the leaderships of the Reykjavik mosques appeared to be in competition over who projects a more pragmatic and pro-integration profile, they distanced themselves from the European Council for Fatwa and Research; at the Grand Mosque, in less explicit terms than its two rivals.

'Askari remembered that he did not think much about fiqh-related issues when he was still living in Morocco, "because someone takes care of that for you."[45] That changed when he moved to Europe. Among the fiqh books he read was al-Qaradawi's *Fi Fiqh al-Aqalliyyat al-Muslima*, a foundational text in the development of *wasati fiqh al-aqalliyyat al-Muslima*. However, the book did not encourage him to affiliate with the Council. Hinting at al-Qaradawi's roots in the Muslim Brothers, he explained that while the idea of European-based panels was positive in principle, the fatwas those councils issue should be critically examined because some of them adhere to specific ideologies and groups, whereas Muslims should follow only the Quran. Distancing himself from defining his mosque as *wasati* and hinting again at his dislike of al-Qaradawi, he noted that the term is used by Islamists who only pretend to be *wasati*. Imam al-Wal'ani has also read *Fi Fiqh al-Aqalliyyat al-Muslima* and considered al-Qaradawi a respected authority but did not privilege the Council or take particular interest in its efforts.[46]

Tamimi, the de-facto imam of his mosque, described the European Council for Fatwa and Research as a failed project because Arab governments financed it, but he did not specify which governments. He said that when he was uncertain about an issue pertaining to shariʻa, he consulted with a friend of his, another hi-tech professional, who had sound knowledge in fiqh, although no academic credentials in the field. He emphasized his complete independence and that, with the Quran by his side, he makes the final decisions himself.[47]

Sadiq based his criticism of the Council on other arguments. He suggested that the notion of uniformed *ifta'* directed by one panel was not in keeping with the way of Islam, and that perhaps a considerably larger panel, with around 100 members, would have allowed the Council to realize its objectives.[48]

Aside from the personal disputes, there is one substantial shariʻa-related issue that divides the mosques. During Ramadan, Muslims who have reached puberty are required to fast from dawn to sunset. They are not to eat, drink, smoke, or have sex. Observing the fast is one of the five pillars of Islam, and an important spiritual experience. The Quran (2:185) explicitly notes two situations that justify breaking the fast and compensating for the days lost during another month: sickness and travel. In the seventh century, not a single Muslim lived in regions where the sun sets late at night during the summers, if it sets at all. With the development of small Muslim communities in Nordic environments, a new challenge called for a solution.

One of the first to address the issue was the grand mufti of Egypt and an intellectual father of contemporary *wasatiyya*, Muhammad ʻAbduh (d. 1905). His fatwa was one of several pragmatic contributions he made concerning the fiqh of Muslim minorities. ʻAbduh wrote that God presented His laws in a way that people can understand; the times of prayer and fasting were based on the conditions that prevailed in most countries of the world, where the length of the day is moderate. Where it is different, there are two prevailing options: either fast the same number of hours as in Mecca and Medina, or the same number of hours in the nearest country in which the length of the day is moderate.[49]

Three decades after its original publication by ʻAbduh's student Rashid Rida in *Al-Manar*, this fatwa was reprinted in the same journal with an addition: Rida emphasized that the option of fasting based on Mecca and Medina times and the option of fasting based on the times in the nearest moderate country are equally permissible because this is not a matter on which a definitive text exists.[50] ʻAbduh's fatwa did not specifically mention the physical burden of lengthy fasts, and seemed

88   Shari'a and Life

more concerned with the difficulty of establishing when the days end during Nordic summers.

In the late twentieth century, as the number of Muslims in Scandinavia grew, the matter became the subject of prolific deliberations by 'Abduh's successors in Egypt. In January 1982, Egypt's grand mufti, 'Ali Jad al-Haqq (d. 1996), advised that Muslims in Norway should begin their fast at dawn but then limit it to the same number of hours observed in Mecca and Medina.[51] Subsequent fatwas issued by Egypt's grand muftis and by Dar al-Ifta' offered similarly lenient opinions, emphasizing that excessive fasting is a health risk.[52]

Contrary to these opinions, both *salafis* and, more surprisingly, the European Council for Fatwa and Research decided against the moderate option. In September 1978, the Saudi Council of Senior Scholars introduced an uncompromising opinion in response to a query sent by the President of Muslim Associations in Malmö, Sweden, as to the times of prayer and fasting in areas where the day is long during the summer and short during the winter. The panel stated that where the night can be distinguished from the day through sunset and dawn, (a) relying on Q. 17:78 and 4:103, as well as several Prophetic traditions, the five prayers must be practiced at their stipulated time whether the day is very long or very short, and (b) relying on 2:187, the fast should be observed through the entire day, even if it is very long, because "the Islamic shari'a is one to all people in all places (*'ammatan li-l-nas*)." However, the panel noted that whoever has reason to believe that the fast would cause their death, or serious medical harm, may break it before its due time and compensate for the days missed in a later month.[53] Other Saudi panels and high-ranking members of its religious establishment issued similar fatwas.[54]

Despite its agenda of making the lives of Muslims in Europe easier, the European Council for Fatwa and Research did not accept the opinion that fasts lasting almost 24 hours should be avoided. It decided to the contrary in its 12th session, held in Dublin from 31 December 2003 to 4 January 2004, and again in a brief fatwa issued during its 20th session, held in Istanbul, in July 2010, as well as during a June 2015 special conference in Stockholm dedicated to the issue.[55]

Three explanations come to mind about its unusual strictness. First, the challenge of long fasts in Nordic countries does not result from the social composition of the societies in which they live but from their geographical position. Even if Iceland or Norway were to become majority Muslim countries, the challenge would remain the same. Second, in instances in which the Council legitimized audacious pragmatic facilitations, the prospect of promoting proselytizing in Europe was a key justification. Unlike these issues, the question of lengthy fasts does not provide a strong context for introducing the justification of proselytizing. A third possible reason is political: the Council addressed the issue of Ramadan in northern countries only after the issuance of several audacious decisions that stirred controversy and undermined its legitimacy. By choosing, in this case, the stricter of the two existing opinions, it signalled that its decisions are evidence-based and do not necessarily always prefer the easier option.

Ramadan functions as a means of bringing Muslims together: mosque attendees meet more often, communally dine in high spirits, and study and pray more extensively than usual; teenagers experience a rite-of-passage by proving their ability to fast like the adults; and appeals for donations to religious causes find more ready audiences. However, a precondition for enhancing social cohesion during that month is for members of the community to agree on the basic rituals of Ramadan, including when the fast begins and when it ends on each day of the month. In Reykjavik, differences in opinion about fasting times give ideological context to, and exacerbate, the divisions between its three mosques.

Al-Nur Mosque has followed the lenient opinion since its establishment. Tamimi said that their preference for mitigated fast was based on the opinion of the Egyptian Dar al-Ifta' and the opinion that excessive fasts were a health risk. In two separate interviews, he offered three additional explanations: first, "it makes sense"; second, "there is no Muslim country that is beyond the 45th latitude line," and thus it is suitable for Muslims living beyond the 45th Parallel to fast in accordance with the number of hours observed along it; third, there is no *fajr* (dawn) in Iceland during the summer, as the light never disappears, meaning that there is no separation between day and night. While Dar al-Ifta' was Tamimi's reference, he did not accept the aforementioned opinions that fasting in situations like Iceland should match the number of hours observed in Mecca. Instead, his mosque adopted the opinion that it should match those observed in the closest country where conditions are not extreme.[56]

Tamimi found an unexpected supporter for the lenient view: Isma'il Malik, an American of Pakistani descent who moved in his teens to Saudi Arabia due to his father's occupation as a professor of engineering. His employment at Al-Nur demonstrated that God works in mysterious ways. In 2012, Malik was dismissed from the Mecca mosque where he was employed. Seeking adventure, he decided to head as far north as possible and Googled the phrase "Islam in Greenland" in the hope of finding a career there. Having learned that there were no mosques

90   Shari'a and Life

in Greenland, he searched instead in Iceland and came across Al-Nur. He contacted Tamimi, who requested video recordings of him reciting the Quran. After reviewing the recordings, Tamimi was impressed and invited Malik to lead the mosque during Ramadan in return for lodging (no travel expenses were covered, nor was a salary provided). As an addendum to his invitation, Tamimi told Malik that Al-Nur's community does not fast in accordance with Saudi jurisprudence and that Malik should be aware of this policy before accepting the invitation.

According to Malik, Tamimi's note alerted him, for the first time, to this religio-juristic polemic and provided the impetus for him to search for opinions that could justify his choice of the more lenient view. His first order of business was to ask for his mother's advice. She told him to study the issue seriously so as not to do anything wrong. Malik said he was assured about the legitimacy of the lenient approach by a professor from the University of Madina, whose opinion he very much respects, and an American-Saudi convert by the name of John, who is a *Madkhali* "and thus is as strict as possible in his religio-juristic approach."

Malik explained that the Prophet and the *salaf* did not fast for 22 hours, so no one should expect Muslims in Iceland to do so. Moreover, "the Prophet was a man who observed reality and acted in accordance with it," and in the context of Iceland, the lenient approach is the more pragmatic one, as a 22-hour fast is too exhausting. He stressed that "Islam is a natural religion, it is a religion that makes sense, and my heart told me to accept this [the lenient approach]."[57]

We heard Malik's sermon against ISIS attacks, in which American internet-slang and Saudi-*salafi* jargon mixed to make an effective appeal to Icelandic Muslims of diverse backgrounds to speak out against terrorism tirelessly. The often-elusive concept of the "globalization of Islam" could not have received a clearer name and face.

When 'Askari and Tamimi were still together at Al-Nur, the month of Ramadan (determined by a lunar calendar) did not coincide with long summer days. The establishment by 'Askari of a new and rival mosque coincided with the shift of Ramadan to the summer. 'Askari determined that his mosque would fast in accordance with Icelandic sunsets, even if that implied a 22-hour-long fast, giving the rivalry between the two mosques an ideological hue.

The founder of the Grand Mosque explained that, in his view, long fasts in Iceland were not a health hazard. For him, their perception as such was another demonstration that muftis must be well acquainted with the realities about which they decide. He argued that in his view, Moroccan muftis, or Egyptians such as Muhammad 'Abduh, were not aware that the weather conditions in Iceland make a summer fast much easier than in their warmer countries. He pointed to an 83-year-old attendee of the mosque who had no problem enduring the long fast.[58]

Indeed, with few exceptions, attendees of the Grand Mosque said that they did not find the long fast too difficult. One of the most impressive scenes we ever witnessed was an *iftar* at the Grand Mosque (then still named Al-Rahman). At midnight, just after the sun, round and majestic, set behind the snowy mountains that surround Reykjavik, thirty men and two brave junior high school students, who had managed to complete yet another day of fasting for 22 hours, sat at three long tables overlooking the prayer hall. Some wore traditional white Moroccan dress, some jeans, and some training suits. On the tables were pitas, cakes, dates, and bottles of Coca-Cola, Fanta, and apple juice. Four minutes later, the moment finally arrived, and, for a short while, nothing but the sound of quiet chewing was heard. Then, the race began: in the little more than two hours remaining, those present were to participate in the Maghrib (evening) 'Isha' (night) and Fajr (dawn) prayers, as well as the *tarawih* (the special Ramadan prayers); eat a meal rich with meat, rice, and potatoes; and struggle with the weariness of a hard day's night. Yet, as far as the eye could tell, they were relaxed and satisfied.

The rigidity of fasting exercised at 'Askari's mosque hardly impressed his rivals at Al-Nur. Malik suggested that choosing the longer fast is an act of "self-righteousness," which only people who live on welfare and may sleep all day can afford to observe. Tamimi, also defending the notion that a 22-hour fast is impractical for most people, stated that many of the attendees of Al-Rahman had actually taken Al-Nur's Ramadan timetable.[59]

Sadiq said he favoured the stricter opinion already before arriving in Iceland. The day he arrived from Egypt and joined 'Askari's mosque happened to be June 21, the longest day of the year. He went to the top of a hill nearby the mosque, took a picture of the sunset, and sent it to the fatwa council of the Saudi-based Muslim World League, which confirmed that indeed the sun sets in the summer and thus fasting according to local time was the correct view.[60]

When Sadiq broke from the Grand Mosque, he maintained the rigid opinion about fasting. Unification between his mosque and Tamimi's mosque could have helped the two compete with 'Askari's richer resources and was negotiated. Sadiq was even invited to give a sermon at Al-Nur. But the Ramadan issue proved an obstacle. Sadiq suggested a possible compromise could be for each community to fast in accordance with its understanding. 'Askari, who also regarded the Ramadan issue as the biggest obstacle to the future unification of his mosque with Al-Nur, suggested that when Tamimi's time comes, and the month of

92 Shari'a and Life

Ramadan shifts again from the summer to less sunny months, a path may open for the two mosques to merge.[61]

As the final draft for this book was prepared, we learned of Tamimi's death. He was 65, and the next Ramadan was to start in April. We did not hear news of imminent unification between any of the mosques, though. It remains to be seen whether nature would allow for what human nature prevented.

As troublesome as internal divisions have been for Muslims in Reykjavik, Islamic life in the city has largely avoided becoming a focus of political debates among the majority society. In 2013, the decision of Reykjavik's municipal council to allocate a plot of land to Al-Nur at the city centre for the construction of a new mosque (which was never built) stirred protests and an internet campaign under the slogan "Stop Islamization of Iceland."

In the capital's local elections, the campaign became the leading and most effective electoral issue raised by the Progressive Party (Framsóknarflokkurinnin). It paid off: the party jumped in the polls and ended with two seats out of 15 in the May 2014 elections, up from no seats in the outgoing Council. The controversy took a particularly ugly turn when a group of Icelanders descended on the proposed mosque site and planted severed pigs' heads and pages of the Quran covered in a red, blood-like liquid.[62]

This remained, however, an isolated incident, and the local campaign did not usher in the rise of a populist anti-migration political party, as was the case in other European countries. The leaderships of the mosques and attendees told us they felt their religious freedom was respected and that it was easier and safer to practice Islam in Iceland than in other European countries. Due to commerce and tourism, Reykjavik attained in recent years an international flair; multiculturalism and respect for different traditions became the official policy. While Iceland's Muslim population has been the fastest growing in the world in relative terms during the first decades of the twenty-first century, it has remained a small minority of less than one per cent of the total population, giving limited credibility to calls against Islamization.

Birmingham, Marseille

Coventry Road, the main street of Small Heath, an area in East Birmingham where 81 per cent of the 21,000 residents are Muslim, provides an Islamic environment few streets in Europe do.[63] Most women passersby don headscarves, and some don niqabs. There are dozens of Islamic-oriented stores, including halal supermarkets, butcheries, restaurants, bridal shops, and bookstores. The largest department store on the street, Al-Manaar, offers a large variety of "everything Islamic," including halal candies, Islamic home decor, traditional garments, congratulation cards, perfumes, toiletry, toys, and religious books.

There could hardly be a more suitable location for Salafi Publications, Britain's most influential *salafi* organization and one of Europe's largest. Along the street resides the Salafi Bookstore it operates and the affiliated Salafi Independent School, a primary school. A converted warehouse on a parallel street is home to the Salafi Mosque (figure 2.4). On an average Friday, the mosque is filled to the brim with some 750 male attendees.

Because attendance for Friday congregational prayer exceeds its capacity, the leadership of the Salafi Mosque opened another, smaller mosque some five kilometres away. Several mosques across Britain are ideologically affiliated with it and recognize its primacy (while not being formally tied to it organizationally). Its conferences, which take place at least once a year, attract *salafi*s from across the country and

Figure 2.4. The Salafi Mosque, Birmingham. The mosque is located in a converted warehouse. On Fridays it is filled to the brim with some 750 male attendees.

Europe at large, and its Eid prayer on the basketball courts in Small Heath Park attracts, even under the threat of severe weather conditions, some 2,500 participants. In recent years, *salafis* from across Europe, including France, Denmark, the Netherlands, Germany, Italy, and Switzerland, have joined the mosque community. City Centre Daʿwah, an on-the-ground proselytizing group affiliated with the mosque, operates a stall several days a week in the commercial heart of Birmingham. It has branches across Britain and also engages in proselytizing overseas.

The mosque is multi-ethnic, with a predominance of first, second, and third-generation subcontinental Muslims, but also a diverse minority of Arabs, Somalis, and others. When sermons are delivered in Arabic, they are translated into English. Most attendees were raised on other ideologies and discovered *salafiyya* at some point in their adult life. The population is relatively young: the questionnaires put the median age at 35 (only attendees who appeared older than 18 were approached).

The diverse operations of Salafi Publications include a publishing house and state-of-the-art advanced media operations, including Twitter, Instagram, and Facebook accounts, as well as an online radio station, all of which are followed by thousands of users. The Salafi Bookstore appears to be self-sustaining – not a small achievement for any independent bookstore in today's world. In dozens of visits, we almost always witnessed at least one paying customer there. In the fiscal year ending 30 September 2020 (the latest available report), the bookstore (registered as the Salafi Bookstore and Islamic Center with the UK charity commission) earned a total of GBP 671,800 from sales and donations.[64]

The bookstore offers a small variety of perfumes, groceries, traditional gowns, and branded stationery, and hundreds of *salafi* titles. These include fatwa compilations and treatises by the luminaries of *salafi* thought, instructional leaflets, and books for young readers. While it is not the only bookstore in the area that offers books that express the *salafi* agenda, it is the only one that restricts its supply to titles that are in line with *salafi* criteria.

The children's books section exhibits *salafi* exceptionalism (figure 2.5). It includes titles such as "Allah Knows All About Me," "My Tawheed Book," "The Way to Jannah [Heaven]," and "A Little Boy Not Too Far Away: A Story About Repentance." *Salafi* books for young readers share four distinct features. First, they emphasize the central tenets of *salafi* doctrine, first and foremost, *tawhid*, regardless of the topic treated. In the everyday world they depict, nothing takes place other than because God wills it to be, and everything is done to please God. Second, these books tend to explicitly state the moral of the story and its educational objectives. Third, in sharp contrast to mainstream Islamic children's literature, Muslims featured in these books do not associate with non-Muslims in a friendly context or assert their identity through social interactions with them. Fourth, humans and animals are drawn without facial features; alternatively, their facial features are defaced or covered. This graphic choice proclaims and delineates to both parents and children the difference between *salafiyya* and other approaches to Islam.[65]

The Salafi Mosque projects both strength and marginality. In Britain, it is the main disseminator of the views and priorities set by the leaders of the Saudi religious establishment and their affiliates in the latter part of the twentieth century, particularly its politically submissive approach, yet is in a fierce rivalry with other groups associated with *salafiyya*, in a way reflective of the divisiveness and animosities that characterized the development of the movement in Europe. It is one of the largest mosques in Britain, yet by the accounts of its leadership, no more than two per cent of Birmingham's Muslim population affiliate with it, and some local Muslims oppose its teachings and the individuals who run it. Despite its strong connections with Saudi Arabia, it is largely self-sufficient, and its infrastructural development has been limited.

The turbulent history of the mosque began in the mid-1980s, when Manwar ʿAli, also known as Abu Muntasir, migrated from Saudi Arabia to Britain, where he established Jamaʿiyyat Ihyaʾ Minhaj as-Sunnah (JIMAS). He advanced the *salafi* approach through study circles in mosques, community centres, and universities all over England.

Abu Khadeejah, a British-born Muslim of Pakistani descent, was one of Abu Muntasir's followers. Reflecting on his childhood in Birmingham in the 1970s, Abu Khadeejah said in an interview with the authors that he was raised as a Muslim "but never went to any mosque, not really," and attended a school where 99 per cent of the pupils were Christian.[66] When studying chemical engineering at Bradford University in the 1980s, he met Arab students, who introduced him to an English translation of ʿAbd al-Wahhab's *Kitab al-Tawhid* and Bukhari's compilation of Prophetic traditions.[67]

According to Abu Khadeejah's account, in 1988, he joined Abu Muntasir's circles, and since the early 1990s, he has studied under *salafi* scholars in Kuwait and Saudi Arabia. These include the Kuwaiti Muhammad al-ʿAnjari and the Saudis ʿUbayd al-Jabiri, ʿAbdallah al-Ghudayan, and Rabiʿ b. Hadi al-Madkhali. The latter, with his adamant voice against the jihadism of al-Qaeda and ISIS and Islamic political insubordination at large, continued to guide Abu Khadeejah in the years that followed.[68]

96 Shari'a and Life

The 1990 Gulf crisis and the presence of US troops on Saudi soil initiated a period of ideological differences within JIMAS between those who openly opposed the invitation of half a million American soldiers to the Kingdom and those who remained loyal to the view that public opposition to political leaders, including those who err, is prohibited. Abu Muntasir sympathized with the massive Saudi movement that protested King Fahd. Abu Khadeejah maintained his support for the Saudi regime and consequently left JIMAS with other activists. According to Hamid, the row between the factions was bitter, leading in some cases even to the breakdown of family bonds.[69]

In May 1996, Abu Khadeejah joined several other *salafi* activists, including some who later became bitter foes, and set up a new group in Manchester, the Organization of Ahl al-Sunnah Islamic Societies (OASIS). In August that year, OASIS held its first conference in Birmingham. It was attended by al-Madkhali and al-'Anjari. At the conference, Abu Khadeejah and others grew suspicious that several of their associates sympathized with the Muslim Brothers and, worse, with its jihadi offspring that followed in the footsteps of Sayyid Qutb. Yet another split followed.

Towards the end of 1996, on the advice of al-Madkhali, al-'Anjari, and other prominent scholars, Abu Khadeejah, Abu Iyad Amjad Rafiq, and two British converts, Abu Talhah Dawud Burbank and Abu Hakim Bilal Davis, established Salafi Publications, dedicated exclusively to the spread of the *salafi* call, and consciously using the term *salafiyya* overtly. Salafi Publications operated at first from Abu Khadeejah's home. Abu Iyad was responsible for managing the website, and, together with Dawud Burbank, he copied and translated material, including fatwas, sent from Saudi Arabia by Abu Hakim, who at the time was still studying at Madina University.[70] Six years later, the Salafi Mosque opened in Small Heath, becoming one of the largest in the city.

The leadership of the mosque supports the dogmatic views of *salafi* muftis on the key issues debated in *fiqh al-aqalliyyat al-Muslima* discourse, including those concerning mortgages, student loans, maintaining a job that requires engaging with haram and avoiding Christmas greetings. It also advances other signature *salafi* views, including that displaying facial features, playing or listening to music, and celebrating birthdays are forbidden, and that Muslim women must wear niqabs.

In responding to *mustaftis*, the leadership only consults with muftis it recognizes as confirmed adherents of *salafiyya*. In practice, it is more independent than its loyalties and affiliations suggest, and allows more room for adjustments of fatwas issued by *salafi* luminaries than the shelves of its bookstore advise. Abu Khadeejah related that when he receives a query and is unsure about the answer, he searches in his fatwa compilations for deliberations on similar issues. If he does not find one, he calls Saudi Arabia. Because the great scholars are usually not available, he often reaches one of the "lesser scholars." He is not committed to a specific mufti or panel, and will insist on getting the reasoning of the fatwa rather than just its conclusion because the *mustafti* might demand it. After receiving the answer, he will examine its applicability to his community, rendering him an authority to a limited extent, rather than a mere transmitter. The explanation he provided suggested that despite his determined dogmatism, he recognized that in some exceptional situations, circumstances in the West necessitate accommodations:

> Let's say a scholar gave a fatwa from Pakistan. Or from India. Or from Saudi Arabia. The fact of its applicability in a minority community living in Birmingham, its applicability and its admissibility is something that I have to judge. So, therefore, to say that I don't issue *fatawa* wouldn't be 100% correct ... Those *fatawa* that have been issued [in Muslim societies], how applicable are those *fatawa* in the UK? The beauty is that most of them are applicable because they are basically halal and haram. But let's say they're *fatawa* that relate to societies as a whole. For example, the fatwa of Shaykh ʾAbd-al ʾAziz Ibn-Baz [in case] there's a magician in our community, what should we do with him? [In Saudi Arabia] This will go up to the authorities. How do you do that in Britain?[71]

Despite its strong ties to Saudi Arabia and the agenda of its religious establishment, the mosque is not directly funded by the Kingdom. Abu Khadeejah explained that when it was established, the leaders approached the Saudi Minister of Religious Affairs and asked if an application for donation would be looked upon positively. The Minister answered in the affirmative, but "we never really went for it, forcefully, ourselves." The reason was a concern for their credibility: the leadership feared people would question their motivations if they were funded by the Saudis. That did not help; in Small Heath and online forums, rumors about the financial motivations of the leadership are widespread.

In line with the teachings of the contemporary luminaries of *salafiyya*, attendees of the Salafi Mosque are instructed that the specific interpretation of Islam taught there is the only true one; if they loyally follow it, they will become part of the Saved Sect that enters Heaven. If they excel in devotion and do more than the obligatory, they will become forerunners who end up in a particularly suitable location in Heaven.

98   Shari'a and Life

On the other hand, if they dissent or divert, they will become part of the 72 deviant sects and will join the infidels in Hell, at least for a time.

The agenda of the mosque is preoccupied with refutations of and distancing from those whom Hell awaits. First, and most obvious, on the lengthy list of rivals is the majority non-Muslim society, morally declining and spiritually void, whose infidelity and promiscuity are a constant threat. In the words of Abu Khadeejah: "We've got a huge battle that we're fighting. And the battle is on every front – psychologically speaking. We have the ideological battle with, you know, the secular society that we live in, a society that is becoming more and more liberal in terms of its morality – sexual morality, other types of morality. It's becoming more godless ... we're losing our own capital, which is our own Muslims, to secularism."[72]

Abu Khadeejah and his fellow imam Abu Hakim associated liberalism with social vices and pointed to the risk that in a democracy, "idiots" would decide the fate of a nation. They noted that it was not a coincidence that the world's largest democracies – the United States, India, and Russia (as they described the latter) – have the highest suicide rates and claimed that in democracies there was, in theory, nothing to prevent the legalization of incest.[73] While they did not deny the potential legitimacy of Muslim electoral participation in Britain if a *maslaha* could be determined (in line with the majority *salafi* views on the matter), they discouraged the participation of mosque attendees in every recent national election. They were equally against participation in the neck-and-neck Brexit referendum because they believed its results would not impact Muslims.[74]

When we suggested that the European Court of Human Rights, for example, does make a difference for religious minorities, Abu Khadeejah responded sceptically. He said that Abu Hamza al-Masri (the imam of Finsbury Park Mosque in London, convicted of inciting violence and then extradited to the United States) and Abu Qatada (the Jordanian radical deported from England following a lengthy legal battle) were not given their day in European courts.[75]

Second on the list of rivals of the Salafi Mosque are non-*salafi* Muslim groups whose deviance and faults the leadership struggles to expose on the shelves of the bookstore, in online articles, in sermons, and in interviews. Along with al-Qaeda and ISIS, these groups include Jama'at al-Tabligh, the Sufis (Abu Khadeejah dedicated an entire treatise to the affinity between the two[76]), and the Muslim Brothers, long-time rivals of the Saudi regime accused of instigating unlawful political subversion.

Refutations of jihadi groups are commensurate with the agenda of the Saudi government and the Saudi religious establishment, particularly since the September 11 attack. They also carry the potential of transforming the *salafi* movement in Britain from being perceived as a threat to the state to being perceived as an asset in the fight against the enemy the public fears most. Being viewed as an asset also directly challenges the Conservative conventional wisdom that intolerant ideologies should no longer be tolerated and specifically calls for the banning of *salafiyya* at large.[77]

One example is a leaflet published by Salafi Publications on *Combating 21st-Century Extremist Terrorism: ISIS and al-Qaeda in Iraq and Syria*, which stresses the importance of presenting youth, particularly in the West, with the appropriate Quranic verses and Prophetic traditions that refute the falsehoods of the jihadis. It emphasizes that it is permissible only for leaders and governments to declare war, that it is prohibited to kill civilians, and that a Muslim army should only engage the enemy in battle if it is strong enough to prevail. It states that "the killings perpetrated by ISIS, al-Qaeda, and other extremist groups is worse than the murder committed by the sinners because the sinners do not claim that they have a license to kill from God, whilst the extremists claim that God Almighty Himself has commanded them with this slaughter, and therefore they believe they are doing God's work!"[78]

Another example is a leaflet entitled *Salafism and Who Are the Salafis in This Era?* by Abu Khadeejah, which suggests that the idea that *salafiyya* is an extreme or radical sect found favour among many Muslims and non-Muslims only due to the propagation of "ill-informed journalists and unscrupulous 'academics.'" It assures that *salafiyya* is, in fact, moderate, "giving leeway where necessary."[79]

A leading book published by Salafi Publications, *The Rise of Jihadist Extremism in the West*, emphasizes the impermissibility of demonstrations, marches, and rallies against political regimes, the duty to accept even tyrannical leaders, and the obligation to inform the authorities about terrorists who plot attacks such as bombings and kidnappings (both in the Muslim world and in the West).[80] In March 2017, the Salafi Mosque condemned a terror attack on the London Bridge that left five dead. In response, a group led by a preacher who supports jihadi-*Salafism*, Abu Haleema (Shakil Chapra), briefly protested against the mosque on Coventry Road, and posted the provocation on YouTube.[81]

High on the list of non-*salafi* Muslims refuted at the Salafi Mosque are also the Muslim Brothers. The era of instability and bloody civil wars that followed the revolutions of the Arab Spring has been seen by *salafis* as vindication of their conviction that submissive loyalty to sinful Muslim leaders is preferable to good (or ill) intentioned Islamist political dissent that aims to bring about ideal Muslim regimes.

100   Shari'a and Life

Abu Khadeejah said it was "clear cut" that the Brothers were one of the 72 deviant sects because they opposed an *asl* (foundation) of shari'a by rebelling against rulers. He described the Brothers, who do not have an affiliated mosque in Birmingham, in conspiratorial terms as being an "enemy within": "as a group [they] probably won't have as many members in the UK, but sympathizers to the cause and the principles of the Ikhwan [the Brothers] – they are by far the biggest ideology. Because a Sufi can be an Ikhwani, a Hanafi can be an Ikhwani, even a Shi'i."[82]

He described al-Qaradawi as deviant and said his books would not be sold at the mosque's bookstore. Explaining what he perceives to be the failure of al-Qaradawi's monopolist *ifta'* ambitions, Abu Khadeejah spoke critically about the independent-minded attitude of Islamist-oriented leaderships, as well as others: "You have to understand, mosques are very territorial places. They don't want any outsiders; even the Ikhwani mosques don't want any outsiders telling the mosque committee what to do ... The European Council [for Fatwa and Research] is seen as a territorial body that wishes to impose its will upon mosques and committees and societies. That's why it doesn't work."[83]

Condemnations of the Brothers dominated the summer 2019 biannual conference organized by the mosque and entitled "Muslim Unity, Splitting of the Ummah and the Methodology of the Scholars of Hadith." The keynote speaker, Shaykh Salim Bamihriz (b. 1950), a Somali-born Saudi-based scholar and a student of al-Madkhali, spoke in Arabic and was translated to English. He dedicated his talk to the evil brought by people who are innovators who appear Muslim but, in fact, are propagators of misguidance. First on Bamihriz's list were the Muslim Brothers; he accused them of calling for *wahdat al-adyan* (the unity of religions) and creating a "cocktail" of Islam and other religions.

Bamihriz pointed to what he described as the misguided words of several Islamist scholars, including the Egyptian Muhammad al-Ghazali, who, according to Bamihriz, cynically addressed a tradition according to which Allah would place his foot over Hell by asking what Allah's shoe size was (a gasp of shock from the audience followed Bamihriz's words at this point). Bamihriz asked the audience to ponder the turbulences wrought by one fruit and vegetable vendor in Tunisia that had led to "the so-called Arab Spring" and argued that the lesson was that Muslims should be obedient to their imam (in this context, political leader) even if he acted unjustly toward them. He warned that Hell awaits Muslims who are not *salafi* and emphasized that being a *salafi* requires unity with those who follow the foundations of religion; it is enough for one not to follow even one of the foundations of religion for one to be discredited as belonging to one of the 72 sects.[84]

Third on the list of rivals of the Salafi Mosque, and subject to equally vicious attacks and counter-attacks, are rival *salafi* groups, particularly the neighboring Green Lane Mosque and the London Ibn Taymiyya Brixton Mosque. Abu Khadeejah accuses those two mosques of having Ikhwani sympathies and being unfaithful to the *salafi* creed.

The roots of the conflict between Green Lane and the Salafi Mosque are difficult to ascertain. That a five-minute walk separates them and they compete for the same population has undoubtedly not helped ease the tensions. At the Salafi Mosque, the story about a sermon at Green Lane, which stated that magic acts are permissible in Islam, a position firmly rejected by *salafis*, is widely told. Abu Khadeejah told us the leaders of Green Lane were closer to Hasan al-Banna than to Ibn Baz and argued that despite its pretenses, it hosts speakers who are not true *salafis* and advances *bid'a*.

The rivalry between the two mosques is ever-present. The Eid prayer marks the annual zenith of the constant struggle for hegemony, with the two mosques organizing mass-attended prayers. 'Abdallah (b. 1967), a convert of Jamaican descent and one of the leading volunteers at the Salafi Mosque, who encouraged us to attend the Salafi Mosque's event, did not fail to point out that while the prayer organized by Green Lane commences only at 9:30, the prayer organized by the Salafi Mosque starts at 7:30, which is, he claimed, not as easy for people, but was in line with the Sunna, which recommends the prayer should commence as early as possible after sunrise.[85]

The discord with the Ibn Taymiyya Brixton Mosque, which has a small publishing operation of its own, is older and has been just as bitter. The two mosques sought the support of al-Madkhali, who sided with the Salafi Mosque and accused the London *salafis* of reaching out to supporters of the Muslim Brothers and distancing themselves from true *salafiyya*. The feud highlighted the expectation of al-Madkhali and his affiliates for exclusivist loyalty to their brand.

One of the imams of the Ibn Taymiyya Mosque, 'Umar Jamayki, told us that leadership of the Salafi Mosque does as it pleases rather than adhering to contemporary *salafi* authorities as it claims to do.[86] Hafeezullah Khan, one of the three imams of the Green Lane Mosque, declined to comment on Abu Khadeejah's accusations against Green Lane. Hinting, perhaps, at the difference between his mosque and the Saudi affiliation of the Salafi Mosque, he emphasized that the three imams of Green Lane respond to queries of *mustaftis* independently. When they struggle with one, they meet together to discuss it but never refer it to an external authority.[87]

Attendees of Green Lane were less restrained in expressing their unease with their big rival. For example, Habib, a seventy-seven-year-old, Pakistani-born retiree we met near the Salafi Mosque, cautioned us to pray only at Green Lane. He accused the Salafi Mosque of exclusively relying on one "Yemeni who moved to Saudi Arabia" and of marrying and divorcing in ways prohibited by shari'a.[88]

The British *salafi* imams that are rivals of the Salafi Mosque were cooperative only to a limited extent in the interviews. It was clear that we would not be able to conduct a meaningful written survey with attendees of their mosques on or near their grounds. Following a meeting of its board, the leadership of the Salafi Mosque gave us such permission, and the imam who gave the Friday sermon even encouraged participation. The leadership did not interfere in any way with the content of the questionnaire.

Thus, to learn more about independent *salafi*s at odds with al-Madkhali, we crossed the channel to Marseille. At the Ali Hacène (Hassan) Blidi Mosque, we met with its imam, Salim Blidi (b. 1972). We

Figure 2.5. The Salafi Bookstore, Birmingham. The children's bookshelf. A signature of Salafi books is that humans and animals appear without facial features.

Across a Wasati-Salafi European Spectrum   103

discovered that the mosque's post-Madkhali turn involved a broader break with *salafiyya*.

The Hassan Blidi Mosque is located in an old building in dire need of repair (for which donations are collected). It accommodates some 350 attendees, most of Algerian descent. The hotline for preventing radicalization at the entrance indicates that the mosque engages in anti-jihadi campaigning like that of the Salafi Mosque (figure 2.6). In other regards, it speaks of disillusionment with the agenda advanced by the British advocates of Saudi-guided *salafiyya*.

According to Blidi, he pursued his undergraduate studies in Syria, when "it was still Syria," and then moved to Mecca and completed an MA in *'aqida* at Umm al-Qura University. There, he embraced the agenda of the Saudi religious establishment and particularly of al-Madkhali. Upon completing his studies, he joined his father, an educator and an official at the Algerian Education Ministry, who was appointed to serve at the Algerian consulate in Marseille. In his first years in Marseille, he was a disciple of al-Madkhali. That caused a rift with his father. However, in 2012 he broke from his Saudi guide. Blidi explained that the reason was personal rather than ideological: al-Madkhali wanted his complete obedience and would not tolerate any disagreement.[89]

Today Blidi defines himself as a *salafi* in the sense that he abides by the Quran and the traditions as interpreted and applied by the *salaf* but is critical of what he identifies as the paranoia and dogmatism of some *salafi*s. In our interview, he emphasized that he issues fatwas independently, without consulting any external muftis, and the need for fatwas to accommodate changing times and places. He said it was crucial that only muftis who were familiar with European realities issue fatwas responding to queries of European Muslims. As an example, he spoke about a woman who did not pray and did not don the hijab. A Saudi or even an Algerian or Egyptian mufti, he said, would advise the husband to divorce her, but a mufti knowledgeable about the liberal environments in Europe would advise the husband to exercise patience. Another example he gave was students who could not pursue their academic studies because classes conflicted with the stipulated times of prayer. He noted that for him, an imam based in France, it was apparent that the students could defer the prayers based on necessity.

Blidi unequivocally opposed the taking of mortgages in any situation other than life-and-death necessity, and opposed electoral participation on the grounds that it was distant from Islamic *shura*, involved Muslims in lies and hate-mongering, and made no difference because all politicians were, in essence, the same.

104 Shari'a and Life

On several other issues debated in *fiqh al-aqalliyyat al-Muslima* discourse, he presented pragmatic opinions that distanced him from *salafi* teachings. These include Christmas congratulations, student loans, and maintaining a job that involved haram until an alternative was found. He insisted that the opinion according to which a person who cannot find another job did not have to resign was supported by al-'Uthaymin (we could not locate such a fatwa). He also accepted the legitimacy of the French hijab ban in public schools as an aspect of the separation of church and state in France and said his daughters take off their headscarves when entering their school. Muslims, he suggested, should ask themselves why they were not able to build private religious schools as the Jewish minority in France did.

Blidi's religio-juristic agenda overlaps, in part, with that of the European Council for Fatwa and Research. Yet he strongly opposes the Dublin-based panel's religio-legal and political arguments. He described the decisions of the Council as deviant, weak, and void, and al-Qaradawi as a barking dog, "the biggest terrorist" of all, who was responsible for the turbulence wrought by the Arab Spring.[90]

Marseille is home to up to 300,000 Muslims[91] – one of the largest Muslim populations in any city in Europe. Directories point to as many as 59 mosques, though the mosques no longer existed at several addresses we visited.[92] Until 2017, Blidi's embrace of an independent version of *salafiyya* faced a challenger at Al-Sounna mosque, a five-minute walk from his. The authorities closed that mosque; and its imam, El Hadi Doudi, was expelled from France. Some reports linked Al-Sounna to violent radicalization, others to al-Madkhali.[93] The distinction between the two is not always clear to Western journalists.

In an interview with the weekly *Marianne*, Blidi said that Doudi spread his venom to such an extent that young people who came to him following the closure asked if it was really prohibited for Muslims to greet non-Muslims with *bonjour*. *Marianne* quoted Blidi as saying that he was no longer a *salafi*, while noting that French authorities still categorized his mosque as such.[94] Blidi's eagerness to show us his integration-mindedness and anti-jihadi campaign aimed, perhaps, at dispelling any doubts as to his agenda.

Despite its large Muslim population, no area of Marseille projects the environment of enhanced Islamic religiosity as Small Heath does. Several of the mosques we visited were converted residential or industrial buildings with sparse facilities, small libraries, and few external observable Islamic signs. The city is not home to a Grand Mosque. The mayor proposed to build one in 2001, but that plan was frustrated due to protests and legal challenges.[95] The closest mosque to this definition is the

Centre Musulman de Marseille, with its marvellous high windows and chandeliers. It is led by the Algerian-born imam Farid Bourouba and is affiliated with the umbrella organization Musulmans de France, which is affiliated with the Federation of Islamic Organizations in Europe, the founding organization of the European Council for Fatwa and Research.

Unlike imam al-Dib of The Stockholm Mosque, imam Bourouba did not consider himself obliged to accept the Council's decisions. Like al-Dib, he told us that it never happened that he rejected one of those decisions, including the 1999 conditional legitimization of mortgages. Muslims in Europe, he explained, are in a situation of weakness, and unless they take mortgages, they will not be able to improve their situation. He did not subscribe to the Council's journal like al-Dib and explained that its copies are available online (we could not locate them). He never referred a query to the Council himself.[96]

Bourouba's mosque was the only one in Marseille where the Council was privileged and its agenda advanced; its existence was not even known in some we visited. Bourouba outlined an approach to fiqh that echoed that of al-Qaradawi, the foundations of *wasatiyya*, and the agenda of the European Council for Fatwa and Research. He noted that the uniformity of *ifta'* sought by the Council was the only way to avoid discord between Muslim communities; fatwas regarding European situations should be issued by muftis acquainted with the environments to which they relate; fatwas should be guided by *taysir*, which is the essence of Islam, and not by hardships added by muftis who were excessively cautious not to transgress; and cross-*madhhab* search is a useful way of establishing *taysir*. He related the case of a Malaysian woman who sojourned in France for studies and stayed with a family that owned a dog. Being a *Shafi'i*, living in proximity to a dog caused her great distress, and she washed her clothes every day until she learned of the more lenient *Maliki* position concerning dogs, and was relieved.

Bourouba was confident that many across the continent subscribe to the religio-legal approach he advanced. He recalled, however, that on several occasions, he offered attendees of his mosque pragmatic fatwas issued by the European Council for Fatwa and Research that they rejected while remaining in his mosque. He had no illusion that the authority of the Council and its fatwas have become a subject for broad agreement – neither in his mosque, nor in France and Europe at large.[97]

Figure 2.6. Hassan Blidi Mosque, Marseille. An anti-radicalization poster greets attendees at the entrance of the post-Salafi mosque. The mosque is located in an old building in dire need of repair.

Chapter Three

The Mustafti Is the Mufti

Navigating through a spectrum of European mosques and their leaderships, the previous chapter presented five main approaches by imams to the ambitions of the European Council for Fatwa and Research to establish itself as a source for uniformed *ifta'* and to advance a pragmatic and integrationist *wasati* approach to the challenges Muslims in Europe face. These include an approach that accepts the Council as an exclusive authority and categorically embraces its ideology and its fatwas; an approach that denies its ambition for exclusive authority, yet views its religio-juristic contributions favourably; an approach that favours pragmatism and integration, yet is critical of the Council's pretenses as well of its religio-legal credibility; an approach that rejects the Council's ideology and methodology, yet recognizes its utility for Muslims of weak faith; and an approach which advances a counter agenda, religio-legal dogmatic and anti-integrationist.

This chapter examines what attendees of the mosques studied made of the Council's ambitions and their imams' approaches to those ambitions. The Council had the potential to make a difference for those of them who care about leading their lives according to the shari'a. First, faced with contesting (often viciously so, as demonstrated) Islamic institutions and ideologies around them, it offered them the option of voluntarily accepting the authority of a single European-based religio-juristic panel, led by a well-known mufti, and finally being relieved of the burden of choosing between conflicting voices. One did not have to be an attendee of a mosque whose imam or leadership was affiliated with the Council to embrace it as an exclusive or at least primary source of instruction.

Second, the Council's view that Muslims in Europe deserve particular facilitations resulted in several original and audacious shari'a-grounded determinations on issues that are potentially life-changing.

108 Shari'a and Life

These include housing, employment, education, inheritance, marriage, interpersonal relations with non-Muslims, and, most importantly, permanent residence in non-Muslim countries. Whether accepted or rejected, a Muslim engaging with these facilitations had, in theory, something to gain. Accepting a facilitating view as correct, or at least legitimate, could provide the confidence and comfort that pragmatic choices do not defy the will of God. Rejecting facilitating views, when conscious of their meaning and that other Muslims promote them, could also be meaningful as a means of enhancing self-perceptions of religious devotion and transforming normative decisions into marks of pure commitment to Islam and its norms.

The more than two decades that have passed since the Council was established do not allow a final verdict as to the success of its ambitions. Yet they allow for meaningful evaluations. The few scholars who have provided theirs offered mixed impressions. Kern described the Council as "the most influential fatwa council in Europe."[1] Other scholars were more reserved, although they agreed that the Council had left a mark. Laurence and Vaisse suggested the Council became a leading voice on shari'a, but a contested one. Among the rivals of its aspirations for hegemony, they mentioned imams at local mosques, *salafi*s, and Muslims who hold that, despite its claims to the contrary, the Council is not familiar with the reality of young European Muslims.[2] Caeiro and al-Saify presented numerous examples of individuals and organizations in Europe who ask for the advice of al-Qaradawi and his Council. Yet their discussion of al-Qaradawi's many rivals on the continent highlighted the obstacles faced by the Council in its efforts to establish uniformity in religious decisions.[3] Van Esdonk interviewed four Dutch imams from communities she believed to be more likely influenced by the Council, who mentioned the panel as a source for advice, albeit of secondary importance. One of them was a Moroccan-Dutch board member of the Federation of Islamic Organizations in the Netherlands and the Council for Moroccan Mosques in the Netherlands, who participated in the discussions that led to the establishment of the Council. He described the panel as a declining project that had failed to realize its objective of attaining uniformity in *ifta'*.[4]

As noted in the Introduction, our survey prioritized mosque populations we considered to be most likely to engage with *fiqh al-aqalliyyat al-Muslima* discourse. This renders its evaluation of the Council's achievements all the more categorical. It points to a threefold failure by the Council across the spectrum studied. First, we found that the Council remained unknown to a majority of attendees approached despite its far-reaching aspirations. Being unaware of its existence, they were neither positive nor negative about its agenda.

Second, even attendees who knew of its existence and thought favourably of its objectives declined to regard it as an exclusive or even primary source of instruction on religio-legal issues pertaining to Muslim minorities, including in a mosque where the leadership commits to its decisions. We found that the Council has completely failed in its effort to establish itself as a disseminator of uniformed *ifta'*.

Analysis of the practices and views of attendees surveyed suggests that alongside its particular limitations, there exist obstacles that are likely to impede any project advancing similar grand ambitions. These include the primacy of ethnic affiliations in defining Islamic religious identities, the pluralistic nature of Islamic online operations and the suspicions regarding them, and, most importantly, the determination of *mustaftis* to have the last word regarding the validity of fatwas and to not commit to any single authority.

Third, the study found that the rich religio-legal output of the Council has had a minor direct impact on the attendees surveyed who were aware of the Council's existence. Almost without exception, they were not familiar with the contours of the *wasati* religio-legal approach to *fiqh al-aqalliyyat al-Muslima* or directly engaged with its fatwas. Not one provided an example for explicitly determining a practice, whether on an existential or a trivial matter, following the reading of a fatwa by the Council.

Also, we found that the polemic between *wasatis* and *salafis* on the legitimacy of pragmatic accommodations in the European context did not play a role, or played a negligible role, in the way interviewees conceptualized their religious identity, including those who are strongly opinionated about the two approaches. That included *salafi* attendees, whom we hypothesized would invoke their opposition to the leniency of the Council as one assertion of their heightened, uncompromising devotion. The minor to non-existent role of *fiqh al-aqalliyyat al-Muslima* in shaping self-perceptions of religiosity reflects a tendency, which was shared by attendees with different orientations for different reasons, not to primarily ground religious identity on approaches to fiqh and not to consider diligent investigations of religio-legal deliberations as a sign of religious devotion.

While the study found almost no evidence for the direct diffusion of the Council's *ifta'* among mosque attendees surveyed, the case study of its signature 1999 mortgages fatwa suggests its efforts may have nevertheless contributed to the limited proliferation of shari'a-grounded pragmatic opinions among the attendees surveyed, including a few

110   Shari'a and Life

who never engaged with any of its writings or were not aware of its existence. The case shows how groundbreaking ideological and methodological argumentations introduced by the Council were reinterpreted and recontextualized in the process of their distorted transmission in a manner that allowed the embrace of facilitating opinions without ascribing to the audacious intellectual project that made them possible.

Who's Heard About al-Majlis al-Urubbi?

The most surprising of our findings about the impact of the European Council for Fatwa and Research was that most attendees surveyed had no idea that it exists. Most of the interviewees in each of the four mosques that were the focus of the study said that they had never heard about the Council or had a very vague idea about a pan-European panel for *ifta'* that exists in one or another city in Europe without being able to mention its name or to say anything meaningful about it. Few who were not familiar with the Council knew al-Qaradawi and that he had engaged with the situation of Muslim minorities. Their main source of information was his television call-in show *Al-Shari'a wa-l-Hayat* that they had watched in the past (but no longer did at the time of the interview). Few interviewees knew about the Council and its objectives, yet not one of them was familiar with the contours of the *wasati* approach or ever systematically engrossed with it.

The written questionnaires asked respondents to note if they were aware of the Council's existence. As table 3.1 shows, more than two decades after it was established with one of the most well-known muftis as its leader, became front-page news, and published groundbreaking

Table 3.1. Knowledge about the existence of the European Council for Fatwa and Research

Mosque	Percentage, %
The Stockholm Mosque	41.7
Al-Nur Mosque, Reykjavik	62.5
The Grand Mosque, Reykjavik	54.2
Markaz Imam Malik, Dortmund	51.5
'Umar Ibn al-Khattab Mosque, Dortmund	34.4
Hassan Blidi Mosque, Marseille	31.3
Husby Mosque, Stockholm	62.1
The Salafi Mosque, Birmingham	19.5

Note: For statistical information about the surveys, see the introduction, note 31.

decisions, in not a single mosque were more than two-thirds of respondents aware that a panel by that name exists, including in mosques where the imams are strongly opinionated about it. The Council was also unknown to a majority of respondents in The Stockholm Mosque, where the imam officially affiliates with it and is committed to its decisions.

This points to a serious marketing failure. Not everyone drinks Coca-Cola, and more than a few disapprove of it, but there is hardly a person in the world who does not recognize the name. If the name of a Council that sought to dominate Islamic life in Europe has not even come to the attention of so many mosque attendees, it means that something has gone terribly wrong in the process of trying to make good on its ambitions.

The roots of this marketing failure are multidimensional. The Council publicizes its views and fatwas through two main channels: new media (websites, social media, and satellite television) and old media (books, a journal, and leaflets). Each has proved of modest efficacy, although for different reasons.

The new media organs the Council operates were, in its early years, poorly designed but have improved since. However, their reach has remained limited. It is still difficult to locate its fatwas through Google searches, including the groundbreaking ones. Its website is in Arabic, and according to traffic-ranking companies, has been consistently low on the lists of the most visited religious websites.[5]

The Council's Facebook page had, as of January 2023, 66,000 'Likes.' These figures are far from impressive for a panel with pan-European ambitions. In comparison, the 'Likes' for Salafi Publications numbered 61,000. One finds Wikipedia entries about the Council in English, French, German, and Swedish, but not in other European languages. The humble achievements of its online platforms testify to the Council's limited financial resources and a lack of youthful enthusiasm among its ranks.

Until 2010, al-Qaradawi supervised Islamonline.net, established in June 1997. This portal included a state-of-the-art, *wasati*-oriented fatwa archive, which also featured fatwas written by the Council and its leading members. According to Alexa.com, an internet ranking company, in 2007, it was one of the two most popular Islamic portals globally.[6] Still, because Islamonline.net featured only Arabic and English pages, some potential readers could not use it. After a managerial dispute led to al-Qaradawi's dismissal from the board of directors in 2010, al-Qaradawi's supporters launched a spin-off site, onislam.net, which became the new platform for *wasati* jurisprudence. (Egypt-based workers argued that

112   Shari'a and Life

the Qatari management of Islamonline.net sought to transform the portal from *wasatiyya* to *salafiyya* and curb its strong anti-Israel agenda.)[7] The new website attracted significantly less traffic, and, in 2015, it ceased operations.

Al-Qaradawi's retirement from *Al-Shari'a wa-l-Hayat*, as part of his gradual retreat from public activities late in life, has denied the Council the most effective means of diffusing its religio-juristic theory. The global ratings of Al Jazeera were and still are difficult to evaluate, as are those of other Arabic satellite channels. Even if claims that *Al-Shari'a wa-l-Hayat* was watched by 40 to 60 million were exaggerated, the program, airing on Sunday afternoons to make it easier for Muslims living in the West to watch, was a novelty and had a loyal viewership in Europe.[8] However, our study and previous studies suggested that, while popular at first, interest in the show waned long before al-Qaradawi left it.[9] With time, the excitement created by the innovation in a mufti answering live queries from around the world in a straightforward manner was gone. At the same time, a plethora of other platforms offered similar discussions.

The circulation of the Council's flagship journal *Al-Majalla al-'Ilmiyya* and its other publications has been even more modest than that of its advanced media operations. On the bookshelves of the eight mosques studied, as well as on those of dozens of other mosques and Islamic-interest bookstores visited, we did not locate copies of the journal and, in total, only a handful of copies of books published by the Council. We did not expect to find the Council's publications in the Salafi Bookstore or other *salafi* mosques, but their absence from large general-interest Islamic bookstores and pragmatic-oriented Arabic-speaking mosques was surprising. Other than in the offices of the Council itself, the only place where we found copies of the Council's journal was the private office of imam Khaled al-Dib at The Stockholm Mosque. However, his mosque's large bookstore did not offer a single copy of the journal (it did have several of al-Qaradawi's books). There is no greater sign of the failure of the Council to publicize itself than that in one of the largest mosques in Europe, where the imam is a committed loyalist, its primary publication is not available for the public.

Laurence and Vaisse pointed to language as a primary and significant problem, noting that Muslims who do not have a good command of Arabic cannot read any of the Council's publications that have not been translated.[10] Indeed, the Council's name recognition may have been improved if its marketing efforts had corresponded with the linguistic realities of European Islam.

In the Babylon that is the Muslim world, Arabic is not the lingua franca of the devout it should ideally be. While all non-Arab Muslims know at least a few words in the language of the Quran, few without religious education have the proficiency to follow a *khutba* or read a fatwa written in Arabic. Ignoring this reality and despite its cross-ethnic ambitions, the Council has deliberated and published mainly in Arabic. The implication, as noted by imam Farid Bourouba of Centre Musulman de Marseille (who privileges the Council), is that its output has been incomprehensible not only for some non-Arab Muslims but also for some second- and third-generation European Muslims of Arab descent who have not mastered Arabic.[11]

The marketing deficiencies of the Council were recognized by one of its leading members already during al-Qaradawi's tenure.[12] The official announcement published in November 2018 marking al-Qaradawi's departure showed that the new leadership was aware of the poor job the Council had done in publicizing its approach and decisions and specifically in utilizing new media. It announced two new projects: a smartphone application, "The Euro Fatwa App," which would contain all the fatwas issued by the Council since its inauguration (the application, offering a rich fatwa archive in Arabic, English, and Spanish, was introduced during 2022) and a Research Committee, which would gather young male and female scholars to explore ways of advancing the cooperation between the Council and educational and governmental bodies as well as search for ways to make the media more aware of its work.[13]

The Limited Appeal of Fiqh al-Aqalliyyat al-Muslima

It is fair to argue that when in dire need of information or for the confirmed articulation of an idea, people will make an effort to find the relevant text, even if it is challenging to access. The history of publishing and ideas is replete with examples. The absence of knowledge by the majority of mosque attendees surveyed about the Council, and the modest to non-existing engagement with its output on the part of those aware of its existence, are thus also the result of limited interest in the main product it offers – fatwas on conflicts between shariʿa norms and the norms in Western countries.

The interviews suggested that (a) a majority of interviewees do not distinguish between shariʿa-related issues resulting from their living in a non-Muslim country and shariʿa-related issues of universal nature as two distinct categories, and, consequently, do not hold that the former deserves special treatment. (b) The specific issues that had dominated

114 Shari'a and Life

fiqh al-aqalliyyat al-Muslima discourse and underlined the debates within it do not preoccupy the *istifta'* of interviewees (to the extent they engage in *istifta'* at all). Interviewees' comments were supported by imams at the mosques surveyed, who said that they rarely received queries on *fiqh al-aqalliyyat al-Muslima*, and pointed to family matters as the main concern of *mustaftis* who approached them. (c) When faced with religio-legal challenges, interviewees resort in some cases to means other than *istifta'* and shari'a-grounded arguments to legitimize or at least make peace with choosing pragmatism over shari'a norms. They do so for various reasons and through various strategies (these reasons and strategies will be discussed in the majority of the next chapter). This being the case, facilitating fatwas like the ones offered by the Council are not crucial for them.

The following list is instructive. Asked to share the most recent shari'a-related issue they researched or asked for expert opinion, some interviewees failed to come up with any specific recollection. Others produced answers that were admittedly not their last inquiry but the most recent one they remembered. The compilation of their queries includes: Is it permissible to eat the meat of an animal that was tranquilized before it was butchered? Is a person considered a traveller, in terms of prayer regulations, if more than three months have passed since arriving at a new destination? What should be done with a five-Euro bill found in a public library? How should the meat of a sheep slaughtered on the occasion of the birth of a child be distributed? Can a Muslim give zakat to a family member in need, or must he give it to a stranger? Is it permissible to marry a Christian woman? Is it permissible to wear garments that are entirely red? If a man discharged sperm in a small amount without climaxing, does he still need a new ablution before praying? If a Muslim accidentally puts food in his mouth and then spits it out during Ramadan, does that constitute a breaking of the fast? Does the Quran really require stoning as the punishment for adultery? If a relative accused a Muslim of stealing money he did not steal and asked him to give an oath before God that he was innocent, should the oath be given? Should a Muslim give zakat on Eid al-Fitr in his home country or in the country where he lives?

The list demonstrates the comprehensiveness of the shari'a and the richness of human actions it is perceived as relevantly addressing. But it also points to the universality of certain Muslim interests and concerns. It is likely that a list assembled by interviewees living in Cairo, Jakarta, or Kabul would not have been much different. The issues broached in *fiqh al-aqalliyyat al-Muslima* discourse are part of the agenda of European

The Mustafti Is the Mufti   115

Muslims but do not preoccupy it, decreasing the essentiality of a panel focused on addressing those issues.

Obscurity in a House of Loyalists

Imams have several means of making a panel of muftis known – through the sermons they deliver, classes they organize, books they encourage followers to read, posters they display, and guidance on shari'a they provide. Given these options, the moderate name recognition of the Council among attendees of The Stockholm Mosque calls for particular explanation. How could it be that so many of the mosque's attendees do not know about the existence of an *ifta'* panel to which their imam commits and which he enthusiastically supports?

Several explanations can be suggested. Because the Council apparently did not supply The Stockholm Mosque (or other mosques we visited) with materials such as posters or leaflets, nothing visible on its grounds advertises its existence. As the previous section informed, imam al-Dib was not frequently approached with queries relating to *fiqh al-aqalliyyat al-Muslima*. The implication is that when advising *mustaftis*, he does not usually have the opportunity to share fatwas issued by the Council with them. He may not even have the opportunity to advise them at all. As a rule, the larger a mosque is, and the more impressive the academic credentials of an imam are, the less likely it is that he will be able to respond to all those who seek his advice.

Imam al-Dib's workload is ambitious. Along with his duties at the mosque and the Imam Association, he is also trained as a marriage counsellor. When advising couples, he acts in that capacity rather than as an *'alim*. The first time we came unannounced to meet with him after Friday's congregational prayer, we waited for over an hour outside his office. Had we come with a question on a non-urgent matter of shari'a, or one we had reason to think could be answered by someone else, we probably would not have waited. It is thus possible that some attendees who wished to consult with imam al-Dib never had a chance to do so, although none of the interviewees at the mosque reported this to have been the case.

Imam Abu Khadeejah is another example of work overload. He said he received some three hundred queries a month, yet he can only reply to one-third of them, "because I have a life to live."[14] Imam Blidi, too, cannot realistically reach out to all those who seek his attention. He estimated that his mobile phone receives over 50 queries on an average day – and that after changing the number! On some days, the number

116   Shari'a and Life

is higher than 200. On top of that, people approach him in person at the mosque.[15]

Yet another possible explanation why the existence of the Council is not familiar to a majority of attendees of a mosque whose imam officially affiliates with it is that many of them pay little or no attention to al-Dib. Mosques serve different functions, broader and narrower. Some Muslims choose their mosque based on what it stands for, its ethnic composition, or ideological tendency; others choose it merely because it is conveniently located or arranged. For some, their mosque of choice is their main hub for socializing: they attend lectures, buy groceries and religious items at the affiliated store, participate in leisure and sports activities, and engage in small talk with friends on the mosque's grounds. For others, on the other hand, the mosque is only a house for prayer, on a frequent or infrequent basis.

Because it is spacious and centrally located in a city with over a hundred thousand Muslims and only a handful of mosques, The Stockholm Mosque is home to a particularly considerable number of prayer-only attendees who visit it mainly during Friday congregational prayer. Several interviewees said they could not understand a word spoken at the sermons because they speak neither Arabic nor Swedish, the two languages spoken at the mosque. They had no idea what its orientation was and were not interested in finding out. Other attendees, who speak Arabic or Swedish, noted the mosque's location and vast space as the reason for choosing it and said they were indifferent to the ideology of the imam, whatever it may be.

The Stockholm Mosque is attended even by Muslims who are consciously and openly resentful of its *wasati* orientation. *Salafi*s we met there did not consider imam al-Dib a credible voice on Islam whose sermons should be heeded. They prayed in his mosque because it was convenient, and based their doing so on the notion that any mosque is a legitimate place of worship. Ironically, we witnessed that the mosque serves as a recruiting ground for the *salafi*s of the Ibn Abbas Center. The previous chapter described how one of the leaders of the *salafi* Center became a *salafi* through contacts he made in the mosque.

During our time at the mosque, we encountered several other examples. Moroccan-born (1975) 'Abd al-Latif, who has lived in Sweden since 1998 and is single, presented unequivocal *salafi* views and said that he was influenced by members of the Ibn Abbas Center and its website.[16] Still, we saw him often wandering around the mosque, alone, and it is where he prays. The *salafi* Husby Mosque is on another side of the city, and the Ibn Abbas Center, which is also far away, is not open every day. Wissam, an undergraduate in physics, who was born in 1995 in Sweden to Libyan parents, began attending The Stockholm Mosque at the age of 19, as he contemplated the meaning of life; it was there that he met students of al-Madina University from the Ibn Abbas Center and embraced the *salafi* approach. He explained that his choice of The Stockholm Mosque as his house of congregational prayer was merely a matter of convenience. The Ibn Abbas Center was too far and the activists go away for lectures on Friday, so the Center is not open.[17]

The phenomenon of partial overlap between the ideology and affiliation of a mosque's leadership and those of its population is not unique to The Stockholm Mosque. In each of the mosques surveyed, larger or smaller segments of the population did not identify with at least some of the views of the leadership, whether pragmatic or dogmatic. None of the interviewees at the pragmatic-inclined Grand Mosque of Reykjavik said they chose it based on its orientation, and several presented views that are at odds with those of the integration-minded and pragmatic-inclined leadership. Interviewees emphasized that the relatively central location of the mosque is convenient and said they appreciated that it was spacious. Several said they purposefully attend all three mosques in the city to make it clear to everyone that they do not take sides in the internal disputes as well as to meet different friends.

At the Hassan Blidi Mosque in Marseille, imam Blidi suggested that some 20 per cent of the attendees are indifferent to his persona and religio-legal approach, while the other 80 per cent would not continue to attend the mosque if someone else took his place.[18] The survey suggested that the number of attendees who do not care about or agree with his views is possibly more significant, or that he was unable to effectively communicate his understanding of shari'a to many of his followers. While, as noted in the previous chapter, he opposed electoral participation, more than 80 per cent of respondents said they hold that Muslims may vote in parliamentary elections in a Western country. Despite his objection to the conditional legitimization of mortgages, almost half of the respondents agreed that Muslims in Europe who have no alternative may purchase a home through a usurious loan (see table 3.2).

Abu Khadeejah, one of the imams of the Salafi Mosque in Birmingham, said that 20 per cent of attendees at his mosque are not *salafis* and pray there only because it is close to their home or workplace.[19] While none of the attendees we interviewed spoke against the religio-legal approach of the mosque, the written survey at the mosque indicated that it is indeed attended by a minority that is not *salafi*. The Salafi Mosque also has attendees who identify with the *salafi* approach and

118   Shari'a and Life

are articulate about it, but resent the imams of the mosque, question the purity of their motivations (without providing any substantive evidence for their allegations), and accuse them of being arrogant, dismissive of dissenting opinions, and self-indulgent.

Obscurity in a House of Antagonists

The lack of familiarity with the existence of the European Council for Fatwa and Research in the Salafi Mosque is noteworthy for different reasons. Only one-fifth of respondents of the written questionnaires at the mosque noted that they were familiar with the existence of the Council. A majority of the interviewees had never heard of it; they were not interested to learn more.

We were surprised by the ignorance about and indifference to the Council, its ideology, and its fatwas because opposing them would have suited the agenda *salafi* interviewees communicated. First, it would fit with their anti-Ikhwani views. Interviewees proved to have internalized *salafi* propaganda against the Muslim Brothers as a deviant, anarchy-spreading sect, some in passionate terms; several expressed a strong dislike of al-Qaradawi: one referred to him as a "crazy old man"; another as "Mickey Mouse." Second, relating to the Council as an 'other' would fit with the sense of elitism and pride in the exemplary practice of Islam interviewees displayed, some in more explicit fashion than others. In defining what their beliefs stand for, it was crucial for some of them that we appreciate not only that their non-compromising understanding of Islam is correct, but is the only correct one.

One example of ignorance of the Council was provided by Sami (b. 1994), a gym and martial arts instructor. Sami is the son of a French-Moroccan mother and a Catholic-born French father who converted to Islam before he was born. He discovered *salafiyya* when he was nineteen, after five years in which he was engrossed with the ideology of the Muslim Brothers. His change of heart owes, in part, to reading 'Abd al-Wahhab's *The Three Fundamental Principles and Their Evidences*. Ironically, the book was handed to him by a Muslim Brothers activist. After one month of additional reading, Sami concluded that the Islam of the Brothers was fundamentally wrong, first and foremost because they tended to embrace Muslims whether they were righteous or not.

Sami approached a *salafi* preacher, Yusuf Abu Anas, who encouraged him to move to Small Heath so that he could gain knowledge at the Salafi Mosque and reside in an Islamic environment. Sami, who said he gave up on managing a family business because he did not want to engage in haram, explained why more Muslims cannot recognize the truth and follow the *salafi* path, in terms celebrating his ability to pay the price in this life for the sake of the afterlife: "Imagine I say to you that you can follow a path where on the first level there is only fire, on the second level you are only allowed to touch your arm, and on the third level all the people you love die. Yet you can follow another path, where you have gold, and then you become king, and then you have 1,000 women. Which path will you choose? Now, if I told you that at the end of the second path, you'll go to Hell, and at the end of the first path, you'll go to Paradise, which one will you choose? [Choosing the right path] is not about intellect … it is about what you really want. Allah has given me the mercy to be on this path."[20] Still, despite his prior Ikhwani connections, and his positioning of his *salafi* identity as contrasting with Muslims (such as the Ikhwanis) who chose easier paths, Sami, like most other interviewees at the Salafi Mosque, responded that he had never heard of the European Council for Fatwa and Research, and was not interested in learning more (he also never heard of al-Qaradawi).

There are several explanations for the Council's obscurity among the majority of *salafi* mosque attendees. The crucial and trivial explanation is cyclical. Because of its lack of publicity, most of the attendees of the Salafi Mosque never heard about the Council, and never came across any of its texts. Some respondents, as will be explored in the next chapter, were never motivated to inquire about any of the key issues debated in *fiqh al-aqalliyyat al-Muslima* discourse, on which *wasati* fatwas were lenient, because they were not personally affected by those issues.

Because those attendees never heard about the Council, let alone came across any of its texts, their imams were rarely confronted with questions about its facilitations and broader ideology. Because the imams were not confronted with the Council's output, which they consider deviant and redundant, they did not regard its pragmatism as a challenge and were not pressed to position it in binary ideological terms and directly attack it. And because they did not attack it, rejection of the Council did not become part of *salafi* identity as the rejection of other affiliations, including with the Muslim Brothers and al-Qaradawi himself, did.

Imam Abu Khadeejah suggested that the differences in *ifta'* between *salafi*s and *wasati*s were of secondary importance. These differences, he explained, are a mere by-product of the Ikhwani misunderstanding of 'aqida (creed), primarily manifested by the Muslim Brothers' support of rebellions against political leaders. He implied that he did not waste time on discussing the Council and refuting it because he recognized that when Muslims are informed and convinced about the crucial differences in creed, they will also appreciate why *wasati* leniency

120 Shari'a and Life

on issues such as usurious loans, the workplace, music, and the shaving of beards is wrong. The secondary importance he attributes to the refutation of wrong practices was also demonstrated by his view that he would rather have children attend gender-separate secular British schools than Islamic Ikhwani schools because it is easier to correct misled understandings of *mu'amalat* (practices related to non-ritualist human actions and interactions) than of *'aqida*.[21]

The Council and the Vatican

Several interviewees across the spectrum of mosques (except for the Salafi Mosque) who were aware of the Council's existence spoke favourably of its approach, agenda, leadership, and pragmatic fatwas. However, none said they were committed to its decisions, regarded it as an exclusive authority, or even privileged it.

Broaching the notion of uniform *ifta'* with the interviewees at large, we learned that with few exceptions, the idea that they should commit to the advice of a specific mufti or panel of muftis seemed peculiar to them. Thus, the failure of the Council to establish itself as a monopoly has to do with more than its particular shortcomings. Rather, regardless of its ideology, methodology, and resources, *any* panel having similar aspirations would likely equally fail. As noted in chapter 1, the Council's project assumed that Muslims in Europe are discouraged by the existence of conflicting and polarizing fatwas and are eager to see the emergence of a unifying, binding panel on *ifta'* on the continent. This assumption did not accord with the majority of interviewees' understanding of *ifta'* and authority, or with their practices of *istifta'*.

If the Council had its way, a papal-like structure would have governed *ifta'* in Europe. Yet as the Marseille-based imam Farid Bourouba, who favours the Council, reminded us when discussing its limited achievements, there has never been a "Vatican" in Islam.[22] The overarching role the Council sought has no precedent in the religio-juristic tradition from which it evolved. Sunni tradition allowed *mustaftis* a great deal of discretion in deciding whom to consult, whether to accept a given fatwa, and how to decide between competing fatwas. The Prophet was reported to have told a woman who wished to consult with him about righteousness and sin that she should ask her heart, as righteousness is what the heart is content with and sin is what the heart is not content with, even if someone passes a fatwa permitting it.[23] With some exceptions, knowledgeable Muslims who issue advice on matters of shari'a were not considered to be inspired through a direct connection to God – and any notion that they were was considered blasphemy.

Muftis were also not part of an organized religious hierarchy whose recognition by the believer was, in and of itself, a foundation of faith. As noted by Abou El Fadl, "growing up in an Islamic religious culture, one is frequently reminded by his teachers that there is no church in Islam and that no one embodies God's Divine authority. The picture conveyed and repeated is one of egalitarianism and the accessibility of God's truth to all," with no one holding exclusive claim to it.[24] Sunni tradition has also not offered an equivalent to a core rabbinical concept, "make for yourself a rav" (a teacher, or a rabbi), that, according to one of its interpretations in Judaism, encourages Jews to refer their queries to one authority and rely on it exclusively so as to avoid confusion and doubt.[25]

There did not emerge a uniform notion of how *mustaftis* should choose muftis and engage with fatwas. The plurality of opinions on these matters allowed inquirers to do pretty much as they deemed fit. Shihab al-Din al-Qarafi (d. 1285), the Cairo-based *Maliki* mufti who expanded the conditions for applying *maslaha* as a means of effecting fatwas, compared the duty of a mufti to that of a translator who translates the words of his patron. The mufti should loyally convey the intentions of God to make it possible for the *mustafti* to understand and apply them.

According to al-Qarafi, if the *mustafti* believes the 'translation' of the mufti to be accurate, he should accept it. If he does not, then he should consult another mufti.[26] The mufti is thus approached like a medical doctor or an engineer: with respect for his hard-earned knowledge, but without a priori commitment that his opinion is correct or will be accepted.

Al-Nawawi (d. 1277), the eminent Hadith scholar and mufti, emphasized that a Muslim who does not have the qualifications of a mufti and is uncertain about the correct practice in a given situation should consult a mufti and follow his advice. If there is not one in his vicinity, then he should travel to find one. If a *mustafti* is uncertain whether a person is indeed a qualified mufti as he claims to be, then it is his responsibility to examine that the mufti is indeed qualified.

It may be the case that a *mustafti* can approach more than one mufti. Al-Nawawi noted that two opinions emerged as to what the *mustafti* should do in this situation. According to one, he is not obligated to examine who of the two is more knowledgeable because a Muslim with a modest education is not expected to engage in *ijtihad*. According to the other, it is the responsibility of the *mustafti* to make a calculated choice between the two because even a Muslim with a modest education can recognize who is a more qualified mufti. Al-Nawawi was inclined toward the former opinion. In a different situation, where the

122 Shari'a and Life

mustafti knows who the more knowledgeable mufti or the more pious one is, he should follow the former.

Exploring the opinions that emerged as to what a *mustafti* should do when faced with conflicting fatwas issued by qualified muftis, al-Nawawi noted there are five options: embrace the strictest, embrace the most moderate, embrace the one issued by the most knowledgeable and virtuous mufti, ask another mufti and accept the majority opinion, or choose whichever fatwa one wishes to select because *mustafti*s are not qualified to engage in *ijtihad*. Al-Nawawi's discussion suggested all these options are legitimate, with the latter the most widely accepted.[27]

With a handful of exceptions, and across the spectrum of mosques studied, the views expressed by interviewees made clear that they cherish the tradition that positions them, individuals without any substantial education in fiqh, as the ultimate arbiters. They emphasized that a *mustafti* cannot accept a fatwa because it was issued by a person with distinguished credentials or because it seems to make sense. Each decision must be subject to examination to the inquirer's best ability.

Textual studies of fatwas demonstrated that *mustafti*s influence the result of their inquiry through their choice of expert and the phrasing of their concern; for example, by highlighting the *maslaha* involved in an impermissible practice under given circumstances.[28] The majority of our interviewees indicated that along with these means of influence, they determine the outcome of *istifta'* by reserving for themselves the task of deciding who is a qualified mufti, which qualified mufti to approach, and whether or not a fatwa is sound.

Asked about their theory and practice of *istifta'*, these interviewees offered one of three ideas. (a) They do not require any advice and can reach correct decisions on shari'a-related issues by themselves. (b) It is their duty to choose one imam who will guide them. However, it is also their responsibility to verify that the evidence in the Quran or the traditions provided by their guide is solid. (c) They should not commit to one authority and can present queries to any person they have reason to believe has sound knowledge. Their responsibility is to verify that the evidence presented from the Quran, or the traditions, is sound.

These statements of autonomy did not imply the embrace of open-ended consultations. Pragmatic and integration-minded interviewees said they would only consult experts who shared their view of Islam as a religion of moderation and common sense and specifically noted their rejection of dogmatic views from muftis unfamiliar with European realities. Some emphasized their disdain for *salafi*s and their approach. On the other hand, *salafi* interviewees mentioned as legitimate guides only names of *salafi* muftis and panels, usually prominent ones. Still, they were clear that they would not commit uncritically to any specific authority within the privileged field, be it as respected and experienced as may be, and would accept or reject fatwas only after examining them.

Only four interviewees in the entire study implied that it was their duty to choose an imam who would guide them and abide by the imam's advice, whatever it may be. They noted that as laymen, it was not their duty to verify that the advice of the imam was credible because they lacked the relevant knowledge and to avoid confusion; or because the practice of soliciting multiple opinions could result in "fishing" for the most lenient answer. However, not one of these interviewees described the existence of an exclusivist, binding relationship of this kind in practice.

An example is Moroccan-born Hisham (b. 1980), who migrated to Spain when he was 28 and moved to Reykjavik when he was 35. Like several other attendees of the Grand Mosque, he works in a pizzeria. He lives in Iceland's capital without his wife. Hisham presented the most rigidly hierarchical concept of authority. He said that once a Muslim has found a mosque, he must adhere to the instructions of the imam of that mosque. He offered a metaphor. Faith is like work. You have your big boss, God, with whom you have no way of connecting to ask what you are required to do. To take the responsibility off your shoulders and be confident that you do not err, you should put trust in your small boss, the imam.[29]

Hisham demonstrated his commitment to the hierarchical model with the following story. When he lived in Spain, there was an argument between several mosques' leaderships as to whether the commencement of Ramadan should be determined based on astronomical calculations or direct observation of the Moon. While he was convinced that the latter was the correct opinion, he followed the imam of his mosque, who preferred the former. Similarly, in Iceland, he fasts according to local time because that is the way of the Grand Mosque, which he attends.

However, the interview suggested that on several important issues, Hisham departed from the pragmatic, integrationist view of the imam of his current mosque, including on electoral participation and Christmas greetings. On major life issues, including his decision to work in a restaurant that sells pork, he decided for himself and did not consult with an expert – *any* expert. He arrived in Iceland shortly before the feud that led Ahmad Sadiq to establish the city's third mosque, but while Sadiq's religio-legal approach was more in line with his, he never

124 Shari'a and Life

considered switching to Sadiq's mosque, explaining that the Grand Mosque was spacious, and the other attendees were friendly.

Non-committed *istifta'* is advantageous for *mustaftis*: It provides the relief of legitimizing potential rejection of advice that does not suit one's expectations and needs and allows one to access authorities based on their availability and responsiveness, an important option considering that the more qualified and distinguished an expert is, the less easy it is to approach him. To accept the Council – or any other panel – as an exclusive authority on *ifta'* would imply giving up on an empowering position despite the absence of a strong normative tradition requiring doing so.

The one potential clear advantage of conformity to one authority is its ability to relieve *mustaftis* of the burden of examining the credibility of the evidence contained in fatwas and the responsibility of choosing between conflicting fatwas. That burden, however, we found remained largely hypothetical, as only a few of the interviewees recalled choosing one fatwa over another based on their careful evaluation, and none presented a structured method and set criteria as to how to evaluate fatwas.

Asked what they would do if faced with a conflict between the conclusions of two fatwas, several interviewees said they would allow their 'heart' to guide them. They argued that God would not allow the heart to mislead a Muslim; or that being a religion of compassion and common sense, the heart is a good compass in Islam (none referenced the aforementioned Prophetic tradition on the matter, but it might have been on their minds). 'Heart' is another word for intuition or decision-making that is not analytic and systematic and privileges pre-existing notions.

The Ethnic and the Global

Other practices and priorities described by interviewees introduced additional obstacles that make the emergence of uniformed *ifta'* in Europe unlikely, regardless of the identity and agenda of the pan-continental panel that would advance it. One is the dominance of ethnic contexts. The founders of the European Council for Fatwa and Research assumed that Muslims in Europe would readily accept the idea of an ethnically neutral panel. Despite its pretenses, since its inception, the Council has been dominated by Arab members, with modest representation for Turks, Pakistanis, Bosnians, and other ethnicities that have a substantial presence in Europe. At the same time, Council members from Arab North-African states have been underrepresented relative to their share of the Muslim-Arab population on the continent.

Yet even if the Council represented the ethnic distribution of Muslims in Europe more faithfully, it is unlikely that its cross-ethnic message would have diminished the dominance of ethnic affiliations. Ethnic-oriented mosques – Turkish, Moroccan, Pakistani, and others – are the norm rather than the exception in Europe. The persistence of this phenomenon owes to the inclination of migrants to socialize and establish communal institutions together, when possible, with people who speak their language and share their culture. It also owes to the direct involvement and investment of governments that seek to exert influence on expatriate communities.

The dominance of the ethnic context in *istifta'* goes beyond ethnically-based mosques such as Dortmund's 'Umar Ibn al-Khattab. Across the spectrum of mosques studied, interviewees agreed that the ethnicity of a mufti or anyone else consulted on a matter pertaining to shari'a was, in and of itself, no criterion for the correctness of the advice given. Neither was a mufti's adherence to a specific *madhhab*. However, in the ethnically-mixed mosques studied in Reykjavik and Stockholm, several interviewees explained that for reasons of custom, familiarity, trust, language, and patriotism, the experts they were in the habit of consulting were always, or almost always, from the same ethnicity. Interviewees at the Salafi Mosque proved an exception.

Another limitation for a uniform, pan-European *ifta'* is how Islamic online media and approaches to these media have developed since the late 1990s. The rise of the internet as a means of Islamic instruction had the potential to be constructive for efforts to create a transnational *ifta'* monopoly. It introduced the possibility for Muslims scattered across dozens of countries to transcend local and national-level authorities, if they so desired, and make a panel or a mufti situated in a distant location their exclusive, or at least primary, authority on shari'a.[30]

Indeed, it was hardly a coincidence that the Council – and al-Qaradawi's grander monopolist ambitions – surfaced at the turn of the century, the time when the internet and satellite television broke through and became widespread. Al-Qaradawi was one of the first in the Muslim world to recognize the potential of the internet to disseminate information on a global scale and establish transnational communities. He referred to online operations as a new form of jihad, a means of spreading Islam. The portal he led, Islamonline.net, represented a sophisticated attempt at constructing a global Islamic imagined community encompassing Muslims living in Muslim and non-Muslim countries alike. But these hopes never materialized.[31]

Competitions between actors in different fields of online operations have produced one of two results. In one, monopolization, one actor

126   Shari'a and Life

manages to assert complete control of a field (it is almost hard to imagine today that twenty years ago, Google was but one of several competing search engines and that Wikipedia was not always the default when searching for encyclopedic entries on anything).[32] In another, pluralization, a highly competitive field emerges, where no single actor becomes dominant.[33]

Online *ifta'*, and Islamic online ventures in general, have followed the latter model. The combination of an already existing dense and polemic field, the pluralistic tradition of shari'a, the low costs of establishing a global presence, and the richly diverse linguistic and ideological milieu that is the Muslim world created a largely democratic market of websites and social media. A virtual ocean of fatwas and Islamic instruction developed, with no single organization hegemonic on a national, let alone global, level, even if some have a much more substantial presence than others. Asked about the websites they visited to explore fatwas in the year before, respondents to the written questionnaires in the eight mosques surveyed presented a plethora of names, with no single one emerging as the most popular. Interviewees either replied that they search through Google or different websites that they pick randomly, or they noted preferred platforms that nevertheless were not privileged exclusively.

Even if transnational simultaneity had resulted in one panel dominating the field of online *ifta'*, that would not have resulted in uniformity because of the strong opposition that still exists to the medium as a means of instruction on religio-legal issues. As table 3.2 informs, in half of the mosques surveyed more than 50 per cent of respondents did not search even once for fatwas online in the previous 12 months; in only one of the mosques surveyed did more than a quarter send a query online during that period. Moreover, in all of the mosques, respondents did not place high confidence in the reliability of websites as a means of learning about shari'a.

Of the interviewees, none was in the habit of regularly examining online religio-legal issues about shari'a (although some said they used to do so in the past). Several opposed using the internet at all as a means of learning about shari'a-related issues (although the interviews suggested that this did not necessarily imply that they had categorically refrained from doing so). Resentment of online *istifta'* was supported by various arguments: (a) users risk falling into the temptation to continue to "fish" for a convenient answer rather than accept the correct one. (b) Unlike when receiving instruction from imams or books, one cannot verify whether a fatwa published online was actually issued by the person to whom it is attributed. (c) Experts need to be familiar with the precise circumstances of the *mustafti*, which cannot happen when soliciting advice online. (d) Users risk landing unintentionally

Table 3.2. Opinions regarding gathering knowledge about Islamic law on the internet

Mosques	Searched at least once for fatwas on the internet during the past year Percentage, %	Sent at least one query to a fatwa council on the internet during the past year Percentage, %	Reliability of websites to learn about Islamic law (1 = very little; 10 = very much) Average	Median
The Stockholm Mosque	52.9	14.3	4.6	5.0
Al-Nur Mosque, Reykjavik	77.8	27.8	5.9	6.25
The Grand Mosque, Reykjavik	45.8	20.8	4.2	4.0
Markaz Imam Malik, Dortmund	35.5	16.7	4.4	4.0
ʿUmar Ibn al-Khattab Mosque, Dortmund	45.2	24.2	4.6	4.0
Hassan Blidi Mosque, Marseille	45.9	21.6	5.0	5.0
Husby Mosque, Stockholm	70.0	23.3	5.1	5.0
The Salafi Mosque, Birmingham	70.2	18.6	5.0	4.5

Note: For statistical information about the surveys, see the introduction, note 31.

on extremist websites without recognizing their true character. Interviewees who invoked this argument cautioned against "snakes" and "crazy" preachers who prey on modestly-educated Muslims to sway them away from the correct path.

The al-Qaradawi Factor

The failure of the European Council for Fatwa and Research to become a more universally recognized brand owes largely to marketing shortcomings and its specific focus on *fiqh al-aqalliyyat al-Muslima*. Its failure to establish uniformed *iftaʾ* owes to objections and conditions that would stand in the way of any other panel with similar ambitions. However, the lack of favour the Council found among some mosque attendees aware of its existence and message, including pragmatic-leaning ones, owes specifically to its leadership – and to its ideology.

The surveys in the eight mosques suggest that among the minority familiar with its existence, including in mosques whose leaderships are pragmatically inclined, and in the mosque where the leadership commits to its decisions, the Council is anything but a matter of consensus.

128   Shari'a and Life

Table 3.3. Opinions about the European Council for Fatwa and Research and the Saudi Council of Senior Scholars

Mosque	European Council for Fatwa and Research		Saudi Council of Senior Scholars	
	Average	Median	Average	Median
The Stockholm Mosque	6.3	6.0	4.6	4.0
Al-Nur Mosque, Reykjavik	5.7	5.5	4.3	3.0
The Grand Mosque, Reykjavik	4.9	5.0	5.4	5.5
Markaz Imam Malik, Dortmund	5.1	5.0	5.3	5.0
'Umar Ibn al-Khattab Mosque, Dortmund	6.4	6.0	7.1	6.0
Hassan Blidi Mosque, Marseille	3.7	3.5	6.0	7.0
Husby Mosque, Stockholm	5.9	6.0	5.3	5.0
The Salafi Mosque, Birmingham	3.8	1.5	9.4	10.0

Note: For statistical information about the surveys, see the introduction, note 31.

Asked to rank their appreciation of the Council on a scale from one to 10, respondents to the written questionnaires who were aware of its existence did not give it a median ranking of more than six in any of the eight mosques surveyed (see table 3.3).

There is reason to argue that detractors of the Council were conscious of their disapproval of the panel, whereas some of those who gave it a favourable ranking possibly did so as a matter of respecting learned scholars in general rather than identifying with its leadership or agenda. Respondents were also asked to rank the *salafi*, Saudi-based Council of Senior Scholars if they were aware of its existence. In Birmingham's Salafi Mosque, attendees who knew of the *wasati* panel gave it distinctly bad rankings, whereas the Saudi Council of Senior Scholars was given distinctly high ones. However, in mosques whose leaderships and populations are relatively integrationist and pragmatically-inclined, including the European Council for Fatwa and Research-affiliated Stockholm Mosque, the ranking of the *wasati* panel was not significantly higher than that of the Council of Senior Scholars.

The controversial persona of the Council's founding leader projected negatively on its popularity. Al-Qaradawi launched the ambitious project of the European Council for Fatwa and Research at the height of his fame, but without the institutional power of a single state behind him, with few widely reputable contemporary muftis on his side, and with his past relations and continuous ideological affinity with a divisive revolutionary mass movement as part of his credentials. In his defense, he was not the first, nor the last, to cultivate delusions of grandeur based on a television show.

While al-Qaradawi was controversial already in the late 1990s, in his declining years he became one of the faces of a political and social tragedy. Shortly after the ousting of Husni Mubarak and the start of what came to be known as the Arab Spring, al-Qaradawi returned to Cairo to a hero's welcome reminiscent of Khomeini's return to Iran. He gave a Friday congregational sermon in front of thousands of enthused supporters at Tahrir Square, where the revolution began.[34]

That reception was the end, rather than the beginning, of his journey to transform Egypt. In the months that followed, he found himself embroiled in internal disputes among the Brothers concerning their choice of a presidential nominee. When a popularly-supported military coup ended the movement's short spell in power, he turned into a declared rival of the new regime, losing whatever influence he had on his homeland's politics.[35] With the Egyptian Muslim Brothers defeated, his homeland again under authoritarian rule, and intensifying civil wars in Libya and Syria, his hopes to be the face of a new Arab, Islamist dawn, if not its actual leader, collapsed.

The turbulent times that followed the eventful months of 2011 have been a living reality for some Muslims in Europe, who learned about events in the Arab world from refugees, families still living in the Middle East, satellite broadcasts, and internet websites (or experienced the tragedy of their homeland firsthand and escaped from it). The interviews demonstrated that al-Qaradawi has not lost his popularity with some, who praised him as a distinguished scholar and a political reformist or both. Yet others spoke about him with contempt.

While *salafi* interviewees were the most expressive in their opposition to al-Qaradawi, several pragmatic-inclined and integration-minded interviewees also did not spare their words. Contrary to his self-positioning as the champion of a balanced, harmonizing approach, they described him as a radical extremist, a political hypocrite, an ideologist who failed to set his priorities right, and an inciter who caused disastrous instability.

For example, at Dortmund's ʿUmar Ibn al-Khattab Mosque, Egyptian-born (1957) Salim, a father of three teenagers who migrated to Germany from Iraq 32 years before the interview, said he used to follow *Al-Shariʿa wa-l-Hayat* until around 2009 and then stopped. He attributed his dislike of al-Qaradawi to the latter's affiliation with the Muslims Brothers, his damaging involvement in politics, and what he described as

130   Shari'a and Life

al-Qaradawi's legitimization of terrorism. Salim wondered why, if al-Qaradawi supported suicide bombers, he did not blow himself up.[36]

Makram (b. 1974) migrated from Tunisia to Austria before settling in Iceland in 1999. At the time, the Muslim population in the country was still in the dozens. He works in tourism, is remarried, and has one son. Makram criticized al-Qaradawi for calling to engage in jihad against the American military in Iraq, whereas the focus of Muslims should be the jihad in Palestine. He emphasized, "I don't listen to anything he [al-Qaradawi] says."[37]

Syrian-born Fahdi (b. 1980), who arrived in Iceland in 2016 after his work visa was not renewed, following a decade in Saudi Arabia, is the father of three young children. He used to watch *Al-Shari'a wa-l-Hayat*, although he no longer did so. Fahdi said he disliked al-Qaradawi's opportunism: the Egyptian scholar was in the habit of fiercely attacking everyone, except the Qatari regime that hosted him. Fahdi resented the notion that there was such a thing as *wasati* Islam. Islam, he said, was Islam. It is possible that Fahdi's change of heart about the civil war in Syria contributed to his apprehension about al-Qaradawi. When the civil war started, he favoured the opposition, hoping to see Bashar al-Assad deposed. Seeing that the Syrian dictator managed to stay put, he no longer supported the rebellion.[38]

The Problem with Leniency

The lack of favour the Council found among some mosque attendees, including pragmatists and integration-leaning ones, also owes to the audacity of several of its fatwas. There was an inherent paradox in the simultaneous quest for reform and consensus-building, in the simultaneous call for advancing *tajdid* and uniformity. Vanguard, groundbreaking opinions can become mainstream at some point. Still, even if efficiently promoted (which was not the case with the Council), this would be a lengthy and divisive process. In retrospect, it was naïve of al-Qaradawi and his colleagues to think that their original, facilitating contributions could be quickly and widely accepted.

The scope of the reception of the notion that mortgages may be legitimized in a broad context demonstrates this point. The Council's 1999 fatwa on mortgages was groundbreaking in both the ideology and methodology it introduced (as explained in chapter 1) and its conclusion (that any Muslim living in Europe who is not a homeowner and does not find other financial means to buy a home may take a mortgage). Its bold approach is why the European Council for Fatwa and Research was initiated in the first place. However, being so far beyond

The Mustafti Is the Mufti   131

the pale of what was considered normative at the time of its publication, and in several different ways, it could not be the stuff from which consensus is built.

The questionnaires asked respondents to state whether it was legitimate for Muslims in Europe who have no alternative to take a usurious loan in order to buy a home. Although legitimization was the determination, the question's phrasing allowed for a more restrictive premise of legitimization than the one presented in the Council's 1999 fatwa (depending on how one understands the term 'no alternative'). The questionnaires also inquired about two issues on which broader agreements exist in *fiqh al-aqalliyyat al-Muslima* discourse: whether Muslims in Europe may vote in a parliamentary election in a Western country; and whether they may congratulate Christians on Christmas. As noted in chapter 1, electoral participation has gained sweeping approval, including by *salafis* (although not all *salafis*). Christmas greetings were encouraged by the European Council for Fatwa and Research and others, but were vehemently opposed by *salafi* muftis, who made their dissent a cornerstone of their ideology and championing of an anti-integration and anti-pragmatism agenda.

Table 3.4 informs that the Council's conditional legitimzation of mortgages remained highly controversial in all but one of the mosques surveyed. The data point to a correlation between the broadness of agreement on the legitimization of a practice in *fiqh al-aqalliyyat*

Table 3.4. Views on controversial religio-legal issues

Mosque	Purchasing a house through a usurious loan if there is no alternative		Congratulating Christians on Christmas		Voting in elections in the West	
	Yes, %	No, %	Yes, %	No, %	Yes, %	No, %
The Stockholm Mosque	50.0	50.0	74.2	25.8	94.1	5.9
Al-Nur Mosque, Reykjavik	85.7	14.3	100.0	0.0	100.0	0.0
The Grand Mosque, Reykjavik	36.4	63.6	38.1	61.9	60.9	39.1
Markaz Imam Malik, Dortmund	33.3	66.7	63.3	36.7	93.3	6.7
ʿUmar Ibn al-Khattab Mosque, Dortmund	34.5	65.5	66.7	33.3	93.9	6.1
Hassan Blidi Mosque, Marseille	45.8	54.2	59.3	40.7	81.3	18.8
Husby Mosque, Stockholm	34.6	65.4	48.1	51.9	81.5	18.5
The Salafi Mosque, Birmingham	10.0	90.0	10.0	90.0	22.5	77.5

Note: For statistical information about the surveys, see the introduction, note 31.

132 Shari'a and Life

al-Muslima discourse and the broadness of agreement on the legitimacy of that practice among mosque attendees. Opinions about the legitimacy of electoral participation were distinctly positive (except for the strong opposition in the Salafi Mosque of Birmingham, where the leadership conditionally approves of it in theory but in practice has opposed it). Opinions about the legitimacy of Christmas greetings suggest that *salafi* opposition has made its mark but that a majority approves of this practice. On the other hand, opinions about the conditional legitimization of mortgages show this practice is broadly rejected. This was the case also in the mosque where the imam affiliates with the Council.[39]

Not only *salafi* interviewees but also several interviewees who presented pragmatic-leaning and integration-minded opinions, including a few who did not resent al-Qaradawi and even appreciated him as a credible religio-legal authority, said they were in total disagreement with the legitimization of usury, regardless of the arguments presented in its favour. They found the idea of paying interest in order to buy a home an outrageous deviation from correct Islam and described the fatwa as an unacceptable and ill-founded statement that human beings can transform the haram to halal using sophisticated terminologies. Their opposition was emotional as much as it was rational. This does not imply that they could not possibly be convinced that the Council's position is justified or at least constitutes legitimate *ijtihad*. It does suggest, however, that breaking taboos is a tough hill to climb.

One example is 'Abd al-Salam (b. 1971) of the 'Umar Ibn al-Khattab Mosque, married with four children, and the son and grandson of imams. He migrated to Germany from Morocco at the age of 22. 'Abd al-Salam used to watch *Al-Shari'a wa-l-Hayat* frequently. He said al-Qaradawi was correct on most issues but noted that he "cannot accept everything" al-Qaradawi had issued. He described usury as a great sin, and added that he was convinced that, regardless of what any fatwa may state, there were no circumstances whatsoever that could legitimize the taking of mortgages in Germany. Many Moroccans, he claimed, own two or three homes in their homeland, and they should sell those homes or return to live there rather than commit a sin.[40]

Somalia-born Hasan (b. 1984), who found refuge in Reykjavik in 2018 after spending a little more than a year in Italy, had never heard about al-Qaradawi or the Council. While mortgages are considered conditionally legitimate by the leadership of the Grand Mosque, Hasan stated they were prohibited under all possible circumstances. He argued that if buying a home without an interest-based loan was impossible, then the Muslim had no alternative but to rent because the Quran is explicit on this point. Hasan assured that "Allah will reward patience." He emphasized that whether one lived in a majority Muslim or non-Muslim country was irrelevant.[41]

Moroccan-born Tariq (b. 1986) is unemployed and single. He left for Italy at the age of 21 and moved to Stockholm in 2018. He said that usury was prohibited under all circumstances, even under an extreme necessity. Tariq noted that the financial crisis in Europe was the result of usury and that even an Italian minister (whose name he could not remember) spoke about the need to abolish usury, as ordained in the Quran.[42]

Rabiʿ (b. 1976), who migrated from Morocco to Reykjavik at 22 to work in the fishing industry and is unemployed due to health problems, is the father of three children. The family lives in a rented apartment. He stated that usury was clearly prohibited in the Quran, and he would never take it for fear of Allah's punishment. Rabiʿ insisted that the only circumstance that could legitimize taking a mortgage – the risk of finding one's family on the street – was irrelevant to European welfare states such as Iceland. He described al-Qaradawi's pragmatism, when inappropriate, as miserable.[43]

The Many Faces of a Fatwa

If one chooses to look at the half-full (or more precisely, one-third full) part of the glass, and search for impact, rather than consensus building, then the support rates for the conditional legitimization of mortgages assume a different meaning. This signature, audacious decision of the Council that addressed one of the biggest challenges Muslims in Europe face has met with objections even within its ranks and is fiercely contested by some of its opponents. This being the case, the approval of its practical implication by a considerable number of mosque attendees, even in mosques where the leadership strongly rejects this fatwa, and even in the Salafi Mosque, is a seeming indication that the Council *did* leave its mark on the religio-legal perceptions of a considerable number of mosque attendees, even if it failed to generate the broad agreement it desired.

However, the interviews indicated that this impact was primarily indirect, where it could be established at all. The explanations provided by attendees who supported the conditional legitimization of mortgages suggested that the text of the 1999 fatwa was not broadly disseminated and that the innovative ideology and methodology that the fatwa epitomizes and upon which it was constructed were not recognized.

134 Shari'a and Life

Where the fatwa helped expand and consolidate the premise that taking a mortgage can be considered legitimate from the point of view of the shari'a, this was done not through engagement with its actual text and embrace of its explicit terms. Rather, paraphrasing and interpretations of the fatwa played a role (in some cases, a role that can only be speculated) in convincing some mosque attendees that paying usury was acceptable under certain circumstances.

This happened through one of two processes of transmission. Several advocates of conditional legitimization said that they made up their mind, at least in part, after they had read or had heard somewhere a qualified opinion or qualified opinions on the matter. They could not remember exactly what they had read or heard, where, or by whom. Given that the Council was not the only authority to suggest that mortgages could be conditionally legitimized (even if its legitimization was the most generous and the most widely publicized), it is very possible but not certain that what these interviewees read or heard was in reference, whether accurate or not, to the 1999 fatwa.

Other supporters of conditional legitimization attested their opinion directly to the Council's fatwa or al-Qaradawi and said they learned about the fatwa from their imam or the media. However, their knowledge of the Council's and al-Qaradawi's position was not loyal to the original text and reflected a more restricted and less audacious understanding than what the fatwa actually stated – either because it was paraphrased to them in a less controversial form by the person who transmitted it, or because they did not grasp its nuances. This narrow understanding, which made accepting the radical legitimizing position easier for them, did not affect the most important outcome of their engagement with the mortgage dilemma: they were convinced that *their* situation justifies taking a mortgage.

The following examples illustrate both these processes. Ahmad (b. 1971) attends the 'Umar Ibn al-Khattab mosque in Dortmund. Born in Morocco, his Berber family migrated to Germany when he was seven, and he does not speak Arabic at all. He is married, the father of three, and works as an electrical engineer. He said he had prayed at 'Umar Ibn al-Khattab since childhood and continued attending it, even though he was living on the other side of the city, because of its open-mindedness. On the weekends, his children attend a local club that teaches Islam in a way that, he said, pleased him because it advanced integration.

While Ahmad agreed, in principle, with the notion that Muslims in Europe should have a fiqh accommodated to their situation, he said that he had never heard about the European Council for Fatwa and Research and was aware of the name al-Qaradawi only from articles he read in *Süddeutsche Zeitung*, *Die Welt*, and other German newspapers. Although he could not remember where, he had heard that a fatwa permitting mortgages had been issued and had welcomed it, although he had never come across the actual text.

It appears that knowledge of the fatwa's existence was welcomed by Ahmad because it supported an opinion he had already established on the matter. Ahmad explained that the world had changed since the time of the Prophet, who, along with not paying interest, also "did not drive a car or eat with a metal spoon." Contemporary Muslims should change accordingly. He and his wife were yet to take a mortgage to buy a home because they had not yet found an apartment to their liking. However, in principle, he said they would not hesitate to do so and had already taken interest-based loans to buy a new car and furniture. In his opinion, taking a loan is better than giving one because a loanee is responsible for paying his debt. In an ideal world, he said, banks would charge interest only for companies, and not for people who wish to buy a home for their families. Yet the world is not ideal.[44]

Mustafa (b. 1970) migrated to Iceland in 2016 and works as a cleaner. His wife and children remained in Morocco. Before he migrated to Iceland, he lived for a few months in the Netherlands. He appreciates al-Qaradawi. While Mustafa did not read his works, he watched *Al-Shari'a wa-l-Hayat* as long as al-Qaradawi appeared on the show. He also ceased to Google search shari'a-related issues, something he was in the habit of doing weekly until two years before the interview. Mustafa explained that he felt that the *wasati* approach to Islam that he crystallized serves as an adequate guide on issues he contemplates. In his understanding, the approach involves coexisting with non-Muslims, avoiding dogmatic positions, and endorsing views that find broad agreement. He did not associate the concept of *wasatiyya* with al-Qaradawi.

While Mustafa heard about the European Council for Fatwa and Research and its conditional legitimization of mortgages (he remembered it being mentioned on television), he had not read the actual 1999 fatwa or any other text by the Council. His understanding of that fatwa and the conditions that legitimize mortgages was more restricted than the text allowed. He held that if a Muslim did not have the option to rent an apartment, or feared he would be evicted, then – and only then – he may take a mortgage to buy a home, as that is a case of necessity. He had not taken a mortgage yet, but intended to do so in the future.[45]

The aforementioned Makram of Reykjavik's Grand Mosque, a sharp critic of al-Qaradawi, discussed his engagement with the Quran as a means of making him a better person. This essence supersedes and

136   Shari'a and Life

marginalizes shari'a-related norms. As Markam put it bluntly: "Islam is not about whether you enter the toilet with your right or left foot." His dislike of al-Qaradawi resonated with his general distrust of religious scholars: "For 200 hundred years, 'ulama had been teaching wrong ideas, and in our day and age, 99.9 per cent of what 'ulama say is wrong." To demonstrate this point, Makram passionately contended that while 'A'isha was twenty rather than eight when she married the Prophet, a majority of religious scholars claim otherwise in order to defend a Prophetic tradition that is not reliable.

Makram was adamant about the ability of his heart to guide him when contemplating his religious practices. His justifications for choices he made on issues debated in *fiqh al-aqalliyyat al-Muslima* discourse involved notions of love, compassion, acting in accordance with nature, and avoiding harm, without reference to specific muftis or panels. On Ramadan fast times during long summer days, he favoured the lenient approach since arriving in Iceland; he did so without engaging with fatwas on the matter because it made sense to him. Fasting, he explained, is about self-contemplation, not about suffering and excessive hunger.

While Makram described himself as a pragmatist (invoking in this context the term *wasati*), he knew little and showed little interest in the "Council in Dublin," as he described the European Council for Fatwa and Research.

Not a homeowner and without prospects to become one unless he took a mortgage, he contemplated taking one when he arrived in Iceland, and reached a conclusion, which he has maintained ever since, that because it was the duty of the Muslim to take care of his family, it was legitimate that he take one. He explained that homeowners can easily evict tenants in Iceland; and finding homes for rent is difficult. If a Muslim family living in a rented apartment were forced to move to another neighbourhood, that would harm the children. Makram added that the Prophet said that the day would come when people would pay interest. He was certain God would forgive any person who has no alternative other than paying interest: "Allah knows that I do not have a choice, and I do the best for my family."

Despite this confidence, and despite his critical observation that in the past Muslims abided by the instructions of the local imam and today they 'fish' for fatwas that fit their needs, Makram did search online for different views on the legitimacy of mortgages *after* he made up his mind on the matter. He said he wanted to be reassured that the opinion he reached was correct. He remembered that one of the opinions he found was by the "Council in Dublin" but did not remember any of its arguments.[46]

The Mustafti Is the Mufti 137

Kabil (b. 1975), married with three children, sojourned to Dortmund from Morocco in 1997 to study telecommunication technologies at the University of Applied Sciences and has remained there ever since. He works for the police and has German citizenship. He champions an integration-minded and pragmatic approach that emphasizes the importance of coexistence and respect for other religions in a globalized world. He said he became a practicing Muslim after years of sinning. For example, he used to secretly drink alcohol and then (he added, smiling) ask God for forgiveness. Kabil shared a joke about the gap between religious ideals and practices:

> A Christian teenager and a Muslim teenager are friends. They go to clubs, drink alcohol, court women, and even eat pork. The Muslim tells the Christian about Islam and invites him to spend Eid with them. At some point, the Christian is convinced to go to the mosque and convert. The imam explains Islam. He tells the Christian it is prohibited to drink, to commit adultery, to eat pork. The Christian is very surprised and tells the imam: No, No. I don't want this kind of Islam. I want the Islam of my friend.

Being today among those who do not take religious duties lightly, Kabil said he never considered taking a mortgage because the Quran clearly stated it was haram and because there is always the option to rent an apartment. Asked again, he admitted that he was almost tempted to take one seven years ago after reading in a newspaper about a fatwa by al-Qaradawi on the matter. He was convinced not to do so by his wife, who insisted that mortgages are haram, and by imams (whose names he did not remember) who told him that al-Qaradawi's fatwa applied only to Muslims with large families. That was also his understanding of the text when he delved into the fatwa. At the time of the interview, he was considering buying a house through a *murabaha* transaction with an Islamic bank based in Brussels.[47]

It is not clear which text of the fatwa the imams discussed with Kabil. However, it appears that the text paraphrased the fatwa and ignored the crucial and controversial notion that individual needs can be regarded as necessities, instead describing a more broadly agreed upon situation of necessity – a large family unable to find an apartment for rent and fearing homelessness. The terms for legitimization presented by the Council and al-Qaradawi were broader; they included the personal situation described by Kabil and any other Muslim who was not a homeowner and did not have access to Islamic banking.

138 Shari'a and Life

'Abd al-Majid (b. 1980), married and the father of three, works for Dominos Pizza. He left Morocco when he was 23, traveled in France, Spain, and Germany, returned to Morocco for five years, and left for Iceland when he was 33, where he has lived ever since. He explained why Muslims should not hesitate to take mortgages to become homeowners: "We must adapt to our new environment now. It is very important … In this land, you must take care of your family … If you are just renting a house, you don't know how much time you will be living in this home. Maybe [the landlord] comes to you and tells you: you must leave my house." 'Abd al-Majid expressed confidence that mortgages were legitimized by several muftis, while recognizing that the issue has remained controversial. While he said he was familiar with al-Qaradawi and the Council, he did not associate them with a fatwa on the matter.[48]

Sufiyan (b. 1988), a single man who hoped to marry soon, was born in Sweden to parents of Tunisian and Algerian descent and has lived his entire life in Stockholm, where he prays at the Council-affiliated Stockholm Mosque. His command of English is better than his Arabic. He works in IT in the financial sector and entered the mosque smartly dressed: button-up shirt, blazer with a handkerchief, and matching pants and shoes.

Sufiyan held that a Muslim should choose an imam and follow his lead. He distinguished, as a matter of fact, between Muslims with little knowledge in religion who chose an imam based on geographical proximity, and Muslims like himself, who apply two additional criteria: the imam shares their approach to fiqh (which, in his case, is *wasati*) and is knowledgeable. He greatly appreciates imam Khaled al-Dib of The Stockholm Mosque and said he consulted with him at least 20 times in his life, including on whether he should maintain his job with a finance company that engages with haram (the imam said he may, noting that he does not directly engage with haram and that the knowledge he gained could be of service to Muslims). Sufiyan was familiar with the European Council for Fatwa and Research and described its merits in terms similar to those invoked by his imam: councils are more qualified to issue fatwas than individual muftis; fatwas must be issued based on qualified knowledge of the relevant realities.

Despite his trust and loyalty to his imam, Sufiyan emphasized he was not a blind follower. He said it was his duty to compare the evidence presented by imam al-Dib with that presented by muftis who reached other conclusions, and only then make up his mind. That was what he did when contemplating the legitimacy of mortgages. It appeared in the interview that Sufiyan never read the Council's 1999 fatwa on mortgages and was not familiar with its specific argumentations – or with any other works by the Council or al-Qaradawi. Yet it also appeared that when he approached imam al-Dib with a query on the matter, hoping to receive a positive answer, he had already learned from one source or another that the discourse offered a controversial legitimization of mortgages, and was acquainted with the notion that advancing certain objectives may justify the suspension of the prohibited.

Sufiyan presented imam al-Dib with the *masalih* that would be advanced through his becoming a homeowner: (a) he wanted to marry soon, and would not like the woman of his choice to reject him just because he is not a homeowner; (b) it is time he stopped being a burden on his parents; (c) it is getting more and more difficult to find apartments to rent in Stockholm; and (d) it is important for him to remain in Stockholm, as he lived there all his life and wants "to give back" to the city. According to Sufiyan, based on these conditions, al-Dib told him that he was in a situation of *darura,* and may thus take a mortgage. Still, the imam told him that there were conflicting opinions and encouraged him to research the matter further. Sufiyan located pertinent fatwas through Google, whose specific details he could not remember, and having read them, was convinced that his imam's view was the correct one.[49]

The latter part of this depiction is confusing. Sufiyan presented a query to his imam, Khaled al-Dib. Imam al-Dib is committed to the decisions of the European Council for Fatwa and Research. The Council issued a fatwa, which explicitly stated that even when becoming homeowners was not a necessity but rather a need, Muslims in Europe may take mortgages because, in the European context, their situation constitutes a need that qualifies as a necessity (unless they already owned a home or could rely on an Islamic bank). Why, then, did al-Dib not provide his wise and loyal adherent with this generous and comprehensive determination, substantiated by the main arguments provided in the fatwa, and instead offered a different kind of legitimization?

In our interviews, imam al-Dib's elaboration on the 1999 fatwa suggested that this was possibly not a case of miscommunication. His interpretation of the fatwa circumvented several of its most controversial aspects. He began by stating that the fatwa was not a "big deal." He emphasized that the fatwa did not say that mortgages were halal, but rather that they were legitimate in a situation of necessity (*wad ' idtar*). He noted that in permitting mortgages for necessity, the fatwa followed the same principle that permits Muslims to eat carcasses to avoid starvation, and noted that the fatwa rendered mortgages legitimate rather than requiring anyone to take interest-based loans. A mufti, he said, was not a *qadi* and could not impose his decisions.[50]

140   Shari'a and Life

The explanation the imam offered us of what constitutes a 'necessity' in the case of Muslims who are not homeowners was generous (as was his application of this term to Sufiyan's situation) and, in essence, overlapped with the terms stipulated by the Council in 1999. (His far more reserved view about student-loans, which the Council also legitimized, suggested that he did not apply an expansive approach to the highest rank of *maslaha* in all cases.) His choice to mediate the fatwa in terms not similar to those used in the original text was possibly not incidental.

By maintaining that the existence of necessity should be weighed individually for each case (rather than that Muslims in Europe, in general, are entitled to take mortgages if they do not have access to Islamic banking), he established a deciding role for himself when such cases are presented to him. By characterizing the fatwa as a legitimization based on necessity (rather than a need that qualifies as necessity), he allowed for a presentation that was relatively simple and grounded in a principle on which there is consensus and which is intuitively understandable, i.e., that necessities legitimize prohibitions. (Follow-up questions indicated that he was aware of the actual content of the fatwa. He noted, correctly, that with regard to 'necessity,' there is a difference between the fatwa and the studies that preceded it, and added that it would take a lot of time to explain the issue convincingly.)

Circumventing two other controversial aspects of the fatwa, al-Dib also failed to mention the fatwa's introduction of proselytization as justification (an aspect of the fatwa that the General Secretary of the Council also denied in an interview; see chapter 1), and the *Hanafi* way of legitimization, which has been the most fiercely debated aspect of the fatwa within the Council.

Interviews with other imams suggested that, as in al-Dib's case, those who accept the fatwa do not necessarily explain their legitimization of mortgages based on the arguments and terms its text presents, and those who reject it do not necessarily deny it potential space in the advice they provide. Rather, imams made of the fatwa something else than what its authors intended.

Salman Tamimi, the founder of Reykjavik's Al-Nur Mosque, said he had read the fatwa years ago and supported its foundations (his was, not coincidently, the only mosque where the majority of attendees surveyed supported the conditional legitimization of mortgages). As noted in the previous chapter, Tamimi was highly critical of the Council and considered it a failed project. He went beyond the limiting conditions proposed in the fatwa, implying a universal, unconditional legitimization of mortgages for European Muslims by noting that when living in Europe, there was no way to avoid usury, so taking mortgages makes no difference.[51]

In contrast, ʿAbd al-ʿAziz al-Walʿani of Reykjavik's Grand Mosque, who also supports the fatwa, offered a restricted interpretation, echoing Stockholm's al-Dib. Al-Walʿani said that the fatwa, which it appeared he had not read, constituted legitimate *ijtihad*, but also emphasized that mortgages should not be universally permitted in Europe to any Muslim who cannot become a homeowner through permissible means. Rather, he argued the fatwa applied only in situations where a person who did not own a home faced a serious problem – for example, the threat of being evicted.[52]

Strong rejection of the religio-legal premise of the fatwa does not imply a categorical rejection of its practical implications. Muhammad al-Makkawi, the *salafi*-inclined imam of the Husby Mosque, identified the groundbreaking leniency of the Council. He said the problem with its terms is that they are too broad, giving carte-blanche to all Muslims in Europe to take a mortgage. He rejected the position that *any* Muslim in Europe who is not a homeowner can take a mortgage if he has no other means. He argued that to determine whether one is in a situation that justifies taking a mortgage, the specifics of one's situation must be evaluated – for example, the situation of a person who has ten children and lives in a three-bedroom rented apartment is not like that of a person with an average-sized family.

However, al-Makkawi said that in answering queries on mortgages, he would consider not only the material situation of the *mustafti* but also his religiosity. He would urge a *mustafti* who is strong in faith to reject the 1999 fatwa and not to take a mortgage unless the *mustafti* was in a situation of necessity. But if a *mustafti* who is weak in faith asks him the same question, al-Makkawi would, fearing that the *mustafti* would take a mortgage one way or another, permit him to take one, based on the Council's fatwa, even if it was not a necessity.[53] Thus, for al-Makkawi, the 1999 fatwa serves as an example of all that is wrong with the Council and al-Qaradawi. But, according to his statements, the fatwa also enables him to respond to Muslims who approach him and whose religiosity he identifies as fragile. His engagement with the fatwa simultaneously manifests his *salafi* inclination and a recognition of the indispensability of pragmatism.

Johannes Klominek, one of the leaders of the *salafi* Ibn Abbas Center, recalled having read the 1999 fatwa a long time ago. When reminded of its content, he said he disapproved of the justifications the fatwa introduced. He sees the position that needs can be regarded as necessities as a slippery slope. Only necessity may justify legitimizing a prohibition, and necessity applies in life-threatening situations only. If one allows taking a mortgage because it is otherwise difficult to buy apartments in

142 Shari'a and Life

Sweden, why not permit eating pork because it is difficult to find halal restaurants?

Klominek was equally dismissive of the argument that mortgages may contribute to proselytizing: "Maybe 10 per cent of the people are active in *da'wa*. There are very few people who really preach Islam on social media and give lectures." He regarded the justification that the laws of *mu'amalat* do not apply outside *Dar al-Islam* as "cherry-picking. In one fatwa, they [the *wasatis*] apply [this justification]; in another, they do not."

His objection to mortgages was not, however, limited to just the lenient terms set in the 1999 fatwa. More broadly, Klominek did not see any scenario that could justify legitimizing the taking of a mortgage in the Swedish context. In his defense of this point, with which he opened his treatment of the Council's fatwa, he noted that Ibn al-Qayyim stated that to issue a fatwa, a mufti must know both the Islamic texts and the relevant reality. If "you have a lot of knowledge about the Quran and the Sunna, but you don't understand the current situation, your fatwa will be wrong. It has to be like this. And if you have knowledge about the current situation, but you don't have any Islamic knowledge, your fatwa will also be wrong from the Islamic point of view."

The thesis that fatwas change in accordance with changing realities is at the heart of *wasati* pragmatism manifested in the 1999 mortgages fatwa. The contrary opinion, which stresses that Muslims in Europe must abide by the same rules Muslims elsewhere abide by, is at the heart of the writings on *fiqh al-aqalliyyat al-Muslima* by the luminaries of *salafiyya*.

In a sophisticated twist, Klominek attributed the pragmatic thesis to Ibn al-Qayyim, one of the scholars *salafis* respect most. Yet he drew on this scholar to explain why there are no possible circumstances that could justify a concession on mortgages in Sweden. In his homeland, he said, renting an apartment is always an option and is not financially damaging:

> I don't speak about other countries; I speak about Sweden. We don't have this issue that you don't have an alternative other than to buy houses. You see that in this suburb and a lot of other suburbs, 95 per cent of the houses are for rent ... So sometimes when I see people say you don't have an alternative, then [I say to them:] stop a second. You have an alternative. You can rent your house ... if you say it is hard to get an apartment in Stockholm, then if you go 50 kilometers, you will find one.

Furthermore, according to Klominek, since the real estate market in Sweden involves life-long monthly payments by homeowners to the builders of some properties, buying an apartment provides no financial relief compared to renting. Still, "in other countries, they may have different (real estate) situations. They can have their scholars and other scholars to speak about it."[54]

In practical terms, Klominek's treatment of interest-based loans was uncompromising. Yet, in discussing the justifications introduced in the 1999 fatwa, which he rejected, his emphasis that his opinion applied to Sweden and to Sweden only, and his broader opinion on the obligation of muftis to respond to local situations, challenged a crucial aspect of the *salafi* approach to *fiqh al-aqalliyyat al-Muslima*. This challenge manifested his position as an independent thinker who is not committed to any specific mufti or panel, including the luminaries of *salafi* thought. Thus, also when rejected, the most controversial and publicized decision of the European Council for Fatwa and Research provides a context through which an approach to shari'a can be individually and pragmatically negotiated and explained.

Chapter Four

There's Shariʿa, and There's Life

One day, a reputable Tunisian-French medical doctor entered the office of imam Salim Blidi at the Hassan Blidi Mosque in Marseille. Apparently, he had heard that interest-based loans can be legitimized based on shariʿa-grounded arguments, and hoped to be reassured by the imam that he could take one, in good conscience, to expand his practice. Blidi, who strongly disapproves of the European Council for Fatwa and Research and its fatwa that conditionally legitimizes mortgages, told him that from the point of view of the shariʿa, the situation he described did not justify taking a usurious loan. The medical doctor angrily left the imam's office and never returned.

Imam Blidi said such incidents had become rarer during his years in office, and not because the people who consulted with him had realized that usury is a grave sin. In the past, he lamented, when local Muslims, born and educated in Muslim countries, considered taking an interest-based loan, they came to consult with him before making the final decision because they were God-fearing. Today, Muslims in Marseille do not bring the matter to his consideration at all. Today, if they want to take a usurious loan, they just do it.[1]

Working in restaurants, supermarkets, hotels, and transportation in Stockholm often requires engagement with haram. Asked how many attendees whose work compelled them to engage with haram approached him to inquire about the legitimacy of keeping their jobs, imam Khaled al-Dib of The Stockholm Mosque said that not a single one did so. He added, laughingly, that those who want to work at McDonald's do so without asking him.[2]

In fact, one interviewee at the mosque – and one only – told us that he approached imam al-Dib with this exact question. Mahmud (b. 1973), who migrated to Sweden from Jordan at the age of 40, works in a security company. His first job in Stockholm was in a restaurant that sold pork and alcohol, and he was not sure whether it was legitimate to maintain it. He remembered imam Khaled had told him that he could keep his job as long as he searched for an alternative and that he should quit the minute he found one. That was what Mahmud did.

Retrospectively reflecting on that turn of events, Mahmud admitted that at the time he presented the query, he would not have quit his job even if the imam had told him he should because he needed the money.[3] In our interview, imam al-Dib presented a slightly stricter view than what Mahmud attributed to him, although still one that did not radically diverge from the view of the European Council for Fatwa and Research, to which he is committed. He said that Muslims were allowed to work in a job where they engaged with haram only if there were no alternatives, but that there were always alternatives in the Stockholm job market. Even if none was available, the state provides unemployment benefits.[4]

The realistic descriptions by the two imams about the exceptionality of *istifta'* on existential issues suggest that attendees who face conflicts between shari'a norms and the pressures of life in Europe follow more than the two paths of resolution offered by *fiqh al-aqalliyyat al-Muslima* discourse. Along with acting in accordance with religious norms (as they understand them) or, conversely, searching and embracing legitimizations grounded in fiqh concepts and mechanisms for otherwise prohibited practices, it is also the case that Muslims who consider themselves to be shari'a-abiding engage in haram without a fatwa or a general sense of shari'a-grounded legitimization to support them. Bluntly put, they sin, without attempting to argue that they do not sin. Instead, they deploy various strategies of negotiation and mitigation to reconcile their practices and their faith.

A premise of the fatwas that comprise *fiqh al-aqalliyyat al-Muslima* is that God-fearing Muslims are dependent on what the religio-legal discourse allows. When conditionally legitimizing mortgages, al-Qaradawi noted that for many years non-*Hanafis* in Europe were severely financially harmed by the absence of a fatwa legitimizing this practice.[5] In essence, he claimed that his religio-legal audacity would be the make-it-or-break-it for Muslims who care about the shari'a and do not have the means to buy a home without a mortgage. Our interviewees suggested this not to be the case. Relying on fatwas and argumentations oriented to fiqh concepts and mechanisms is one strategy some of them apply when seeking pragmatic accommodations for practices recognized as prohibited by the shari'a. Yet, it is not the *only* way. This being the case, lenient solutions are not dependent on engagement with and acceptance of a lenient religio-legal discourse.

146 Shariʿa and Life

In the previous chapter, we demonstrated that mosque attendees reject exclusivist *iftaʾ* and maintain for themselves the role of ultimate arbiters as to what is acceptable from the standpoint of shariʿa. They do so even if they are pragmatic-inclined and know of the existence of a pragmatic-inclined panel. The strategies of negotiating conscious transgressions explored in this chapter represent another form of independence. Not the independence of the *mustafti* from the authority of specific muftis, but the independence from acting as a *mustafti* at all when a potential conflict between the pressures of life and shariʿa norms arises.

This chapter demonstrates that in the self-perception of transgressors, engaging in a practice they recognize as impermissible without *istiftaʾ* does not signify a retreat from their Islamic identity, but is a way of defining and asserting it, and part of a developing relationship with God. The chapter also shows that the different strategies for dealing with conflicts between shariʿa norms and the challenges of life in Europe are not systematically adhered to and applied. Rather than be consistently guided by *istiftaʾ* or do without it, some mosque attendees transition between the options in response to changing conditions and circumstances. Moreover, where the religio-legal sphere is engaged with as a means to form an opinion, a transitioning of different sorts was applied in the case of some interviewees. Rather than consistently embrace a pragmatic or dogmatic approach, they are dogmatic on issues that have no personal bearing and pragmatic on those that do. Transitioning maximizes the potential for a sense of moral commitment to coexist alongside practical concessions. It is, perhaps, indefensible from a theoretical point of view. Yet as the following pages show, the shariʿa is not always engaged with coherently or persistently.

The final section of the chapter demonstrates that, for various reasons, including their application of strategies external to *istiftaʾ* and their transitioning between moderate pragmatism and dogmatism, even mosque attendees who wholeheartedly identify with the *salafi* approach are not as dogmatic as that approach's theoretical presentations imply. In practical terms, adherence to the *salafi* approach involves lesser material and social injuries than what is inferred from textual comparisons between what the luminaries of that approach expect of Muslims in Europe and what the pragmatic *wasati* approach allows.

The composition of the sample should be emphasized again. There are, in Europe as elsewhere, Muslims who do not accept the idea of revealed law. This does not imply that practices grounded in the shariʿa have no place in their lives as a matter of habit, tradition, folklore, or cultural acculturation; it does mean that, at least in the intellectual sense, they do not see acting against the stipulations of the shariʿa as defiance of a set of codes to which they are committed.

Because we interviewed only mosque attendees, located through their attendance of mosques, our interviewees included, almost without exception, Muslims who believe that the permissible and prohibited are from God, and that God punishes those who transgress. They also had at least a basic knowledge about what constitutes haram and what constitutes halal. Still, in addressing situations where shariʿa norms, as understood by them, conflicted with pressures of life, they did not (or did not always) resort to inquiries directed at finding a fiqh-oriented "way out" and did not act as *mustaftis*.

The prevalence of engaging in prohibited practices without grounding them in pragmatic fatwas points to the caveat of privileging the *wasati-salafi* polemic – and fiqh discourses at large – as a means of understanding the relationship between religious identity (and especially levels of religiosity) and everyday life practices of Muslims in Europe. Resolutions of conflicts between shariʿa and life that are external to *mustafti*-mufti communications leave no textual records. Rather, they are the result of personal contemplations and, possibly, discussions among family and friends. However, given their essential role in determining actual everyday life practices, the reality of being a Muslim in Europe cannot be understood without recording them.

Transgressions Explained

Admitting personal failures when speaking to strangers is not easy, although it is sometimes easier than doing so with friends or while soul-searching. The written questionnaires asked respondents to describe their level of commitment to shariʿa norms. As table 4.1 informs, while a negligible number of respondents noted that they do not regulate any aspect of their life according to the shariʿa, a considerable minority in all the mosques studied noted that they regulated only *some* aspects of their lives according to the shariʿa. The interviews informed that, when asked methodologically about their practices, some admit that they do not conduct every aspect of their lives entirely in accordance with what the shariʿa (as they understand it) allows.

Interviewees who explicitly noted situations in which they breached the boundaries of the shariʿa, fully conscious of doing so, and without resorting to *istifta'* to examine whether their prohibited practice could be case-based legitimized in shariʿa-grounded terms, introduced four main strategies to explain their transgressions: (a) **Confession of sin** – acknowledging that an unlawful act is committed and that the potential

148 Shari'a and Life

Table 4.1. The role of shari'a in everyday life

Mosque	I direct all aspects of my life based on the shari'a, %	I direct some aspects of my life based on the shari'a, %	I don't direct any aspect of my life based on the shari'a, %
The Stockholm Mosque	54.8	41.9	3.2
Al-Nur Mosque, Reykjavik	87.5	12.5	0.0
The Grand Mosque, Reykjavik	60.0	35.0	5.0
Hassan Blidi Mosque, Marseille	44.4	37.0	18.5
Husby Mosque, Stockholm	64.3	35.7	0.0
The Salafi Mosque, Birmingham	75.6	24.4	0.0

Notes: Because of a technical error, this question was not asked in the two Dortmund mosques surveyed. We could not explain the relatively high percentage of participants in Marseille who stated they did not direct any aspect of their lives according to the shari'a. For statistical information about the surveys, see the introduction, note 31.

consequence could be a divine punishment, although God, the merciful, might forgive. (b) **Minimization of sin** – explaining that while the prohibited is committed, the greatest effort is made to minimize the scope of the transgression. (c) **Universalization of sin** – stating that the prohibited could not have been avoided even in a Muslim land. (d) **Separation of spheres** – arguing that while the shari'a should in principle be respected, it is impossible to abide by it in every aspect of life; thus, some of its requirements must be overlooked.

The four strategies are not mutually exclusive. Several interviewees joined two and even three kinds of arguments together when discussing and explaining their failures to abide by Islamic norms. With different nuances, the four strategies make the similar point that human beings can only strive to match normative ideals but never quite fully do so – let alone in Europe, where the challenges are more formidable.

From the standpoint of attendees who spoke in these terms, being Muslim implies that you recognize the supremacy of the shari'a and that you abide by the shari'a, but that sometimes you do not – sometimes life gets in the way. Interviewees who presented one or more of the four strategies agreed that God gave humanity laws through His final Prophet, and that it was their duty, ideally, to lead their lives by each of the revealed laws. They nevertheless contended that they were not always able to do so. It is possible that socially desirable responding, which has been claimed to be more dominant in the reports of religious individuals about their moral behaviour than in those of secular individuals[6], resulted in moderated and selective depictions of the scope and nature of transgressing.

The strategy of plainly admitting sin involved implied, or explicit, statements that a prohibited practice was, or was about to be, committed. Because the transgression was understood as just that – an act that conflicts with the norms set by the divine Lawgiver and cannot be justified within the premise of the shariʿa – the transgressor believed it might inflict on him some kind of divine punishment in this life or the afterlife. Still, because confessions of this kind were contextualized as part of a submissive relationship with God – the punisher, the forgiver, or both – and as part of a spiritual struggle between the pressures of life and the Islamic ideal, they did not injure interviewees' self-perceptions of devotion. Ironically, in some cases, they even appeared to enhance such self-perceptions. Interviewees stated that sinning is a failure that could be avoided if they improved their character, while placing trust in the mercifulness of the divine Lawgiver and hinting that their improvement is possible. A more complicated argument implied that the shariʿa is a normative system whose integrity requires the occasional breaching of its demands. Interviewees described their moral imperfection as an aspect of the God-created nature of humans and suggested that sinning and asking for forgiveness please God. They even went as far as suggesting that a human being who aspires to avoid sinning altogether is, in fact, sinning by aspiring for Godly perfection.

The conscious and regulated manner in which they sinned may have contributed to, rather than disturbed, the ease with which those interviewees related to their behaviour. As Grubbs et al. demonstrated, contrary to the conventional wisdom in religious writing, the perception of uncontrolled surrender to desires is a better predictor of the existence of feelings of a religious and spiritual struggle than the scope of doing so.[7] Perhaps because the interviewees who spoke about sinning were in control of their wrongdoings (with their pros and cons) and already fit them within a narrative regarding their relationship with God, sinning pained less.

Statements about minimizations of sin framed transgressions in lighter contexts. They suggested that while the shariʿa was not observed to the full in the circumstance discussed, an effort was made to minimize the level of breach. Minimization was introduced either by scaling down the physical involvement with the prohibited practice or by separating between the technical aspect of involvement and the intention (*niyya*) motivating the practice. The transgression was thus relativized not only to the ideal, but also to a greater sin that could have been committed but was avoided. This effort of minimizing, in itself, spoke for the religious, conscious, and continued commitment of the occasional transgressor.

150   Shari'a and Life

Analogies to conditions in Muslim lands were intended to dispel suspicions – self-imposed or believed to be externally implied – that haram is committed due to living in the West. While it is easier to avoid certain pressures leading to transgressions when living in a majority-Muslim society, these societies, without exception, are not modelled in their entirety according to shari'a regulations. Still, there is arguably a higher probability that a Muslim would find a haram-free job in services, a separate-gender swimming pool, or an Islamic bank when living in a Muslim society, even if none of these can be taken for granted.

From a normative point of view, a reality of corrupt conduct in one place does not justify, in and of itself, corruption in another. Still, the implication that life in the homeland would have forced similar conflicts and similar breaches reassured the person invoking the universalizing argument that his life-changing decision to move to a non-Muslim society, particularly if motivated by financial considerations, was not an "original sin" that resulted in continued and inevitable moral deterioration. Conversely, the strategy of separating spheres reduced the shari'a unapologetically to a code that is applied only in *some* aspects of life and is denied regarding others. The separation was not explored or constructed in conceptual, coherent terms, or as a distinct category of religiosity.

Those who introduced that strategy did not describe themselves in terms analogous to traditionalist Jews, whose self-identity draws on consciously fluid and compromised engagement with religious norms that often involves appreciation and even awe of religious identities that require more rigid forms of engagement. Rather, and without theoretically denying the overarching authority of the divine Lawgiver, they noted, as a statement of fact and without resorting to shari'a-grounded terms, that the shari'a can only be given certain space in their everyday life practices. Where they cannot, they do not apply it. These points of view may sound paradoxical, and, indeed, philosophically, they are. But as a psychological state of mind, they can coexist. One can believe that a corpus of laws is divine and that an ever-present God observes its application, and at the same time, defy God-given laws in certain contexts without *necessarily* fearing punishment and feeling unease.

The Prophet Muhammad spoke of the greater jihad as one's constant struggle against desires and temptations.[8] Human beings are prone to err, fall into temptation, and aspire to an ideal but never fully realize it. This is true for Muslims in Europe as it is for Muslims in majority Muslim countries as it is for adherents of any other faith. Yet, although divine forgiveness is always a possibility – and possibility is a keyword, as no believer can rest assured about God's final judgment – the choice of God-fearing mosque attendees to transgress without at least searching for potential religio-legal legitimizations for committing what they recognize as sins is curious, considering the abundance of such legitimizations.

It is even more curious when transgressing due to challenges resulting from the minority situation and pertinent to the field of *fiqh al-aqalliyyat al-Muslima*. Why speak of compromise, of imperfection, why have a guilty conscience and hope for compassion, why minimize or relativize – where one can *potentially* situate one's choices within the boundaries of the shari'a by engaging in *istifta'*? Why not, at the very least, explore whether *ifta'* allows for legitimization, and then make up one's mind?

The interviews pointed to several explanations. Some who transgress hold firm to a notion of shari'a as an unequivocal guide, a corpus of commands that, whether light or imposing, cannot be understood in more than one way. This position was dominant in *salafi* narratives but also resonated in the words of several interviewees who were not *salafis*. They resented the notion that what the divine Lawgiver ordered could be mitigated or compromised through what they perceived, intuitively, to be over-creative, human-made hermeneutics.

In one of the greatest and earliest modern novels on sin and punishment, Daniel Defoe's *Roxana*, the protagonist creates at a certain point her own interpretation of God's expectations to convince herself that her illicit transgressions are legitimate in His eyes. She ends up regretting her choice to make up the rules.[9] Some interviewees who could not make peace with muftis' fiqh-oriented legitimizations found the idea that divine rules could be mitigated and applied differently in different situations based on human discretion contradictory to the revealed essence of the shari'a. They saw any conditional legitimization by humans of a prohibition as stripping the divine reward-and-punishment system of its absolutist, reassuring essence. They were more at peace with recognizing their own imperfection and transgressions, contextualizing it in spiritually comforting terms, and hoping for forgiveness, than dealing with the potential confusion that multiple interpretations allow.

Another situation that discouraged interviewees from searching for a legitimizing fatwa on a specific prohibition was being convinced (whether rightly or not) that the search would be in vain. This conviction was encouraged by the gravity of the prohibition, or, conversely, by a prohibited practice being related to the spheres of leisure or indulgence and thus perceived as unlikely to justify facilitations. Where that appeared to be the case, the options were reduced to two only – refrain from the desired practice or engage in it consciously, knowing that a sin is committed.

152   Shari'a and Life

Modest knowledge of fiqh as an art and practice is another factor. Several interviewees were utterly unfamiliar with the existence of concepts and mechanisms that carry the potential to legitimize otherwise prohibited practices in shari'a-grounded terms. Others had a vague notion that situations of extreme necessity allow compromise, but often, it fell short of a systematic understanding of the field. They mentioned the transgression discussed in terms alluding to *maslaha mursala*, either for the Muslim community at large or for themselves and their families. Still, they did not rely on this or another fiqh concept to justify their transgression in shari'a-grounded terms.

It was not only that these interviewees knew nothing about the project of al-Qaradawi and the European Council for Fatwa and Research, the innovative ideology and methodology it introduced as a means to suspend prohibitions and make the lives of European Muslims easier, and the existence of a corpus of fatwas that have the potential to situate their transgression within the boundaries of shari'a-grounded legitimacy. Rather, they were unaware that fiqh, as a discipline, is engaged with by some muftis in a way that allowed for the conditional legitimization of the prohibited practices that concerned them.

None of the interviewees in any of the mosques studied Islam at a university. The plurality of sources from which they accumulated their knowledge of fiqh – their family and friends, their mosque, their school, and the media – provided all of them with the practical know-how of what is prohibited and what is permissible. But it provided only some with substantial knowledge in fiqh and its mechanisms. Moroccan interviewees, for example, mentioned classes on *tarbiyya Islamiyya*, Islamic education, taught from elementary school to high school as one of their sources of information about shari'a. Our analysis of Moroccan state-regulated textbooks for this class, including those that prepare high school students for their baccalaureate, informs that they hardly discuss the foundations and mechanisms of fiqh. Pupils receive only limited instruction on – among other topics – *ijtihad*, the qualifications required of a mufti, *maqasid al-shari'a*, and *maslaha mursala* and its ranks.[10] Interviews with graduates of the Moroccan school system who mentioned *tarbiyya Islamiyya* as their source of knowledge suggested that some of that limited information had been lost through the years. That not all that is taught in high school is ingrained and remembered in later stages in life was hardly one of the more surprising findings of the study.

The blurring of cultural and religious norms is another reason for not searching for shari'a-based legitimizations for transgressions. From a religious point of view, a revelation-based law is precisely that: the eternal command of God. Any such law may be of greater or lesser importance and applied differently under different circumstances; yet, its status differs from that of endeared traditions or habits because of its revealed nature. However, when discussing their practices, several interviewees applied different approaches to prohibitions that they exclusively grounded in the revelation, and prohibitions that they understood as reflecting cultural traditions passed on from parent to child *as well as* what God requires of them. The conflation of the revealed and the traditional helped downscale the graveness of transgressions.

Searching for religio-legal legitimizations for prohibited practices was discouraged in some cases also because of moderate social pressures to conform. Obedience to divine laws is encouraged by two types of relationships. One is a metaphysical, authoritative entity who reduces one's conflict between norms and desires by externalizing the demand to obey.[11] Another is with a community to which the believer belongs.

Belonging to a religious community encourages compliance with religious norms through psychological and material rewards offered. As Self-Categorization Theory informs, identification with a group enhances the self-esteem of the individual.[12] Such identification involves the accentuation of intra-category similarities, which, in religious groups, implies engaging in certain practices and avoiding other practices.[13] Where education and indoctrination fail to accomplish a religious community's desired conformity, it can apply, potentially, other means of persuasion, including granting or denying permission to use the facilities of the group, marrying into the group, sending children to a school administrated by the group, and receiving relief money.

Without exception, social pressures were irrelevant or moderately relevant to interviewees across the spectrum of mosques surveyed. Those who regarded their mosque merely as a house of prayer did not self-categorize their Islamic identity by accentuating the norms preached there. Those for whom the mosque was a hub of socialization and who identified with its ideological orientation were hardly, if at all, subject to rewards or sanctions based on their public conduct, including with relation to their right to pray there (this, as explored below, is the case also for the Salafi Mosque of Birmingham). Thus, they had no reason to be concerned that by being seen in public doing something that they and the group believed the shari'a prohibited, they would face retributions.

Haram in Everyday Life

The accounts of several interviewees who explained transgressions of the boundaries of shari'a through one or more of the aforementioned strategies follow. Moroccan-born (1980) 'Abd al-Majid, a father of three

154 Shari'a and Life

who ultimately settled in Iceland at the age of 33 after many sojourns in Europe, spoke in the previous chapter about taking mortgages as a reflection of the need to adapt to a receiving country and to avoid the risks of eviction from rented apartments. 'Abd al-Majid takes great pride in his work as assistant manager at a Domino's Pizza, where he touches and sells pork products as part of his duties on the job.

'Abd al-Majid never engaged in *istifta'* on the permissibility of his job, although he recognized that it was problematic from the point of view of the shari'a. He justified his choice through the minimizing, universalizing, and separating strategies, while also alluding to *maslaha*. He explained that (a) while he sells the pork, he does not eat it and washes his hands thoroughly after handling it; "I clean my hands, with the cream, with the soap, with everything." (b) "If I know a Muslim is coming to me, I clean the knife for cutting the pizza and I make it nicely, to respect him also." (c) Restaurants in Morocco also sell haram products to attract tourists: "our country, now, it has a minibar and many restaurants with pork … Morocco, Algeria, Tunisia – everyone now [sells pork]." (d) Muslim-owned restaurants in Iceland also engage with haram products, so working in one of them is not really an alternative ('Abd al-Majid accused one of the most well-known, Muslim-owned restaurants in the city of selling pork, which is less expensive than beef and lamb, as though it was halal kebab). (e) Muslims should be employed rather than rely on welfare money; "If I stay at home, and I go just always to the social service – 'help me' – this is a bad thing." (f) When you live in Europe, you cannot "comply a full hundred per cent" with Islamic norms.

Prompted to answer why, while he engaged in *istifta'* about the proper duration of the Ramadan fast in Iceland and other issues, he never took the time to consult an authority on fiqh regarding whether his personal situation justified his choice of working in a restaurant that sold pork, 'Abd al-Majid said a mufti or a fatwa could not change his mind. "Look, when we were younger, we believed in some persons who show us the way. But when we start growing, we see [for ourselves]. Tell him [the mufti who condemns engaging with haram in the workplace]: come help me first, give me the money first. Tell him: 'come,' I will [ask him] 'Can you get me a very good job' [instead of my job at Domino's Pizza]? You are opposed [to what I do]? If you want me to stop these things [working with haram products], help me."[14]

Our travels across Morocco's touristic hubs in 2018 informed that, indeed, there are restaurants and supermarkets that sell haram products. However, not all do. The chances for someone like 'Abd al-Majid to find a permissible job in his homeland are considerably higher than in Iceland, where finding a restaurant or supermarket that does not sell pork or alcohol is almost impossible.

Muhammad (b. 1982) left Pakistan for Northern Italy when he was 25. When he was 35, he moved to Sweden, where he works in deliveries. His wife and two young boys were still in Pakistan at the time of the interview, and he hoped they would join him in Sweden in a year and a half. They were able to meet only once a year, but frequently chatted via Skype.

In theory, Muhammad, who described himself as a "common Muslim" who never studied fiqh, holds that one must abide by what one's imam says. He explained that if imam Khaled al-Dib of The Stockholm Mosque, where he occasionally prayed, told him, for example, to quit his job, he would. That is, however, just in theory.

When Muhammad first arrived in Sweden, he washed dishes in a restaurant owned by a Muslim where pork and alcohol were served. He explained that he needed the money and could not find an alternative job. He felt troubled while working there, but also felt that "When I live in this society, in Europe, then I adjust in this situation."

Muhammad had in mind what a friend told him in Italy when he considered taking a loan to buy a car. This friend told him that there was a principle in Islam according to which a person who suffers from hunger may even eat pork. However, he did not consult with imam al-Dib, or anyone else, whether his specific situation legitimized keeping the prohibited job at the restaurant. He ultimately quit, but he admitted that it was not because of shari'a-grounded considerations but because his boss would not raise his salary. "Had my boss given me more money, I would have maintained it," he confessed.

Muhammad said that his decisions as to when to comply with the shari'a and when to breach it were, in the end, guided by his sense that full adherence was not realistic: "Islam is too big. If I go too fast, step, step, step, there is no end. No one follows 100 per cent of the rules. Imam Khaled [al-Dib] would not say that he follows 100 per cent of the rules."[15]

'Abdallah (b. 1995) is a Syrian, born and raised in Dubai. He migrated to Sweden in 2016 with his sister to pursue a degree in architecture. At the time of the interview, he was engaged to a Swedish Christian girl whom he met on campus, and they planned to marry soon. The couple considered moving to Dubai after they marry, depending on the job market. 'Abdallah said that the Quran permitted this kind of marriage and that he was certain of this fact because he saw interfaith marriages in feature films.

His knowledge of fiqh was modest. He was aware that there was a concept according to which when something was of necessity, it may

156   Shari'a and Life

become legitimate, but did not know the relevant terminologies or mechanisms. To the best of his memory, he picked up this concept from friends around the age of 15.

To finance his studies, 'Abdallah took out a loan that carried interest. He said he was compelled to do so because otherwise, he could not build a future for himself. However, while having a general idea that necessity can legitimize suspensions of prohibitions, he avoided exploring with the pragmatic imam of his mosque or with any other expert whether taking the loan was legitimate under his specific circumstances. 'Abdallah explained that he thought that if he had inquired, he would have been advised not to take the loan, which he badly needed, and which he decided to take no matter what. (This may have indeed been the case if he approached imam al-Dib, as demonstrated in chapter 2, but if 'Abdallah had done his research, he could have relied on the generous terms with which the European Council for Fatwa and Research addressed the issue in its July 2008 session).

When hearing about his decision, several of 'Abdallah's friends, Syrians raised in Saudi Arabia who moved to Sweden, told him that he should fear the Day of Judgment and not take the loan. Their warning did not deter him and did not encourage him to engage in *istifta'* on the matter. He said their opinion was strict not because they were strict (*mutashaddidun*) but because they were rich and could pay tuition without taking a loan. He was confident that they would have done what he did if they had been in his financial situation.

A matter-of-fact approach, conscious yet unapologetic, underlines 'Abdallah's depiction of his haram deeds. Ideally, shari'a and life would always overlap; realistically, they do not. That is just the way things are. He related that he was in the habit of meeting with Swedish friends in places where alcohol is served. While he knew it was prohibited to do so, he liked his friends and respected them (he, himself, does not drink).

During the Ramadan before the interview, he did not fast and instead gave charity to the poor. The reason was that he was practicing boxing for one hour per day and did not want to impede on his training. His father called him and asked: "Son, are you fasting?" 'Abdallah answered that he was not, but instead would give charity. His father reprimanded him and told him that giving money to the poor was a lesser fulfilment of Ramadan and that 'Abdallah's younger sister was fasting.

Reflecting on that conversation, 'Abdallah said he respected his father and knew that boxing was just a hobby. Ultimately, he admitted, he would have to answer to his Creator for making the wrong call. However, boxing was important to him, and he simply prioritized it over his religious duties.[16]

In the previous chapter, we met Moroccan-born Hisham (b. 1980), who migrated to Spain when he was 28 and moved to Reykjavik when he was 36. Hisham was one of the few interviewees who supported the idea that a Muslim should find a mufti and abide by that mufti's decisions, even if the *mustafti* disagreed with some decisions. However, his experiences suggested that he did not have such an authority in Reykjavik. On some issues, including his continued work in a restaurant that engages with haram products, he decided for himself without consulting with texts or experts.

Hisham goes swimming with his five-year-old son Muhammad. Swimming is one of Iceland's most cherished leisure activities, and pools serve as hubs for socialization. All pools are mixed-gender, none offers separate-gender hours, and all require visitors to shower naked in gender-separate communal showers, a practice strictly monitored due to the moderate usage of chlorine in Icelandic pools and reflecting Icelandic society's egalitarian tradition. In the pluralistic ocean of contemporary fiqh, the total impermissibility of mixed-gender swimming and same-gender exposure of private parts is one issue on which almost all muftis agree. It is likely that a brief visit to an Icelandic swimming pool would not change their mind.

The implication is that there is no way to swim in an Icelandic pool and fully respect shariʿa norms. Several interviewees in Reykjavik told us that swimming was out of bounds for them, noting both the norms expected from Muslims and the disgust they felt about seeing nakedness.

Others said they go swimming anyway. One of them was imam Ahmad Sadiq. Sadiq said there was no problem with swimming because it was possible to lower the gaze (to avoid seeing naked bodies) and shower and change in cubicles (so that others do not see one's naked body).[17] Salman Tamimi, the founder of the pragmatic-inclined Al-Nur Mosque, said he was an avid swimmer and suggested there was no problem with this practice, invoking the same arguments imam Sadiq invoked.[18] On the other hand, imam ʿAbd al-ʿAziz al-Walʿani of the Grand Mosque, a relative newcomer to the country and not a swimmer himself, was more ambiguous. He said that Islamic norms require that men and women did not swim together, but also that it was expected of Muslims to adhere to the norms of the country in which they live.[19]

To minimize the impermissibility of the choice to attend a public pool, Hisham and his son make sure to use enclosed shower cubicles. Still, unlike imams Sadiq and Tamimi, Hisham was unequivocal that he breached shariʿa norms by swimming in mixed-gender pools and walking through locker rooms where other men are naked. Asked why,

158   Shari'a and Life

then, he engaged in a practice he knew was prohibited, he explained, as a matter of fact, that there was a difference between what Islam commands and what people actually do in their lives.

Hisham's treatment of mortgages was similar. He opposed the notion that interest-based loans could be legitimized in the case of European Muslims. When told about the 1999 mortgage fatwa (of which he had never heard), he said it was wrong because necessity can only apply in life and death situations, such as when a starving person wanders in the desert and finds pork. He emphasized that taking a mortgage was equally impermissible as drinking alcohol.

Still, Hisham, who was never in a financial position to seriously consider taking a mortgage, argued that if given the opportunity, he would take a mortgage and buy a home. He said he would do so for the same reason that some people drink alcohol, even though it is haram: "there is shari'a, and there is life" and "in life, sometimes people do things which they know shari'a does not permit."[20]

A few days after our first interview, we asked Hisham to reflect on his answers. Does he not fear divine punishment for consciously committing what he understands to be sins? The question made him uncomfortable. At first, he answered in abstract terms and argued that our questions were uncommon; then, he turned to another topic.

It is far from obvious that had Hisham remained in Morocco, he would have had access to a permissible loan for the purchase of a home. Islamic banks did not open in Morocco until 2017. Ibrahim al-Wah, Personal Assistant to the General Secretary of the Supreme Council of 'Ulama in Morocco told us in an interview that the state does not refer to those banks as Islamic banks but rather as *bunuk tasharukiyya*, so as to not discredit the traditional banks that engage with *riba*. The religio-legal permissibility of the operations of these banks is supervised by the Supreme Council. Muhammad Khayari, the Supervisor of Religious Guides in Morocco (*al-Mushrif 'ala 'amal al-Murshidin wa-l-Murshidat fi l-Maghrib*, the office responsible for religious guidance in mosques, hospitals, welfare societies, prisons, and other institutions) emphasized in the same interview that 80 per cent of the operations of the other banks are commensurate with the shari'a.[21]

Syrian-born (1980) Fahdi of Reykjavik's Grand Mosque, with whom we were briefly acquainted in the previous chapter, was painfully sincere about the possibility that he just might not resist an opportunity to buy a house through a usurious loan, and that if he did, he would not be able to justify his decision. Fahdi, the father of three, said that his parents were culturally but not religiously conservative. At age 14 and still in Homs, he began memorizing the Quran, a task he never completed.

In his twenties, he became more religious, searched for fatwas online, read books on religious topics, and occasionally attended lessons in his mosque.

Fahdi said paying interest on a loan was impermissible in any situation because usury harmed the community. However, he confessed that in the past, he considered transgressing. "Satan told me: 'all people do it – you can do it;' then an Angel came and said, 'it is not good.'" He estimated that if the option became practical, there was a 30 per cent chance he would not resist the temptation and take a mortgage. He added, out of context, that even Saudi Arabia was not an interest-free economy. Asked what he thought would happen if the devil would eventually manage to tempt him, Fahdi said that the sin would bother him and his mistake would stay with him for a long time, and maybe, when his time to account for his deeds in this life would come, he would be punished.[22]

Munir, born in 1983, is single. He is the son of Palestinian refugees who lived in Gaza until the mid-1980s and then moved to Libya. In 2005, he left for Italy, where he lived for ten years. Life there was good for him, but in 2015, the economic crisis left him without a job or prospects, and he was forced to try his luck in Stockholm. He found a part-time job in cleaning.

Methodologically opinionated about competing approaches to politics and fiqh, Munir shared his resentment of *salafi* views. He argued that the notion that congratulating Christians was a form of asserting another religion was something that the *salafis* had begun to spread in recent years, causing nothing but discord, and it was not sound. He suggested *salafis* spread this and other false fatwas because they did not want Muslims to be enlightened and to get along with others. Rather, they desire Muslims who are backward. The reason is that they are servants of the Saudi regime, whose sole objective was to remain in power and who was supported by the United States, which created al-Qaeda and supported the Islamic State as a means of weakening the Muslims and asserting its global hegemony.

On the other hand, Munir greatly appreciated al-Qaradawi as a personality, both as a mufti and as a champion of political reforms in the Arab world. Munir's opinions – that Muslims who could not buy a home or attend university without taking interest-based loans may take them, and that Muslims who could not find an alternative may temporarily maintain jobs that engage with haram – were commensurate with those of the European Council for Fatwa and Research and al-Qaradawi, as was his opinion about Christmas greetings. However, the decade-long sojourner in Europe had never heard of the Dublin-based panel.

160 Shari'a and Life

Despite his engagement with fiqh and pragmatic inclination, Munir was not encouraged to explore shari'a-grounded legitimizations when faced with conflicts between religious norms and Western practices, or any other matter. He could not remember a single issue about which he engaged in *istifta'*. Munir defined himself as a Muslim "who does not observe religion a hundred per cent." This was not a position he justified, but neither a position about which he was apologetic or defensive. It was simply the reality of his life.

An avid swimmer who loves the Stockholm beaches, a friend advised him not to participate in mixed-gender swimming. When he heard that friendly reprimand, he thought about the matter, but he stopped thinking about it the next day and continued going to the beach: "you know what it is like in Europe," he explained. After further thought, he said that mixed-gender swimming was *makruh* (disliked) rather than haram and not an important issue in general, and detailed how he minimized the transgression (he talks to women at the beach, but remembers there is a line he must not cross; in any case, he finds Swedish women less attractive then Italian ones).

During the Ramadan before the interview, which overlapped with long, hot summer days, Munir only managed to fast for two weeks and then stopped. The fast could have been more bearable if Munir had adopted one of the fatwas according to which while living in a Nordic country, Muslims may fast in accordance to a time zone where the duration of the fast was more moderate. While Munir had heard of this option, he did not study relevant fatwas. He said that because his roommates at the time fasted according to local time, he decided that was how he should fast as well, and when he discovered it was too difficult, he quit.[23]

Moroccan-born (1971) 'Abd al-Salam was briefly introduced in the previous chapter. After migrating to Germany in 1992, his first job was in a restaurant in the former capital Bonn. He was a cook and had to handle pork and alcohol.

'Abd al-Salam knew his job conflicted with his duties as a Muslim. At the time, his faith was not strong. While exploring the religio-legal discourse on the matter could have provided him with a legitimizing context, he did not ask an imam or any other person whether what he was doing could be legitimized. He explained that he wanted to make money, was extremely busy, and made an easy choice rather than a correct choice. Moreover, he did not confer with anyone because he was convinced his employment could not be legitimized within the boundaries of shari'a. Later he worked as a waiter at a conference centre and then began working in construction. At the time of the interview, he was unemployed due to a herniated disc.

Several years ago, ʿAbd al-Salam began leading a more religious life. He said he had given up on certain vices; for example, he no longer flirts with women. He read the Quran more attentively and understood how grave a sin flirting is. However, he was not avoiding all transgressions.

ʿAbd al-Salam said that he was in the habit of visiting a mixed-gender swimming pool with his children. He did not examine the permissibility of this practice because he was convinced that the norms at the swimming pool did not accord with shariʿa modesty requirements between the genders and within the genders. Like other Moroccan-born interviewees, he invoked a universalizing argument when discussing this choice, noting that mixed-gender swimming is also the norm in Morocco. (In our travels in Morocco, we found this is the case in some, although not all, pools).

Asked if he did not fear being condemned to Hell because of the sins he committed, ʿAbd al-Salam said that he did. He was quick to add that in life, people make mistakes, and that he had asked God for forgiveness. He suggested that sinning and asking for forgiveness is an aspect of being a good, devout Muslim: "Allah likes that people make mistakes and ask for forgiveness"; in fact, he said, it was a form of *shirk* (denying the oneness of God) to try and lead a perfect life, because only Allah and the angels are perfect.[24]

Yusuf was born (1986) in Germany to Moroccan migrants and has MA degrees in mechanical engineering and welding technology. His father financed his studies. Yusuf, who has five siblings, is very thankful for that. He planned to find a job and then get married – preferably to a Moroccan, because, he explained, it would be easier to observe traditions and religion with a Muslim wife, "but, maybe, I will fall crazily in love with a Christian."[25] Yusuf has decided to take a mortgage to buy an apartment when the opportunity arises. He developed this opinion through debates with his father, who paid rent for thirty years and never became a homeowner: "my father just said it's haram, and that was it."[26]

While Yusuf believed that given the negative media portrayals of Islam, there was reason for Muslims to fear eviction from rented apartments, he also contended that buying an apartment could not be justified as a necessity, and thus legitimate from a shariʿa-based perspective. Instead, he invoked his upbringing as the reason for parting with his father on mortgages. He explained that being born and socialized in Germany, he developed a different opinion than the one grounded in the shariʿa about banks and usury. Unlike his father, he realized that in a globalized economy, "strictly speaking, you can't eat a single potato anymore" if you want to avoid dealing with haram.[27] He added

162   Shari'a and Life

that *murabaha* transactions offered by Islamic banks are, in essence, not better because the customer ends up paying much more than the actual cost of the apartment. Invoking the universalizing argument (but out of context), he noted that Islamic countries were not really Islamic because they allowed the sale of alcohol.[28]

Tunisian-born (1948) Habib did not argue with his son about mortgages as Yusuf's father did. A pensioner who migrated to Sweden in 1970, he used to work in nightclubs and casinos. When his married son approached him with his decision to buy a house through a usurious loan, Habib, alarmed by the high prices of rent in Stockholm, advised him that it was the right call.

Habib was critical of the local *salafis*: "You cannot have an imam from Saudi Arabia telling you what to do in Sweden."[29] He said he supported the European Council for Fatwa and Research "100 per cent" because it was familiar with European realities. He was particularly content with its decision that Muslims in Nordic countries should fast during long summer days in accordance with the local times of dawn and sunset, which he believed was the correct view.

Despite his favourable opinion of the Council, and despite his presence at a lecture al-Qaradawi delivered at the mosque in 2005, in which (so Habib remembered) he addressed the legitimization of mortgages, Habib emphasized that his approval of his son's decision had nothing to do with the 1999 fatwa. It would have been the same even if the fatwa had never been issued. His explanation described shari'a norms and the realities of life in Sweden as two separate spheres that at times overlap and at times do not. When they do not, Muslims need to decide which to prioritize. In his son's case, the need to take care of the family was rightly prioritized.

Habib's view about mixed-gender swimming was another demonstration of this approach. His justification for attending local pools was triple-fold: first, when in Europe, Muslims should act like Europeans rather than try to change their societies and impose alternatives to the European lifestyle – just as they should expect Europeans who move to Muslim lands to respect their religion, traditions, and culture. Second, people who object to mixed-gender swimming on religious grounds confuse religion with tradition, just as people who object to shaking the hands of women do. Third, he goes to the pool to relax rather than flirt with women, and there is nothing wrong with that.[30]

The Tunisian-Algerian-Swede Sufiyan (b. 1988) was introduced in the previous chapter as a keen *mustafti*. He received from his imam, Khaled al-Dib of The Stockholm Mosque, the advice he hoped for – that due to his personal situation, it was legitimate that he took a mortgage.

Interest-based loans were not the only crucial issue on which Sufiyan resorted to *istifta* in the hope of receiving a response in line with his pragmatic standpoint. He also asked imam al-Dib whether he could maintain his job in his IT firm. The firm engages with haram financing practices. The imam assured him that indeed he could, for two reasons: The job did not require him to directly engage in haram (for example, he was not required to sell interest-based loans himself); and the knowledge he acquired in the firm could help other Muslims in the future. Sufiyan assured us that had the imam told him to quit, he would have.

Along with resorting to *istifta* as a means of legitimizing pragmatic choices or applying dogmatic views, there are occasions when, faced with a conflict between Swedish realities and his understanding of shari'a norms, Sufiyan also chooses to transgress, mindful that he does so. In this way, the sense of guilt is compromised by a sense of imperfection, a self-recognition that asserts his humaneness and personal connection to God. Sinning gives God the opportunity to forgive Sufiyan and, at the same time, gives Sufiyan the opportunity to be forgiven.

Sufiyan attends mixed-gender pools. He said he would have chosen separate-gender pools if they existed in Stockholm, but they do not (Khaled al-Dib advised us that there are pools that offer separate swimming hours). Unlike Habib, he was convinced this practice conflicts with shari'a norms. However, he did not seek legitimization as he did when dealing with other prohibitions and did not believe that he could find one.

While Sufiyan admitted that he could avoid pursuing this leisure activity, he contextualized his transgression as part of his religious identity. God, he said, created man weak, and He knows that humans can make mistakes. A righteous path acquired through self-reflection and self-improvement is even more cherished than that easily earned because "Allah loves me more when I come back to my religion."[31]

The absence of sufficient modesty in swimming pools strikes Sufiyan as an inconvenience and unfamiliarity caused by cultural differences, as much as it is understood as a breach of the divine Lawgiver's demands. The blurring of the lines between the two aspects makes transgressing easier. To address both, Sufiyan applied the minimizing strategy. He said he tried to "minimize contact with ladies" in the pool (he was quick to add that he loves women but always makes sure not to cross any lines when talking to them). He also tried to visit the pool early in the morning or late at night, when there were fewer swimmers. He would wait until the communal showers were empty to enter and would not take off his swim trunks there. He also would wait for the locker room to empty before changing. Sufiyan recalled that he once went with two

164 Shari'a and Life

friends to Eriksdalsbadet, Stockholm's largest and most crowded swimming pool. Seeing that the locker room was full of naked men, they decided to visit only smaller pools from that point forward.[32]

When You Must, When You Can

Sufiyan's depictions reflect a fluid way of dealing with haram practices. On a leisure-related matter, he had been consciously transgressing without engaging in *istifta*'. On existential housing and employment matters, he approached his mufti and grounded his choices in the advice the mufti offered him, as well as fiqh concepts.

The transition between consciously transgressing and finding advice that places practices within the fold of legitimacy empowers him. While Sufiyan reserves the option to sin and contextualize the sin as part of a relationship of forgiveness from his Creator for himself, it is an *option*, rather than a way of life. Transgression is something that happens occasionally, rather than something that characterizes his engagement with religious norms.

It would be misleading to describe Sufiyan as a Muslim who abides by normative boundaries resulting from *istifta*', or to describe him as the opposite. As was the case of other interviewees who, on some dilemmas, inquired with experts and on some issues, did not, he shifts between the categories, and in doing so expands his ability to maintain his religious identity while leading an integrating, comfortable, and ambitious lifestyle in Sweden. Equally misleading would be a description of Sufiyan as someone who, when engaging with religio-legal discourse, always chooses the most lenient and pragmatic opinion. While Sufiyan shined in the interview as systematically inclined to religio-legal pragmatism, he advocated the dogmatic view on the duration of Summer Ramadan fasts in Nordic countries. He was not aware that this was the opinion of the European Council for Fatwa and Research. Fully confident about this position, he did not even discuss it with his imam. Sufiyan argued that no matter how long the day was, the fast should last from dawn to sunset, as stated in the Quran. He described the lenient view about Nordic fasts as unsound and added that he had never heard from anyone a precise definition of what the maximum duration of fasts should be. He suggested that if exceptionally long days during Nordic summers call for moderating the fast, then exceptionally short days during Nordic winters should, in kind, require extending the fast.[33]

However, his choice of the dogmatic view on this issue did not come at the same expense favouring dogmatic views on other issues would have. Sufiyan related with pride that he played football during that year's Ramadan while fasting and was surprised to see how easy it was. (Imam al-Dib told us he subscribed to the opinion of the European Council for Fatwa and Research on this issue as well. When we mentioned that the great Muhammad 'Abduh introduced the facilitating option, he answered, similar to the Reykjavik-based 'Askari, that 'Abduh was not familiar with the weather conditions in Sweden. Nevertheless, he advised university students that they could defer the fast if they had to take exams, and gave the same counsel to a member of Sweden's national football squad.[34])

Transitions between pragmatism and dogmatism were inferred from the narratives of other interviewees as well. In some cases, their transitions were more radical than Sufiyan's, who presented articulate and methodological explanations for each opinion. Transitioning interviewees expressed adamant, non-compromising views on certain issues and pragmatic views on other issues without reconciling the variations in theoretical terms.

The shifts followed a pattern. Interviewees who shifted between the two approaches tended to advance dogmatic views on issues that had no immediate implications for them and to support pragmatic views on issues that did. Where dogmatism involved a sense of high personal cost, they spoke like *wasatis* – and even went beyond what *wasatiyya* allowed; where it did not, they sounded like *salafis*.

A crucial distinction should be drawn here. All theories of fiqh suggest that adjustments are case-based (individually or communally). The most effective means muftis have for legitimizing conditional suspension of prohibitions, *maslaha mursala*, applies only where necessity or need arises concerning given conditions (including potentially broad conditions, such as being a Muslim in Europe). It is thus perfectly logical and theoretically coherent for Muslims to deny themselves facilitations when they are not in a situation of need or necessity and accept them when they are. For example, to argue that it is legitimate that they take a mortgage if they do not have an alternative means for buying an apartment, and at the same time insist that it is not legitimate for them to do so if they are already homeowners.

The ideological flexibility our discussion points to is different. We refer to interviewees who supported pragmatic facilitations on issues that affected them, but, discussing similar yet theoretical situations that did not affect them, insisted that applicable prohibitions should be abided by under all circumstances; or, who systematically sided with dogmatic views on debated issues, and expressed pragmatism, in a way that was not methodologically constructed, when discussing matters that were meaningful to them. Transitioning provided a benefit.

166   Shari'a and Life

It allowed interviewees to manifest absolute loyalty to the letter of the Quran and maintain and project an image of strong religious commitment in the face of the challenges of living in the West while pursuing pragmatism where it matters most.

To argue that there is a measure of hypocrisy in shifting between pragmatism and dogmatism would not do the practice injustice. To imply that it is a unique phenomenon would. One of the facts of life is that it is easier to hold abstract moral values than to live by them. Tom Wolfe's celebrated observation that a conservative was a liberal who has been mugged and a liberal was a conservative who has been arrested reflected a truth that transcends time and ideological orientations: in most cases, our social existence determines how we reflect on spiritual, moral, and ethical demands. This being the case, it should not seem awkward that some advocates of dogmatic opinions were attentive and welcoming of pragmatic fatwas only when these made a difference for them.

Aside from the human inclination to care for oneself more than for one's neighbour, which prophets and sages cautioned against, the transition by some interviewees between the theoretically dogmatic and practically pragmatic positions can also be explained by the different ways in which people relate to immediate and remote situations, as illustrated by Construal-Level Theory (CLT). The theory suggests that the more distant (in time and space alike) people are from other people, objects, and events, the more they tend to think about them in abstract rather than practical terms.[35] For example, a person who plans a vacation for the coming year would imagine it in emotional and general terms (i.e., sense the pleasure of basking in the sun and the joy of seeing new landscapes). Conversely, a person who goes on vacation the next day would be mainly preoccupied with tasks such as withdrawing money from an ATM or washing underwear and socks.

In the same way, a person considering whether a religious prohibition should be applied under all circumstances will be more likely to address the question in idealistic and unequivocal terms, insensitive to specific practical nuances and implications, when the relevancy of the prohibition is potential and distant. If the prohibition presents a real and imminent challenge that carries material or psychological injury for oneself, a greater tendency to treat it in detailed and pragmatic terms is expected.

Lack of theoretical engagement with fiqh also encourages transitions between dogmatism and pragmatism. A fatwa draws from and reflects an approach to the essence of Islam and the priorities of contemporary Muslims and a specific understanding of fiqh concepts and mechanisms.

The more an approach is coherently internalized and applied, the more likely it is that those who hold it would issue similar fatwas. Where engagement with shari'a norms is not grounded in a structured ideology and methodology, and views echo personal sentiments and preferences assembled through non-hierarchical exposure to experts situated along a spectrum of approaches, the ability to simultaneously advance views that accord with conflicting approaches without being conscious of the conflict is greater.

Several examples follow. Somalia-born (1984) Hasan, a single man who found refuge in Iceland, was briefly introduced in the previous chapter expressing his view that mortgages could not be legitimized under any circumstances. At the time of the interview, he had not acquired a work permit and was yet to explore the local job market and establish contacts in the Icelandic society.

Hasan presented religious devotion as a struggle between temptation and abstention and offered unequivocal dogmatic opinions on most issues debated in *fiqh al-aqalliyyat al-Muslima* discourse. He argued that it was not permissible under any circumstances to work in a job that requires engaging in haram, adding that it was always possible to find another job; it was not permissible to congratulate a Christian on Christmas, as that would imply recognition of the false belief that Christ was the son of God; one must fast in accordance with the local time in Iceland – even if it is very difficult to do so, the reward, Paradise, is worth it. He also made clear that listening to music is strictly prohibited and that birthdays should not be celebrated.

Throughout the interview, Hasan highlighted the importance of following the letter of the Quran without applying human-made interpretations. He emphasized that all the answers a person needed were in the Quran, and that strictly observing religious norms paid off, no matter the difficulties, because Muslims who do so enter Heaven. The question of whether he ever changed his mind about a religio-legal issue sounded strange to him. Islam, he said, was not about opinions but about abiding by God's commands, which could not be understood in more than one way.

Hasan, who said he gained his knowledge about Islam in a madrasa in Somalia, never engaged with *fiqh al-aqalliyyat al-Muslima* literature. He was not familiar with the terms *wasati* or *salafi* and did not know al-Qaradawi, the European Council for Fatwa and Research, or any of the eminent *salafi* muftis or panels. Neither could he mention the name of any Somali mufti he trusted.

It appeared, however, that he was aware that polemics surround the issues about which he was asked. He became defensive when told that

168   Shari'a and Life

some Muslims would argue that he was a *mutashaddid*, a hardliner. He said that he had heard that term before, and its intention was to paint Muslims like him, who abide by the laws of their religion, as radicals and terrorists. He emphasized that while he would not like to change the rules of Iceland, the instructions of the Quran and the traditions apply universally.

Though dogmatic throughout, on one issue, Hasan presented an unequivocally pragmatic view. He said that he intended to stay in Iceland for good. Asked whether he did not consider that, being a refugee in Iceland, it would be his duty to migrate to a Muslim land when that became possible, he answered that Iceland was created by God as all other lands were. This being the case, it was a legitimate place of residence for Muslims, as all other lands were. The terminology Hasan invoked, obliterating any notional difference between Muslim and non-Muslim lands, was generous even in *wasati* terms.

There was a crucial difference between the issues Hasan was dogmatic about and the one issue on which he was pragmatic. Implying that his permanent presence in Iceland conflicted with shari'a norms would have gravely conflicted his sense of uncompromising devotion with his concrete, immediate plans to make a land he grew fond of his home. The one issue on which Hasan was creative and embraced change was the one that actually mattered to him.[36]

Earlier in the chapter we met 'Abdallah (b. 1995), the Syrian student raised in Dubai, who migrated to Sweden to pursue a university degree in architecture and took a loan that carried interest to finance his studies. He justified his decision by arguing that he was compelled to take the loan because otherwise, he could not build a future for himself. He also mentioned that he avoided engaging in *istifta'* on the matter because he feared the advice would be not to take the loan.

At a different point in the interview, we asked 'Abdallah what he thought of taking a mortgage in Europe if there were no alternative means to buy a home. Young 'Abdallah, who was never in a position to consider buying an apartment, made clear that he would not take one; taking mortgages was unequivocally prohibited under any circumstances, he said.[37] It seemed that the (potential) parallelism between the two situations did not occur to him; neither did he deduce from his general understanding of necessity that there can be situations – for example, fear of eviction – that would compel Muslims living in Europe to take a mortgage.

Yusuf, born in 1984, is a Pakistani who moved to Sweden for the first time in 2009 to pursue an MA degree in electrical engineering. He moved back to his homeland in 2012 and intended to complete his MA there, but then married and "and life got in the way."[38] Four years later, he returned to Sweden with his wife and finally completed his studies. He has a daughter, four years old at the time of the interview, and a son, two years younger.

Employed as an electrical engineer in a telecommunications company, Yusuf is yet to decide whether to settle down with his family in Sweden permanently. Alternatives considered were the United States, returning to Pakistan, or moving to another Muslim country, preferably in the Gulf, where, according to Yusuf, they would enjoy more of an Islamic atmosphere and where one's family is what matters most. Before arriving in Sweden for the first time, Yusuf heard rumors that concerned him about how Muslims were treated. He feared, for example, that he would have to shave his beard.

In Stockholm, Yusuf split his mosque attendance between The Stockholm Mosque, which is close to his workplace, and a Pakistani mosque in Märsta, a city suburb. He did not establish one primary authority to advise him on shari'a-related issues. He attended The Stockholm Mosque only because of its location and had never spoken to imam Khaled al-Dib, and he did not consider the imam at Märsta to be more than a *hafiz*. Thus, when uncertain about a religio-legal issue, he conferred either with members of Jama'at al-Tabligh at Märsta, online sources, or a friend with better knowledge in fiqh who had lived in Europe for a long time.

Asked about the legitimacy of mortgages, Yusuf, who had never considered buying a home, stated that interest-based loans were prohibited under any circumstances. He explained that even though it was challenging to find an apartment to rent in Stockholm, "Allah will provide."[39]

On other prohibitions that personally affected him, his views were pragmatic. Yusuf held that paying commercial insurance was haram (because it is a form of gambling). Still, to buy a car, he was required to breach the prohibition. Yusuf admitted that owning a car was not a necessity for him. He grounded his choice to pay the insurance in the Prophetic tradition (narrated by Sa'id al-Khudri) according to which, "Whoever sees an evil, let him change it with his hand; if he is not able to do so, then with his tongue; and if he is not able to do so, then with his heart – and that is the weakest of faith."[40] This *hadith*, which usually serves to legitimize inaction in the face of governmental transgressions, is not an obvious justification for engaging in an avoidable prohibited transaction. One way or another, if one applies this *hadith* to legitimize the suspension of one form of haram transaction that is not a necessity, then it should logically at least be considered applicable to other forms of haram transactions.

170   Shari'a and Life

Mixed-gender swimming is another issue on which Yusuf chose a lenient, matter-of-fact approach. He offered a mix of justifications, including that he needed to lose weight, that he made sure to lower his gaze, and that there were different levels of purity. Further, he admitted he would indeed be purer if he avoided swimming, but he had not reached that level of purity yet.[41]

Moroccan-born Radwan (b. 1965) moved to Iceland in 1990, where he joined his father. At the time, he remembered, there were only around 20 Muslims in the country. He first worked in the fishing industry, then in a restaurant, and ultimately became co-owner of a pizza place, while also volunteering in the mosque and becoming Chairman Karim 'Askari's second-in-command at what became the Grand Mosque. Shortly before our interview, he had returned from a visit to Norway, where he joined members of Jama'at al-Tabligh to learn how to engage in da'wa.

Radwan was strongly opposed to swimming in mixed-gender Icelandic pools. As noted earlier in the chapter, the two imams of the rival mosques in the city attend local swimming pools, while the imam of Radwan's mosque was apprehensive about this practice. Radwan said that he used to work as a lifeguard at swimming pools and beaches in Morocco. During his first years in Iceland, he attended local pools but stopped doing so in 1995 after he got married and became more religious so as to avoid *shaytan* (the devil). He explained that women in Icelandic pools are "almost naked," which results in temptation, and thus "when the faith increases, you stop going."[42] It appeared that Radwan did not greatly miss his swimming days.

On other issues, Radwan presented pragmatic opinions. On one, which particularly concerned him, he went beyond what the pragmatic end of the religio-legal spectrum allows. The restaurant he partly owned sold ham and alcohol. While *wasati* fatwas conditionally legitimized employment that required engaging with haram, they did not legitimize ownership that did the same.

Radwan justified his long-time engagement with pork and alcohol in his partially owned pizzeria through four arguments. (a) Having realized that there was no future for him in the fishing industry, he understood that the only way to provide for his family was to open a pizza place. The only way for the pizza place to be profitable in Iceland is to sell ham and alcohol. (b) In Morocco, too, there are restaurants that sell haram. (c) It is not possible to obtain halal meat in Iceland. (d) Through the sacrifices he makes by operating a haram restaurant, Muslims in Iceland will be able to enjoy a fully halal life in ten or twenty years.[43]

When we spoke, Radwan was in the process of leaving the pizzeria and assuming a full-time position as the manager of the hostel affiliated with the Grand Mosque (and located on its lower floor). When giving us a tour of the hostel, he demonstrated the integration-minded tendency of the administration by stating that bringing haram food onto the premises was permissible and that, as a matter of principle, the dormitories are mixed-gender.

Radwan's views on the permissible and prohibited in the workplace were easy prey for his rivals in other mosques. When we asked the founder and leader of Al-Nur Mosque, Salman Tamimi, a "dear friend" as Radwan described him, his opinion on engaging with haram, Tamimi endorsed the *wasati* view that it was legitimate to work in a place that sold such products only as long as the Muslim had no alternative and searched for an alternative halal job. Tamimi could not resist adding that it was not legitimate to own a pizza restaurant that sold haram products. This was a thinly veiled reference to Radwan. When asked about it, Tamimi was quick to say that, indeed, his comment was directed at Radwan's pizza place.[44] He added that the hostel run by Radwan permitted residents to bring in wine and allowed the mixing of genders. That the restaurant was not run in a proper Islamic way epitomized, for him, the hypocrisy of the leadership of the Grand Mosque, which is dogmatic about Ramadan fasting times, but not on other issues. Still, our interviews at the Grand Mosque revealed that Radwan's Islamic credentials had not been injured by his professional choices.

The Limited Implications of Dogmatism

Becoming *salafi* implies embracing an approach to Islam that prohibits certain fields of activity that others allow, narrows the options for adjustments that others open, and limits the space for interactions with non-Muslims that others encourage. The implications would seem particularly harsh in a non-Muslim environment. Because the ascendance of the *salafi* approach in Europe is a relatively new phenomenon, most *salafi*s adopted it rather than were raised on it. It is no wonder, then, that researchers of the *salafi* movement wondered why some Western Muslims, including second- and third-generation Muslims in Europe, chose to become *salafi* when "many (perhaps most) other groups require their adherents to make fewer sacrifices and take fewer risks."[45] Why be a *salafi* when you can be, say, a *wasati*, pragmatically oriented and integration inclined?

The answer calls for an evaluation of the benefits gained and the injuries incurred by affiliating with *salafiyya*. Interviewees at the Salafi Mosque suggested that the former are considerable. One benefit is clarity and unequivocalness grounded in a sense of authenticity. As other

172 Shari a and Life

studies on *salafiyya* found, our *salafi* interviewees were satisfied with what they understood as the evidence-based rigidity of the approach, which they contrasted with relaxed, cultural, folkloristic, localized, and other "non-authentic" manifestations of Islam on which they were raised.[46]

Another benefit is the constant challenge of personal moral and ritualist improvement. *Salafiyya* calls upon Muslims to perfect different aspects of their daily practices and rituals, including some which are relatively trivial. When met with success, the effort carries a sense of accomplishment.

Yet another benefit, which was more observable in the case of some interviewees than others, was the speedily-attained sense of elitism the self-congratulatory self-depiction of a "saved sect" infuses. As noted in the previous chapter, it was crucial for some *salafis* not only that we see them as good but also that we see them as *better*.

There are few more comforting and flattering notions than one's conviction that one was fortunate enough to have discovered and become a member of a tiny minority-within-minority that is exclusively destined for Heaven, whereas the rest would meet hellfire. Whereas affiliating with an elite community other than through birthright is usually a gruelling process, *salafi* interviewees' sense of belonging and elitism was acquired in a swift and almost effortless way. The teachings embraced, usually conveyed in a simple, straightforward manner, did not require them to engage with nuanced theological or religio-legal deliberations. On the contrary, they were asked to a priori reject the dense and intellectually demanding bookshelf of old and modern texts that are allegorical, contextual, and rational. Neither were they required, as will be explored below, to sever ties with family members and friends, commit financially to the group, or change their place of residence.

Studies on *salafiyya* in Europe described the embrace of this approach as a response to a crisis of identity. *Salafis* were depicted predominantly in two ways. One, as "former users of cannabis or alcohol or members of street gangs" who accepted Islam as "an answer to all of their life problems."[47] Another, as second- and third-generation migrants who, raised in the West and having limited contact with their homelands, were not comfortable with the hyphenated identities of their parents (e.g., "Moroccan-French" or "Turkish-German") and at the same time, felt they did not fully belong, or have been fully accepted, in their receiving societies.[48]

We did not find this necessarily to be the case. With few exceptions, our *salafi* interviewees did not experience a crisis of identity of any sort and did not actively seek to radically break from their past before becoming *salafi*. Rather, a coincidental acquaintance with a *salafi* person or text convinced them that they did not practice Islam correctly. Encouraged to learn more, they were impressed with the textual clarity of the approach, ready for the moral improvement it required, and, to some extent, flattered by the sense of elitism it allows, and thus affiliated with it. They did not experience *salafiyya* as a complete transformation but as a personal reformation.

The example of Fawaz (b. 1986) is illustrative. Married and the father of a ten-year-old daughter, he was born in England to parents who migrated from Pakistan. As a schoolkid, he went to a local, ethnically-Pakistani mosque on Fridays, fasted on Ramadan, and recited verses from the Quran, though without understanding their meaning. When he was sixteen, he became more curious about the meaning of life and decided to search beyond Islam. He read about Christianity but remembers being discouraged when noticing, so he said, that Christians do not worship God alone. He remained a Muslim and, for a decade, was satisfied with his knowledge and practices.

At the age of twenty-seven, Fawaz, who works as a mechanic, discovered *salafiyya*. He said that a Muslim co-worker in the garage where he used to be employed enlightened him about the errors in the ways Muslims practice Islam. The first issue brought to his attention was that it was wrong to touch the ears when praying, as the Sufis do. At that time, he did not even know that there was such a thing as *salafiyya*.

Fawaz was convinced that his way of praying was wrong because the co-worker pointed to evidence from the Quran and the traditions for everything he said. He joined his co-worker in praying at the Salafi Mosque, which is situated some fifteen kilometres from his home, and became a regular. At first (he recalled with a smile), he used to come to the mosque all the time and present imam Abu Khadeejah with queries about his practices. With time, the eagerness for self-improvement did not decline, but his self-confidence did, and when uncertain about something, he began to search for answers on the Mosque's website before approaching the imam.

Fawaz displayed an intense missionary zeal and elitist pride in the advantage of *salafiyya*. He noted a *hadith* according to which only one of a thousand Muslims would enter Heaven. Asked why he, with modest religious education and modest education in general, was able to see the truth that so many other Muslims (and the rest of humanity) were not able to see, he suggested that it was a blessing; that his heart was open; and that what matters is not how intellectually brilliant one is, or how many degrees one holds, but whether one is able to recognize the simple truth when it is presented. When asked to explain what the

174 Shari'a and Life

faults of the Muslim Brothers were, Fawaz emphasized their inclination to cooperate with anyone who can make them more influential, whereas loyalty to the truth, rather than popularity, is what should matter. It was evident that Fawaz did not have the tiniest doubt that he had come to possess the truth in its most clear and authentic expression and found much comfort in this conviction.[49]

So much about the benefits attained by choosing to be a *salafi*. Yet this choice also comes at a price. Several interviewees spoke about difficulties they faced with their partners and their parents (which, at the very least, required them to exercise much patience). Several mentioned cherished habits they gave up after becoming *salafi*. Giving up listening to music, which *salafi* fatwas strongly prohibit, and others, including those of *wasatis*, conditionally permit, was the most common concession mentioned. It was particularly painful for people who played an instrument or whose adolescence was defined in part by their love of music.

Yet while the costs of becoming *salafi* were measurable, interviews with attendees at the Salafi Mosque informed that they were significantly less profound than what could be inferred from a reading of *salafi* texts. With one exception, interviewees' embrace of *salafi* teachings did not result in serious, permanent injury to their material situation or interpersonal relations. Securing a good place in the afterlife did not involve giving up a comfortable existence in this life.

One reason for the limited impact is that while the *salafi* approach is dogmatic, *salafi*s occasionally apply, as other Muslims do, strategies that are external to *istifta'* to deal with practical challenges. Also, some shift between approaches, making pragmatic choices on crucial issues and invoking shari'a-grounded arguments that counter *salafi* dogmatism in their support. Thus, while they are less likely to find on the list of privileged *salafi* experts fiqh-oriented facilitations on conflicts between religious norms and pressures of everyday life, they do compromise.

We did not document *salafi*s who invoked the arguments that similar transgressions to those they commit are unavoidable in Muslim lands, or that the shari'a can only be applied in certain spheres of life. These two positions defy the core of *salafi* teaching, which stresses the duty of Muslims to abide by the divine Lawgiver wherever they are and take every one of God's laws seriously. Interviewees did, however, confess to consciously sinning occasionally and to transgressing in minimizing ways, although on issues non-*salafi*s would not even necessarily consider transgressions.

Recognition of consciously transgressing was contextualized within a broader sense of imperfection and a constant striving for improvement.

This was an admission we heard from almost all the interviewees of the Salafi Mosque. One said he could not resist occasionally watching the football team he roots for on television, although he knew he should avoid watching football (because the players are wearing shorts that are not modest). Another said he sometimes listened to music, although he knew it was prohibited. Some were more reluctant than others to detail any of their failings but admitted that they transgressed.

Anik (b. 1989) is single and works in homes for the mentally challenged. He left Bangladesh with his parents for Italy when he was 13, returned to his homeland, and settled in Italy at 17. In his mid-20s, he joined his father in Cologne, and, at 28, he moved to Birmingham, in no small part because he had heard about the Islamic environment in Small Heath and the multicultural, tolerant nature of British society.

Growing up in what he described as a very conservative family, Anik was confident he had a good grasp of what constitutes halal and haram. As a boy in Bangladesh, he was active in the Islamist Jamaat-e-Islami, and while in Italy, he was still active with the organization and also joined the Tablighis. Already in his teens, he came to believe that Bengali Islam was "mumbo-jumbo Islam," a mixing of religion and culture.

Anik attends the Salafi Mosque, which is across the corner from his home, but said it was important for him also to attend other mosques, as not committing to one mosque is a guarantee against being radicalized. Still, his views on religio-juristic issues were at the *salafi* dogmatic end of the spectrum. He said that when engaging in *istifta*ʾ, he favoured the fatwas of the Saudi Permanent Committee, which he usually finds on the website Islam Question and Answer. He heard that a fatwa was issued that legitimized mortgages but never bothered to read it because, in his opinion, there was no need to read a text that legitimized the haram to know it was wrong. "If you shop around, you will find anything," he lamented.[50]

Anik also strongly objected to interest-based student loans, explaining that if students could not afford tuition fees, they could always attend the Open University or move to a country with no tuition. He opposed Christmas greetings because, in his view, they implied recognition of the false claim that Christ was the son of God. He would not listen to music. He would never attend a mixed-gender swimming pool or swim during separate-gender hours where men do not comply with same-gender modesty norms. He held that no matter the circumstances, a Muslim must never engage with haram in his workplace.

While Anik was knowledgeable about and loyal to *salafi* dogmatism, he admitted that he was in the habit of doing "a lot of things which are haram."[51] He did not contextualize this confession in any mitigating

176   Shari'a and Life

way; rather, it implied that he recognized he had failed to be the exemplary Muslim he would wish to be and can only hope to repent and be forgiven. The example Anik was willing to provide for his transgressing was that he did not refrain from shaking the hands of women in his workplace.[52]

Handshakes with the opposite sex proved a sensitive issue and a major point of friction in the mosques surveyed. Some Europeans interpret avoidance of handshakes as a grave insult, an implication that women are impure and lesser beings.[53] Wissam, the young Libyan we introduced in the previous chapter, a *salafi* who prays at the *wasati*-oriented Stockholm Mosque, said, with pride, that he lost his last job at a restaurant owned by a Muslim lady on his very first day because he refused to shake her hand. He did not regret the cost of his insistence because of his conviction that God would reward those who follow the righteous path.[54]

The position of Khaled al-Dib, the imam of The Stockholm Mosque, is that handshakes could, possibly, be legitimized as serving a *maslaha*.[55] His rivals at the *salafi*-inclined Husby Mosque see this position as an example of The Stockholm Mosque's *Ikhwani*, politicized opinions. The Chairman of the Grand Mosque in Reykjavik, Karim 'Askari, invoked the opposition of the former imam and current rival, Ahmad Sadiq, to shake women's hands as an example of Sadiq's *salafi* inclination that caused the leadership of the mosque to sever ties with him.[56] Salman Tamimi, the founder of Al-Nur from which 'Askari split, directed the same allegation against 'Askari. He argued that 'Askari and his followers advanced opinions that impeded the prospects for Muslim integration and assertion of their presence in Iceland, noting opposition to shaking the hands of women as an example.[57]

Unlike Wissam in Stockholm, Birmingham-based Anik said he did not manage to avoid this cordial gesture at his workplace. He did not search for potential fiqh-oriented legitimizations of his practice. He explained this transgression as resulting from a personal weakness: "I don't want to do it [shake the hands of female colleagues], but I also don't want to explain why I don't want to do it."[58]

As in other mosques, *salafis* also invoked minimizing strategies to argue that while a choice they made did not fully accord with the normative ideal, the transgression involved was drastically moderated. Swimming is an example. Unlike in other mosques, without exception, interviewees at the Salafi Mosque said they would never swim in mixed-gender pools, no matter what. However, a few avid swimmers said they were content with swimming during men-only hours in pools that do not regulate same-sex modesty norms (i.e., where men expose the area between the navel and the knee before other men, including in the locker room).

One of them is Yemen-born Muhammad (b. 1985), married and the father of three, who justified swimming during male-only hours, where some do not abide by modesty codes, as a means to remain healthy. He emphasized that he made sure to lower his gaze to avoid "wicked thoughts." Muhammad said he and his friends used to advise Muslim swimmers who did not respect (their understanding of) same-gender modesty codes, but he stopped doing that because some responded aggressively.[59]

Salafi Mosque interviewees also found a way around the dogmatism of their approach by choosing leniency on certain issues. Because the mosque does not ask affiliates to abide by hierarchically-structured *ifta'* (and both ideologically and operationally does not encourage such obedience), embracing opinions that contradict the views of luminary *salafi* muftis and those of the leadership does not necessarily involve a notional conflict.

Ahmad (b. 1982) is married with children. His Bengali family migrated to Britain when he was eight. He used to work as a bus driver but was let go because he insisted on praying within the stipulated times. Then he became an Uber driver, enjoying the privilege of being his own boss.

Ahmad was aware that this job was also problematic because of its *potential* to involve assisting haram. As an Uber driver, he has the option to decide not to take rides to prohibited venues such as pubs. Still, if a passenger changed his destination during a ride, he would be forced to take him to the new destination of choice, wherever it may be (it had not yet happened at the time of the interview). The case is borderline, and if the imams at the mosque or *salafi* muftis were asked about it, they would have likely advised Ahmad to search for a job where he could not meet a situation of this kind. Ahmad avoided the dilemma by determining, for himself, that being an Uber driver was a form of *maslaha* because it involved less harm than any alternative, constituting a "lesser of two evils."[60]

Somali-born Muhammad (b. 1987) is a lorry driver. His family migrated to the Netherlands when he was a child, with refugee status. In 2004, he left for Small Heath after becoming acquainted with *salafi* ideology. Several of his colleagues transfer haram meat and are also required to carry it into supermarkets. Because, at the time of the interview, he had always had the choice of which products to deliver, he never found himself assisting haram. Yet, siding with the *wasati* opinion on haram in the workplace, he was confident that if this were to be the case, it would still be legitimate for him to maintain his job. He said

178 Shari'a and Life

he had once heard a mufti or read a fatwa (he could not remember which of the two and by whom) from which he learned that if he were required to handle haram, he would not have to resign as long as he searched for an alternative job.[61]

Along with occasionally acting through different strategies of engagement externally to what *salafi* fatwas dictate, *salafi* dogmatism also appeared to impact interviewees' lives minimally because several uncompromising opinions on issues debated in *fiqh al-aqalliyyat al-Muslima* discourse turned out to be inconsequential for their actual, practical realities. They chose dogmatic over pragmatic opinions, but were not personally affected by those choices. The job market, and the *salafi* prohibition of workplaces that engage in haram or do not allow fully abiding by religious norms, are one example. Only three attendees of the Salafi Mosque shared experiences of losing jobs or job opportunities because of their beliefs. In contrast, the others made clear that their convictions never harmed them financially. The above-mentioned driver, Ahmad, is one. Another interviewee gave up prospective ownership of a family-owned café that sold alcohol, while another quit his job in a British bank after learning that it was impermissible to work in a place that engages in usury (he became a social worker).

Seeing the scope, passion, and thoroughness of *salafi ifta'* on Christmas greetings, one can get the impression that it tops the list of concerns of Muslims in Europe. Table 3.4 informed that the vast majority of attendees at Birmingham's Salafi Mosque conform to the *salafi* view on the matter and oppose Christmas greetings. Interviewees at the mosque were unanimous in their opposition to the salutations. They cited arguments prevalent in *salafi* discourse, predominantly that Christmas greetings constitute an assertion of falsehood.

Still, not a single interviewee recalled that avoiding cordial seasonal phrases resulted in dismissal, reprimand, or even inconvenience. There are several reasons why this was the case. First, it is not likely that a person who knows that the acquaintance before him is a Muslim would offer a seasonal Christmas greeting that calls for a mutual greeting in return. Thus, to start with, avoiding the gesture can become an "issue" only in interpersonal relationships where the Christian party has a reason to expect a greeting initiated on the part of the Muslim.

Second, while non-Muslims are hardly aware of the specific *salafi* position on Christmas greetings, they are not necessarily offended by explanations on the matter. Muhammad works in a café in Birmingham. Born in 1991 in England to Pakistani parents, married and the father of three, he discovered *salafiyya* four and a half years before the interview. Muhammad said he used to offer Christmas greetings to colleagues, but having learned that it was haram because it equated to accepting the false notion that Christ was God's son, he stopped doing so. No harm was caused: he explained his position to his boss, and his boss accepted it.[62]

Salafi fatwas on Christmas greetings can, in fact, be read in a way that does not entirely close the door to cordial conduct during the holiday season. While they prohibit any greeting involving explicit religious connotations, they can be understood as allowing statements such as "have a nice holiday." As Abu Khadeejah and Abu Hakim of the Salafi Mosque explained, this phrase constitutes no more than recognition of a vacation from work.[63] We heard similar legitimizations of generic holiday greetings from several other *salafi* leaders, including Stockholm's Ibn Abbas Center's Johannes Klominek, who said that wishing a nice holiday, which is anyhow the norm in Sweden, is a good way of avoiding being rude to non-Muslims.[64] Nasir al-'Isa, imam of the largest *salafi* mosque in Germany, Berlin's Al-Nur Mosque, said it was permissible to say "to you as well" to a Christian who wishes a nice holiday to a Muslim on the occasion of Christmas.[65]

On the Christmas-related issue that matters most, the permissibility of accepting a Christmas bonus, the opinion taught at the Salafi Mosque is seemingly harsh, but in practice, pragmatic. According to Abu Khadeejah, it is impermissible to accept a bonus described as a Christmas gift, but it is permissible to accept a bonus related to increased business activity during the holiday period.[66] 'Abdallah, the convert and dedicated volunteer briefly mentioned in chapter 2, summed it up as follows: "I've never been offered one [Christmas bonus], but I wouldn't accept it. [However] if you wanted to give me [the bonus] in January, not related to Christmas, then I'd take it."[67]

All the interviewees at the Salafi Mosque dismissed the notion that mortgages could be legitimized under any circumstances. Not one of them could conceive of committing the grave sin of taking a usurious loan and then hope for God's forgiveness. However, this position bore no practical implications on any of the interviewees, either because they were too poor to have the capital sum needed to be eligible for a mortgage, too young to consider buying an apartment, or uncertain that they would remain in England in the near future (or all of the above).

In the case of two interviewees, accepting the dogmatic opinion regarding mortgages was inconsequential (at least in this life) for another reason: they already took one before they embraced *salafiyya*. When a person committed the haram act of taking a usurious loan and only later discovered he sinned, *salafi* muftis call to repent and pay off the loan as early as possible. However, they do not ask the transgressor

180 Shari`a and Life

to sell or demolish the apartment. This was the experience of the aforementioned Fawaz, who took a mortgage when he got married because
"some people" told him it was acceptable to do so. When he learned
about his grave error, he decided on the advice of Abu Khadeejah to pay
off the loan sooner than the stipulated time. He intended to then sell the
house and buy a new one without taking a loan.[68]

Table 3.4 informed that the vast majority of attendees shared the
Salafi Mosque's leadership's de-facto opposition to electoral participation. Interviewees at the mosque explained that democracy and Islam
are inherently incompatible and spoke of their distrust in "the system."
For example, the aforementioned `Abdallah, one of the most dedicated
volunteers at the mosque, said: "I don't vote because it's a democracy
and I don't deal with democracy. It's un-Islamic; it's not from Islam."[69]

For a small religious community such as the Salafi Mosque that faces
multiple attacks, including by other *salafis*, political participation would
seem, in theory, crucial in order to gain the friendly ears of the member
of parliament representing their constituency and those of their local
councillors. In practical terms, however, *salafi* votes would hardly make
a difference. The Labour Party enjoys one of its safest national margins
in the constituency to which Small Heath belongs, and that majority is
also reflected when electing Small Heath's two local councillors. Even if
all the attendees of the Salafi Mosque voted, and all voted for the same
political party, their votes would most likely not provide them with
leverage and influence in local or national politics.

Another reason for the mitigated effect of *salafi* ideology on the daily
lives of attendees is that affiliates of the mosque and their families are
not segregated from other Muslims and non-Muslims as *salafi* texts
imply they should be. The Salafi Mosque projects an enclave mentality
without actually maintaining an enclave, partly due to its slow infrastructural development, but also for other reasons.

Douglas introduced the "enclave" in her typology of the ways social
groups remain together to describe communities that choose to disen-
gage from mainstream society. Lacking the coercive authorities of the
state and in the face of an outside world rich with potential material
rewards, these groups struggle to prevent defections by asserting their
ideological superiority and the spiritual gains that await members.
They nurture notions of "us" against "them" and embed the image of
the outside world as corrupting and evil.[70]

Scholars invoked the typology to make comparative sense of the rise
of anti-modernist, literalist-leaning religious groups and explore the
structures and institutions that make the endurance of the social order
tied with their ideologies possible. One example is ultra-Orthodox Jews,

who, like the *salafis*, manage to thrive in modern society. The structures and institutions that maintain the separation between their communities and the outside world include: the concentration of the faithful in specific areas in a way that minimizes their contact with people of other persuasions; the social expectation that the faithful adhere to norms stipulated by specific authorities; dress codes, terminologies, and physical gestures that distinguish members of the enclave from others; mouthpieces that strictly accord with the norms of the enclave and delegitimize other ideologies, and the exclusion of media that speak for the outside world; arranged marriages between members; the facilitation of social spheres that encourage exclusive in-group socialization; and the establishment of heterogeneous educational institutions in which articulations of moral superiority assert the loyalty of the next generation and its rejection of the outer world.[71]

Salafi ideology involves an "us" against "them" rejection of liberal values and modern practices, calls upon Muslims to distance from non-Muslims ("loyalty and disavowal"), and condemns all Muslims who are non-*salafi*. However, in practice, rather than theory, the Salafi Mosque's community is far more flexible and permeable compared to ultra-Orthodox communities one finds in Jerusalem or Brooklyn. There are psychological – but not physical – walls that separate *salafis* from non-Muslims and non-*salafis*, and even these are not as strict as what *salafi* texts advise.

Affiliates of the mosque are not required to pay membership fees or donate a frequent sum of their income, although small donations are welcomed. They are not centred in one neighbourhood, let alone one compound. The leadership provides limited space for in-group socialization. The mosque offers few activities, all of which are strictly in the realm of learning and proselytizing. It does not operate many of the same institutions that encourage in-group socialization seen in some other large mosques, such as a grocery store, sports teams, a gym, a barbershop, a cafeteria, or a library. The bookstore, while spacious, does not have a table or sofas that enable visitors to sit and study together. The layout of the mosque's exterior, which does not have a large yard or a cafeteria, makes it difficult for attendees to sit together and have friendly conversations before or after the prayer, as is customary in some large mosques. None of our interviewees said that his social life revolved around bonds established in the mosque.

Segregated education is the key for groups that desire to shelter their community from external influences. Since 2002, the Salafi Mosque has operated the Salafi Independent School, a primary school for children aged four to eleven with a capacity of around 150 pupils. The annual

182   Shari'a and Life

fee is GBP 2,640, beyond the means of some parents, though the school awards scholarships to needy families. The demand is higher than the school's capacity, a situation the mosque's leaders have recognized, but which they have not amended and are not in the process of amending. Homeschooling is the alternative encouraged, but not all parents have the time, or the academic skills, to pursue that option. The mosque does not operate a secondary school. Abu Khadeejah acknowledged that a majority of parents who attend the mosque send their children to state schools.[72]

Several attendees legitimized their children's education in British state schools by alluding to *maslaha*. The aforementioned Fawaz had a ten-year-old daughter who attends a state primary school. He explained that there was no room for the daughter at the Salafi School, homeschooling was not an option because he was busy at work and his Pakistani-born wife does not have a good command of English, and sending the daughter to a non-*salafi* Islamic school was not an option because those schools do not follow the ways of the *salaf*. He compared sending his child to a secular school, where gym classes are mixed, among other evils, to being photographed when issuing a passport: a transgression legitimized based on necessity because the state imposes it.[73]

Other *salafi*s stated that they were not overly concerned about the implications of secular education. 'Abdallah, the aforementioned dedicated volunteer at the mosque, went so far as to suggest that his six- and eleven-year-old sons were better off in the state school than in the *salafi* one: "I want them to experience life and make choices of their own, but I give them the education that they need with regards to belief."[74] He said he allowed his younger son to watch cartoons with friends, but he would not join him because these programs involve "sorcery and magic."[75]

The previously mentioned Somalia-born Muhammad sent his children to state schools because he could not afford the tuition at the Salafi School. Shortly before the interview, he was alarmed when he learned that teachers use dolls to explain the body's private parts to first graders. Still, he remained confident that his children's religiosity would not be harmed because of his own childhood experiences in the Netherlands, where he participated in sex education and mixed-gender swimming classes, yet ended up a faithful Muslim.[76]

While the mosque's leadership is ideologically intolerant to other views, it is tolerant of the presence of non-Muslims and non-*salafi*s on its premises. As noted in the previous chapter, among the attendees, there is a considerable population of Muslims who are not *salafi* or who are *salafi* yet hostile to the leadership. The volunteer security guards will not allow the independent circulation of leaflets on the mosque's grounds or the deliberate propagation of what they deem false ideas. Other than that, the mosque attaches no conditions for entering it or participating in any of its activities. Anyone, including Muslims whose rituals during prayer contradict those applied by *salafis*, is welcome to join. So are non-Muslims. The aforementioned ʿAbdallah gave us an example of the tolerance applied: "A man was praying next to me once, and I was trying to advise him about joining the feet together, and he just stood there like this and prayed differently, so afterward I advised him, but he's kept doing it, and that's why I dislike praying next to him. I disliked it – I didn't ban him. So, when he came and stood next to me once [again], I moved to the other side because I wanted to pray like the Prophet prayed."[77] The aggressive manner in which we were approached, on three different occasions, by one of the volunteers reveals that not everyone is happy with the leadership's open-door policy. Soon enough, we learned, however, that the leadership is determined to maintain that policy.

While the leaders of the mosque do not facilitate interfaith encounters, they accept that socializing with non-Muslims is part of the reality of life in Birmingham. Abu Khadeejah made clear in two separate interviews that he was not opposed to Muslim and non-Muslim children being friends or to interfaith friendships in general. He did not consider this an opinion in which he adjusted fatwas in light of local realities because of his insistence that one strict criterion is preserved:

> Yes, of course [my child can have non-Muslim friends]. The issue of engaging with non-Muslims, whether it be Christians, Hindu, whatever, sitting with them, talking with them, even having a joke with them, you know – we've had a conversation, you're not Muslim, right? (Laughing) Well, this type of engagement that we have, even if we go for a meal, even if we go for a coffee, there is no problem with it whatsoever. Not for myself, not for my children … The line is drawn when my *mahabba* for [the non-Muslim], my love or allegiance for him, is greater than for my religion. How do I know if I crossed that line? [If] I will disobey Allah for my friendship and for my allegiance [with the non-Muslim].[78]

The disparity between the ideological fervour of Salafi Publications and the low-intensity of its in-group activities and infrastructural development that limits its ability to shelter affiliates from the outside non-*salafi* world is a consequence of the group's ideological priorities and financial constraints. The *salafis'* agenda encourages the neglect of worldly matters. We learned that it was easier to engage attendees in

184 Shari'a and Life

discussions on certain Prophetic traditions than on pressing everyday life issues. Their ambition to shine as forerunners (*sabiqun*), exemplary Muslims who dedicate every moment of their lives to pleasing God, discourages indulgence in forms of leisure activities, even if regulated by the mosque and according to strict *salafi* criteria.

In any case, even if the leadership was interested in promoting more group activities, a lack of financial resources limits its ability to do so. The same problem constrained the infrastructural development of the mosque, including the expansion of schooling. Abu Khadeejah told us that he and his colleagues never appealed intensely with the Saudi government or Saudi donors for support, but was not clear why they did not.

The gap between the "us" against "them" preaching, and the laxity practiced at the gates and beyond them, is explained by several factors. While the Salafi Mosque is home to one of the oldest *salafi* communities in Europe, it is still in the early stages of its existence. Its first generation comprises people who voluntarily forsook other affiliations and joined *salafiyya* and, thus, is less likely to find the "outside world" appealing. Due to the relatively young age of affiliates, the second generation mainly comprises primary school children who have yet to reach their (potentially) rebellious phase of life. Another factor is the public benefits of transparency. No policy is more effective for a group whose premises are suspected by some in the media as breeding grounds for extremism and intolerance than to open its gates to anyone who wishes to visit.

Yet another reason is that some members of the mosque actively engage in proselytizing among non-Muslims and Muslims alike. The community's prospects for recruiting new members (and being competitive with other *salafi* mosques) require that its gates remain open to all who wish to enter and that affiliates will not shelter from the outer world. That also explains why those who wish to attend lectures or seminars do not have to pay a fee to do so – a gesture much appreciated by some attendees with whom we spoke.

Chapter Five

A Mission with Few Missionaries

The first to offer the transformation of migrants into a missionary force was the Egyptian Muhammad al-Ghazali. In 1984 he authored a book after several years of Saudi-sponsored visits to Muslim communities in Europe, *Islam beyond Its Boundaries: How to Think about It?* Despite his expulsion from the Muslim Brothers in 1953, al-Ghazali became one of the leading and most prolific voices of mainstream Islamism in the second half of the 20th century and an inspiration and helpful source for al-Qaradawi's crystallization of *wasatiyya*. His life project was to revive Islam as an all-encompassing way of life, an alternative to doubt-based, secular societies.

During his visit to France, al-Ghazali recognized something that was far from evident in the 1960s and early 1970s: millions of Muslim migrants were there to stay. He was impressed with the number of converts to Islam he witnessed.[1] Still, he viewed with grave concern how some among the second generation, devoid of religious education at school and living in an environment with few public expressions of Islam, were drifting away from their religion and assimilating.

There was something more significant that concerned him. The massive voluntary settlement of Muslims in societies with Christian pasts and secularizing presents conflicted with his strong belief that the future was for Islam, not for the West. Al-Ghazali, who was convinced that secular societies, despite their achievements, were hopeless, had to reconcile the cognitive dissonance. The choice, by millions of Muslims, of the West as their permanent home had to fit somehow the notion that God promised Islam an ultimate victory, and that victory is soon to come.

Al-Ghazali could have responded in different ways. He could have urged migrants to return to the Abodes of Islam. Such a call would have most likely fallen on deaf ears, and he knew it. He could have

186   Shari'a and Life

ignored what he saw. Such silence would border on indifference to the fate of millions of migrants. He could have reflected on the historical reasons why so many Muslims chose to live in the West. Such soul searching could raise some inconvenient observations, as well as political complications.

Instead, al-Ghazali presented a twofold vision. It was introduced almost in passing and not grounded in religio-legal terms. He argued that Muslims should live in the West as if they had never left their homelands. They should have schools where their children can learn their religion, traditions, and language, as well as clubs with a proper Islamic atmosphere that would encourage the marriage of Muslim men to Muslim women rather than their falling to temptations. He also emphasized that Muslims who cannot protect their and their families' religious identity must return to their homelands. He urged Muslim governments and peoples to contribute to developing Islamic textures of life in the West, and suggested that if they were to develop, not only would Muslim migrants maintain their religiosity, but they would also be pioneers in spreading their religion.[2]

In the following two decades, as a distinct religio-legal discourse dealing with the challenges of living in non-Muslim countries emerged, al-Ghazali's early contemplations were developed and systemized in fatwas and treatises. Muslims living in the West or planning to migrate there were informed about the religio-legal criteria for doing so.

As explored in chapter 1, contributors to *fiqh al-aqalliyyat al-Muslima* discourse agreed that living in Western societies involved grave risks. Still, there were few dissenting voices to the notion that living in the West could be legitimized if religious identity was strictly preserved and shari'a-grounded objectives were advanced. Foremost among these legitimizing objectives was proselytizing among non-Muslims. *Wasati* fatwas went so far as to reflect positively on a Muslim presence in the West as a means of spreading Islam, explicitly tasking all Western Muslims with proselytizing and considering *da'wa* a reason for granting facilitations. *Salafis*, who emphasized the undesirability of living among the infidels, nevertheless left proselytizing as an almost exclusive justification for residing in the West.

The ideal presented in fatwas and treatises that conditionally legitimized migration to and residence in the West was that of a devout Muslim migrant whose practices are regulated strictly by the criteria of shari'a, whose family's religious identity is sheltered, and who helps lead the Islamizing of Christian, secularized lands. The narrative about the potential – and the importance – of that Muslim transformed danger into opportunity, and individuals who sought financial improvement into members of a religious vanguard. It reinterpreted Islamic histories and myths to address an unprecedented phenomenon in ways that were simultaneously pragmatically adjusting and consistent with the core belief in a universal religion destined to prevail.

It was not a coincidence that *wasatis* were the most prolific, systematic, and explicit in advancing these prospects, both in broad theorizing about the legitimacy and meaning of migration and in fatwas that discussed the importance of spreading Islam. The art of transforming unmatched Western advancements into proof for the inevitable superiority and triumph of Islam as part of a call for the conditional integration of those advancements into Muslim societies was one they mastered and one that had underscored their intellectual project for decades. The emphasis on proselytizing corresponded with their rich literature anticipating the downfall of the morally declining West and the ascendance of Islam.[3] By elevating the spread of Islam to a primary objective of the divine Lawgiver, they were able to offer a particularly radical synthesis: issue groundbreaking pragmatic fatwas that facilitate integration into European societies, such as the conditional legitimization of mortgages, in religiously triumphant terms.

That *salafis* articulated similar notions, even if in much narrower and reluctant terms, suggests that they, too, realized that permanent Muslim presence in the West is an irreversible phenomenon and thus it would be better to defend the migrants' religious identity and utilize them in the service of Islam than to alienate them. The influence Islamists established in the Muslim World League and other Saudi-based and -financed, globally-oriented Islamic institutions contributed to the prevalence of pragmatism on this issue.

The premise that permanent Muslim residence in the West is legitimate was essential to institutionalizing Islamic life in Europe. Muslim governments, religious foundations, and private donors, especially Saudi-affiliated, would have found it more difficult, if not impossible, to offer financial support and foster contacts with European Muslim communities if the religio-legal discourse had established that the existence of those communities was illegitimate. Graduates of Islamic universities would have found it equally difficult to assume positions in mosques in Europe if that had been the case. In itself, the development of a religio-legal discourse dedicated to the challenges arising from migration would not have been possible if that discourse had not contained the foundation that living in the West was conditionally legitimate.

The promise to European Muslims was profound. The "missionary migrant" concept suggested that whatever challenges and frustrations they faced in their receiving societies were merely obstacles in their path

188   Shari'a and Life

to fulfilling a sublime task – leading Islam to its ultimate and promised victory. It elevated them to potential world-changers, the lauded poor who will inherit the earth if only they guard their religiosity and share it with others. Max Frisch critically commented about the European treatment of migrants: "We wanted a labor force, but human beings came."[4] Contributors to *fiqh al-aqalliyyat al-Muslima* discourse offered those human beings a new way of interpreting their minority status: if they engaged in some form of proselytizing, their presence in Europe would become a service to their religion and humanity.

In the more than three decades that followed, much has changed since the legitimizing fatwas began to surface and the "missionary migrant" concept crystalized. The Islamic infrastructure across the continent developed rapidly. Thousands of mosques, fully packed during Friday congregational prayers, indicated that living in a non-Muslim country did not erode religious sentiments for many. Some first-generation migrants from Muslim countries had already become grandparents to a third generation born on European soil; the temporariness of their and their family's residence became a forgotten memory. On the other hand, anti-multicultural and anti-Islamic sentiments have also been on the rise in European societies, restricting the observance of certain religious norms, causing unease about the practice of others, and raising doubts about whether European majorities had truly accepted Islamic identity as a legitimate part of European existence.

This chapter examines the impact, across the spectrum of mosques studied, of the most socially and politically charged option offered in *fiqh al-aqalliyyat al-Muslima* discourse. What do imams and mosque attendees know about the notion that their presence in Europe needs to meet certain shari'a-grounded criteria? How does it factor in constructing their identity and practices? How many of them became "missionary migrants"? And of those who did, how many assuaged any concerns they may have had regarding the permissibility of their presence in Europe through proselytizing efforts?

The chapter argues that the impact has been minimal. It exposes profound differences between what the foundational texts of *fiqh al-aqalliyyat al-Muslima* required of Muslims living in the West and the realities of imams and mosque attendees interviewed. Those foundational texts have received meagre attention and have had a meagre influence on decisions and practices.

With one exception, imams interviewed across the spectrum of mosques studied related to the discussion about the permissibility of permanent Muslim residence in the West as archaic and distanced themselves from the notion that Muslims in majority non-Muslim societies should act as missionaries. Their position was encouraged by concerns about the political explosiveness of the issue. It was also encouraged by their growing accustomed to seeing their communities as a normal phenomenon, their recognition that living in Muslim lands is no longer advantageous for Muslims compared to life in the West, and their judgment that only those thoroughly trained to do so can proselytize effectively.

A majority of the attendees interviewed across the spectrum of mosques studied, who settled in Europe from the early 1970s to as late as 2018, never inquired about the legitimacy of migration to or permanent residence in the West. The rich literature on the subject did not reach them. Some were surprised to learn that such literature exists at all. This was also the case of interviewees who were highly opinionated and very passionate and articulate about their religiosity. Only a handful of interviewees engaged in *istifta'* on the matter. Broaching the issue with them demonstrated yet again that the existential (and what is more existential than deciding where to live?) is rarely determined by a hierarchic process of submitting a query and receiving advice. Their inquiries awarded them, immediately or ultimately, with arguments that corresponded with and supported their original needs and wishes, which saw them living on European soil.

The idea that migrants should act as missionaries – and in so doing, legitimize their presence in the West – was rejected by most of the interviewees whom we introduced to it. Those who did not see anything problematic in the Muslim presence in Europe defied the idea that, as a minority, they have any particular duty, and were wary of the potentially grave political and social implications of open missionary zeal and activism. On the other hand, some of those who did see something problematic about living in the West denied that missionary work could amend it. Both were highly sceptical that Muslims who are not academically trained in that field can efficiently spread the word of Islam; they considered the "missionary migrant" an idea that sounds theoretically appealing but detached from European realities.

A few interviewees did relish the thought that they were tasked with a sacred mission, and found in it a justification for their continued presence in the West and reassurance of their loyalty to Islam, although they could not ascribe it to a specific mufti or fatwa. Yet, only one of them actualized, rather than merely embraced, the terms of the "missionary migrant." Ironically, those who accepted that proselytizing legitimized living in Europe did not necessarily engage in active *da'wa*. Where we found organized *da'wa* to exist, it was not primarily motivated by a need for religio-legal legitimacy.

The Blurring of the Abodes

Imams interviewed across the spectrum of mosques surveyed, including several *salafi*-inclined, distanced themselves from the idea that permanent Muslim presence in the West is legitimate only if specific shari'a-grounded criteria are met and that the primary legitimization for Muslim migration to the West is proselytizing. Instead, they suggested that living in the West was equally permissible as is living in Muslim lands and stated that members of their communities who did not have the relevant expertise should not engage in *da'wa*. The imams appeared to be familiar, albeit not extensively, with *fiqh al-aqalliyyat al-Muslima* discourse about the permissibility of living in non-Muslim lands. They invoked arguments introduced in the discourse, for example, that the world had become a global village or that today, Muslims are safe in non-Muslim countries. However, they did so without the requirements for caution and duty that fatwas and treatises in *fiqh al-aqalliyyat al-Muslima* discourse emphasized.

It was evident that the imams' positions were, in some part, politically motivated. Our inquiries were interpreted as ill-intentioned attempts at depicting them and their communities in a negative light, implying that their civil commitment was ambivalent and their hidden agenda was to convert as many Christians as possible. The spectre of the "Islamization debate" hovered; they knew well what the public implications could be of echoing the missionary, triumphal statements with which *fiqh al-aqalliyyat al-Muslima* literature is dense.

Yet there were other motivations. Our impression was also that the imams felt that discussing the terms of permanent Muslim presence in Europe was anachronistic. They related to the topic as a relic from a distant, formative past when massive voluntary Muslim migration was a confusing new phenomenon conceptualized apologetically from afar in utopian religio-legal terms. In their eyes, those conceptualizations were detached from the reality that developed, in which a second and third generation of Muslims was born on European soil, citizenship was acquired, and Islamic life flourished in greater freedom than what their homelands allowed. It seemed that the imams were not often approached by attendees of their mosques with queries about the conditions for living in the West, an impression which interviews with attendees, as will be elaborated below, substantiated. Therefore, those imams were not encouraged to crystalize their thoughts on these matters in a systematic fashion.

The imams also made it clear that they regarded the notion that *every* Muslim should actively proselytize as ludicrous wishful thinking, implying that their first-hand knowledge of the field (as opposed to agendas introduced from afar) advised them that only a skilled elite should be involved in presenting Islam to non-Muslims. The exception to this was the late Salman Tamimi, the pragmatic-inclined founder and imam of Al-Nur Mosque in Reykjavik. The occasion was his Friday sermon, which he delivered in Arabic and translated into English, shortly after an interview in which we discussed his integration-minded approach, and with him knowing we were in attendance. He preached that it was the duty of Muslims to teach Islam to Muslims who were weak in faith, as well as to non-Muslims, so that they escape hellfire, and added that no human being would like to end up in Hell – not the Muslim, not the Christian, not the Jew, not the Buddhist.[5]

The notional obliteration by several imams of the classic religio-juristic differentiation between Muslim and non-Muslim lands, based on the notion that the former are not properly Islamic and the latter allow religious freedom, was original and digressed even from the broadest legitimizations by *wasatis*. Al-Qaradawi, al-ʿAlwani, and others went so far as to suggest that given the global leadership of the West and the duty to proselytize there, migration was not only legitimate but should be encouraged. Still, in laying the foundations to their approach to *wasati fiqh al-aqalliyyat al-Muslima*, even those *wasati* muftis held that it was easier for Muslims to preserve their religious identity and adhere to shariʿa norms in majority Muslim lands and that, ideally, Muslims should reside there. They tied their legitimization to specific, even if almost all-inclusive, shariʿa-grounded criteria and maintained the view that majority Muslim and majority non-Muslim lands are two distinct categories, even when rejecting the notion that the latter constituted Abodes of War.

Ironically, the premise that Muslim countries are not Islamic, to the point that eradicates the conceptual and practical distinction between them and non-Muslim countries, was a foundation of Islamist-jihadi excommunicating groups associated with the legacy of Sayyid Qutb. The imams who pointed to the dire situation of Muslim lands eliminated the distinction between the two abodes to make the opposite argument: Not that Muslims should be equally at war with all the political regimes on earth, but that they may be equally at peace with them.

In part, these positions are explained by the sense of normalcy the imams' religious identity acquired. Unlike the muftis who laid the foundations for *fiqh al-aqalliyyat al-Muslima* in the 1980s and 1990s, they no longer feared that Muslim presence in the West would result in complete assimilation and the loss of the next generation to secularism. While critical of some aspects of their societies and aware of the challenges living in the West poses, they projected a sense of confident belonging and took pride in the development of their communities.

Tragic events in the second decade of the twenty-first century, including the deterioration of the Arab Spring uprisings into bloody civil wars or authoritarianism, the rise of ISIS, and the dire situation in Somalia and Afghanistan (to note just a few), have given the imams reasons to be suspicious of the idea that it is, in principle, better for Muslims to live in Muslim lands. Moreover, the influx of Muslim refugees to Europe during this recent period of unrest exposed an inconvenient truth: rich Muslim countries are less understanding and less hospitable to their desperate fellow Muslim brothers than rich European countries are. This discovery caused resentment and alienation and discredited notions of the Abode of Islam as an actual entity and a universal Islamic fraternity as a meaningful concept. In practical terms, it transformed the West from an option for the desperate to the *only* option.

The sentiment that denied the relevancy of conditioning permanent residence in the West and of the concept of the "missionary migrant" was not expressed by imams in equally engaging terms. In the case of some, our questions started an elaborate, dialectic exchange. Others impatiently dismissed our attempts to take the interview in that direction.

Sweden-born convert Johannes Klominek, one of the leaders of the *salafi* Ibn Abbas Center in Stockholm, addressed the legitimacy of migration and the duty to proselytize in a way that demonstrated his independent thinking and his critical contextualization – in light of Swedish realities – of fatwas issued by distinguished *salafi* authorities. Klominek accepted that, in *some* sense, it *might* be better for Muslims to live in Muslim countries. In a Muslim country, it would be easier to raise children according to Islamic norms and avoid employment that engages with haram. However, while it *might* be better to live in a Muslim country, this does not imply that it is prohibited or not desired to live in a non-Muslim one.

Klominek offered two explanations for this position. First, the *Maliki* fatwas that called on Muslims to move from Christian-occupied lands to Muslim lands were issued at a time when Muslims were tortured and persecuted by Christian regimes, following the Reconquista. The situation in present-day Europe is very different (shortly before the interview, he had returned from a visit with his father to Spain, where he had learned about that period). Second, "not many Muslim countries are really Muslim," and Sweden allows greater religious freedom than they do. To demonstrate his point, he spoke about a Tunisian friend who described how the Tunisian police arrested him and his friends after they completed their *fajr* prayer because the police assumed that anyone who woke up so early to pray was radical. In addition, he noted that while Muslim soldiers serving in the Syrian army were not allowed to pray, Muslims serving in the Swedish army had that option.

The most effective *salafi* missionary in Sweden dismissed the notion that Muslims in Europe should engage in proselytizing:

> [To] say to [Muslim] people here in Sweden that they should go preach, I think it is ridiculous because not everybody is a preacher. Any organization that has everybody preaching is not good. You can preach with your good deeds ... you can show a good picture of Islam. A lot of people have a distorted picture of Islam, so [Muslims] can show with deeds and actions that Islam is not violent and all of this terrorism thing. That's good. If you call this preaching, then it is preaching. But [the notion that] everybody should preach and speak and [distribute] pamphlets – no. [Proselytizing] is not a condition for a person to be here [in Sweden], and I think it would be ridiculous to say [that it is], to make all of the one million or 700,000 to 800,000 people with Muslim background in Sweden preachers.[6]

Asked to explain the discrepancy between his views and the emphasis placed in fatwas on proselytizing as a main legitimization for residence in the West, Klominek explained those fatwas were attempts to treat a situation that several decades ago was new and unprecedented to muftis. He argued that notions that seem very logical at a particular time look different in hindsight, giving the example of a politician who, when the internet started to evolve, said the innovative technology would wear itself out after several years.

The leadership of Stockholm's *salafi*-inclined Husby Mosque addressed the legitimacy of migration and the duty of proselytizing in similar terms. As the interview with imam Muhammad al-Makkawi and his colleagues at the mosque's *da 'wa* board developed, their anger with what they interpreted as the hypocrisy of Swedish liberalism became increasingly evident. Al-Makkawi complained about policies such as prohibiting young girls from wearing a headscarf in schools, even if those girls desire to do so. One of his colleagues intervened and said that children should do what their parents tell them until the age of 18, so whether the girls desire to wear the headscarf or not is irrelevant. The two described Swedish society as rapidly becoming more promiscuous, invoking gay marriage as one example.

Despite this harsh criticism and his alignment with the luminaries of *salafi ifta'* on most issues discussed, al-Makkawi departed from foundational *salafi* writings on the legitimacy of permanent residence in Sweden and did so in terms similar to those used by Klominek. He said he

194 Shari'a and Life

was aware that some scholars hold that *Dar al-Islam* was where Muslims were in the majority. However, he felt more of a Ramadan atmosphere in parts of Sweden than in the Arab world and felt safer wearing traditional attire in Sweden than in certain Arab countries, where he would be labelled a radical.

His approach to proselytizing was somewhat more positive than Klominek's, but still reserved. He agreed that *da'wa* was a duty for a Muslim, but to each according to his ability. Only those with solid knowledge should actively spread Islam, whereas the rest should testify to Islam through their good morals and conduct. He added that when meeting with Christians, he did not encourage them to convert, but rather to return first to their own religion so that they become closer to God and to the morals all religions preach, such as not to lie, not to steal, and not to commit adultery.[7]

Hafeezullah Khan, one of the three imams of the *salafi* Green Lane Mosque, the main rival of the Salafi Mosque in Birmingham's *salafi* scene, said that he had never received queries on the permissibility of living in the West. He contended that Muslims who live in Small Heath should recognize their good fortunes and that "they would face many problems" if they moved back to their countries of origin. He referred to Britain as *Dar al-Aman* – a country where Muslims can live in safety and practice Islam (yet still a separate category from *Dar al-Islam*).

Khan argued that engaging in *da'wa* was the duty of all Muslims, regardless of where they lived, yet Muslims should engage in it according to their ability. Being nice to others is a form of *da'wa*. He suggested that proselytizing in the West is a means of fending off the proselytizing of the other side.[8]

Imam Salim Blidi of Marseille's post-Madkhali Hassan Blidi Mosque approached the legitimacy of migration and permanent residence in the West in a pragmatic, matter-of-fact way that highlighted his departure from what he came to understand as *ifta'* that is not grounded in reality and is thus invalid. He said that migration to and settlement in the West were permissible. Whatever the reasons for migrating in our time were, Muslims migrate in one direction – to Europe, because their oppressive societies have no education, no schooling, and no work to offer them and their families. He asked, rhetorically and sarcastically, why those who had been speaking for decades about the impermissibility of living in the West had remained in the West themselves.

Noting that the *sahaba* (the Companions of Prophet Muhammad) traded and married with people from distant countries, Blidi challenged those who argue that migration to the West conflicted with shari'a to provide evidence. We offered him evidence commonly used in *salafi* literature to delegitimize financially motivated migration: the tradition according to which the Prophet said he disavowed Muslims who reside among polytheists. He replied that this reference was an example of the need to accommodate Quranic verses and traditions to changing times and places.

Asked whether Muslims have a role in Europe, Blidi did not mention proselytizing. Rather, he spoke of his 24/7 work in his community, attending to those who approach him with their concerns. He suggested that if all imams were as helpful as he was, the problems of Muslims in Europe would have been solved.[9] Several additional questions about *da'wa* as a duty indicated that he interprets this notion as extremist and thus as belonging to radical convictions he held in his youth and abandoned.

The imam at Dortmund's 'Umar Ibn al-Khattab, the young 'Abd al-'Ali, who was the last of the constantly changing imams we met there, made no effort to hide that he regarded the question about the conditions for living in the West as absurd. He mentioned that earlier in the discussion he had said that voting in German elections was permissible because Muslims should wish the best for the countries where they reside. How, then, could he think that living in Germany could be considered, under certain terms, impermissible? Germany, he added, is his home; the Prophet acted kindly to Christians and Jews, and that implied that it was permissible to live among them.[10]

Imam 'Abdallah, who preceded 'Abd al-'Ali and left his post in haste, understood the topic as political and said he would rather not address it. He apologetically emphasized that Muslims came to Germany to earn money and not fight the Germans.[11] Moroccan-born Bin Nasir (b. 1949), who acts as an understudy imam at the mosque and has lived in Germany since 1970, flatly dismissed the notion that Muslims in the West needed to meet certain criteria or perform specific duties, including proselytizing. While Bin Nasir said he was concerned about the future of his family in Germany (he explained that since his migration to the country in the early 1970s, attitudes towards Muslims had worsened, although the situation in Dortmund was better), he was confident that he and his children would stay there permanently. He prided himself on his recently attained German citizenship, having passed the citizenship test with distinction, and said he was eager to exercise his right to vote for the first time. Bin Nasir argued that proselytizing efforts were futile; whenever he had talked about Islam with colleagues at work, they were not interested.[12]

Imam Khaled al-Dib of The Stockholm Mosque contextualized his own migration to Sweden in shari'a-grounded terms. He justified his

196 Shari'a and Life

migration as altruistically serving a communal *maslaha*. He emphasized that his material situation in Egypt was better. He owned a private school with 300 pupils and 25 employees and worked in an Islamic research centre, aside from his employment as an imam in the ministry of *awqaf*. When he visited Stockholm to assist Islamic centres during Ramadan, he realized that he was needed in Sweden more than in Egypt and decided to make it his home.

However, in generally addressing Muslim migration to and permanent presence in Sweden, al-Dib did not refer to shari'a-grounded justifications. He emphasized that Muslims did not migrate to Sweden temporarily to make gains and profits and then return to their countries of origin. Sweden, he said, became their homeland; they are there to stay, and they have a duty towards its society. It seemed it was not a matter that he attended to recently. It was also clear that he was concerned that questions in this regard intended to portray him and his mosque negatively.

Asked whether the shari'a attached any conditions to Muslim residence in Sweden, for example, the ability to manifest religion, al-Dib answered that manifestation of religion implied only that a person had the right to perform religious rituals in places designated to that end, but not the right to impose his religion on a society that was not Muslim. He added that Muslims came to Sweden because its constitution guaranteed freedom of religion for all. Asked whether Muslims had a role in Sweden, he said it was to help society and twice repeated that it was not acceptable for a person to help only himself and distance himself from a society that benefited him. Asked more specifically if Muslims have a duty to proselytize, he implied that explicit proselytizing was not desired, stating that Muslims should positively reflect Islam in their deeds rather than their speech. He added that if a Muslim did not act in accordance with Islam, that should not bear on the image of other Muslims, just as if a citizen of Sweden broke the law, that did not indicate that Sweden as a whole is an evil society.[13]

The Algeria-born imam Farid Bourouba of Centre Musulman de Marseille said that it was apparent Muslims can live in France and added that they should behave well, work for the common good, and participate in elections. He explained that the world had become a global village. He did not suggest that migration to, and permanent presence in, France was conditioned by any shari'a-grounded stipulations, including active proselytizing.

The issue was not always so simple from his standpoint. Bourouba, who originally traveled to France in the 1980s to write a PhD in linguistics, decided upon completing his studies that he would like to make

France his home. He wrote to the Lebanese mufti Faysal Mawlawi (d. 2011), who in 1997 became al-Qaradawi's deputy at the European Council for Fatwa and Research. Bourouba asked Mawlawi whether it was permissible for him to attain French citizenship and remain in France. Mawlawi answered that he must return to Algeria, noting, among other reasons, that French family laws were not commensurate with the shariʿa. Still, Bourouba stayed. He said that later, in the 1990s, Mawlawi changed his mind and told him he must stay in France to help *da ʿwa* efforts among its Muslims. Bourouba agreed with our suggestion that Mawlawi's change of heart was encouraged by his realization that it was impossible for all Muslims in France to return to their homelands.[14]

Al-Dib and Bourouba's positions were detached from the formative treatises and fatwas of al-Qaradawi and the European Council for Fatwa and Research, to which the former is committed and which the latter privileges. Al-Qaradawi and the Council were unequivocal about the duty of migrants to meet certain (generous) shariʿa-grounded criteria and their role as missionaries. Still, the imams' caution was not out of touch with that of the Council's more recent treatments of *da ʿwa*. As noted in chapter 1, while the concept was never revoked, the Council's deliberations throughout the 2000s all but neglected the ideal of migrants as proselytizers, and it did not invest funds or intellectual energy in programs to bring the message of Islam to non-Muslims.

The Case for Impermissibility

Imam Abu Khadeejah of Birmingham's Salafi Mosque also parted from *fiqh al-aqalliyyat al-Muslima* discourse on the legitimacy of migration, but in the opposite direction. Rather than argue, as did other imams, including *salafi*s, that discussing the terms of permissibility became obsolete, he introduced terms for migration that were more restrictive than those originally offered by *salafi* luminaries. He described most Muslim migrants as careless sinners whose migration could not be retroactively justified through their service to Islam in the West and suggested the imminent prospect of a forced total exodus, also by Muslims whose residence in the West is legitimate.

Abu Khadeejah's views reflected doubts about the ability of his community to maintain *salafi* norms in Britain. In presenting them, he sought to highlight the uncompromising, ready-to-sacrifice virtues of his approach to Islam, its shying away from seeking popularity, and its insistence on loyalty to correct understandings of religious duties. He said these updated opinions were informed by his consultations with

198   Shari'a and Life

muftis in Saudi Arabia, which apparently were yet to be articulated in the form of written fatwas.

According to Abu Khadeejah, it is permissible for Muslims to move from a Muslim land to a Western country only temporarily and in connection to a legitimate objective – including trade, political persecution, academic studies, and proselytizing. While *salafi* fatwas have left, even if inconclusively and in a highly restrained manner, a door open for invoking proselytizing as a retrospective, acquired justification, Abu Khadeejah held that impermissibly-motivated migration could not become retrospectively legitimate if the Muslim migrant begins to proselytize actively. Thus, even devotion to *da'wa* does not "launder" the transgression of abandoning *Dar al-Islam* based on an impermissible reason: "the thing is that if they were to do that to justify their presence here, then they've put the cart before the horse. Because their initial journey from the Muslim country should have been for a particular purpose."

Firmly rooted in Britain, where he was born, as were all other active proselytizers affiliated with his mosque, Abu Khadeejah was anyhow sceptical about the potential of Muslim migrants to be effective proselytizers. He held that those migrants were not rooted enough in British society and that if *da'wa* was dear to them, they should advance it in their homelands. He emphasized that proselytizing was not an individual duty but rather a communal duty.

According to Abu Khadeejah, a Muslim who was not aware of what shari'a norms were when migrating for financial benefit, and then became more religious and realized that he had sinned, was still required to move back to his homeland or another Muslim country, unless there are political circumstances that hinder his return. This, he said, is a common and rather unfortunate situation, putting Muslims at a difficult choice between abiding by what their religion commands and giving up on their life in Britain:

> Remember there are people whom I've met that came to this country 10 or 15 years ago – non-practicing, they fled from their country, paid someone to get out of their country, they came in the back of a container, or in a lorry, they came to this country only for economic reasons, there was no danger in their country – and some of them, I mean, I've met a person in [the] city centre of Birmingham, more than one person – I don't ask you to believe me or not – and he said I'm not Afghani, but when I came here I pretended to be an Afghani; I'm not Iraqi, but when I came to this country I pretended I was from Iraq. And they came, and they spent 10 thousand dollars to come to this country, illegitimately. Once they've come to this country,

maybe through *da'wa* … they become religious. When they become religious, they realize that they shouldn't have left their country. So now they have two choices in front of them – now they have to relinquish their right of residency in the UK and go back, and some of them do, I've met Syrians who've come back [to their homeland] … If they stay, then … if you ask me a straight question then – [it is] haram … They are in a problem.

The case of Muslims who were born in the West, such as himself, is different. According to Abu Khadeejah, it is recommended (*mustahab*) that they migrate to a Muslim country, but it is not obligatory (*wajib*) that they do so.

This position legitimizes the residence of the leadership and most active affiliates of the community in Britain. Yet it may be on the verge of changing. Abu Khadeejah stressed that he was "leaning towards the position that if the continual changing of the goal-posts of the Western education system for children continues in its present state," then migration to Muslim countries would become obligatory, rather than recommended, also for Muslims like himself born in the West.[15]

Contrary to muftis and community leaders who addressed the issue of permissibility in a way intent on affirming their civic commitment to their receiving states, it appeared that Abu Khadeejah wanted to make the point that the continued presence of his community in Europe should not be taken for granted and that there was a limit to their endurance in the face of what they interpret as Islamophobia. His main concern was that the British government would require faith-based schools, like the one his mosque operates, to teach that homosexuality is religiously permissible, noting such a development would constitute the crossing of a "red line." He said that if faith-based schools were required to teach Evolution Theory and Big Bang theory as facts rather than theories, that would also constitute a "red line" whose crossing made migration to a Muslim land obligatory, also for Muslims born in the West.

Abu Khadeejah disagreed with the comment that the return of millions of Muslim migrants back to the Muslim world was not realistic. He suggested that there was nothing to hinder a Muslim return to the homelands, except in the case of Muslims who live in countries where they faced dangers: "If you cannot flee – then you're stuck. Like you look at some of the *sahaba*, they were not able to flee Mecca. Right? They were chained, they were imprisoned, they were not able to flee."[16] When we argued that Morocco could not absorb millions of expats, he agreed that any exodus would have to be gradual and added that the legitimacy of advancing a phased exodus was a demonstration of the rationality and pragmatism of Islam.[17]

In Europe to Stay

The religio-legal discussion about living in the West was not familiar to a majority of the mosque attendees interviewed. Some who never gave the matter a thought appeared to be surprised to learn from us that it is discussed in religio-legal discourse at all. They were confident that their presence in Europe did not require *istifta'*, or strategies external to *istifta'*, because it never occurred to them that the issue is problematic from a religious point of view. When asked to contemplate whether their decision to remain in a European country was justifiable, they were quick to provide arguments why it is, similar in essence to those provided by imams. There is no more explicit demonstration of the limited diffusion of the foundational texts of *fiqh al-aqalliyyat al-Muslima* than European mosque attendees who have never been exposed to the notion that their living in Europe could be problematic from the point of view of the shari'a, or that as Muslims in the West they have certain religious duties. Because living in Europe has been the reality of their existence, and no one told them that muftis had some ideas about it, they did not think of it in religious terms.

A few attendees did recall engaging in *istifta'* as to whether they may reside in a non-Muslim country. None of them changed his mind about migrating to Europe or living there following the advice he received. It is not clear how they would have acted if their inquiry had led to a conclusion they did not favour; yet those who came across advice to leave, continued their search until they found a different opinion. The shari'a-grounded justifications *mustafti*s received, in their first inquiry or ultimately, reassured them that they were not transgressing in making a Western country their home. The question did not seem to be high on their agenda, and they would have most likely not broached it unless asked specifically about their opinion.

Obviously, Muslims who moved from Europe to a Muslim land could not be expected in a European mosque. Still, in all the mosques studied, including the Salafi Mosque, we did not come across a person who was in a practical process of moving to a Muslim country based on *istifta'* regarding the legitimacy of staying in Europe.

One of the interviewees who never gave his migration to Europe a second thought is Moroccan-born (1971) Muhammad, who moved to Germany at the age of 20. He is married, the father of four children, and works as a driver in a logistic company. Muhammad was not aware that the migration of Muslims to and settlement in Europe was deliberated in the religio-legal discourse. He could not understand why his choice should be questioned. He was equally surprised to learn that he was expected to act as a proselytizer, suggesting that only those trained to bring the message of Islam should do so.[18]

Jordan-born (1973) Mahmud, who moved to Sweden in 2013, had not given the permissibility of migrating any thought before or after leaving his homeland. He never came across pertinent fatwas or debates on the matter. Asked to reflect on his decision to leave Jordan, he came up with two justifications: he can make more money in Sweden than in Jordan; Jordan, too, is home to many migrants.[19]

Moroccan-born (1968) Mustafa migrated to Germany when he was 23. He is married, has three children, and works as a steel trader. He has been with the 'Umar Ibn al-Khattab mosque since he migrated to Germany. Referring to *salafi* activists, he spoke passionately against Muslims who "do not even know how to write their names" and advance radical notions, such as that Christians should not be invited to mosques and that they should not be congratulated on Christmas.[20] Mustafa said that one of the reasons he liked the 'Umar Ibn al-Khattab mosque was that radicals were hardly present there.

Asked about the permissibility of living in the West, Mustafa, who appeared to have never engaged with the discourse on the matter, argued that living in Morocco was not more permissible than living in Germany. He noted the firm hand with which the Moroccan government treated protestors, its corruption, and his homeland's failed health system. Introduced to the idea that Muslim migrants have a religious task to proselytize, he responded that they had no duty other than to be respectful and lead good lives. Only Muslims with great knowledge and patience should engage in *da'wa*; if Muslims like him, who lack both, try to contribute, their efforts would be counter-productive.

Chapter 3 briefly introduced Morocco-born (1970) Mustafa, who migrated to Iceland in 2016 without his family. Until two years before the interview, he used to Google search religio-legal issues. He gave up on the practice, having, so he said, acquired the confidence to decide on issues for himself based on his understanding of Islam as a religion of leniency and coexistence with non-Muslims. It appeared that Mustafa never engaged with fatwas on the permissibility of migrating to a non-Muslim land for financial motivations. He said that he was satisfied that because his homeland was weak, did not apply Islam fully, and was not democratic, it was legitimate that he moved to a financially strong and democratic land.[21]

Mustafa (b. 1988) left Morocco for Naples in 2007. Three months before the interview, he moved to Sweden because Italy's economic crisis left him jobless. In Italy, he worked in a slaughterhouse where he handled pork. Mustafa, who said that he had only an elementary education and

202 Shari'a and Life

no knowledge of fiqh, was assured by friends that working there was legitimate because it was a means of providing for his basic needs. In Sweden, he had yet to find a job. He explained that he had the necessary documents, but it was difficult to find work without "contacts." Asked whether his presence in the West was legitimate, Mustafa, who noted that he had never consulted an imam in his life, responded that this was "the first time in 11 years of migration that I have thought of that." He explained his migration as a matter of necessity, without contextualizing the necessity as a condition that legitimized living in the West: "I moved to Italy in order to survive. To have a roof over my head, clothes. Whether it is permissible – this Allah knows."

After some contemplation, the theme rang a bell. Mustafa remembered something he once read or heard, although he could not remember where: "The Prophet, peace be upon him, said that it is permissible to migrate to any place in the world in order to engage in *da'wa*. But to migrate to America just to make a dollar – that is not permissible." He never engaged in proselytizing himself.[22]

The few interviewees who remembered engaging in *istifta'* on the legitimacy of residing in the West were not convinced, following their investigation, that *any* Muslim can, under any circumstances, live in a non-Muslim country. They were, however, conveniently persuaded that *their* specific situation justifies remaining in a European country. Abu Khadeejah suggested that he and his colleagues are rarely approached with queries about this issue, because the answer is too hard for *muftis* to accept: "I mean if you go to our website, and type in *hijra*, you'll see that I've given two or three talks about this – ten or twenty minutes [each]. But the thing is, predominantly, a lot of people are rooted here. And they're afraid of leaving."[23] Still, interviews with attendees who did inquire about the legitimacy of living in the West, including in his mosque, demonstrated that they had no inhibitions about continuing searching until they found answers that support their inclination to remain in the West, at least for the foreseeable future.

We briefly encountered Muhammad (b. 1985) in the previous chapter. The Yemen-born and Birmingham-raised affiliate of the Salafi Mosque is married and the father of three. Muhammad, who grew up in Birmingham in a practicing family, volunteers with City Centre Da'wah, the proselytizing group affiliated with the Salafi Mosque, which has branches across Britain, including London, Oxford, Manchester, and Leeds, as well as vibrant online operations.

The group's declaration of principles, "Our Da'wah, Our Call," written by Abu Khadeejah, details the foundations and priorities of *salafiyya* as taught at the Salafi Mosque and by Salafi Publications. It aims to bring non-Muslims to Islam and bring Muslims to "true Islam."[24] Birmingham volunteers operate a stall once or twice a week at the centre of the city, offering passersby free copies of the Quran in English as well as a variety of free booklets and leaflets by Salafi Publications, including those opposing al-Qaeda and ISIS.

The volunteers also travel once a week to other cities in England to proselytize, and several times a year, they travel abroad; Muhammad has travelled with the group as far as New Zealand. Their activities are the public face of the Salafi Mosque in Britain's second-largest city and across the country. Our observations of the booth suggested that it attracts mainly the attention of Muslims, and our observations of the mosque suggested that proselytizing efforts have not yielded more than several dozen converts in Birmingham.

In 2014, Muhammad was in the process of moving with his family to Yemen. His motivation was that he wanted to be close to *salafi* scholars of prominence who live there and that he realized it would be easier to raise his children properly in a Muslim country, where, for example, the *adhan* is heard everywhere. Then the civil war in the country deteriorated, and Muhammad determined to remain in Britain for the time being. He engaged in *istifta'* about his decision. He found a sermon on Google by Nasir al-Din al-Albani, from which he understood that he must not remain in Britain under any circumstances. Yet, following additional inquiries, he decided to stay. Reading the opinion of Rabi' al-Madkhali, and consulting with imam Abu Hakim of the Salafi Mosque, convinced Muhammad that it was permissible to remain in Britain as long as he was able to manifest Islam, engaged in proselytizing, and did not abandon his intention to leave for a Muslim country ultimately. Muhammad remembered that Abu Hakim advised him that there was a difference between the situation of Muslims in France, where they were oppressed and therefore must leave, and Muslims in Britain, who were not oppressed.

Muhammad added to the list of justifications for remaining one which he appeared to have thought of himself, and that significantly decreased the feasibility of a future migration to Yemen. He said that in deciding about migrating to a Muslim country, one should consider whether that would significantly diminish the situation of one's spouse. For example, if one's wife is used to living in a spacious apartment and migration would result in her living in a muddy hut, then that is an argument for remaining because of a husband's duty for the welfare of his wife and family.[25]

'Abd al-Majid of Reykjavik's Grand Mosque, whom we met in the previous chapters, remembered engaging in *istifta'* twice since he

204   Shari'a and Life

migrated. He explained: "sometimes we need help. Because we don't know 100 per cent everything about the Quran."

One issue he inquired about has divided Icelandic Muslims – whether fasting should be in accordance with local time during long summer days. The answer he received from the Moroccan Ministry of Endowments advised him that he should fast in accordance with local time, even if the day was extremely long, as long as sunset was observable. He said he examined the evidence provided for that fatwa and was satisfied with it.

The other query 'Abd al-Majid sent was about the legitimacy of residing and working in a Western country. What unsettled him was a video he watched online where a shaykh, whose name he could not remember, said that it was not. 'Abd al-Majid first phoned a call-in advisory *ifta'* forum in Saudi Arabia (he could not remember its name). Asked why he chose a Saudi forum, he noted the advanced academic quality of Islamic studies in the Kingdom and that "Mecca is where God put the special things."[26] After some additional thought, he recalled that the phone number was handed to him and some friends by Saudis who visited the mosque. However, no one answered the phone in Saudi Arabia, so he called the Moroccan Ministry of Endowments instead. It appeared that the idea that there could be a difference in how Moroccan and Saudi panels address this existential matter and that the latter do not agree with the ideological preference for *taysir* he articulated did not occur to 'Abd al-Majid.

As 'Abd al-Majid recalled, the fatwa he received reassured him that he may stay in Iceland. It advised that Muslims were permitted to live in every corner of the earth, and wherever they are, they should have good morals and values, show that Muslims are good people, and help those in need, Muslims and non-Muslims alike. 'Abd al-Majid found these terms correct. He noted that whenever he saw people whose cars were stuck in the snow, he helped them; the last was a woman he saved with his 4x4 at 02:00 in the morning. He implied that if Muslims acted in this manner, that would help spread Islam in the West. To demonstrate the point, he told us about an Englishman he knew who travelled to Egypt every year, for fifteen years, for one-and-a-half-month holidays. The positive interactions of that Englishman with Muslims led him to convert. The last time the Englishman was in Egypt, the taxi driver asked him for a fare that was three or four times higher than the normal price. The Englishman told the driver: "If I had known you before I converted, I would have never become Muslim."[27]

Gambia-born 'Uthman (b. 1975), who works in a restaurant, moved to Sweden in 2010. He consulted with his mosque's imam in Ghana before migrating. The imam explained that if one migrates to pursue an objective such as caring for family, then moving to a non-Muslim land is permissible. He cautioned 'Uthman that he must meet his wife at least once every four months, or else she must join him.

We asked 'Uthman whether his continued presence in the West required that he be able to manifest his religion; for example, obtain halal food? His answer was cyclical: first, halal food was accessible everywhere; second, where that would not be the case, eating haram would be a necessity.[28]

Muhammad (b. 1967), born in Britain to parents who migrated from Pakistan, said that he had never read fatwas on the permissibility of living in the West and implied that the Islamic character of Small Heath legitimizes making it his permanent home. He remembered that Abu Hakim (Bilal Davis), one of the three imams of the Salafi Mosque, once advised that it was preferable for Muslims who have children to migrate to a Muslim land in order to preserve the children's religious identity. However, according to Muhammad, because he did not have children, he was convinced the advice did not affect him.[29]

Bangladesh-born Anik (b. 1988), also of the Salafi Mosque, whom we encountered in the previous chapter, said that when he was 20, he began examining through Google the legitimacy of living in the West. The first fatwas he found stated that it was "haram, haram, haram" and that he "cannot live in the *kuffar* society." Then, when he read more, he learned that it was permissible.

According to Anik, his homeland Bangladesh was not more Islamic than England was, and, in fact, no country, including Saudi Arabia (which he visited for the hajj), was entirely Islamic: "See how they treat the people there [in Saudi Arabia]. For example, they treat Bangladeshis like dogs."[30] It was evident that he did not regard moving to a Muslim country as a viable option. When asked whether it would not be easier to preserve his children's religious identity in a Muslim country, he said he would trust God that their identity would be protected in England.

While Anik considered proselytizing among non-Muslims to be a duty, he suggested this duty was universal for all Muslims and did not, in and of itself, justify residence in Europe. He said that his way of fulfilling this duty was not to distribute leaflets but to use every opportunity to tell non-Muslims about Islam. For example, when he asked his boss to go on holiday so that he could perform the hajj, the boss asked him to explain what the hajj meant, and he was happy to oblige.

Anik said that the examples set by the Prophet and his Companions also support his choice to continue living in Britain. He offered evidence underlined in *wasati*, rather than *salafi*, texts on migration to the

206 Shari'a and Life

West: The Prophet lived in a non-Muslim society and migrated to a non-Muslim society; he allowed some of his followers to migrate to Abyssinia, where Muslims lived alongside Christians in peace; after the Hijra to Medina, some Muslims remained in Mecca.

Returning to the First Hijra

The Abyssinia model, which Anik alluded to, refers to the first migration of Muslims. According to Prophetic traditions and biographies, in years 615–16, when the persecutions in Mecca intensified, the Prophet Muhammad permitted the migration of some 100 Muslims to Abyssinia (Ethiopia; more precisely, the Christian Axumite Kingdom located in modern-day Eritrea and Northern Ethiopia). The Prophet chose Abyssinia because he considered its Christian King, the Negus (Ar. *Najashi*), to be a just ruler; or because he held Christianity to be closer to Islam than the hegemonic faiths of other potential shelters; or because its commercial ties with the Meccans were weaker than those of other states; or because of all the above. The migrants included 'Uthman b. 'Affan, later the third *khalifa,* and his wife, Ruqayya.

When the Prophet and his Companions migrated to Medina in 622, some Muslims immediately left Abyssinia and joined them. However, others remained in Abyssinia for seven more years, i.e., long after an Islamic state where God's rules prevailed was established. A result of the first migration was the conversion of the Negus to Islam.[31]

Analogies to the first Hijra attained primacy in the contemporary discussion on the legitimacy of Muslim settlement in the West because they could support many agendas. This migration took place during the Meccan period, a formative time in the establishment of Islamic faith and law; it also involved prominent Companions and other Muslims who abided by the Prophet's commands. Thus, its credibility as an example to follow is undeniable.

The migration involved a settlement of Muslims in a Christian society and a movement from one non-Muslim society (Mecca at the time) to another (Abyssinia). The Muslim migrants in Abyssinia shined as constructive contributors to their host society. They offered their political support to the Christian King, who gave them refuge, while maintaining absolute loyalty to the requirements of their religion. Their exemplary conduct ultimately led to the conversion of the Negus, demonstrating what Muslim migrants who are loyal to their religion can achieve.[32]

Along with religio-legal treatises, the Abyssinia model was a centrepiece of one of the most popular sermons on the future of Islam and Muslims in Europe, Amr Khaled's "Between Integration and Introversion" (or

Integration im Islam in its German version). Khaled delivered it to three packed stadiums in Germany in 2003. The Egyptian-born, accountant-turned-television preacher, who rose to prominence in the late 1990s with his dynamic, straightforward style, invoked the first Hijra to support his call for European Muslims to strengthen their religious identity and act as loyal representatives of the good that is in Islam through constructive integration and excelling in assisting non-Muslims. He was careful not to argue that the objective of representing Islam was to convert others. His model introduced migrants as ambassadors rather than as missionaries, although the difference between the two is not always easy to distinguish.[33]

Other than Anik, only three of our interviewees related to the Abyssinia model. Other stories mentioned in *fiqh al-aqalliyyat al-Muslima* discussions about the legitimacy of migration and integration, for example, the imprisonment of Prophet Joseph and the crucial help he offered the infidels who wronged him, were not mentioned by any of them. This was another indication that the direct and indirect diffusion of texts discussing migration in religious terms has been limited, even if these texts did leave some mark.

Exposure to the Abyssinia model had a particular impact on Sami (b. 1994) of the Salafi Mosque, whom we met in chapter 3. Sami offered several motivations for migrating alone from France to Small Heath, including the discrimination he experienced in France; the limitations on practicing Islam freely there; the inability to apply certain norms Islam allows, such as polygamy; the desire to study at the Salafi Mosque; and the enhanced Islamic environment in parts of Birmingham.

Sami was one of several attendees of the Salafi Mosque we met who migrated to Small Heath, or were in the process of doing so, from France, the Netherlands, Denmark, Germany, Italy, and Switzerland. Concerned about growing intolerance towards Islam in their homelands, these attendees were also aware that, according to *salafi* muftis, it was recommended, though not obligatory, that they move to a Muslim land. Being unprepared or unwilling to do so at that time, they turned to Birmingham as a compromise, transforming it into a modern-day version of Abyssinia – a Christian land privileged over other non-Muslim lands as a safe-haven of religious freedom.

We asked Sami if he was aware of the small Hijra to Abyssinia. He replied: "This is why I'm here, because of this story! … Some people say it's not a Hijra to go from a non-Muslim country to a non-Muslim country, but they are wrong because they don't understand the first Hijra (to Abyssinia). When the Prophet's peace be upon him [Companions] went from Mecca to Abyssinia, it was called a Hijra – it was to a non-Muslim country. So, this is exactly what I have done."[34] The validity of the analogy did not imply, according to Sami, that it was legitimate for him to remain in Britain for the rest of his life. He said that "for every Muslim, it is a duty to go to a Muslim country" and that he intended to leave Britain for a Muslim country as soon as it would be possible for him (he needed to pay off some debts): "If you really want to live your Islam in a good way, you have to go in a Muslim country."[35]

Sami agreed that certain conditions legitimize continued residence in Europe – for example, if a Muslim has a sick daughter who needs high-quality medical treatment. Asked if proselytizing could serve as an additional justification, he said that it could – but only for "real" proselytizers. He did not consider himself one.

Perhaps because Sami was so engaging and kind, we tried another argument to legitimize his continued stay in Britain. We mentioned that after the Prophet migrated to Medina, and the reality of persecution ended, some Muslims remained in Abyssinia. Was that not evidence that he, too, could remain in the non-Muslim land he migrated to from another non-Muslim land? Sami replied that it was not. First, because the permission the Prophet granted applied only to the Companions. Second, the Muslims who remained in Abyssinia proselytized, a capacity which, as he had already mentioned, was beyond his skills.[36]

Other *salafis* who sought in Birmingham an enhanced religious environment and shelter from perceived persecutions in their European societies did not relate their story to the Abyssinia example as Sami did. They justified their migration as the best *practical* option they had. One is Swiss-German 'Abd al-'Aziz (b. 1986), born and raised in Bern. Discussing his conversion, 'Abd al-'Aziz recalled being the only one in his family who believed in God. At school, he attended Kirchlichen Unterricht (Church Class), where he was learning for confirmation. It was at this time, however, that 'Abd al-'Aziz had an epiphany. He stated: "and then I realized that this entire concept of God having a son, and the son is, on the one hand, God and nevertheless dies on the cross as a human ... all these contradictions I never believed. That's why I said I wanted to leave this class. Back then I was maybe 11 or 12 years old."[37]

'Abd al-'Aziz converted to Islam in his final year of high school. A new student from Afghanistan had joined his class. 'Abd al-'Aziz was curious to learn about that country, and when he read on the internet that the religion there was Islam, he began to read more about that religion. Soon enough, he thought: "Hey ... It's like when someone tells you who you are ... When I read about Islam and also about the proofs for Islam, I thought that this is what I have always been, I just didn't know it."[38]

At the age of twenty-eight, ʿAbd al-ʿAziz became a *salafi*. In 2017, he moved to Birmingham with his Muslim wife. He splits his time between the Salafi Mosque and its Green Lane *salafi* rival and prefers the latter because it offers more activities and, so he finds, is more embracing. ʿAbd al-ʿAziz works in human resources for a large company. Relating to his migration, he explained:

> I moved here [Birmingham] because it is hard to practice Islam in Switzerland. Even in Germany it is hard to practice Islam. A lot of brothers from Germany, the Netherlands, or France, move here now. Because in the UK, they give Muslims more opportunities to practice religion. For example, in Switzerland, it was hard to get any job with a beard. Even in Germany, it is getting hard … Just one example is the niqab. In Switzerland, it is not officially banned, but the thing is that people spit at you, they insult you, everything. So, I didn't see my future in Switzerland. And also [I moved] for the education of my children and everything. And also, to be able to learn the religion properly …

Asked about the permissibility of living in the West, ʿAbd al-ʿAziz suggested that his migration to Birmingham was the best he could do, at least for the foreseeable future. He explained that the Quran and the Hadith forbid Muslims to live under oppression. The situation in Britain is different from that on the Continent because his religious freedom is respected, and he is treated well.

Moving to a Muslim land is desirable for him in principle but is not a concrete or feasible plan: "If I have the opportunity, definitely [we will migrate to a Muslim country]. [However] for example, in Morocco, it will be very hard to be employed. Normally, you need to have a business. The first criteria [for moving to a Muslim land] is that I am able to stay in this country. That they don't say: 'you need to leave the county after a certain period.' The second thing is that you [need to be sure that you] have the opportunity to survive, that you have the opportunity to work."[39]

ʿAbd al-ʿAziz was the most eager, and at times aggressive, *salafi* proselytizer we met. From the moment we saw him at the Salafi Bookstore and asked for an interview, he passionately tried to save us from hellfire, confident that "in half an hour I could prove to anyone that God exists, and that Islam is the right path." He said that proselytizing was the duty of every Muslim and that he used to participate in distributing copies of the Quran in Switzerland. Still, he did not mention *daʿwa* as a legitimization for his continued residence in the West, and his answers implied that he was no longer active in group proselytizing activities.

Duty and Reward

The concept of the "missionary migrant" was a trade-off of sorts. Muftis offered migrants religious legitimization in return for, in part, commitment to services to the greater Muslim cause. These kinds of 'deals' are common in diasporic relations. The diaspora is encouraged to advance the broader interests of the homeland. In return, it is offered gratitude from the community it left behind and recognition of its belonging to that community. The analogy did not escape and even encouraged several formulators of the "missionary migrant" concept, including al-Qaradawi. His succinct fatwa about the "duties of Muslims living in the West" called upon Muslim migrants to follow the example of Jewish Diasporas that assist Israel.[40]

It is possible that muftis who formulated the concept of the "missionary migrant" hoped for the proliferation of small and large networks of European Muslims who, thankful for the opportunity to assert their religious credentials and prove that earning more money was not their primary motivation in life, would spend their free time in *da'wa* activities and contribute to a speedy Islamization of the continent. Still, the minimal involvement of authors of pertinent fatwas and treatises in facilitating programs to that effect suggests that their theorizing was not motivated by concrete plans for action. The concept of migrants as missionaries originated from their wishful thinking, their ideals. It was, first and foremost, a means of reconciling a theological conflict.

The discussion above suggested that the modest presence of "missionary migrants" in Europe could be explained by the limited diffusion of the concept; the reluctance of imams to accept its terms, including because of its political sensitivity; the absence of a sense of wrongdoing on the part of some Muslims who chose (where it was a choice) to make a European country their home; and the conviction that proper training is essential for effective proselytizing. A Muslim who is not told that he is expected to act as a missionary cannot respond to that expectation.

We found, however, that it is also the case that Muslims who were familiar and content with the notion that it was their duty to proselytize, and that fulfilling this duty was the primary legitimization for living in the West, were not necessarily involved in any actual *da'wa* efforts. In fact, the above-mentioned Yemen-born Muhammad, who was convinced through *istifta'* that proselytizing legitimizes his remaining in a non-Muslim country, was the exception. Other attendees interviewed who accepted the concept of the "missionary migrant" explained why it was true in principle but also had reasons why *they* could not take part in active proselytizing efforts themselves, at least for the time being. It seemed that recognition that they potentially had a religious task satisfied their anxiety about living in the West, at least for the time being. None was able to attest these views to a specific author or text or recalled a process of inquiring about his personal situation.

Muhammad was born (2000) in Sweden to parents who migrated from Somalia. At the time of the interview, he was working with the postal service and was about to start summer school to improve his grades, with the hope of being accepted to university. Muhammad grew more religious in his teens and began voluntarily attending The Stockholm Mosque's Quran School, where he learned some Arabic. He developed a strong sense that being born and raised in Sweden, his religiosity was somewhat compromised. Reflecting on his habit of swimming at Stockholm's beaches, he admitted that he sometimes stared at female swimmers. This practice he explained by noting that having lived all his life in Sweden, his mindset was different from that of people raised in Muslim countries.

Muhammad had a prompt answer when asked whether Muslims have a role in Sweden: to bring non-Muslims to Islam. He said that when a person dies, his good and bad deeds are balanced in front of God. Converting non-Muslims counts as a good deed. Muhammad could not remember where he heard this idea – perhaps from his parents, perhaps in a sermon given at the mosque a few years ago, and perhaps on the internet.

Despite this conviction, Muhammad said he had not engaged in proselytizing. The reason was that he feared being labelled as a radical. He did witness one conversion, though: at his high school, a Christian pupil who used to follow him and his friends during the breaks when they prayed, ultimately became a Muslim.

We provoked young Muhammad: In Sweden, the quality of life is better than in Somalia. Why, then, was he so sure that Swedes should convert to Islam? Perhaps it is the Somalis who should accept the ways of the Swedes? He answered that our premise was wrong. It was true that in Sweden, people have more money, but in Somalia, they were happier because they had faith.[41]

Nasser (b. 1955), married and the father of three, migrated to Sweden from Tunisia when he was 23. He worked as a taxi driver until his retirement. He recounted that as a child in Tunisia, religion classes did not "get to his head," but he developed an interest in Islam as he grew older. While he displayed meagre knowledge of fiqh concepts during the interview, he said he had not once consulted imam Khaled al-Dib or any other imam. There is haram, there is halal, and there are exceptions to the rules; it is all in the Quran, and there is no need to inquire further.

212 Shari'a and Life

Asked if he ever contemplated the permissibility of living in the West, Nasser was quick to answer that it was not only permissible, but that for leading an Islamic life in Sweden while living among the *kuffar*, Muslims gain a greater reward from God than if they had done so in a Muslim country. The reason is the potential that their deeds would encourage one of the *kuffar* to convert. Nasser insisted that he developed this concept himself. Still, he was not an active proselytizer. He explained that actions, being a model Muslim, counted more than words. He added that God knows if the example he set led someone to convert or not.

We challenged Nasser, too, to reflect whether there was not a measure of hypocrisy in his words. Given that Sweden provided him with a better life and that he appreciated his life there, was it sensible for him to desire its ultimate Islamizing? Nasser answered that Swedish society was indeed better than that of the homeland he had left. Yet the Quran stated that the entire world would become Muslim, and thus, eventually, that would happen. He invoked the Abyssinia example, noting that the Companions of the Prophet went to the Christian country to escape the persecution of the idol-worshippers of Mecca. The result was the conversion of the Negus.[42]

Wissam (b. 1995), a physics undergraduate *salafi* attendee of The Stockholm Mosque, was briefly acquainted in the previous chapters. Born to Libyan parents in Stockholm, he became a *salafi* at the age of 19 through the influence of members of the Ibn Abbas Center whom he met, ironically, at the *wasati* mosque. Throughout the interview, Wissam presented dogmatic *salafi* views on various issues in an eloquent, systematic manner that made the engaging young man sound like a walking testimony of *salafi* textbooks and sermons. He said that he began inquiring about the legitimacy of his living in Sweden after he became religious. He reached the conclusion, which he did not ascribe to a specific source, that Muslims (such as his parents) who migrated to a Western country erred in not giving thought to the implications of their action. Also, it was better for Muslims born in the West, such as himself, to migrate to Muslim countries.

Nevertheless, Wissam was also convinced that there was an 'excuse' (that was the word he used) for him to remain in Sweden: that he will engage in *da'wa* and share the light he had, the light of Islam, with others. This legitimization was, however, prospective. Wissam emphasized that his knowledge had not reached the level of knowledge required to proselytize, but he hoped that the day would come when he would be capable of preaching about Islam, as the members of the Ibn Abbas Center who showed him the righteous path do. He was not certain whether, when the day came, he would focus his efforts online or on traditional preaching.

Wissam explained that some Swedish realities were difficult for him. For example, during Ramadan, he saw drug addicts and women who were not dressed modestly on his way to the mosque. Still, he argued that he preferred Sweden to Muslim countries where there was no religious freedom, such as Tunisia, where his long beard could get him in trouble. Having visited Saudi Arabia for the umrah, his dream was to make the Kingdom his home. That being unrealistic, at least for the time being, the prospect of leaving Sweden, his country of birth, was entirely hypothetical. The practical plans he shared with us, such as becoming a physics teacher, were grounded in the reality of his life in Sweden.

We asked Wissam, too, to reflect on the one-sidedness of migration. Muslims like his parents move to the West, but Westerners do not migrate to Muslim countries. Does that not suggest that a change in Sweden was not desired? He answered that the problem of Muslim countries was not that they were Muslim, but that they were not really Muslim. Money in and of itself does not make people happy. Moreover, he said, people in Sweden are not really happy. There are drug addicts, and there are rapes. Things would have been better if shariʿa was applied in Sweden, and he hopes that one day it would.[43]

While adopting the "missionary migrant" concept did not necessarily encourage active proselytizing, being active in proselytizing did not rely on adopting the concept, and in some cases, even involved negating it. Muhammad (b. 1990) is the son of a Jamaican father and a white mother, and he volunteers with City Centre Daʿwah. His parents were members of the Pentecostal Church, and he grew up in Birmingham. He believed in God and used to talk to Him in a way not related to Christian teachings. He did not occupy himself with doctrine.

At 22, Muhammad began to ask more questions about religion and a personal relationship with God. The trigger was reading about Freemasons and the Illuminati. The more he read, the more he was convinced that the leader of those societies must be Satan; the implication was that there indeed must be a God. Then came another realization: it is not logical that his personal relationship with God is different from everyone else's.

One of Muhammad's friends was a non-practicing Muslim. One day, he visited his friend's home. Muhammad remembered he did not want to discuss religion with the friend's father for fear of being influenced, but a conversation ensued, nevertheless. The father asked him to think about the bee. The bee travels around flowers, collects nectar, and brings the nectar back to the hive. Everything has a clear purpose: the bee, the flower, the nectar, the hive. Is it possible that only humans have no purpose?

214 Shari'a and Life

The metaphor encouraged Muhammad to turn to the scriptures. He began to read the Bible as well as the Quran. He remembers realizing even before he finished the Quran that it must be the word of the Creator. One verse that impressed him, in particular, was Q. 2:2, "this is the Book about which there is no doubt, a guidance for those conscious of Allah."[44] He understood it to imply that God encourages humans to test the content of the Quran, which is evidence of its truth. Muhammad spent the next six months reading more about Islam. Even before formally converting, he began inviting others to convert.

Muhammad knew nothing about *salafis* when he began to engage with Islam. After reading the Quran, he asked Muslim friends of his, also of Jamaican descent, to take him along to an Eid prayer. While the friends were not *salafis*, they went to the Salafi Mosque's Eid prayer at the Small Heath Park basketball courts – the annual high point of the mosque's activities. After the prayer, Muhammad took the *shahada*. He said that on the spot, he felt that the Salafi Mosque was suitable for him and never found the need to examine other mosques or groups.

Following his conversion, Muhammad married a convert from a similar background, and together they have a son, who was two years old at the time of the interview. Asked if living in a non-Muslim country was permissible, Muhammad first answered, laughing: "It has to be permissible because I am here." Muhammad then added that indeed it was desired for a Muslim to migrate to a Muslim country, but two conditions needed to apply before he could personally do so. First, he would need to have enough money and a job in the destination country so that he can provide for his family. Second, he would need to ask permission from his parents (who are still Christian, and maintain good relations with him) and make sure that they would be taken care of in his absence. He said this condition was based on a *hadith*: The Prophet Muhammad was approached by someone who wanted to migrate and told him that he needed permission from his parents.

Muhammad accepted that every Muslim in the West who had sufficient knowledge should engage in proselytizing.[45] However, he did not argue that his volunteer work with City Centre Da'wah should factor in his – or others' – decision on whether to remain in the West. The issue appeared alien to him, as leaving Britain was not in any way on his agenda.

Usama (b. 1994) was the most dedicated of the volunteer proselytizers we met at Muslims Love Jesus, the *da 'wa* booth affiliated with the Green Lane Mosque at the centre of Birmingham. He fled war-torn Libya in 2014 with his family. We met him while he was waiting for passersby to approach and receive freely distributed copies of the Quran. Less than five years after his migration, he spoke perfect English with a local accent and an indefatigably pleasant smile.

The booth Usama led operates on different days at the same central location of the Salafi Mosque's City Centre Daʿwah. Asked why two groups of *salafi* activists who share the goal of spreading Islam could not work together, Usama argued that Abu Khadeejah would not approve such cooperation because the volunteers from Green Lane would not declare their loyalty to him. He accused the imam of the Salafi Mosque of being a political agent of the Saudi government.

Despite his impressive integration and the freedom with which he proselytized, Usama said it was impermissible for Muslims to make non-Muslim countries their permanent home. He held it was legitimate for Muslims to reside in Europe only temporarily and for legitimate objectives such as medical treatment, studies, and finding refuge. He argued that proselytizing could not justify continued presence in Britain because the Muslim who remains in the West is exposed to the proselytizing of non-Muslims, which could undermine his identity. Thus, he intended to return to Libya, although he still did not know when.[46]

Conclusion

The debate about migration policies and the limits of multicultural-ism has become a defining feature of European politics. It is largely about the extent to which shari'a norms should be permitted in pub-lic spheres – schools, workplaces, leisure centres, sidewalks, or parks. Voices that call to ban or restrict expressions of Islamic identity com-prise an unusual coalition of secular liberals and Christian conserva-tives, feminists and populists, socialists and libertarians.

Discontent has been directed towards specific practices. Yet, in essence, concerns raised are not about the implications of one or another norm set by an interpretation of the shari'a, but about the presence of the shari'a itself in modern-day Europe. A revelation-based corpus of codes in the eyes of those who abide by it, the shari'a is seen by some Euro-peans of diverse orientations as a direct challenge to the achievements of the Enlightenment. The existence of shari'a norms in their proximity has fascinated and troubled so many non-Muslims (as well as some Muslims) because they believe those norms belong to a past from which their individualist, rationalist, and democratic societies have advanced.

Perhaps because of this combination of fascination and fear, the authors of this study have had more opportunities in recent years to speak before general audiences than professors usually have. Often, when presenting the contours of *fiqh al-aqalliyyat al-Muslima* and the ways Muslims in Europe engage with it – i.e., the main conclusions of this study – we are met with surprised responses. These responses adhere, more or less, to the following lines: Until today, says the per-son in the audience, I was under the impression that the shari'a is a rigid, static code, which devout Muslims insist on following because they believe in its revealed origins. If so many different and conflicting things can be made of it, how is the shari'a different from any other human ideology or preference? If the shari'a can be anything a person

Conclusion   217

wants it to be, why should those who deny its relevancy give it a privileged status of any sort?

To be sure, not anything can be made of the shariʿa. More often than not, the permissible and the prohibited are clear-cut. It is, however, true that Muslims who accept the shariʿa as a revelation-based corpus and consider themselves committed, in principle, to its terms as they understand them, can engage with it with a great degree of individual discretion and flexibility. These qualities are of particular utility when living in the West, a situation that presents constant conflicts between religious norms and the norms of the majority society. Based on interviews and written questionnaires in a spectrum of European mosques regarding options opened by *fiqh al-aqalliyyat al-Muslima* discourse, this book presented the different aspects of pragmatic engagement with the shariʿa by Muslims in England, France, Germany, Iceland, and Sweden.

One is enabled by the existence of lenient (and controversial) fatwas, including those springing from a systematic facilitating religio-legal approach that is determined to make the lives of Muslims in the West easier within the boundaries of religio-legal legitimacy. Those fatwas offer a way of treating practices that are strictly prohibited in the shariʿa, such as taking mortgages, as conditionally legitimate in the case of Muslims living in non-Muslim countries. As demonstrated in the study, facilitating fatwas may have an impact also on people who were never directly exposed to them. This is done through paraphrased and even distorted variations that evolve from the dissemination of their contents.

Mosque attendees were found to engage with the religio-legal discourse, where they do, in a manner that gives them the final word. The book demonstrated their insistence to preserve for themselves the role of ultimate arbiters as to what the correct understanding of the shariʿa is in different situations. They grant themselves the discretion to decide when, and if, to ask or search for religio-legal advice, whom to consult, and whether or not to accept the advice given.

Many explanations could be attributed to the failure of the transnational European Council for Fatwa and Research to become the exclusive or at least a primary authority on religious law for Muslims in Europe that it sought to become, including its marketing deficiencies, focus on a narrow field of jurisprudence, controversial leadership and ideology, the dominance of ethnic affiliations in defining European Muslim identities, and the competitive pluralism of Islamic online operations. Yet the most fundamental hindrance, which would likely frustrate any similar ambition by other panels, is that the concept of exclusive authority in itself is rejected. Throughout the spectrum of mosques studied, and almost without exception, attendees interviewed were adamant that they would not commit to or even privilege any individual expert or panel. Their view was inspired by a Sunni tradition that privileged the strength of the evidence over the status of the expert. It bestowed them with complete independence. That independence comes with a burden of responsibility. Yet, the empowering prize it carries for those advancing it is that their religious practices are free from commitment to any individual or group.

Transitioning between approaches is another enabler of pragmatism. Anthropologists of religion have established that rigid categories of religiosity, such as orthodox, traditionalist, and modern, fail to exhaust the nuances of religious sentiments, practices, and affiliations, and that an instructive continuum must recognize the continued emergence of in-between categories. This book introduced a bolder complication. It demonstrated that rather than adhere to either pragmatic or dogmatic approaches to the shariʿa, some Muslims shift between approaches in response to different personal circumstances. They are neither coherently pragmatic nor coherently dogmatic. Transitioning helps them to preserve a self-perception of uncompromising religiosity while compromising where it matters most.

One implication is that self-ascribed categories of affiliation have limited power to predict life-decisions. Yes, there are people whose inclination is towards pragmatism and there are the dogmatic-inclined; there are those who attend mosques where the leadership advocates facilitations and those who attend mosques whose spirit is different. Yet the pragmatists are not always pragmatic, and the dogmatists are not always dogmatic.

Other than the flexibility allowed by certain fatwas and the ways through which the religio-legal discourse is engaged, the book demonstrated that pragmatic navigations of shariʿa norms may also be enabled, and indeed often are, through strategies external to fatwa-grounded legitimizations of practices believed to contradict the shariʿa. Such strategies do not rely on religio-legal mechanisms or confirmed textual analyses; rather, they represent individual negotiations of normative expectations that reconcile sentiments of doubts and concerns. These include plain confession of sinning, presented in a way that affirms submission to God and the task of improving; minimizations of the gravity of the transgression, which bestow a sense of commitment even when transgressions occur; statements that transgressions committed could not have also been avoided in a Muslim land, which disassociate offences from the decision to settle in the West; and blunt recognition that humans cannot fully actualize the ideals set by the shari'a. The strategies of repenting and relativizing were found to be applied – moderately – even by *salafi* mosque attendees. Their utilization is one of the reasons why principal adherence to dogmatic and segregationist *salafiyya* involves less practical injury than what the rigidity of *salafi* texts suggests.

Just as there is shifting between fatwa-grounded pragmatic and dogmatic approaches, so were some mosque attendees documented to shift between multiple ways of addressing normative concerns. They neither ignore *istifta'* as a means to settle normative religious concerns, nor rely on it exclusively. Rather, they at times search for religio-legal expert opinions, and at times come up with individual arguments to assuage concerns.

The leading muftis who contributed to *fiqh al-aqalliyyat al-Muslima* and constructed its contesting contours did not direct their contributions toward small elites. Regardless of their orientation, they dealt with common, everyday life issues; wrote mostly in accessible, straightforward language; and desired to bring their specific agendas and priorities to the attention of as large a public as possible through modern and post-modern media (whether successfully or not). The vast majority of mosque attendees who participated in the study indicated that they consider the shari'a a corpus that regulated all or at least some aspects of their lives. They also revealed without exception that their education in fiqh was not academic.

One could expect that these two factors would establish an animated and intensive relationship between readers and texts, *mustaftis* and muftis. That *fiqh al-aqalliyyat al-Muslima* discourse would have a powerful presence in the minds and hearts of those for whom it was intended. Yet this has not been the case. The study found that the foundational texts of the discourse were almost, without exception, not read by mosque attendees, including those who were deeply immersed in studying their religion in their free time, and did not particularly intrigue them. It also found that some of the issues prolifically and profusely debated in the discourse, such as the legitimacy of living in the West or Christmas greetings, were of little concern to most interviewees. This does not mean that *fiqh al-aqalliyyat al-Muslima* is detached from the realities of Muslims in Europe – their priorities, concerns, and hopes. It means, however, that this discourse should not be seen as a loyal and comprehensive reflection of those priorities, concerns, and hopes, let alone as the decisive agent that shapes them.

The study was based on a particular sample and treated a particular question: male mosque attendees in Arabic-speaking European mosques and how they engage with the religious law of Muslim

220 Shari'a and Life

minorities. Additional studies of other Muslim populations will be needed to inform whether the patterns exposed, or some of them, are universal.

There are, however, those who can no longer be anthropologically explored – the *mustaftis* and the muftis of past generations. Perhaps this book will contribute to historical studies in the sociology of religion as well, by offering another call for caution as to how much can be inferred from fatwas about the social realities of their times.

Along with contributing to the understanding of the sociology of shari'a, in Europe and at large, we hope that the analyses presented in the book will contribute to the public discourse on integration. Not a day passes without a story from somewhere across the continent about the parents of a schoolkid who appealed to the courts to have their son or daughter exempted from mixed-gender swimming or gym class or to allow them to pray on school grounds during the regulated times; or the employee who was fired for insisting on wearing a hijab, refusing to sell a bottle of vodka, or continuing to grow a thick beard; or the football player who faces sanctions for refusing to wear a jersey marketing beer or to break the fast before a crucial match during Ramadan.

The prevalence of such reports and their, at times, cynical political usages create the impression that devotion to Islam leads unavoidably to insolvable conflicts. However, while many, perhaps a majority, of the Muslims in Europe consider themselves committed to the shari'a as a principal guide, and while there are indeed contradictions between certain shari'a norms and certain everyday life realities in Europe, conflicts of the nature described above are the exception, not the norm. Most Muslims who care about shari'a manage to preserve a sense of religious commitment and practice without ending up in direct conflicts with employers, educators, and other officials. Studying processes of *istifta'* in their fullness and the strategies Muslims in Europe deploy beyond these processes can help make sense of how contradictions between shari'a and Western norms are negotiated. It can also make sense of why they are more often than not resolved in mutual agreement, or at least moderated.

A fair conclusion to draw is that wherever and whenever non-Muslim majorities deny shari'a norms space in the public sphere, Muslims who abide by these norms will find ways to compromise without necessarily feeling that they injured their principal loyalty to their religion and its revealed laws. The book introduced numerous pertinent examples. The imams of Reykjavik and the attendees of their mosques would have, no doubt, preferred if the city offered separate-gender swimming hours where Islamic same-gender modesty codes are applied. In the absence of such options, they find ways to justify swimming in the mixed-gender pools with everyone else. Some attendees of the Salafi Mosque in Birmingham would have preferred to send their children to the local Salafi School. Not being able to do so, they find ways to explain why their kids' attending state schools constitutes no injury to their religious beliefs.

Perhaps some readers of this book will understand it as suggesting that non-Muslim majorities can rest assured that by refusing to accommodate shariʿa-related norms, they do not categorically breach Muslims' right to religious freedom. After all, if there are so many ways for Muslims to navigate those norms and compromise, what differences do refusals make? We take the liberty to offer a different approach, one that puts a greater burden on liberals. Indeed, because of the accommodating nature of the shariʿa and of engagements with the shariʿa, liberal societies can expect Muslims to be the ones who resolve conflicts between their religious norms and the expectations of the majority. Yet, these kinds of expectations, let alone when articulated in the form of regulations and legislation, should be reserved only for the most crucial and clearly defined breaches of core liberal values and interferences with the public order. Shariʿa-grounded expressions should not be denied because they make the majority uncomfortable or puzzled. They should only be denied where they negate the essences of society.

That, to be sure, is easier said than done. Determining what these essences are could be a painful task for Europeans. It forces revisiting the meanings of liberalism and national identity and asking questions that have long been avoided – for a reason.

Liberalism developed as an ideology that defends two core values – freedom and equality. Historically, the progression of both in Europe was interrelated. Women's rights are a primary example. The more legal and social norms guaranteed equality between men and women, the more women were able to exhaust their potential and pursue their dreams as men could. Thus, liberals were led to believe that the link between freedom and equality is deterministic.

Muslim migration proved this not always to be the case. Headscarves are the most common demonstration. The religio-legal justification for hijabs is that women are a cause of temptation for men, and it is their responsibility to avoid temptation. Thus, this practice can be viewed as an injury to the core liberal value of equality. It is less evident that it is an injury to the core value of freedom. To the extent that women decide independently to cover themselves, they exercise a fundamental right that liberal ideology guarantees: to practice a belief in a way that does not directly infringe on the freedom of others.

In their effort to assert the link between freedom and equality, some liberals insist that women do not freely choose to don the hijab. Rather, they are forced to do so. This is not true, at least not in all cases. There is indeed a strong element of religious and cultural indoctrination encouraging the decision to cover, but indoctrination also greatly impacts the choice of women to wear bikinis. No matter how one spins the debate about the headscarf, it forces an inconvenient dilemma upon liberals who took for granted that freedom facilitates progression towards equality – can the two be separated? And if they cannot, then how much can a liberal society impose without becoming illiberal?

National identity is also an essence that cannot be easily defined. For some Europeans, "core national values" are inseparable from Christianity. They believe that their societies are at least to some extent characterized by their Christian heritage and ethics.

The proliferation of Islamic institutions and norms in public spheres is seen by those who hold this view as an assault on the Christian character of their nation. For example, debates about the broadcasting of calls to prayer were encouraged not only by environmental concerns but also by sentiments of dismay and offence that the sounds of another faith are infringing upon a landscape dominated by church bells. These concerns underscored an expectation that Christianity be privileged over other religions.

Should it, indeed? For a long while, the tension between a secular present and a Christian past was dormant in European societies because, as the only major religion, Christianity enjoyed a de-facto privileged status. Religious conservatives and secularists were both at peace with that status because the meaning of its expressions could be interpreted differently. Christmas markets or coronations rich with Christian symbols could equally be seen as manifestations of an actual, viable national affinity to a religious doctrine or as harmless commercialized folklore. Determining whether Islamic norms contradict an essence of national identity or not forces more definite answers to questions Europeans have skilfully avoided for so long: Is their nation Christian? Does Christianity have a special status?

There is a belief in Europe that greater integration of Muslim minorities would do away with conflicts between shari'a norms and Western norms because it would do away with code-based religiosity. That is unlikely to be the case. Ironically, part of the reason why, in recent years, more European Muslims are standing up for their right to practice religious norms, as they understand them, is that they feel more integrated and secure in their receiving societies.

Conclusion 223

To launch a legal appeal, speak up in the media, or plead with local politicians, one must possess certain skills and resources – financial, logistic, linguistic, and other. Newcomers to Europe did not have these assets. As the years went by, some among the first generation of migrants naturalized, learned the local language, obtained job security, and developed social networks. Second and third generations were born and educated on the continent. Religious life institutionalized on transnational, national, and local levels, and a competitive field of Islamic organizations triggered struggles for influence and provided new resources and confidence for social activism.

For Muslims who have always been devout, or who found their way back to the fold of religion, enhanced social status implied, among other things, greater opportunities to advance Islamic causes. From their point of view, demanding space for Islam is not a provocation against European norms because they are confident that their religious norms are part of the European story, whether the majority likes it or not. It is misleading to think of integration as a one-dimensional process in terms of its impact on religious practices. Among the European Muslims who demand space for their norms are individuals who are highly educated, do well financially, and have non-Muslim friends. Some asserted their Islamic identity not because they were withdrawn from the mainstream secular society, but in response to intense interactions with that society and concerns about its values. There are many good reasons why European governments should insist that every child commands the language spoken by the majority and learn the history and traditions of their receiving states. However, it is fanciful to think that Islamic norms would disappear from public spheres if that happened.

Muslims will remain a sizeable minority in Europe. This implies that the shariʿa will remain a part of life in Europe. Understanding the dynamics through which shariʿa and life impact one another is a key for informed public debates on migration, integration, and religious freedom. Equally important are goodwill and resolute minds.

Notes

Introduction

1 Zweig, *Magellan*, 5.

2 The terms dogmatism and pragmatism are used throughout the book to differentiate between an ideological system of beliefs and ideas that is resistant to change and one that is more inclined to accommodation. The former results in greater isolation from other systems of beliefs and ideas. Rokeach, "Nature and Meaning of Dogmatism," 196–8. While the terms may be understood as normative and pejorative, they describe well the core difference between *salafi* and *wasati* approaches respectively.

3 Examples include: Caeiro, "Power of European Fatwas," 435–49; Caeiro, "Transnational Ulama," 121–41; DeLorenzo, "Fiqh and the Fiqh Council," 193; Duderija "Minority Fiqh," 209–29; Fishman, *Fiqh Al-Aqalliyyat*; Ghadban, "Fiqh Al-Aqalliyyat," 30–7; Hassan, *Fiqh al-Aqalliyyat*; March, *Islam and Liberal Citizenship*; March, "Sources of Moral Obligation," 34–94; Parray, "Legal Methodology," 88–107; Rohe, *Muslim Minorities*, 146–54; Shadid and van Koningsveld, "Loyalty to a Non-Muslim," 85–114; Shavit, "Wasati and Salafi," 416–57; Shavit, "Can Muslims Befriend Non-Muslims?" 67–88; Shavit, *Shariʿa and Muslim Minorities*.

4 Calder, *Islamic Jurisprudence*, 116–17; Masud, "Significance of Istiftaʾ," 341–66.

5 Asad, *Genealogies of Religion*, 36.

6 On the difficulty of ascertaining the authenticity of fatwas or their reflecting of actual social realities, see: Skovgaard-Petersen, *Defining Islam for the Egyptian State*, 5–6.

7 Larsen, *How Muftis Think*, 7.

8 Allievi, "Muslim Voices, European Ears," 39.

9 An example is the compilation of anthropological studies by Dessing, Jeldoft, and Woodhead, *Everyday Lived Islam in Europe*.

226 Notes to pages 7–17

10 Holland, *5 Readers Reading*, ix.
11 Holland, 113–29.
12 Ginzburg, *The Cheese and the Worms*.
13 Liebes and Katz, *The Export of Meaning*, 68–81.
14 Radway, *Reading the Romance*, 60–3.
15 For example, Pinchevski and Brand, "Holocaust Perversions," 387–407.
16 For example, Burtăverde et al., "Why Do People Watch Porn?," 1–15.
17 For example, Sauerberg, "Literature in Figures," 93–107.
18 For example, Spence, *Watching Daytime Soap Operas*.
19 Stubbersfield, Tehrani, and Flynn, "Serial Killers, Spiders and Cybersex," 291, 298.
20 Masud, Messick, and Powers, "Muftis, Fatwas, and Islamic Legal Interpretation," in *Islamic Legal Interpretation*, 3–4.
21 Schacht, *An Introduction to Islamic Law*, 69–75; Hallaq, *Shari'a*, 110–12, 153, 176–7; Calder, *Islamic Jurisprudence*, 116–46.
22 Tamanaha, *General Jurisprudence of Law*, 155–65, 235.
23 Agrama, *Questioning Secularism*, 34–6, 123, 170–5.
24 Shavit, "Muslim Brothers' Conception," 601–3.
25 Skovgaard-Petersen, *Defining Islam for the Egyptian State*, 100–45.
26 Al-Atawneh, "Is Saudi Arabia a Theocracy?" 721–37; Mouline, "Committee of Grand Ulama," 146–70.
27 Bruinessen, "Producing Islamic Knowledge," 8.
28 Yayciolgu tells about a sixteenth-century Ottoman mufti who dangled a basket from his balcony. *Mustafti*s would approach and place their queries in the basket. The mufti would then pull up the basket, issue his fatwa, and lower the basket again: Yaycioglu, "Ottoman Fatwa," 45.
29 Bunt, *Islam in the Digital Age*, 125–33; Campbell, "Who's Got the Power?" 1051–2; Echchaibi, "From Audio Tapes," 26–33; Miladi, Karim, and Athambawa, "Fatwa on Satellite TV," 133, 138–40.
30 At the 'Umar Ibn al-Khattab Mosque in Dortmund, 15 attendees were interviewed, as well as three (changing) imams and the chairman; at The Grand Mosque of Reykjavik, 15 attendees were interviewed, as well as the imam and the Chairman; at The Stockholm Mosque, 20 attendees were interviewed, as well as the imam; at The Salafi Mosque, Birmingham, 20 attendees were interviewed, as well as the imam.

Attendees at the 'Umar Ibn al-Khattab Mosque, with its constant change of imams, were approached during different periods in 2016–19, but particularly from 28 August to 19 September 2018. The study in Reykjavik's Grand Mosque was done from 17 September to 15 October 2017, and was supported by a previous study there conducted in June and October 2015. The study in The Stockholm Mosque was conducted from 6 July to 5 August 2018. The study in Birmingham's Salafi Mosque was conducted from 18 July to 17 August 2019, and supported by previous visits to the mosque in August 2013 and October 2015.

31 ʿUmar Ibn al-Khattab Mosque, Dortmund, 26 August 2016, 200 attendees present, 50 approached, 33 participated; Markaz Imam Malik, Dortmund, 2 September 2016, 90 attendees present, 43 approached, 33 participated; The Grand Mosque Reykjavik, 100 attendees present, 34 approached, 24 participated; Al-Nur Mosque, Reykjavik, 50 attendees present, 25 approached, 18 participated; The Stockholm Mosque, 1,200 attendees present, 110 approached, 38 participated; Husby Mosque, Stockholm, 400 attendees present, 50 approached, 31 participated; The Salafi Mosque, Birmingham, 750 attendees present, 75 approached, 47 participated; Hassan Blidi Mosque, Marseille, 350 attendees present, 50 approached, 42 participated. The aggregated number of respondents is 266.

At a confidence interval of 85%, margins of error for the samples are 3.6% to 10.4%; at a confidence interval of 95%, they are 3.6% to 16.4%. We are thankful to Hakan Yar for advising and supervising the statistical analysis of the surveys.

Not all respondents answered all questions included in the surveys respectively. We note here only those cases where more than three respondents did not answer specific questions. The question whether respondents searched at least once for a fatwa on the internet during the past year was not answered by four respondents at The Stockholm Mosque and by five at the Hassan Blidi Mosque in Marseille. The question whether respondents sent at least one query to an online fatwa council during the past year was not answered by five respondents at the Hassan Blidi Mosque and by four at The Salafi Mosque. The question regarding purchasing a house through a usurious loan was not answered by eight respondents at The Stockholm Moque, by four at the Al-Nur Mosque in Reykjavik, by six at Markaz Imam Malik in Dortmund, by four at the ʿUmar Ibn al-Khattab Mosque in Dortmund, by 18 at the Hassan Blidi Mosque, by five at the Husby Mosque in Stockholm, and by seven at The Salafi Mosque. The question regarding Christmas congratulations was not answered by seven respondents at The Stockholm Mosque, by 15 at the Hassan Blidi Mosque, by four at the Husby Mosque, and by seven at The Salafi Mosque. The question regarding voting in elections was not answered by four respondents at The Stockholm Mosque, by 10 at the Hassan Blidi Mosque, by four at the Husby Mosque, and by seven at The Salafi Mosque. The question regarding directing one's life according to the shariʿa was not answered by seven respondents at The Stockholm Mosque, by four at The Grand Mosque in Reykjavik, by 15 at the Hassan Blidi Mosque, and by six at The Salafi Mosque.

228   Notes to pages 19–25

32 An example for a study based in part on online circulation of questionnaires through networks established through a snowballing effect is Brekke's "Halal Money," 2–4. The method allowed for a large sample, with the limitations noted in our above discussion.

1. The Religious Law of Muslim Minorities

1   Asad, *Genealogies of Religion*, 210.
2   Portions of this chapter draw on and update sections in Uriya Shavit's *Shari'a and Muslim Minorities*.
3   Rida used the term *wasatiyya* to describe balanced reformism that is an alternative to blind *taqlid*, which is not capable of absorbing modernity, and to Muslims who reject shari'a as incapable of accommodating modernity. However, the term was not common to his writings: Rida, "Kitab Yusr al-Islam," 63–70. Al-Qaradawi considered Rida one of the intellectual fathers of *wasatiyya*: Al-Qaradawi, *Fiqh al-Wasatiyya*, 106–8. On al-Ghazali's account of Rida's importance as a proponent of Muhammad 'Abduh's reformism: Al-Ghazali, *Al-Ghazwu al-Thaqafi*, 37.
4   Al-Qaradawi, *Fiqh al-Wasatiyya*, 26–32; Bettina Gräf, "The Concept of Wasatiyya," 218.
5   Al-Qaradawi, *Al-Sahwa al-Islamiyya*, 33–60.
6   For example, in a lengthy interview for Al Jazeera, al-Qaradawi defined *wasatiyya* as the trend that reflects the truths of Islam: Mansur, "Al-Wasatiyya fi l-Islam."
7   Al-Ghannushi, "Al-Wasatiyya fi l-Fikr," 294–345; Husyan, "Faqih al-Wasatiyya," 376–88; Haydar, *I'tidal am Tatarruf?*, 28–32, 44; Tayi, "Al-Shaykh al-Qaradawi," 877–912.
8   Ali, *Al-Qur'an*.
9   Al-Qaradawi, *Fiqh al-Wasatiyya*, 61–99; al-Qaradawi, *Min Ajl Sahwa Rashida* (Cairo: Dar al-Shuruq, 1988), 138; Tayi, "Al-Shaykh al-Qaradawi," 881, 905; Al-Lafi, "Al-Khitab al-Dini," 250.
10 'Imara, *Al-Istiqlal al-Hadari*, 19–21.
11 Hallaq, *Authority, Continuity and Change*, 86–120.
12 'Abdallah, "Al-Salat fi l-Masjid al-Aqsa," 48; al-Qaradawi, *Khitabuna al-Islami*, 28, 59; al-Qaradawi, *Fiqh al-Wasatiyya*, 209; al-Qaradawi, "al-Wasatiyya wa-Dawr al-I'lam;" Al-Majlis al-Urubbi li-l-Ifta' wa-l-Buhuth, "al-Bayan al-Khitami li-l-Dawra al-'adiyya al-Thaniyya 'Ashara," 457.
13 Al-Qaradawi, *Al-Halal wa-l-Haram*, 13.
14 As al-Qaradawi noted in *Taysir al-Fiqh li-l-Muslim al-Mu'asir fi Daw' al-Qur'an wa-l-Sunna – Fiqh al-Siyam* (this book preceded the publication of

Notes to pages 26–8   229

what he described as his great project on the subject of *taysir*, ultimately presented in his book *Taysir al-Fiqh li-l-Muslim al-Mu'asir fi Daw' al-Qur'an wa-l-Sunna*, which he completed in July 1996 and was published in 2000), 5.

15 Al-Qaradawi, *Taysir al-Fiqh* (2000), 15–35; al-Qaradawi, *Fiqh al-Wasatiyya*, 124–33; al-Qaradawi, *Khitabuna al-Islami*, 145–8. On the centricity of *taysir* in al-Qaradawi's thought, see: Kassab, *Al-Manhaj al-Da'wi*, 237–43. On the need for *taysir*, and specifically lifting *haraj* as a *wasati* fundamental, see also Abu l-Majd, *Ru'ya Islamiyya Mu'asira*, 28.

16 Al-Qaradawi, *Taysir al-Fiqh* (2000), 19–20.

17 Al-Qaradawi, 28.

18 Al-Qaradawi, 32.

19 Al-Qaradawi, 29.

20 Al-Qaradawi, 33.

21 Al-Qaradawi, 28–9.

22 Al-Qaradawi, 113–14; Al-Qaradawi, *Min Ajl Sahwa Rashida*, 46.

23 Al-Qaradawi, *Taysir al-Fiqh* (2000), 31.

24 Al-Qaradawi, *Khitabuna al-Islami*, 149–51; *Fiqh al-Wasatiyya*, 235. On the centricity of *tabshir* in al-Qaradawi's teachings, see: Kassab, *Al-Manhaj al-Da'wi*, 244–8; on the importance of gradualism in the application of Islamic law by governments, see: Al-Qaradawi, *Taysir al-Fiqh* (2000), 28.

25 For his earlier view, see al-Qaradawi, *Al-Halal wa-l-Haram*, 38. For his later view, see al-Qaradawi, *Taysir al-Fiqh* (2000), 96–101; *Al-Siyasa al-Shar'iyya*, 84, 90–2; *Fiqh al-Wasatiyya*, 235.

26 Al-Qaradawi, *Al-Siyasa al-Shar'iyya*, 84.

27 Al-Qaradawi, *Taysir al-Fiqh* (2000), 35.

28 Al-Qaradawi, *Min Fiqh al-Dawla*, 36, 144–6; 'Imara, *Al-Islam wa-Huquq al-Insan*, 60–1; Abu l-Majd, *Ru'ya Islamiyya Mu'asira*, 30–1; Huwaydi, *Al-Qur'an wa-l-Sultan*, 20–6.

29 'Imara, *Al-Islam wa-Huquq al-Insan*, 61; al-Qaradawi, *Al-Khasa'is al-'Amma li-l-Islam*, 87; al-Ghazali, *Azmat al-Shura fi l-Mujtama'at*, 14; Huwaydi, *Al-Islam wa-l-Dimuqratiyya*, 8–9, 113.

30 Al-Qaradawi, *Al-Halal wa-l-Haram*, 181–2; Abu l-Majd, *Ru'ya Islamiyya Mu'asira*, 44; Al-Hawari, "Usus al-Bina' al-Usari," 164.

31 Al-Qaradawi, *Al-Halal wa-l-Haram*, 134–8.

32 On the *wasatis'*, and particularly al-Ghazali's, view regarding equal rights in education and the job market, see: Baker, *Islam without Fear*, 49–50, 93–100. On al-Qaradawi's views regarding women, higher education, and the job market: 'Abdallah, "Fasahtu Khitbat Ibnati," 109–10. In the interview, he took pride in his daughter's academic achievements

230   Notes to pages 28–32

in the exact sciences. On al-Qaradawi's views regarding the political participation of women: Barbara Freyer-Stowasser, "Yusuf al-Qaradawi on Women," 913, 921.

33   Al-Ghazali, *Al-Sunna al-Nabawiyya*, 44–58. Al-Ghazali did not encourage the election of women as heads of state but argued that the fittest person of the nation, whether male or female, should be elected. He noted the examples of the successful reigns of the Queen of Sheba, Queen Victoria, Margaret Thatcher, Golda Meir, and Indira Gandhi. See also on Benazir Bhutto: al-Ghazali, *Qadaya al-Mar'a*, 16; on al-Qaradawi's opinion: Freyer-Stowasser, "Yusuf Al-Qaradawi on Women," 206; Fahmi al-Huwaydi called for full participation of women in public life based on the example of the early Muslims: Huwaydi, "Risala fi Tahrir al-Mar'a," 7.

34   Al-Qaradawi, *Al-Halal wa-l-Haram*, 143; Abu l-Majd, "Qadiyyat al-Hijab wa-l-Niqab," 9.

35   Al-Qaradawi, *Al-Halal wa-l-Haram*, 261–5.

36   Mawlawi and 'Atiyya, "Watching Football."

37   Abu l-Majd emphasized the equality of all citizens of Egypt, regardless of their religion, and urged that the term *dhimma* be rethought: Abu l-Majd, *Ru'ya Islamiyya Mu'asira*, 38. Al-Qaradawi suggested replacing *dhimma* with the term "citizens," arguing that this term does not contradict the *shari'a* in any way: al-Qaradawi, *Khitabuna al-Islami*, 50–1. On *wasati*s and minorities in non-Muslim societies, see: Baker, *Islam without Fear*, 106–10. On the *wasati* approach to Egyptian Copts: 'Abd al-Fattah, *Taqrir al-Hala al-Diniyya*, 365–6.

38   Ali, *Al-Qur'an*.

39   Al-Qaradawi, *Al-Halal wa-l-Haram*, 290–2.

40   For a reference about the king's speech in November 1946: AbdusSalam, *To Be a Serious Salafi*, 23.

41   Al-Akhdar, *In Defense of Islam*, 25.

42   Ibn Jibrin, "Advise to Those," 200–2. On the Saudi rejection of the term *Wahhabiyya*: Armanios, "Islamic Traditions of Wahhabism," 1–3.

43   Al-Khadar, *Al-Sa'udiyya Sirat Dawla*, 224–8.

44   Wiktorowicz, "Anatomy of the Salafi," 208.

45   Hegghammer, "Jihadi-Salafis," 251–5.

46   Wiktorowicz, "Anatomy of the Salafi," 221–5.

47   'Abd al-Wahhab, *Kitab al-Tawhid*. For an overview of his concept of *tawhid* and its reception: Commins, *The Wahhabi Mission*, 7–70.

48   Ibn Baz, *The Legislation of Islam*, 12. Note: This publication uses the alternative spelling of Ibn Baaz.

49 Al-Fawzaan, "Why Do the 'Wahhabis'," 4. On the essentiality of establishing *tawhid* and the risk of engaging in *shirk* by, for example, supplicating to the Prophet, see also Al Bur'ee, *A Concise Manual*, 8.

50 Islam Question & Answer, "What Is the True Meaning," 22–32. Al-ʿUthaymin, "Anwaʿ al-Shirk," 56–7.

51 Ibn Baz explained that "loyalty and disavowal" means loving the believers and being their friend (or ally), while despising the infidels, spurning them and their religion: Ibn Baz, "Al-Walaʾ wa-l-Baraʾ," 174. See also Ibn Baz, *The Correct Belief*, 24–25. The Permanent Committee for Scholarly Research and Iftaʾ argued that infidels, including Jews and Christians, are the enemies of Allah and His Prophet and are doomed to hellfire: Al-Lajna al-Daʾima li-l-Buhuth wa-l-Iftaʾ, "Hukm al-Daʿwa," 16–20. The glossary of a master's dissertation on the meaning of *al-walaʾ wa-l-baraʾ*, written by Muhammad Saʿid al-Qahtani and approved in June 1981 at Umm al-Qura University in Mecca, defined *walaʾ* as "loyalty, holding fast to all that is pleasing to Allah" and *baraʾ* as "withdrawing from and opposing all that is displeasing to Allah and His messenger." See: Al-Qahtani, *Al-Walaʾ Wal-Baraʾ*, 118, 129–30. The dissertation was supervised by Muhammad Qutb (d. 2014), a former member of the Muslim Brothers and the brother of Sayyid Qutb, who escaped execution, was released from Egyptian prison in 1972, and found academic shelter in Saudi Arabia. A member of the dissertation's examining committee, who also endorsed the book version, was ʿAbd al-Raziq ʿAfifi, Deputy President of the Departments for Guidance, Iftaʾ, Daʿwa, and Scholarly Research. In referencing Sayyid Qutb and *salafi* sources, the dissertation demonstrates the blending of Islamist and *salafi* ideas among a generation of Saudi university graduates. An introduction by an England-based president of a *salafi* organization to a treatise on *al-walaʾ wa-l-baraʾ*, first published in 1997, explained that "in the context of Islam, *al-walaʾ* is loyalty to Allah and whatever He is pleased with as well as friendship and closeness to the believers, whereas *al-baraʾ* is freeing oneself from that which is displeasing to Allah and disowning the disbelievers": ʿAli, "Introduction," 4–5.

52 Al-Qahtani, *Al-Walaʾ Wal-Baraʾ*, 115. See also Ibn ʿAbd al-Khaliq, "Al-Walaʾ wa-l-baraʾ"; Al-Arshani, *Al-Walaʾ wa-l-Baraʾ*.

53 Al-Fawzan, "Ahkam al-Tashabuh."

54 Al-ʿUthaymin, "Benefiting from What," 39.

55 Al-Fawzan, "Ahkam al-Tashabuh," 5.

56 In warning against imitating Jews and Christians, Ibn Taymiyya explained that customs – clothes, food, housing, etc. – affect beliefs and wishes, and vice versa. A person who wears the clothes of a

232 Notes to pages 33–6

certain group identifies with that group: Ibn Taymiyya, *Al-Sirat al-Mustaqim*, 56–8.

57 Al-Fawzan, "Ahkam al-Tashabuh," 6–8.
58 See the words of ʿAbd al-Wahhab and al-Fawzan's contemporary elaboration on them: Ibn ʿAbdul Wahhab, *The Best Religion*, 79–82; also Ibn Baz, *Correct Islamic Aqidah*, 43–54; Ibn Adam, ed., *Crime of Hizbiyyah*, 4–5, 24–5, 57–60.
59 Ibn Taymiyya, *The Friends of Allah*, 92–107.
60 Ibn Baz, *The Legislation of Islam*, 18–28. Note: This publication uses the alternative spelling of Ibn Baaz.
61 Al-ʿUthaymin, "Don't Be Such a Fanatic!" 3.
62 Al-Khudayr, "Is It Permissible," 93.
63 Al-ʿUthaymin, "Ma Huwa al-Wasat," 151–2.
64 Al-Fawzan, *Al-Wasatiyya fi l-Islam*, 27, 32.
65 Al-Fawzan, *Wujub al-Tahakum*, 10–11.
66 Ibn Baz, "There Are No Trivial Issues," 194–6.
67 AbdusSalam, *To Be a Serious Salafi*, 60; Al-Madkhali, *The Necessity of Conforming*, 24–5; al-Tibi, *Fatawa al-Shaykh al-Albani*, 135–48.
68 Without referencing Ibn Taymiyya specifically, Ibn Baz asserted the utility of the fiqh of balances through the example of a man who will start murdering people if he stops drinking. Ibn Baz argues that in this case it is better to refrain from denying the potential murderer his drink: Ibn Baz, *The Legislation of Islam*, 52–3. Note: This publication uses the alternative spelling of Ibn Baaz.
69 An example is Ibn Baz's approval of the invitation of American soldiers to Saudi Arabia following Saddam Hussein's occupation of Kuwait on 2 August 1990, which provided religio-juristic legitimization for the House of Saud at a critical historical juncture. Based on Q. 6:119, he argued that necessities permit the otherwise impermissible, including the assistance of an infidel army in defending against a corrupt regime: Ibn Baz, "Hukm al-Tashkik." See the discussion in: Al-Atawneh, *Wahhabi Islam*, 43–4.
70 Ibn Baz, "Mawqif al-Muslim," 941; Al-Khudayr, "Is It Permissible," 93.
71 As explained by al-Fawzan in an edition of Ibn ʿAbdul Wahhab, *The Best Religion*, 72.
72 Al-Atawneh, *Wahhabi Islam*, 73.
73 Al-Atawneh, *Wahhabi Islam*, 74.
74 Al-Atawneh, *Wahhabi Islam*, 70–7.
75 Al-Munajjid, "Does Islam Regard Men," 57–67.
76 Rawas, *Mawsuʿat Fiqh Ibn Taymiyya*, 582.
77 Al-Lajna al-Daʾima, "Ruling on Making Fun of the Hijab," 75–6.

78 Al-Fawzan, *Rulings Pertaining to Muslim Women*, 15–17. Note: This source uses an alternative spelling of the author's name: Saleh Fauzan Al-Fauzan.

79 Ibn Taymiyya, *The Friends of Allah*, 341.

80 Ibn Baz, "Ruling Concerning Listening," 324.

81 The Permanent Committee, "Ruling on Children's Songs," 220–1.

82 Islam Question & Answer, "Bodybuilding."

83 See discussion in Shavit, "Raising *Salafi* Children," 346.

84 Islam Question & Answer, "Ruling on Democracy"; Shavit, "Is Shura a Muslim Form," 358–60, 366–8.

85 Ibn Taymiyya, *Al-Siyasa al-Shar'iyya*, 161; Al-Enazy, *Creation of Saudi Arabia*, 14–19; Rawas, *Mawsu'at Fiqh Ibn Taymiyya*, 1:285–300.

86 Al-Harithi, ed., *Al-Fatawa al-Muhimma*, 15–40, 97, 102, 106; Ibn Adam, *Crime of Hizbiyyah*, 54; Al-'Uthaymin, "*Hukm Ta'at*", 172–3; Al-Ghunayman, "The Kufr of Those," 131; AbdusSalam, *To Be a Serious Salafi*, 84; Al-Haddaadee, ed., *Book of Forty Hadeeth*, 32.

87 Al-Qaradawi, "Introduction," 9–10.

88 European Council for Fatwa and Research, *Fatwas*, 1–2.

89 A copy of Rawi's speech, which was not published, was obtained by Alexandre Caeiro, "Transnational Ulama," 123.

90 Interview by Uriya Shavit (together with *qadi* Dr. Iyad Zahalka), Dublin, 13 February 2012.

91 Al-Qaradawi, *Fi Fiqh al-Aqalliyyat al-Muslima*, 50–2.

92 Al-Qaradawi, 53. On the importance of gradualism in Muslim minorities' fiqh. see also Al-Bishri, "Muntalaqat li-Fiqh," 213–15.

93 Al-Majlis al-Urubbi li-l-Ifta' wa-l-Buhuth, "Fatwa No. 6."

94 Abou El Fadl, "Islamic Law," 146–7.

95 Abou El Fadl, 159.

96 Al-Qaradawi, *Fi Fiqh al-Aqalliyyat al-Muslima*, 33.

97 Al-Qaradawi, "Duties of Muslims."

98 Al-Nayfar, "Al-Tajannus bi-Jinssiya," 177–252. For discussion of his essay and similar opinions: Shavit, *Shari'a and Muslim Minorities*, 104–8.

99 Al-Qaradawi, *Taysir al-Fiqh* (2000), 35–9; Al-Qaradawi, *Fi Fiqh al-Aqalliyyat al-Muslima*, 57–60; Al-Najjar, *Fiqh al-Muwatana*, 108.

100 European Council for Fatwa and Research, *Fatwas of European Council for Fatwa and Research*, 3.

101 European Council for Fatwa and Research, 31–4.

102 Al-Qaradawi, *Fi Fiqh al-Aqalliyyat al-Muslima*, 55.

103 Al-'Alwani, *Fi Fiqh al-Aqalliyyat*.

104 Lewis and Algaoud, *Islamic Banking*, 52–5; Abdullah, *Islamic Banking and Interest*, 76–95; Balala, *Islamic Finance and Law*, 28–9.

234   Notes to pages 44–51

105   For the full text of the fatwa, see: Imam, "Fatwa Tujizu Shira' al-Manazil," 25; al-Qaradawi, *Fi Fiqh al-Aqalliyyat al-Muslima*, 174–9. For an English translation: European Council for Fatwa and Research, *Fatwas*, 160–8.
106   For his earlier opinion: Al-Qaradawi, *Al-Halal wa-l-Haram*, 230–3.
107   Al-Qaradawi, *Fi Fiqh al-Aqalliyyat al-Muslima*, 169–70.
108   Al-Qaradawi, 154–61.
109   Muzammil Siddiqi, "Necessity' That Allows Buying."
110   Al-Shaykhi, "Hukm al-Qurud al-Tulabiyya," 432–4.
111   Nafi, "Fatwa and War," 80–2.
112   Group of Muftis, "Ulama's Fatwas."
113   Al-Qaradawi, *Fi Fiqh al-Aqalliyyat al-Muslima*, 60.
114   Al-Qaradawi, 105–6.
115   Al-Qaradawi, 106–25.
116   Al-Majlis al-Urubbi li-l-Ifta' wa-l-Buhuth, "Qararat wa-Fatawa," 4–5.
117   Al-Qaradawi, *Fi Fiqh al-Aqalliyyat al-Muslima*, 126–31.
118   European Council for Fatwa and Research, *Fatwas*, 148–9.
119   European Council for Fatwa and Research, *Fatwas*, 49–50.
120   European Council for Fatwa and Research, *Fatwas*, 100.
121   Al-Majlis al-Urubbi li-l-Ifta' wa-l-Buhuth, "Al-Bayan al-Khitami li-l-Dawra al-Sabi'a wa-l-'Ashara," 511.
122   Badawi, "'Alaqat al-Muslim bi-Ghayr al-Muslim," 71-81.
123   Jaballah, "Al-Wasatiyya bayna Muqtadayat al-Muwatana," 264–8.
124   For example, Dar al-Ifta' al-Misriyya, "Is It Permissible to Send." In 2007, Malaysia's National Fatwa Committee permitted Christmas greetings as long as the greetings did not glorify non-Muslim faiths or use their religious symbols. In 2016, the chief mufti of Kuala Lumpur, Zulkifli Mohamad al-Bakri, relied on that fatwa to reiterate that Christmas greetings are permissible: The Straits Times, "KL Mufti: Okay."
125   European Council for Fatwa and Research, *Fatwas*, 177, 183.
126   European Council for Fatwa and Research, "Ruling on Offering Congratulations," 181–2.
127   European Council for Fatwa and Research, "Ruling on Offering Congratulations," 182.
128   Al-Qaradawi, "Tahni'at Ahl al-Kitab bi-A'yadihim," in *Fi Fiqh al-Aqalliyyat al-Muslima*, 145–50.
129   See discussion in Shavit, *Shari'a and Muslim Minorities*, 134–7.
130   Al-Najjar, "Ma'alat al-Af'al," 198–9. In his 2011 treatise, al-Najjar claimed a "civilizational dialogue" takes places in which Muslims in the West take from it material advances and endow it with Muslim values that are essential to resolving their problems. He called for the establishment of *da'wa* institutions that would present Islam as the

practical solution to the West's problems: Al-Najjar, "Al-Dawr al-Hadari," 156–7, 174. This kind of rhetoric has become, as noted, more exceptional in the Council's discourse than it was at the turn of the century, when it was founded.

131 Interview by Uriya Shavit, Dublin, 13 February 2012 (with *qadi* Dr. Iyad Zahalka).
132 Hanafy, "European Council."
133 Al-Majlis al-Urubbi li-l-Ifta' wa-l-Buhuth, "Al-Bayan al-Khitami li-l-Dawra al-'Adiyya al-Tasi'a wa-l-'Ishrin Li-l-Majlis."
134 Al-Majlis al-Urubbi li-l-Ifta' wa-l-Buhuth, "Al-Bayan al-Khitami li-l-Dawra al-Hadiyya wa-l-Thalathin."
135 Al-Shithri, *Hukm al-Luju'*, 69–70.
136 As quoted in the introduction to Al-Shithri, 6–7.
137 Al-'Uthaymin, "Al-Safar ila Bilad al-Kuffar," 189.
138 Al-'Uthaymin, "Al-Safar ila Bilad al-Kuffar"; Al-Lajna al-Da'ima, "Ma Hukm al-Safar," 191–2.
139 Ibn Baz, "Al-Safar Kharij," 187–8.
140 Al-'Afifi, "Hukm al-Safar," 68.
141 Al-'Uthaymin, "Question 17," 77. Note: This source uses alternate spelling of author's name, al-'Uthaymeen.
142 As quoted in: Al-Shithri, *Hukm al-Luju'*, 11–13.
143 Ibn Baz, "It Is Not Permissible."
144 Ibn Baz, "It Is Not Permissible."
145 Al-'Uthaymin, "Al-Iqama fi Bilad al-Kufar," 189–91.
146 Al-Shaykh, "A Tunisian Wishing."
147 Islamway, "Advice to Muslims in the West."
148 Al-Atawneh, *Wahhabi Islam*, 121–34; Al-Fawzan, *Al-Ribba*, 18, 24–5; Islam Question & Answer, "Ruling on Dealing."
149 Islamweb, "Fatawa bi-Sha'n Shira'."
150 Al-Lajna al-Da'ima, "Hukm Akhdh al-Qard," 133–4.
151 Islam Question & Answer, "Hukm al-Qurud."
152 Quoted in Al-Munajjid, "Military Service," 137–8.
153 Al-'Uthaymin, "Idha Aslamat al-Zawja," 278–80.
154 Al-Fawzan, *Al-Ribba*, 59–60.
155 Al-Munajjid, "Inheritance from a Non-Muslim."
156 Al-'Uthaymin, "Al-Ikhtilat fi l-Ta'lim," 281.
157 Islamweb, "Services."
158 Islamweb, "Working as a Waiter."
159 The Permanent Committee for Scholarly Research and Ifta', "Fatwa 5651."
160 See also: Al-Majma' al-Fiqhi al-Islami, "Musharakat al-Muslim."
161 Ibn Baz, "Hukm Musahabat al-Kafir," 241.
162 Al-'Uthaymin, "Doesn't the Hadeeth," 34.

236   Notes to pages 60–70

163   Al-ʿUthaymin, "Hukm Qawl Akhi," 186.
164   Al-ʿUthaymin, "Tawdih al-Walaʾ wa-l-Baraʾ," 175–6.
165   Ibn Baz, "Al-Walaʾ wa-l-Baraʾ"; Ibn Baaz, "The Importance of Muslim Minorities Adhering to Islam," in *Muslim Minorities*, a compilation of fatwas and sermons by Ibn Baz and al-ʿUthaymin (London: Message of Islam, 1998), 20. The sermon included in this compilation uses the alternative spelling Ibn Baaz, while the cover uses Ibn Baz.
166   Al-Fouzan, *"Al-Walaaʾ Wal-Baraaʾ,"* 13, 24; al-Fawzan, *"Ahkam al-Taʿamul,"* 20.
167   Al-ʿUthaymin, "Al-Tahniʾa bi-ʿid," 183–5.
168   Islamhouse, "His Company Gives."
169   Islam Question & Answer, "It Is Not Permissible."
170   Islam Question & Answer, "It Is Not Permissible."
171   Al-ʿUthaymin, "Al-Tahniʾa bi-ʿid," 183–5.
172   Al-ʿUthaymin, "Ruling on Celebrating."
173   Al-Munajjid, "Selling Greeting Cards."
174   Al-Munajjid, "Collecting Donations."
175   Al-ʿUthaymin, "Tahniʾat al-Kafir," 185.
176   See for example a compilation of sermons and fatwas by two *salafi* luminaries: Ibn Baz and Shaykh Uthaymeen, *Muslim Minorities*.
177   Ar-Rayyis, *Beautiful Advice*, 3.
178   Ar-Rayyis, 5–6, 20–1.
179   On the biography of al-Madkhali, his ideology, and its focus on the duty to obey the political leaders and refutation of Muslim Brothers, the controversy about him in Saudi Arabia, and his influence in Europe: Meijer, "Politicising al-Jarh," 375–99.

2. Across a Wasati-Salafi European Spectrum

1   Bosnic Musovic, "Omstridd Moské Invigs i Dag."
2   Hackett, "5 Facts."
3   Stockholms Stad, *Statistical Year-Book.*
4   Hammargren, "Fatwor utfärdas i Stockholm."
5   For a translation of his speech, see: MEMRI, "Al-Qaradhawi Speaks in Favor." See also Malm, "Massmordspredikan i Svensk Moské."
6   Karam, "Dubbla Budskap i Moskén."
7   Chavez Perez and Boucheloukh, "Moské Säljer Judefientligt Material."
8   The Local, "Mosque swastika attack"; Matt Payton, "Nazi Swastikas Painted."
9   Interviews, Stockholm, 6, 13 July 2018.
10   As per a flyer distributed by the Rinkeby-Kista District Council. The figure includes first-generation migrants and those born in Sweden whose parents were born abroad: Rinkeby-Kista District Council, "Welcome to Rinkeby-Kista," 7.

Notes to pages 70–87   237

11 Orange, "Swedish Riots Spark Surprise."
12 Interview, Stockholm, 27 July 2018.
13 Interview, Stockholm, 27 July 2018.
14 Interview, Stockholm, 3 August 2018.
15 Interview, Stockholm, 25 July 2018.
16 Forschungsgruppe Weltanschuungen in Deutschland, "Dortmund: Religionszugehörigkeiten 1910–2018."
17 Dortmunder Statistik, "Hauptwohnbevölkerung in Dortmund am 31.12.2020."
18 Kohlstadt, "Jeder fünfte Schüler."
19 Moscheesuche, "Moscheen in Dortmund."
20 Schmoll, "Wo landen die Koran-Bücher."
21 Bandermann, "Neue Beratungsstelle."
22 During the Covid-19 pandemic, the municipality allowed only registered members to attend houses of worship for prayer. Visiting the mosque again in July 2021, we learned that because of this, the number of registered members had doubled to 300.
23 Interview, Dortmund, 19 August 2016.
24 Interview, Dortmund, 19 August 2016.
25 Interview, Dortmund, 21 September 2018.
26 Interview, Dortmund, 21 August 2019.
27 Interview, Dortmund, 30 August 2016.
28 Interview, Dortmund, 30 August 2016.
29 Kettani, "Muslim Population in Europe," 158.
30 Al-Kittani, *Al-Muslimun fi Urubba*, 298.
31 Interview, Reykjavik, 13 October 2017.
32 Kettani, "Muslim Population in Europe," 158.
33 Interview, Reykjavik, 19 September, 2017.
34 Interview, Reykjavik, 13 October 2017.
35 Interview, Reykjavik, 19 September 2017.
36 Interview, Reykjavik, 13 October 2017.
37 Interview, Reykjavik, 19 September 2017.
38 Interview, Reykjavik, 6 October 2017.
39 Interview, Reykjavik, 14 October 2017.
40 Interview, Reykjavik, 19 September 2017.
41 Interview, Reykjavik, 18 September 2017.
42 Interview, Reykjavik, 19 September 2017.
43 Interview, Reykjavik, 6 October 2017.
44 Interview, Reykjavik, 14 October 2017.
45 Interview, Reykjavik, 19 September 2017.
46 Interview, Reykjavik, 18 September 2017.
47 Interview, Reykjavik, 13 October 2017.
48 Interview, Reykjavik, 6 October 2017.

238 Notes to pages 87–99

49 ʿAbduh, "Tafsir al-Qurʾan al-Hakim," 641–60.
50 Al-Manar, "Tafsir al-Qurʾan al-Hakim," 762–3.
51 Jad al-Haqq, "Badʾ al-Siyam wa-Intihaʾuhu."
52 Dar al-Iftaʾ al-Misriyya, "Fasting in Countries"; "The Fasting Hours."
53 Quoted in Ibn Baz, "Siyam Man Yatul," 95–8.
54 Ibn Baz, 95; al-Zarqa, *Al-ʿaql wa-l-Fiqh*, 119–23; Islamweb, "Difficulty Fasting in Norway."
55 Al-Majlis al-Urubbi li-l-Iftaʾ wa-l-Buhuth, "Qarar 2, al-Dawra al-ʿadiyya al-Thaniyya ʿashra'"; Al-Majlis al-Urubbi li-l-Iftaʾ wa-l-Buhuth, "Qarar 7, al-Dawra al-ʿadiyya al-ʿIshrin," European Council for Fatwa and Research, session held 24–27 July 2010; Al-Majlis al-Urubbi li-l-Iftaʾ wa-l-Buhuth, "Al-Siyam wa-Ahkamuhu."
56 Shavit, "Ramadan in Iceland," 409.
57 Shavit, 410.
58 Interview, Reykjavik, 19 September 2017.
59 Shavit, "Ramadan in Iceland," 411.
60 Interview, Reykjavik, 6 October 2017.
61 Interview, Reykjavik, 19 September 2017.
62 Holbrook, "A Cold Reception."
63 Strategic Research Team, Birmingham City Council, "2018 Birmingham Ward Profiles."
64 Charity Commission for England and Wales, "Salafi Bookstore and Islamic Centre."
65 Shavit, "Raising *Salafi* Children," 347–8.
66 Interview, Birmingham, 29 July 2019.
67 Interview, Birmingham, 29 July 2019.
68 Abu Khadeejah Abdul-Wahid, *Insight to the Manhaj*.
69 Hamid, *Sufis, Salafis and Islamists*, 60–2.
70 Abu Khadeejah Abdul-Wahid, "May 1996: OASIS & Salafi Publications"; Birt, "Wahhabism in the United Kingdom," 170–2.
71 Interview, Birmingham, 29 July 2019.
72 Interview, Birmingham, 29 July 2019.
73 Interview, Birmingham, 19 July 2013.
74 Interview, Birmingham 29 July 2019.
75 Interview, Birmingham, 29 July 2019.
76 Abu Khadeejah Abdul-Wahid, *What Are the Core Mistakes?*
77 For extremism in general: Commission for Countering Extremism, "Commission Releases First Round". For *salafiyya* specifically: Mortimer, "It's Time Europe"; Awan, "I Watch the Growing"; Dale, "Why Wahhabi/ Salafist Mosques."
78 See *Combating 21st-Century Extremist Terrorism*.
79 Abu Khadeejah Abdul-Wahid, *Salafism*.

Notes to pages 99–115   239

80 Salafi Publications (name of author not mentioned), *The Rise of Jihadist*.
81 Layton, "Mosque Leader Welcomes YouTube."
82 Interview, Birmingham, 29 July 2019.
83 Interview, Birmingham, 29 July 2019.
84 Lecture attended 19 July 2019.
85 Interview, Birmingham, 2 August 2019.
86 Interview, London, 20 July 2013.
87 Interview, Birmingham, 1 August 2019.
88 Interview, Birmingham, 7 August 2019.
89 Interview, Marseille, 10 October 2019.
90 Interview, Marseille, 10 October 2019.
91 Ceilles, "A Marseille, les Musulmans."
92 Trouve Ta Mosquée, "Les 59 Mosquées Trouvées."
93 For radicalization: Leroux, "Procédure d'Expulsion Engagée." For al-Madkhali: AFP, "Le Salafisme, une Nébuleuse."
94 Bonnefoy, "Bouches-du-Rhône."
95 Azadé, "Marseille's Muslims Need."
96 Interview, Marseille, 14 October 2019.
97 Interview, Marseille, 14 October 2019.

3. The Mustafti Is the Mufti

1   Kern, "Europe's Fatwa Factories."
2   Laurence and Vaisse, *Integrating Islam*, 130–1.
3   Caeiro and al-Saify, "Qaradawi in Europe," 118–23.
4   Esdonk, "European Fatwas," 48–66.
5   According to Similarweb, a company that tracks and researches internet traffic, in 2022 the Council's website registered on average 82,000 visitors per month. In comparison, two of the leading *salafi* websites, islamqa.info and islamweb.net, registered 18.1 million and 30.9 million visitors per month, respectively. See: Similarweb, "Website Performance."
6   Shavit, *New Imagined Community*, 129.
7   Abdel-Fadil, "The Islam-Online Crisis," 24.
8   Esposito et al., eds., *500 Most Influential*, 36; Smoltczyk, "Islam's Spiritual 'Dear Abby'"; Cherribi, *Fridays of Rage*, 60; Galal, "Yusuf al-Qaradawi," 150.
9   Shavit, *New Imagined Community*, 161.
10 Laurence and Vaisse, *Integrating Islam*, 130–1.
11 Interview, Marseille, 14 October 2019.
12 Al-Najjar, *Fiqh al-Muwatana*, 69–70.
13 Hanafy, "European Council."
14 Interview, Birmingham, 29 July 2019.

240 Notes to pages 116–32

15 Interview, Marseille, 10 October 2019.
16 Interview, Stockholm, 12 July 2018.
17 Interview, Stockholm, 23 July 2018.
18 Interview, Marseille, 10 October 2019.
19 Interview, Birmingham, 29 July 2019.
20 Interview, Birmingham, 4 August 2019.
21 Interview, Birmingham, 29 July 2019.
22 Interview, Marseille, 10 October 2019.
23 Reported by imam Ahmad and others and determined sound by al-Nawawi. On the 'heart' versus the intellect as a guide, see: Schimmel, "Reason and Mystical Experience," 132–3.
24 Abou El Fadl, *And God Knows*, 24.
25 Sivan, "Aliyat Ma'amado shel HaRav," 131.
26 Jackson, "The Second Education," 202–3.
27 Al-Nawawi, *Adab al-Fatwa*, 73–4.
28 For example, Muhammad Khalid Masud's analysis of a query sent to Ibn Baz about visiting countries of disbelief, "Significance of Istifta'," 39–50. The discussion of mortgages later in this chapter also provides an instructive example.
29 Interview, Reykjavik, 28 September 2017.
30 Bunt, *Islam in the Digital Age*, 167–80; Campbell, "Who's Got the Power?" 1054–6; Echchaibi, "From Audio Tapes," 35, 40; Mariani, "Cyber-Fatwas, Sermons, and Media Campaigns," 148–52; Sisler, "Internet and the Construction," 211–12.
31 Shavit, *The New Imagined Community*, 127–31; Shavit, "Postmodern Reconstitution of an Islamic Memory," 176–7.
32 Haucap and Heimeshoff, "Google, Facebook, Amazon, eBay," 50–1; Taplin, *Move Fast and Break Things*, 14, 18, 84.
33 Haucap and Heimeshoff, "Google, Facebook, Amazon, eBay," 52–4.
34 Warren, *Rivals in the Gulf*, 43–4.
35 Warren, 59–64.
36 Interview, Dortmund, 17 September 2018.
37 Interview, Reykjavik, 22 September 2017.
38 Interview, Reykjavik, 1 October 2017.
39 Two studies of Norwegian Muslims also indicated that the Council's conditional legitimization of mortgages remained highly controversial. Eighty-eight percent of Torkel Brekke's sample of Muslims approached in mosques, Muslim organizations, and online agreed or strongly agreed that "Conventional banks provide interest-based loans, which are totally forbidden in Islam." Seventy-two percent agreed or strongly agreed that they have actively searched for interest-free loans: Brekke, "Halal Money," 4–5. Borchgrevink and Birkvad argued that the leaderships of

Notes to pages 132–52   241

Pakistani mosques in Norway accepted the European Council for Fatwa and Research's fatwa on mortgages, whereas the leadership of Somali mosques did not. Several of their Pakistani-Norwegian interviewees rejected the fatwa: Borchgrevink and Birkvad, "Religious Norms and Homeownership," 1–18.

40 Interview, Dortmund, 29 August 2018.
41 Interview, Reykjavik, 27 September 2017.
42 Interview, Stockholm, 15 July 2018.
43 Interview, Reykjavik, 2 October 2017.
44 Interview, Dortmund, 15 September 2018.
45 Interview, Reykjavik, 24 September 2017.
46 Interview, Reykjavik, 22 September 2017.
47 Interview, Dortmund, 2 September 2018.
48 Interview, Reykjavik, 4 October 2017.
49 Interview, Stockholm, 9 July 2018.
50 Interview, Stockholm, 6 July 2018.
51 Interview, Reykjavik, 13 October 2017.
52 Interview, Reykjavik, 18 September 2017.
53 Interview, Stockholm, 27 July 2018.
54 Interview, Stockholm, 25 July 2018.

4. There's Shariʿa, and There's Life

1 Interview, Marseille, 10 October 2019.
2 Interview, Stockholm, 6 July 2018.
3 Interview, Stockholm, 14 July 2018.
4 Interview, Stockholm, 6 July 2018.
5 Al-Qaradawi, *Fi Fiqh al-Aqalliyyat al-Muslima*, 154.
6 Shariff, "Does Religion Increase," 109.
7 Grubbs et al., "Internet Pornography Use," 1741.
8 Schleifer, "Understanding Jihad," 125.
9 Defoe saved the readers from learning precisely what catastrophes Roxana met in the final years of her life. The moral of his story lies in the punishment, but the story itself is a celebration of the benefits of sinning – and that is possibly one of the reasons for its popularity. Defoe, *Roxana: The Fortunate Mistress*.
10 Our survey included analysis of the contents of the following school textbooks, purchased in a second-hand bookstore: Muhammad b. ʿAbd al-Wahhab et al., *Murshidi fi l-Tarbiyya al-Islamiyya al-Sana al-Thaniyya min al-Taʿlim al-Ibtidaʾi*, (2016). The book presents instruction about the truth of the Creator and the revelation, and the life of the Prophet, as well as the proper procedures of prayer, table manners, and hygiene.

242 Notes to pages 153–8

Muhammad Binjadida et al., *Al-Munir fi l-Tarbiyya al-Islamiyya al-Sana al-Thalitha al-Ibtida'iyya*. The book instructs about the proper manner of praying, presents the biographies of major *sahaba*, and emphasizes the importance of compassion, including towards animals. Muhammad al-'Asli et al., *Munir fi l-Tarbiyya al-Islamiyya al-Sana al-Sadisa al-Ibtida'iyya*. The book focuses on creed, but includes also certain social instructions, including a rather insensitive elaboration against excessive eating during *iftar* on the days of Ramadan. Name of author not mentioned, *Al-Tarbiyya al-Islamiyya al-Sana al-Thalitha min al-Ta'lim al-Thanawi al-I'dadi* (2010). The book emphasizes the balanced and pragmatic nature of Islam and its preference for *taysir*. It includes a lengthy explanation about the prohibition of usury and the reasons for that prohibition. Muhammad al-Hadrati et al., *Fi Ruhab al-Tarbiyya al-Islamiyya: al-Sana al-'Ula min Silk al-Bakaluriya*. Significant portions of the book are dedicated to the social virtues that faith in and practice of Islam enhance. More than a third of it deals with Islamic norms regarding finances, but with little attention to usury. The book emphasizes the balanced and pragmatic nature of Islam. Yusuf b. 'Ajiba et al., *Fi Ruhab al-Tarbiyya al-Islamiyya: al-Sana al-Thaniyya min Silk al-Bakaluriya, Kitab al-Talmidh wa-l-Talmidha*. The book, targeting pupils towards the end of their high school years, covers a range of fiqh-related issues in more elaborate fashion than any of the other books surveyed, including the notion that the *shari'a* has primary objectives and that new circumstances at the rank of necessity may require the application of *ijtihad* and *maslaha mursala*. Still, these complicated issues are related to in telegraphic manner. The book emphasizes the *wasati* nature of Islam, the Prophet's warnings against exaggeration, and the duty to shy away from interpretations of the Quran issued by those not qualified to do so.

11 Beit-Hallahmi and Argyle, *Psychology of Religious Behaviour*, 22–4.
12 Hogg, "Social Identity," 101–2.
13 Mael and Ashforth, "Identification in Work," 209.
14 Interview, Reykjavik, 4 October 2017.
15 Interview, Stockholm, 7 July 2018.
16 Interview, Stockholm, 13 July 2018.
17 Interview, Reykjavik, 6 October 2017.
18 Interview, Reykjavik, 13 October 2017.
19 Interview, Reykjavik, 18 September 2017.
20 Interview, Reykjavik, 28 September 2017.
21 Interview, Rabat, 19 February 2018. Asked to address that the laws of Islam are not fully implemented in his country, Khayari explained that in Morocco the 'ulama issue fatwas, not laws. The Supreme Council gives the King advice if he desires it, but there is no concept of *wilayat*

al-faqih, like in Iran, or of Supreme Guide, like in the Muslim Brothers. He said the experts at the Supreme Council exercise their duties with wisdom, and that wisdom sometimes dictates not to answer certain queries – sometimes, *Al-samt huwa al-hikma*, 'Silence is wisdom.' Khayari informed that the King asked the Supreme Council to advise whether it was permissible to issue laws based on *maslaha mursala*, noting that the deliberation was needed in response to those in Morocco, first and foremost the *salafis*, who hold that anything not explicitly legislated in the Quran constitutes *bid'a*.

22 Interview, Reykjavik, 1 October 2017.
23 Interview, Stockholm, 8 July 2018.
24 Interview, Dortmund, 29 August 2018.
25 Interview, Dortmund, 28 August 2018.
26 Interview, Dortmund, 28 August 2018.
27 Interview, Dortmund, 28 August 2018.
28 Interview, Dortmund, 28 August 2018.
29 Interview, Stockholm, 11 July 2018.
30 Interview, Stockholm, 11 July 2018.
31 Interview, Stockholm, 9 July 2018.
32 Interview, Stockholm, 9 July 2018.
33 Interview, Stockholm, 9 July 2018.
34 Interview, Stockholm, 6 July 2018.
35 Trope and Liberman, "Construal-Level Theory," 448.
36 Interview, Reykjavik, 27 September 2017.
37 Interview, Stockholm, 13 July 2018.
38 Interview, Stockholm, 13 July 2018.
39 Interview, Stockholm, 13 July 2018.
40 Interview, Stockholm, 13 July 2018.
41 Interview, Stockholm, 13 July 2018.
42 Interview, Reykjavik, 7 October 2017.
43 Interview, Reykjavik, 7 October 2017.
44 Interview, Reykjavik, 13 October 2017.
45 Inge, *The Making of a Salafi*, 20.
46 Doyle, "Lessons from France," 484–5; Hamid, "The Attraction of 'Authentic,'" 49.
47 Wiedl, *The Making of German*, 31. See also Damir-Geilsdorf and Menzfeld, "'Looking at the Life," 446.
48 Wiedl, *The Making of German*, 32; Pall and De Koning, "Being and Belonging," 78–9; De Koning, "Changing Worldviews and Friendship," 375.
49 Interview, Birmingham, 22 July 2019.
50 Interview, Birmingham, 1 August 2019.

244   Notes to pages 175–83

51   Interview, Birmingham, 1 August 2019.
52   Interview, Birmingham, 1 August 2019.
53   See, for example, the discussion of one of the more well-known incidents: O'Grady, "After Refusing a Handshake."
54   Interview, Stockholm, 23 July 2018.
55   Interview, Stockholm, 6 July 2018.
56   Interview, Reykjavik, 19 September 2017.
57   Interview, Reykjavik, 13 October 2017.
58   Interview, Birmingham, 1 August 2019.
59   Interview, Birmingham, 20 July 2019.
60   Interview, Birmingham, 26 July 2019.
61   Interview, Birmingham, 27 July 2019.
62   Interview, Birmingham, 1 August 2019.
63   Interview, Birmingham, 29 July 2019; interview, Birmingham, 19 July 2013.
64   Interview, Stockholm, 25 July 2018.
65   Interview, Berlin, 1 August 2013.
66   Interview, Birmingham, 29 July 2019.
67   Interview, Birmingham, 2 August 2019.
68   Interview, Birmingham, 22 July 2019.
69   Interview, Birmingham, 2 August 2019.
70   Douglas, *In the Wilderness*, 42–58.
71   Almond, Appleby, and Sivan, *Strong Religion*, 23–89; Davidman, "The Transformation of Bodily," 209–19; Neriya-Ben Shahar, "The Medium Is the Danger," 27–38.
72   Interview, Birmingham, 10 October 2015; 29 July 2019.
73   Interview, Birmingham, 22 July 2019.
74   Interview, Birmingham, 2 August 2019.
75   Interview, Birmingham, 2 August 2019.
76   Interview, Birmingham, 27 July 2019.
77   Interview, Birmingham, 2 August 2019.
78   Interview, Birmingham, 29 July 2019. Similar opinions were articulated by other *salafi* leaders. For example, Johannes Klominek of the Stockholm-based Ibn Abbas Center emphasized that based on Q. 60:8, Muslims should always be good to non-Muslims who do not wage war against Muslims. If that principle is breached, there is the danger that they would be led astray to ISIS. There are, though, limits to interfaith interpersonal contacts according to Klominek: "I think, like, socialize, to hang around, to help people at work, to be good with them, to be friendly to people, to your neighbors, I say no problem. But to have somebody as a very close friend, usually, he will affect your way of thinking about God and so on. I think this can be hard for a Muslim. If this is your close friend, that you take and you share your sorrows, and happy times with, I think this will affect you

Notes to pages 185–202   245

a lot … but at the same time I think it is very important that you can be friendly (to non-Muslims)." These limitations, however, do not apply to children according to Klominek: "No, I do not believe in preventing people in this sense, I am not that kind of guy." Interview Stockholm, 25 July 2018.

Still, not all *salafi*s we met were equally at ease with their children forging friendships with non-Muslims. In a *salafi* mosque visited in London, Masjid Dar us-Sunnah in Shepherds Bush district, Nur al-Din Abu ʿAbdallah, one of two imams, said he would not allow his 18-month-old son to befriend a non-Muslim child in the future. Relating to Christian dogma, he explained: "If a boy will tell your son that his father does not exist and that his mother is a whore, will you allow him to be friends with your son?" ʿAbdallah held that befriending Muslims who are innovators and who can negatively affect children's understanding of Islam is even *more* dangerous. Asked whether this opinion could not result in *salafi* children having no friends, he said this was not a problem. *Salafi*s have large families, and the children of the community would always find enough friends in their age group. Interview London, 7 October 2015.

5. A Mission with Few Missionaries

 1 Al-Ghazali, *Mustaqbal al-Islam Kharij Ardihi*, 5–11.
 2 Al-Ghazali, 77–80.
 3 Shavit, *Islamism and the West*, 97–138.
 4 Frisch, *Öffentlichkeit als Partner*, 100.
 5 Attendance of Tamimi's sermon, Reykjavik, 13 October 2017.
 6 Interview, Stockholm, 25 July 2018.
 7 Interview, Stockholm, 27 July 2018.
 8 Interview, Birmingham, 1 August 2019.
 9 Interview, Marseille, 10 October 2019.
10 Interview, Dortmund, 21 August 2019.
11 Interview, Dortmund, 21 September 2018.
12 Interview, Dortmund, 18 September 2018.
13 Interview, Stockholm, 6 July 2018.
14 Interview, Marseille, 14 October 2019.
15 Interview, Birmingham, 29 July 2021.
16 Interview, Birmingham, 29 July 2021.
17 Interview, Birmingham, 29 July 2021.
18 Interview, Dortmund, 10 September 2018.
19 Interview, Stockholm, 14 July 2018.
20 Interview, Dortmund, 11 September 2018.
21 Interview, Reykjavik, 24 September 2017.
22 Interview, Stockholm, 15 July 2018.

246   Notes to pages 202–15

23   Interview, Stockholm, 15 July 2018.
24   Abu Khadeejah Abdul-Wahid, "Our Da'wah, Our Call," CCDa'wah n.d.
25   Interview, Birmingham, 20 July 2019.
26   Interview, Reykjavik, 4 October 2017.
27   Interview, Reykjavik, 4 October 2017.
28   Interview, Stockholm, 18 July 2018.
29   Interview, Birmingham, 23 July 2019.
30   Interview, Birmingham, 1 August 2019.
31   Siddiqi, Muhammad Yasin Mazhar, *The Prophet Muhammad*, 55–86; Mansour, "The Immigration to Abyssinia," 57–69; Saritoprak, "Migration, Feelings of Belonging," 45–6.
32   Shavit, "Europe, the New Abyssinia," 374–6.
33   Khaled, *Integration im Islam*, 16–20.
34   Interview, Birmingham, 4 August 2019.
35   Interview, Birmingham, 4 August 2019.
36   Interview, Birmingham, 4 August 2019.
37   Interview, Birmingham, 2 August 2019.
38   Interview, Birmingham, 2 August 2019.
39   Interview, Birmingham, 2 August 2019.
40   Al-Qaradawi, "Duties of Muslims," 7 May 2006.
41   Interview, Stockholm, 16 July 2018.
42   Interview, Stockholm, 18 July 2018.
43   Interview, Stockholm, 23 July 2018.
44   Saheeh International, *The Quran*.
45   Interview, Birmingham, 8 August 2019.
46   Interview, Birmingham, 29 July 2019.

Bibliography

Arabic

ʿAbd al-Fattah, Nabil. *Taqrir al-Hala al-Diniyya fi Misr*. Vol. 2. Cairo: Markaz al-Dirasat al-Siyasiyya wa-l-Istratijiyya bi-l-Ahram, 1998.

ʿAbdallah, Hasan. "Al-Salat fi l-Masjid al-Aqsa ... Haram." *Nisf al-Dunya*, 16 August 1998, 45–9.

‒ "Fasahtu Khitbat Ibnati li-anna Khalibha Rafada an Taʿmalu." *Nisf al-Dunya*, 23 August 1998, 106–10.

ʿAbd al-Wahhab, Muhammad b. *Kitab al-Tawhid*. Riyadh: Imam Muhammad b. Saʿud University, n.d.

ʿAbd al-Wahhab, Muhammad b., Sufyan Nawal, Yusuf Takamanat, and Muhammad Akanidar. *Murshidi fi l-Tarbiyya al-Islamiyya al-Sana al-Thaniyya min al-Taʿlim al-Ibtidaʾi*. Casablanca: Afrikiyya al-Sharq, 2016.

ʿAbduh, Muhammad. "Tafsir al-Qurʾan al-Hakim." *Al-Manar* 7, no. 17 (1904): 641–60.

Abu l-Majd, Ahmad Kamal. *Ruʾya Islamiyya Muʿasira: Iʿlan mabadiʾ*. Cairo: Dar al-Shuruq, 1991.

‒ "Qadiyyat al-Hijab wa-l-Niqab." *Al-Wafd*, 28 January 1994, 9.

ʿAjiba, Yusuf b. et al. *Fi Ruhab al-Tarbiyya al-Islamiyya: Al-Sana al-Thaniyya min Silk al-Bakaluriyya, Kitab al-Talmidh wa-l-Talmidha*. Casablanca: Maktabat al-Salam al-Jadida, al-Dar al-ʿAlamiyya li-l-Kitab, 2014. First published in 2007.

ʿAfifi, ʿAbd al-Razzaq al-. "Hukm al-Safar ila Bilad al-Kufr li-l-ʿAmal." In *500 Jawab fi al-Buyuʿ wa-l-Muʿamalat*, edited by Ahmad b. ʿAbdallah al-Shafiʿi, 68. Cairo: Dar Ibn Hazm, 2010.

Al-Lajna al-Daʾima li-l-Buhuth wa-l-Iftaʾ. "Hukm Akhdh al-Qard al-Ribawi li-l-Haja al-Massa." In *Fatawa al-ʿUlamaʾ hawla l-Aqalliyyat al-Muslima fi l-ʿAlam*, edited by Salah al-Din Mahhmud al-Saʿid, 133–4. Alexandria: Dar al-Imam, 2004.

248 Bibliography

- "Hukm al-Da'wa ila Wahdat al-Adyan." In *Fatawa al-Balad al-Haram*, 16–20. Cairo: Al-Maktaba al-Tawfiqiyya, n.d.
- "Ma Hukm al-Safar wa-l-Dirasa fi Bilad al-Kuffar." In *Fatawa al-Balad al-Haram*, 191–2. Cairo: Al-Maktaba al-Tawfiqiyya, n.d.

Al-Majlis al-Urubbi li-l-Ifta' wa-l-Buhuth. "Al-Bayan al-Khitami li-l-Dawra al-'Adiyya al-Tasi'a wa-l-'Ishrin li-l-Majlis." European Council for Fatwa and Research, 20 July 2019. https://www.e-cfr.org/blog/2019/07/20/29-البيان-الختامي-للدورة/.

- "Al-Bayan al-Khitami li-l-Dawra al-Hadiyya wa-l-Thalathin." European Council for Fatwa and Research, 20 December 2020. https://www.e-cfr.org/blog/2020/12/21/البيان-الختاميّ-للدورة-الحادية-والـ/.
- "Al-Bayan al-Khitami li-l-Dawra al-'Adiyya al-Thaniyya 'Ashara." *Al-Majalla al-'Ilmiyya li-l-Majlis al-'Urubbi li-l-Ifta' wa-l-Buhuth*, nos. 4–5 (2004): 457.
- "Al-Bayan al-Khitami li-l-Dawra al-Sabi'a wa-l-'Ashara." *Al-Majalla al-'Ilmiyya li-l-Majlis al-'Urubbi li-l-Ifta' wa-l-Buhuth*, nos. 12–13 (2008): 399–513.
- "Al-Siyam wa-Ahkamuhu al-Fiqhiyya fi l-Duwal al-Iskandanafiyya wa-min Hukmiha." European Council for Fatwa and Research, 9 June 2015. https://www.e-cfr.org/blog/2015/06/09/الصيام-وأحكامه-الفقهية-الدول-الإسكند/.
- "Fatwa No. 6." In *Qararat wa-Fatawa al-Majlis al-Urubbi li-l-Ifta' wa-l-Buhuth*. Cairo: Dar al-Tawzi' wa-l-Nashr al-Islamiyya, n.d.
- "Qarar 2, al-Dawra al-'Adiyya al-Thaniyya 'Ashara." *Al-Majalla al-'Ilmiyya li-l-Majlis al-Urubbi li-l-Ifta' wa-l-Buhuth*, nos. 4–5 (2004): 460–3.
- "Qarar 7, al-Dawra al-'Adiyya al-'Ishrin." European Council for Fatwa and Research, 24–27 July 2010. https://www.e-cfr.org/blog/2017/05/15/حول-اختلاف-ساعات-الصيام-البلدان-ذات-خط-2/.
- "Qararat wa-Fatawa al-Majlis min al-Dawra al-Thamina ila l-Khamisa 'Ashara." European Council for Fatwa and Research, n.d. Accessed 13 September 2010. https://www.e-cfr.org/.

Al-Majma' al-Fiqhi al-Islami. "Musharakat al-Muslim fi Intikhabat ma'a Ghayr al-Muslimin." *The Muslim World League*, 8 November 2007. Accessed 5 May 2012. http://www.themwl.org.

Al-Manar. "Tafsir al-Qur'an al-Hakim: Hukm Mawaqit al-Salah wa-l-Siyam fi l-Qutbayn wa-ma Yaqrabu Minhuma." *Al-Manar* 34, no. 10 (1935): 761–3.

Al-Tarbiyya al-Islamiyya al-Sana al-Thalitha min al-Ta'lim al-Thanawi al-I'dadi. N.p.: Al-Dar al-'Alamiyya li-l-Kitab, 2010.

'Alwani, Taha Jabir al-. *Fi Fiqh al-Aqalliyyat al-Muslima*. 6th October City: Nahdat Misr li-l-Tiba'a wa-l-Nashr wa-l-Tawzi', 2000.

Arshani, Murshid al-. *Al-Wala' wa-l-Bara'*. Sanaa: Maktabat Khalid b. al-Walid, 2004.

Badawi, Jamal. "'Alaqat al-Muslim bi-Ghayr al-Muslim: Nazarat fi Kitab Allah Ta'ala." *Al-Majalla al-'Ilmiyya li-l-Majlis al-'Urubbi li-l-Ifta' wa-l-Buhuth*, no. 6 (January 2005): 69–99.

Binjadida, Muhammad et al. *Al-Munir fi l-Tarbiyya al-Islamiyya al-Sana al-Thalitha al-Ibtida'iyya*. Casablanca: Dar al-Nashr, 2015–16. First published in 2004.

Bishri, al-'Arabi al-. "Muntalaqat li-Fiqh al-Aqalliyyat." *Al-Majalla al-'Ilmiyya li-l-Majlis al-Urubbi li-l-Ifta' wa-l-Buhuth*, nos. 4–5 (June 2004): 201–18.

Fawzan, Salih b. Fawzan b. 'Abdallah al-. "Ahkam al-Tashabuh bi-l-Kuffar." The Official Website of His Eminence Shaykh Abdullah bin Saleh al-Fawil, n.d. Accessed 10 November 2013. http://alfuzan.islamlight.net.

Ahkam al-Ta'amul ma'a Ghayr al-Muslimin. Riyadh: Dar Kunuz Ishbiliyya li-l-Nashr wa-l-Tawzi', 2009.

– *Al-Wasatiyya fi l-Islam*. Riyadh: Dar Kunuz Ishbiliyya li-l-Nashr wa-l-Tawzi', 2010.

– *Al-Ribba wa-Ba'd Suwariha al-Mu'asira*. Cairo: Dar al-Imam Ahmad, 2005.

– *Wujub al-Tahakum ila ma Anzala Allah wa-Tahrim al-Tahakum ila Ghayrihi*. Riyadh: Dar al-'Asima, 1993.

Ghannushi, Rashid al-. "Al-Wasatiyya fi l-Fikr al-Siyasi li-l-Qaradawi." In *Yusuf al-Qaradawi: Kalimat fi Takrimihi wa-Buhuth fi Fikrihi wa-Fiqhihi*, 294–345. Cairo: Dar al-Salam, 2004.

Ghazali, Muhammad al-. *Al-Ghazwu al-Thaqafi Yamtaddu fi Faraghina*. 2nd printing. Cairo: Dar al-Shuruq, 1998.

– *Al-Sunna al-Nabawiyya bayna Ahl al-Fiqh wa-Ahl al-Hadith*. 3rd ed. Cairo: Dar al-Shuruq, 1989.

– *Azmat al-Shura fi l-Mujtama'at al-'Arabiyya wa-l-Islamiyya*. N.p., 1990.

– *Mustaqbal al-Islam Kharij Ardihi: Kayfa Nufakkiru fihi?* Cairo: Dar al-Shuruq, 1984.

– *Qadaya al-Mar'a bayna l-Taqalid al-Rakida wa-l-Wafida*. Cairo: Dar al-Shuruq, 1994.

Hadrati, Muhammad al- et al. *Fi Ruhab al-Tarbiyya al-Islamiyya: Al-Sana al-'Ula min Silk al-Bakaluriya*. Casablanca: Maktabat al-Salam al-Jadida, al-Dar al-'Alamiyya li-l-Kitab, 2014. First published in 2007.

Harithi, Abu Farihan Jamal b. Farihan al-, ed. *Al-Fatawa al-Muhimma fi Tabsir al-Umma*. Cairo: Maktabat al-Hadi al-Muhammadi, 2009.

Hawari, Muhammad al-. "Usus al-Bina' al-Usari fi l-Islam." *Al-Majalla al-'Ilmiyya li-l-Majlis al-Urubbi li-l-Ifta' wa-l-Buhuth*, no. 7 (July 2005): 119–72.

Haydar, Khalil Ali. *I'tidal am Tatarruf? Ta'ammulat Naqdiyya fi Tayyar al-Wasatiyya al-Islamiyya*. Kuwait: Qurtas-Publishing, 1998.

Husyan, 'Adil. "Faqih al-Wasatiyya al-Islamiyya fi 'Asrina." In *Yusuf al-Qaradawi: Kalimat fi Takrimihi wa-Buhuth fi Fikrihi wa-Fiqhihi*, 376–88. Cairo: Dar al-Salam, 2004.

Huwaydi, Fahmi. *Al-Islam wa-l-Dimuqratiyya*. Cairo: Markaz al-Ahram li -l-Tarjama wa-l-Nashr, 1993.

– *Al-Qur'an wa-l-Sultan*. 4th printing. Cairo: Dar al-Shuruq, 1999.

250 Bibliography

- "Risala fi Tahrir al-Mar'a." *Al-Ahram*, 14 May 1991, 7.
Ibn 'Abd al-Khaliq, 'Abd al-Rahman. "Al-Wala' wa-l-Bara'." Al-Mustafa
Electronic Library, n.d. Accessed 10 September 2012. https://al-mostafa
.com.
Ibn Baz, 'Abd al-'Aziz b. 'Abdallah. "Al-Safar Kharij al-Bilad al-Islamiyya." In
Fatawa al-Balad al-Haram, 187–8. Cairo: Al-Maktaba al-Tawfiqiyya, n.d.
- "Al-Wala' wa-l-Bara' wa-Ahkam al-Kuffar." In *Fatawa al-Balad al-Haram*,
174–5. Cairo: Al-Maktaba al-Tawfiqiyya, n.d.
- "Hukm al-Tashkik bi-Sha'n al-Isti'ana bi-Ghayr al-Muslimin fi Qital Taghiyyat
al-'Iraq." Al-Mawqi' al-Rasmi al-Samaha al-Shaykh al-Imam Ibn Baz, n.d.
https://binbaz.org.sa/fatwas/1568/حكم-الاستعانة-بغير-المسلمين-في-قتال-طاغية-العراق.
- "Hukm Musahabat al-Kafir." In *500 Jawab fi l-Buyu' wa-l-Mu'amalat*, edited
by Ahmad b. 'Abdallah al-Shafi'i, 241. Cairo: Dar Ibn Hazm, 2010.
- "Mawqif al-Muslim min al-Khilafat al-Madhhabiyya al-Muntashira." In
Fatawa al-Balad al-Haram, 941. Cairo: Al-Maktaba al-Tawfiqiyya, n.d.
- "Siyam Man Yatul Naharuhum Jiddan wa-Kadha Man Yaqsur Naharuhum."
In *Fatawa al-'Ulama' hawla l-Aqalliyyat al-Muslima fi l-'Alam*, edited by Salah
al-Din Mahhmud al-Sa'id, 95–100. Alexandria: Dar al-Iman, 2004.
Ibn Taymiyya, Taki al-Din Ahmad. *Al-Sirat al-Mustaqim*. Cairo: Dar al-Futuh
al-Islamiyya, 1995.
- *Al-Siyasa al-Shar'iyya fi Islah al-Ra'i wa-l-Ra'iyya*. Cairo: Dar al-Kitab al-
'Arabi bi-Misr, 1969.
Imam, Imam Muhammad. "Fatwa Tujizu Shira' al-Manazil bi-Qard Ribawi
li-l-Muslimin fi Ghayr Bilad al-Islam." *Al-Sharq al-Awsat*, 3 October 1999, 25.
'Imara, Muhammad. *Al-Islam wa-Huquq al-Insan Darurat La Huquq*. Damascus:
Markaz al-Raya, 2004.
- *Al-Istiqlal al-Hadari*. 6th October City: Nahdat Misr li-l-Tiba'a wa-l-Nashr
wa-l-Tawzi', 2007.
Islam Question & Answer. "Hukm al-Qurud allati Tumnahu li-Ajl al-Dirasa."
Islam Question & Answer, 10 July 2012. https://islamqa.info/ar/181723.
Islamweb. "Fatawa bi-Sha'n Shira' Manzil bi-Qard Ribawi." Islamweb, n.d.
Accessed 8 April 2013. https://islamweb.net.
Jaballah, Ahmad. "Al-Wasatiyya bayna Muqtadayat al-Muwatana fi 'Urubba
wa-l-Hifaz 'ala al-Huwiyya al-Islamiyya." *Al-Majalla al-'Ilmiyya li-l-Majlis
al-'Urubbi li-l-Ifta' wa-l-Buhuth*, nos. 12–13 (July 2008): 255–72.
Jad al-Haqq, 'Ali. "Bad' al-Siyam wa-Intiha'uhu fi l-Nurwij." Islam Port, n.d.
Accessed 16 August 2021. http://islamport.com/.
Kassab, Akram. *Al-Manhaj al-Da'wi 'ind al-Qaradawi*. Cairo: Maktabat Wahaba,
2006.
Khadar, 'Ali al-. *Al-Sa'udiyya Sirat Dawla wa-Mujtama'*. Beirut: Arab Network
for Research and Publishing, 2010.

Kittani, ʿAli Ibn al-Muntasir al-. *Al-Muslimun fi Urubba wa-Amrika*. Beirut: Dar al-Kutub al-ʿIlmiyya, 2000.

Lafi, Muhammad al-Fadil al-. "Al-Khitab al-Dini al-Islami." *Al-Majalla al-ʿIlmiyya li-l-Majlis al-Urubbi li-l-Iftaʾ wa-l-Buhuth*, no. 6 (January 2005): 209–58.

Mansur, Ahmad. "Al-Wasatiyya fi l-Islam." Interview by Ahmad Mansur. *Al Jazeera*, 26 October 1997. Accessed 6 November 2013. https://www.aljazeera.net.

Najjar, ʿAbd al-Majid al-. "Al-Dawr al-Hadari li-l-Waqf al-Islami bi-l-Gharb." *Al-Majalla al-ʿIlmiyya li-l-Majlis al-Urubbi li-l-Iftaʾ wa-l-Buhuth*, no. 18 (July 2011): 151–82.

– *Fiqh al-Muwatana li-l-Muslimin fi-Urubba*. Dublin: Al-Majlis al-Urubbi li-l-Iftaʾ wa-l-Buhuth, 2009.

– "Maʿalat al-Afʿal wa-Athruha fi Fiqh al-Aqalliyyat." *Al-Majalla al-ʿIlmiyya li-l-Majlis al-Urubbi li-l-Iftaʾ wa-l-Buhuth*, nos. 4–5 (June 2004): 147–200.

Nawawi, Abu Zakariyya Yahya Ibn Sharaf al-. *Adab al-Fatwa wa-l-Mufti wa-l-Mustafti*. Limassol: Al-Jaffan & Al-Jabi, 1988.

Nayfar, Muhammad al-Shadhili al-. "Al-Tajannus bi-Jinsiyya Ghayr Islamiyya." *Majallat al-Majmaʿ al-Fiqhi al-Islami* 2, no. 4 (1989): 177–252.

Qaradawi, Yusuf al-. *Al-Halal wa-l-Haram fi l-Islam*. Cairo: Maktabat Wahaba, 2004. First published in 1960.

– *Al-Khasaʾis al-ʿamma li-l-Islam*. Cairo: Maktabat Wahaba, 1977.

– *Al-Sahwa al-Islamiyya wa-Humum al-Watan al-ʿArabi wa-l-Islami*. 2nd printing. Cairo: Dar al-Shuruq, n.d.

– *Al-Siyasa al-Sharʿiyya fi Dawʾ Nusus al-Shariʿa wa-Maqasidiha*. Beirut: Muʾassasat al-Risala, 2001.

– "Al-Wasatiyya wa-Dawr al-Iʿlam fi Ibraziha." *Mawqiʿ al-Qaradawi*, 15 October 2006. Accessed 10 September 2012. http://www.qaradawi.net/.

– *Fi Fiqh al-Aqalliyyat al-Muslima*. Cairo: Dar al-Shuruq, 2007. Originally published in 2001.

– *Fiqh al-Wasatiyya al-Islamiyya wa-l-Tajdid: Maʿalim wa-Manarat*. Cairo: Dar al-Shuruq, 2010.

– *Khitabuna al-Islami fi ʿAsr al-Awlama*. Cairo: Dar al-Shuruq, 2009.

– *Min Ajl Sahwa Rashida*. Cairo: Dar al-Shuruq, 1988.

– *Min Fiqh al-Dawla fi l-Islam*. Cairo : Dar al-Shuruq, 2001.

– *Taysir al-Fiqh li-l-Muslim al-Muʿasir fi Dawʾ al-Qurʾan wa-l-Sunna – Fiqh al-Siyam*. Beirut: Muʾassasat al-Risala, 1993.

– *Taysir al-Fiqh li-l-Muslim al-Muʿasir fi Dawʾ al-Qurʾan wa-l-Sunna*. Beirut: Muʾassasat al-Risala, 2000.

Rawas, Muhammad. *Mawsuʿat Fiqh Ibn Taymiyya*. Vol. 1. Beirut: Dar al-Nafaʾis, 1998.

Rida, Muhammad Rashid. "Kitab Yusr al-Islam wa-Usul al-Tashriʿ al-ʿamm." *Al-Manar* 29, no. 1 (22 March 1928): 63–70.

252 Bibliography

Shaykhi, Salim al-. "Hukm al-Qurud al-Tulabiyya fi Urubba." *Al-Majalla al-*
Ilmiyya li-l-Majlis al-Urubbi li-l-Ifta' wa-l-Buhuth, nos. 14–15 (July 2009): 411–58.

Shithri, Salih b. Muhammad al-. *Hukm al-Luju' wa-l-Iqama fi Bilad al-Kuffar.*
Riyadh: Dar al-Habib, 2001.

Tayi, Hani Muhammad. "Al-Shaykh al-Qaradawi wa-Minhaj al-Wasatiyya
al-Islamiyya." In *Yusuf al-Qaradawi: Kalimat fi Takrimihi wa-Buhuth fi Fikrihi*
wa-Fiqhihi, 877–912. Cairo: Dar al-Salam, 2004.

Tibi, 'Ukasha 'Abd al-Manan al-. *Fatawa al-Shaykh al-Albani wa-Muqaranatuha*
bi-Fatawa al-'Ulama'. Beirut: Dar al-Jil, 1995.

'Uthaymin, Muhammad b. Salih al-. "Al-Ikhtilat fi l-Ta'lim wa-l-'Amal." In
Fatawa al-'Ulama' hawla l-Aqalliyyat al-Muslima fi l-'alam, edited by Salah al-
Din Mahhmud al-Sa'id, 281. Alexandria: Dar al-Iman, 2004.

– "Al-Iqama fi Bilad al-Kuffar." In *Fatawa al-Balad al-Haram,* 189–91. Cairo: Al-
Maktaba al-Tawfiqiyya, n.d .

– "Al-Safar ila Bilad al-Kuffar." In *Fatawa al-Balad al-Haram,* 189. Cairo: Al-
Maktaba al-Tawfiqiyya, n.d.

– "Al-Tahni'a bi-'id al-Krismas." In *Fatawa al-Balad al-Haram,* 183–5. Cairo: Al-
Maktaba al-Tawfiqiyya, n.d.

– "Anwa' al-Shirk." In *Fiqh al-'Ibadat li-l-Shaykh Muhammad b. Salih al-*
Uthaymin, edited by Muhammad Tamir, 56–7. Cairo: Dar al-Risala, 2003.

– "Hukm Qawl Akhi aw Sadiqi aw al-Dahk li-Ghayr al-Muslimin li-Talab
al-Mawadda." In *Fatawa al-Balad al-Haram,* 186. Cairo: Al-Maktaba al-
Tawfiqiyya, n.d.

– *"Hukm Ta'at al-Hakim alladhi La Yahkumu bi-Kitab Allah wa-Sunnat Rasulihi."*
In *Fatawa al-Balad al-Haram,* 172–3. Cairo: Al-Maktaba al-Tawfiqiyya, n.d.

– "Idha Aslamat al-Zawja wa-Jawzuha lam Yaslam." In *Fatawa al-'Ulama'*
hawla l-Aqalliyyat al-Muslima fi l-'alam, edited by Salah al-Din Mahhmud al-
Sa'id, 278–80. Alexandria: Dar al-Iman, 2004.

– "Ma Huwa al-Wasat fi l-Din?" In *Fatawa al-Balad al-Haram,* 151–2. Cairo: Al-
Maktaba al-Tawfiqiyya, n.d.

– "Tahni'at al-Kafir." In *Fatawa al-Balad al-Haram,* 185. Cairo: Al-Maktaba al-
Tawfiqiyya, n.d.

– "Tawdih al-Wala' wa-l-Bara'." In *Fatawa al-Balad al-Haram,* 175–6. Cairo: Al-
Maktaba al-Tawfiqiyya, n.d.

Zarqa, Mustafa al-. *Al-'aql wa-l-Fiqh fi Fahm al-Hadith al-Nabawi.* Damascus:
Dar al-Qalam, 1996.

Other Languages

Abdel-Fadil, Mona. "The Islam-Online Crisis: A Battle of Wasatiyya vs. Salafi
Ideologies?" *Cyber Orient* 5, no. 1 (May 2011): 4–36. https://doi.org/10.1002/j
.cyo2.20110501.0001.

Bibliography 253

Abdullah, Saeed. *Islamic Banking and Interest: A Study of the Prohibition of Riba and Its Contemporary Interpretation*. Leiden: Brill, 1996.

AbdusSalam, As-Sihaymi. *To Be a Serious Salafi*. London: Jamiah Media, 2011.

Abou El Fadl, Khaled. *And God Knows the Soldiers: The Authoritative and Authoritarian in Islamic Discourses*. Lanham, MD: University Press of America, 2001.

– "Islamic Law and Muslim Minorities: The Juristic Discourse on Muslim Minorities from the Second/Eighth to the Eleventh/Seventeenth Centuries." *Islamic Law and Society* 1, no. 2 (1994): 141–87. https://doi .org/10.1163/156851994x00011.

Abu Khadeejah Abdul-Wahid. *An Insight to the Manhaj of the Early Salaf – ʿAqida*. Troid, 10 July 2013. https://soundcloud.com/troidorg/an-insight-into -the-manhaj-of-the-early-salaf-and-their-aqidah-2.

– "May 1996: OASIS & Salafi Publications – Spreading Salafi Daʿwah." Abukhadeejah.com, 18 December 2013. https://abukhadeejah.com/may -1996-oasis-salafi-publications-a-new-approach-to-salafi-dawah/.

– "Our Daʿwah, Our Call." CCDaʿwah, n.d. Accessed 31 December 2022. https://www.ccdawah.co.uk/our-call/.

– *Salafism and Who Are the Salafis in This Era?* Birmingham: Salafi Publications, n.d.

– *What Are the Core Mistakes of the Tablighi Jamaʿat of Today?* Birmingham: Salafi Publications, 2018.

AFP. "Le Salafisme, une Nébuleuse Fondamentaliste en Croissance en France." *Le Point*, 15 June 2018. https://www.lepoint.fr/societe/ le-salafisme-une-nebuleuse-fondamentaliste-en-croissance-en -france-15-06-2018-2227557_23.php.

Agrama, Hussein Ali. *Questioning Secularism: Islam, Sovereignty, and the Rule of Law in Modern Egypt*. Chicago: The University of Chicago Press, 2012.

Al-Akhdar, Abdul-Hasan Maalik. *In Defense of Islam in Light of the Events of September 11th*. Toronto: T.R.O.I.D Publications, 2002.

Al-ʿAsli, Muhammad et al. *Munir fi l-Tarbiyya al-Islamiyya al-Sana al-Sadisa al-Ibtidaʾiyya*. Casablanca: Dar al-Sharq, 2017–18.

Al-Atawneh, Muhammad. "Is Saudi Arabia a Theocracy? Religion and Governance in Contemporary Saudi Arabia." *Middle Eastern Studies* 45, no. 5 (September 2009): 721–37. https://doi.org/10.1080/ 00263200802586105.

– *Wahhabi Islam Facing the Challenges of Modernity: Dar Al-Ifta in the Modern Saudi State*. Leiden: Brill, 2010.

Al Burʿee, ʿAbdul ʿAzeez Bin Yahyaa. *A Concise Manual for the New Muslim*. Orlando: Salafi Ink Publications, 2012.

Al-Enazy, Askar H. *The Creation of Saudi Arabia*. London: Routledge, 2010.

254 Bibliography

Al-Fauzan, Saleh Fauzan. *Rulings Pertaining to Muslim Women*. Riyadh: Darussalam, 2003.

Al-Fawzaan, Saleh. "Why Do the 'Wahhabis' Always Talk about Tawheed?" *The Ark* 21 (August 2007): 4.

Al-Fouzan, Saalih bin Fouzan. *Al-Walaa' Wal-Baraa': Allegiance and Association with the People of Islaam and Eeman and Disassociation and Enmity with the People of Falsehood and Disbelief in Islaam*. Translated by Abdur-Rahman Bansfield. Ipswich: Jam'iyyat Ihya' Minhaj al-Sunna, 1997.

Al-Ghunayman, 'Abdallah. "The Kufr of Those Who Rule by Man-Made Laws." In *Islam: Questions and Answers – Polytheism and Its Different Forms*, edited by Muhammad Saed Abdul-Rahman, 131. London: MSA Publication, 2003.

Al-Haddaadee, Alee bin Yahyah, ed. *The Book of Forty Hadeeth Regarding the Madhab of the Salaf*. Birmingham: Minhaj al-Sunnah Publications, 2005.

'Ali, Abu Muntasir ibn Mohar. "Introduction." In *Al-Walaa' Wal-Baraa': Allegiance and Association with the People of Islaam and Eeman and Disassociation and Enmity with the People of Falsehood and Disbelief in Islaam*, translated by Abu 'Abd al-Rahman Bansfield, 4–5. Ipswich: Jam'iyyat Ihya' Minhaj al-Sunna, 1997.

Ali, Ahmed. *Al-Qur'an, a Contemporary Translation*. Princeton: Princeton University Press, 1993.

Al-Khudayr, 'Abd al-Karim. "Is It Permissible for a Muslim to Choose the Easiest Scholarly Opinion." In *Islam: Questions and Answers – Basis for Jurisprudence and Islamic Rulings*, edited by Muhammad Saed Abdul-Rahman, 93. London: MSA Publication, 2007.

Al-Lajna al-Da'ima. "Ruling on Making Fun of the Hijab." In *Islam Questions and Answers – Polytheism (Shirk) and Its Different Forms*, edited by Muhammad Saed Abdul-Rahman, 75–6. London: MSA Publication, 2003.

Allievi, Stefano. "Muslim Voices, European Ears: Exploring the Gap between the Production of Islamic Knowledge and Its Perception." In *Producing Islamic Knowledge: Transmission and Dissemination in Western Europe*, edited by Martin van Bruinessen and Stefano Allievi, 28–46. Abingdon: Routledge, 2011.

Al-Madkhali, Rabee Bin Haadi. *The Necessity of Conforming to the Understanding of the Salaf*. Jedda: Miraath Publications, 2012.

Almond, Gabriel A., R. Scott Appleby, and Emmanuel Sivan. *Strong Religion: The Rise of Fundamentalisms around the World*. Chicago: University of Chicago Press, 2003.

Al-Munajjid, Muhammad Salih. "Collecting Donations to Give Gifts to Poor Families at Christmas." Islam Question & Answer, 25 December 2009. https://islamqa.info/en/8375.

- "Does Islam Regard Men and Women as Equal?" In *Islam: Questions and Answers – Basis for Jurisprudence and Islamic Rulings,* edited by Muhammad Saed Abdul-Rahman, 57–67. London: MSA Publication, 2007.
Al-Munajjid, Muhammad Salih. "Inheritance from a Non-Muslim." Islam Question & Answer, 4 March 1998. https://islamqa.info/en/ref/428.
- "Military Service in Kaafir Armies and Working as a 'Chaplain' in Those Armies." In *Islam: Questions and Answers – Alliance and Amity, Disavowal and Enmity,* edited by Muhammad Saed Abdul-Rahman, 137–8. London: MSA Publication, 2003.
- "Selling Greeting Cards for Christian Holidays." Islamway, 27 December 2007. https://en.islamway.net/article/8318/selling-greeting-cards-for-christian-holidays.
Al-Qahtani, Muhammad Saeed. *Al-Wala' Wal-Bara' According to the 'Aqeedah of the Salaf.* London: Al-Firdous, 1993.
- "Duties of Muslims Living in the West." On Islam, 7 May 2006. Accessed 14 June 2013. http://www.onislam.net/.
- "Introduction." In *Fatwas of European Council for Fatwa and Research,* translated by Anas Usama al-Tikriti and Shakir Nasif al-Ubaydi, vii–xii. Cairo: Islamic Inc., 2002.
Al-Shaykh, 'Abdul-'Aziz. "A Tunisian Wishing to Migrate to France Where Things Are Tough on Muslims." Al Fiqh, n.d. Accessed 31 December 2022. https://www.al-feqh.com/en/a-tunisian-wishing-to-migrate-to-france-where-things-are-tough-on-muslims.
Al-'Uthaymin, Muhammad b. Salih. "Benefiting from What the Kaafirs Have." In *Islam: Questions and Answers – Alliance and Amity, Disavowal and Enmity,* edited by Muhammad Saed Abdul-Rahman, 39. London: MSA Publication, 2003.
- "Doesn't the Hadeeth 'Do Not Initiate the Greeting with a Jew or a Christian' Put People off Islam?" In *Islam: Questions and Answers – Alliance and Amity, Disavowal and Enmity,* edited by Muhammad Saed Abdul-Rahman, 34. London: MSA Publication, 2003.
- "Don't Be Such a Fanatic!" In *Islam: Questions and Answers – Islamic Politics,* edited by Muhammad Saed Abdul-Rahman, 3. London: MSA Publication, 2003.
- "Question 17." In *Muslim Minorities,* a compilation of semons and fatwas by Shaykh Ibn Baz and Shaykh Uthaymeen, 77. London: Message of Islam, 1998.
- "Ruling on Celebrating Non-Muslim Holidays and Congratulating Them." Islam Question & Answer, 28 March 1998. https://islamqa.info/en/947.
Armanios, Febe. "The Islamic Traditions of Wahhabism and Salafiyya." *Congressional Research Service Reports,* December 2003.

256 Bibliography

Ar-Rayyis, ʿAbdul-Aziz. *The Beautiful Advice to the Noble Salafis of the West.* Translated by ʿAbd al-Haqq Al-Ashanti. London: Jamiah Media, 2010.

Asad, Talal. *Genealogies of Religion: Discipline and Reasons of Power in Christianity and Islam.* Baltimore: Johns Hopkins University Press, 1993.

– "The Idea of an Anthropology of Islam." *Qui Parle* 17, no. 2 (2009): 1–30. https://doi.org/10.5250/quiparle.17.2.1.

Awan, Shazia. "I Watch the Growing Puritanical Attitudes of Young Muslims With Apprehension," *HuffPost UK*, 26 September 2016. https://www .huffingtonpost.co.uk/shazia-awan/i-watch-the-growing-purit_b_12134378 .html.

Azadé, Annabelle. "Marseille's Muslims Need Their Grand Mosque – Why Is It Still a Car Park?" *The Guardian*, 3 March 2015. https://www.theguardian .com/cities/2015/mar/03/marseille-muslim-community-grand-mosque.

Baker, Raymond William. *Islam without Fear: Egypt and the New Islamists.* Cambridge, MA: Harvard University Press, 2003.

Balala, Maha-Hanaan. *Islamic Finance and Law: Theory and Practice in a Globalized World.* London: I.B. Tauris, 2011.

Bandermann, Peter. "Neue Beratungsstelle soll Einstieg in den Salafismus verhindern." *Ruhr Nachrichten*, 4 December 2015.

Beit-Hallahmi, Benjamin, and Michael Argyle. *The Psychology of Religious Behaviour, Belief, and Experience.* London: Routledge, 1997.

Birt, Jonathan. "Wahhabism in the United Kingdom: Manifestations and Reactions." In *Transnational Connections and the Arab Gulf*, edited by Madawi al-Rasheed, 168–84. London: Routledge, 2004.

Bonnefoy, Coralie. "Bouches-du-Rhône : Quand le Venin Salafiste se Diffuse." *Marianne*, 15 June 2018. https://www.marianne.net/societe/marseille -bouches-du-rhone-la-diffusion-du-venin-salafiste.

Borchgrevink, Kaja, and Ida Roland Birkvad. "Religious Norms and Homeownership among Norwegian Muslim Women." *Journal of Ethnic and Migration Studies* 48, no. 5 (April 2022): 1–18. https://doi.org/10.1080/136918 3x.2021.1965866.

Bosnic Musovic, Alisa. "Omstridd Moské invigs i Dag." *Dagens Nyheter*, 8 June 2000. https://www.dn.se/arkiv/stockholm/soders-nya-profil-omstridd -moske-invigs-i-dag/.

Brekke, Torkel. "Halal Money: Financial Inclusion and Demand for Islamic Banking in Norway." *Research & Politics* 5, no. 1 (January–March 2018): 1–7. https://doi.org/10.1177/2053168018757624.

Bruinessen, Martin van. "Producing Islamic Knowledge in Western Europe: Discipline, Authority and Personal Quest." In *Producing Islamic Knowledge: Transmission and Dissemination in Western Europe*, edited by Martin van Bruinessen and Stefano Allievi, 1–27. Abingdon: Routledge, 2011.

Bunt, Gary R. *Islam in the Digital Age: E-Jihad, Online Fatwas and Cyber Islamic Environments*. London: Pluto Press, 2003.

Burtăverde, Vlad, Peter K. Jonason, Cezar Giosan, and Cristina Ene. "Why Do People Watch Porn? An Evolutionary Perspective on the Reasons for Pornography Consumption." *Evolutionary Psychology* 19, no. 2 (April–June 2021): 1–15. https://doi.org/10.1177/14747049211028798.

Caeiro, Alexandre. "The Power of European Fatwas: The Minority Fiqh Project and the Making of an Islamic Counterpublic." *International Journal of Middle East Studies* 42, no. 3 (August 2010): 435–49. https://doi.org/10.1017/s0020743810000437.

– "Transnational Ulama, European Fatwas, and Islamic Authority: A Case Study of the European Council for Fatwa and Research." In *Producing Islamic Knowledge: Transmission and Dissemination in Western Europe*, edited by Martin van Bruinessen and Stefano Allievi, 121–41. Abingdon: Routledge, 2013.

Caeiro, Alexandre, and Mahmoud al-Saify. "Qaradawi in Europe, Europe in Qaradawi? The Global Mufti's European Politics." In *Global Mufti: The Phenomenon of Yusuf al-Qaradawi*, edited by Bettina Gräf and Jakob Skovgaard-Petersen, 109–48. London: Hurst, 2009.

Calder, Norman. *Islamic Jurisprudence in the Classical Era*. Edited by Colin Imber. Cambridge: Cambridge University Press, 2010.

Campbell, Heidi. "Who's Got the Power? Religious Authority and the Internet." *Journal of Computer-Mediated Communication* 12, no. 3 (April 2007): 1043–62. https://doi.org/10.1111/j.1083-6101.2007.00362.x.

Ceilles, Mathilde. "A Marseille, les musulmans déplorent un manque de mosquées." *20minutes*, 18 September 2018. https://www.20minutes.fr/marseille/2338611-20180918-marseille-manque-mosquees-fait-musulmans-ville-etroit.

Charity Commission for England and Wales. "Salafi Bookstore and Islamic Centre." n.d. Accessed 31 December 2022. https://register-of-charities.charitycommission.gov.uk/charity-details/?regid=1083080&subid=0.

Chavez Perez, Inti, and Nedjma Boucheloukh. "Moské säljer judefientligt material." *Sveriges Radio*, 27 November 2005. https://sverigesradio.se/artikel/742418.

Cherribi, Sam. *Fridays of Rage: Al Jazeera, the Arab Spring, and Political Islam*. Oxford: Oxford University Press, 2017.

Combating 21st-Century Extremist Terrorism: ISIS and al-Qaeda in Iraq and Syria. Birmingham: Salafi Publications, n.d.

Commins, David. *The Wahhabi Mission and Saudi Arabia*. London: I.B. Tauris, 2006.

Commission for Countering Extremism. "Commission Releases First Round of Evidence of Extremism." 19 July 2019. https://www.gov.uk/government/news/commission-releases-first-round-of-evidence-of-extremism.

258 Bibliography

Dale, Iain. "Why Wahhabi/Salafist Mosques Should Be Banned from Receiving Foreign Funding." *Iain Dale* (blog), 28 June 2015. https://www.iaindale.com/articles/why-wahhabi-salafist-mosques-should-be-banned-from-receiving-foreign-funding.

Damir-Geilsdorf, Sabine, and Mira Menzfeld. "'Looking at the Life of the Prophet and How He Dealt with All These Issues.' Self-Positioning, Demarcations and Belongingness of German Salafis from an Emic Perspective." *Contemporary Islam* 10, no. 3 (September 2016): 433–54. https://doi.org/10.1007/s11562-016-0361-7.

Dar al-Ifta' al-Misriyya. "The Fasting Hours of This Year's Ramadan Will Exceed 19 Hours in My Country. How Could We Endure Fasting – Decision 8057." n.d. Accessed 5 July 2015. http://www.dar-alifta.org.

– "Fasting in Countries Where the Nights Are Short – Decision 2806." n.d. Accessed 5 July 2015. http://www.dar-alifta.org.

– "Is It Permissible to Send Christmas Greetings to Christian Friends." 25 July 2013. https://www.dar-alifta.org/en/fatwa/details/5982/is-it-permissible-to-send-christmas-greetings-to-christian-friends.

Davidman, Lynn. "The Transformation of Bodily Practices among Religious Defectors." In *Embodied Resistance: Challenging the Norms, Breaking the Rules,* edited by Chris Bobel and Samantha Kwan, 209–19. Nashville: Vanderbilt University Press, 2011.

Defoe, Daniel. *Roxana: The Fortunate Mistress.* Oxford: Oxford University Press, 2008.

De Koning, Martijn. "Changing Worldviews and Friendship: An Exploration of the Life Stories of Two Female Salafists in the Netherlands." In *Global Salafism,* edited by Roel Meijer, 372–92. London: Hurst, 2009.

DeLorenzo, Yusuf Talal. "Fiqh and the Fiqh Council of North America." *Journal of Islamic Law* 3 (1998): 193.

Dessing, Nathal M., Nadia Jeldoft, and Linda Woodhead, eds. *Everyday Lived Islam in Europe.* Abingdon: Routledge, 2016.

Dortmunder Statistik. "Hauptwohnbevölkerung in Dortmund am 31.12.2020." Stadt Dortmund, 26 April 2021. Microsoft Word document recieved from the municipality.

Douglas, Mary. *In the Wilderness: The Doctrine of Defilement in the Book of Numbers.* Oxford: Oxford University Press, 2001.

Doyle, Natalie J. "Lessons from France: Popularist Anxiety and Veiled Fears of Islam." *Islam and Christian–Muslim Relations* 22, no. 4 (October 2011): 475–89. https://doi.org/10.1080/09596410.2011.606194.

Duderija, Adis, and Halim Rane. "Minority Fiqh (Fiqh al-Aqalliyyat)." In *Islam and Muslims in the West: Major Issues and Debates,* edited by Adis Duderija and Halim Rane, 209–29. Cham: Palgrave Macmillan, 2019.

Echchaibi, Nabil. "From Audio Tapes to Video Blogs: The Delocalisation of Authority in Islam." *Nations and Nationalism* 17, no. 1 (January 2011): 25–44. https://doi.org/10.1111/j.1469-8129.2010.00468.x.

Esdonk, Susanne Elisabeth van. "European Fatwas in the Netherlands: An Exploratory Qualitative Study among Dutch Imams on the Influence the European Council for Fatwa and Research Has upon the Muslim Community in the Netherlands." Master's thesis, University of Amsterdam, 2011.

Esposito, John, Ibrahim Kalin, Ed Marques, and Ursa Ghazi, eds. *The 500 Most Influential Muslims in the World*. Amman: The Royal Islamic Strategic Studies Centre, 2009.

European Council for Fatwa and Research. *Fatwas of European Council for Fatwa and Research*. Cairo: Islamic Inc., 2002.

– "The Muslim Inheriting His Non-Muslim Relative." In *Fatwas of European Council for Fatwa and Research*, 148–9. Cairo: Islamic Inc., 2002.

– "Ruling on Offering Congratulations to Non-Muslims on Their Festive Occasions (Decision 3/6)." In *Fatwas of European Council for Fatwa and Research*, 177–84. Cairo: Islamic Inc., 2002.

Fishman, Shammai. *Fiqh al-Aqalliyyat: A Legal Theory for Muslim Minorities*. Washington: Hudson Institute, 2006.

Forschungsgruppe Weltanschauungen in Deutschland. "Dortmund: Religionszugehörigkeiten 1910–2018." fowid (Forschungsgruppe Weltanschauungen in Deutschland), 4 September 2019. https://fowid.de/meldung/dortmund-religionszugehoerigkeiten-1910-2018.

Freyer-Stowasser, Barbara. "Yusuf Al-Qaradawi on Women." In *Global Mufti: The Phenomenon of Yusuf al-Qaradawi*, edited by Bettina Gräf and Jakob Skovgaard-Petersen, 181–211. London: Hurst, 2009.

Frisch, Max. *Öffentlichkeit als Partner*. Frankfurt am Main: Suhrkamp, 1967.

Galal, Ehab. "Yusuf al-Qaradawi and the New Islamic TV." In *Global Mufti: The Phenomenon of Yusuf al-Qaradawi*, edited by Bettina Gräf and Jakob Skovgaard-Petersen, 149–80. London: Hurst, 2009.

Ghadban, Ralph. "Fiqh al-Aqalliyyat and Its Place in Islamic Law." *Orient* 2 (2010): 30–7.

Ginzburg, Carlo. *The Cheese and the Worms: The Cosmos of a Sixteenth-Century Miller*. Baltimore: Johns Hopkins University Press, 2013. First published in 1976.

Gräf, Bettina. "The Concept of Wasatiyya in the Work of Yusuf al-Qaradawi." In *Global Mufti: The Phenomenon of Yusuf al-Qaradawi*, edited by Bettina Gräf and Jakob Skovgaard-Petersen, 213–38. London: Hurst, 2009.

Group of Muftis. "Ulama's Fatwas on American Muslim Participating in US Military Campaign." *Islam Online*, 16 October 2001. Accessed 12 September 2013. http://www.onislam.net/.

260 Bibliography

Grubbs, Joshua B., Fred Volk, Julie J. Exline, and Kenneth I. Pargament. "Internet Pornography Use: Perceived Addiction, Psychological Distress, and the Validation of a Brief Measure." *Journal of Sex & Marital Therapy* 41, no. 1 (January 2015): 1733–45. https://doi.org/10.1080/0092623x.2013.842192.

Hackett, Conrad. "5 Facts about the Muslim Population in Europe." Pew Research Center, 29 November 2017. https://pewrsr.ch/2i3TIim.

Hallaq, Wael B. *Authority, Continuity and Change in Islamic Law*. New York: Cambridge University Press, 2001.

– *Shari῾a: Theory, Practice, Transformations*. Cambridge: Cambridge University Press, 2009.

Hamid, Sadek. "The Attraction of 'Authentic' Islam: Salafism and British Muslim Youth." In *Global Salafism*, edited by Roel Meijer, 384–403. Oxford: Oxford University Press, 2014.

– *Sufis, Salafis and Islamists: The Contested Ground of British Islamic Activism*. London: I.B. Tauris, 2016.

Hammargren, Bitte. "Fatwor Utfärdas i Stockholm." *Svenska Dagbladet*, 8 July 2003. https://www.svd.se/a/37a493cd-5c7f-38d8-a77f-68c2a05212ba/fatwor -utfardas-i-stockholm.

Hanafy, Khaled. "The European Council for Fatwa and Research: Renewed Leadership, Renewed Hopes." European Council for Fatwa and Research, 16 December 2018. https://www.e-cfr.org/blog/2018/12/16/european-council -fatwa-research/.

Hassan, Said Fares. *Fiqh Al-Aqalliyyat: History, Development, and Progress*. New York: Palgrave Macmillan, 2013.

Haucap, Justus, and Ulrich Heimeshoff. "Google, Facebook, Amazon, eBay: Is the Internet Driving Competition or Market Monopolization?" *International Economics and Economic Policy* 11, nos. 1–2 (February 2014): 49–61. https:// doi.org/10.1007/s10368-013-0247-6.

Hegghammer, Thomas. "Jihadi-Salafis or Revolutionaries? On Religion and Politics in the Study of Militant Islamism." In *Global Salafism: Islam's New Religious Movement*, edited by Roel Meijer. London: Hurst, 2009, 244–66.

Hogg, Michael A. "Social Identity and Group Cohesiveness." In *Rediscovering the Social Group: A Self-Categorization Theory*, edited by John C. Turner. Oxford: B. Blackwell, 1987.

Holbrook, Donald. "A Cold Reception: The Rise of Anti-Islamic Sentiments in Iceland?" openDemocracy, 12 June 2014. https://www.opendemocracy.net/ en/can-europe-make-it/cold-reception-rise-of-antiislamic-sentiments-in -iceland/.

Holland, Norman N. *5 Readers Reading*. New Haven: Yale University Press, 1975.

Ibn ῾Abdul Wahhab, Muhammad. *The Best Religion for Mankind, Explained by Saalih Ibn Fawzaan Ibn ῾Abdullah al-Fawzaan*. New York: Daarul Isnad, 2010.

- *The Three Fundamental Principles and Their Evidences: Workbook for Germantown Masjid's Summer Seminar*. Edited by Anwar Wright and translated by Moosaa Richardson. N.p.: Independently Published, 2019.
Ibn Adam, Abu al-Hasan Malik, ed. *The Crime of Hizbiyyah against the Salafi Da'wah*. Grand Rapids, MI: Sunnah Publishing, 2009.
Ibn Baaz, 'Abdul Azeez. "The Importance of Muslim Minorities Adhering to Islam." In *Muslim Minorities*, edited by Shaykh Ibn Baz and Shaykh Uthaymeen, 4–21. London: Message of Islam, 1998.
Ibn Baz, 'Abd al-'Aziz b. 'Abdallah. *The Correct Belief and Its Opposite and What Negates al-Islam*. Translated by Muhammad 'Abd al-Rahman Abu Hamza Maghribi. London: Al-Firdous, 1996.
- *The Legislation of Islam*. Translated by Abu Sumayya 'Aqil Walker. Grand Prairie: Ibnul Qayyim Publications, 2006.
- "It Is Not Permissible to Reside in a Country Where Disbelief Is Prevalent Except for the Call of Allah." Al-Ifta, n.d. Accessed 25 September 2011. http://www.alifta.org/.
- "Ruling Concerning Listening to Radio Programs that Contain Music." In *Islamic Fatawa Regarding Women*, edited by Muhammad bin Abdul-Aziz Al-Musnad, 324. Riyadh: Darussalam Publishers & Distributers, 1996.
- "There Are No Trivial Issues in Islam." In *Islam: Questions and Answers – Basis for Jurisprudence and Islamic Rulings*, edited by Muhammad Saed Abdul-Rahman, 194–6. London: MSA Publication, 2007.
- *The Correct Islamic Aqidah*. Birmingham: Daar us-Sunnah Publishers, 2008.
Ibn Baz, Shaykh, and Shaykh Uthaymeen. *Muslim Minorities*, a compilation of sermons and fatwas. London: Message of Islam, 1998.
Ibn Jibrin, 'Abdallah. "Advice to Those Who Do Not Recognize the Salafi Scholars and Call Them Wahhabis." In *Islam: Questions and Answers – Inviting Others to Islam*, edited by Muhammad Saed Abdul-Rahman, 200–2. London: MSA Publication, 2007.
Ibn Taymiyya, Taki al-Din Ahmad. *The Friends of Allah & The Friends of Shaytan*. Translated by Abu Rumaysah. Birmingham: Daar us-Sunnah Publishers, 2005.
Inge, Anabel. *The Making of a Salafi Muslim Woman: Paths to Conversion*. Oxford: Oxford University Press, 2017.
Islamhouse. "His Company Gives Its Employees a Christmas Bonus." IslamHouse, 2012. Accessed 31 December 2022. https://d1.islamhouse.com/data/en/ih_fatawa/single/en_islam_qa_146328.pdf.
Islam Question & Answer. "Is Bodybuilding Haram?" Islam Question & Answer, 16 September 2003. https://islamqa.info/en/ref/40527.
- "It Is Not Permissible to Eat Foods That Are Prepared by the Kuffaar for Their Festivals." Islam Question & Answer, 27 December 2011. https://islamqa.info/en/answers/12666/it-is-not-permissible-to-eat-foods-that-are-prepared-by-the-kuffaar-for-their-festivals.

262   Bibliography

- "Ruling on Dealing with Mortgages in a Non-Muslim Country." Islamway, 4 February 2013. https://en.islamway.net/fatwa/41459/ruling-on-dealing -with-mortgages-in-a-non-muslim-country.
- "Ruling on Democracy and Elections and Participation in That System." Islam Question & Answer, 8 October 2008. https://islamqa.info/en/ answers/107166/ruling-on-democracy-and-elections-and-participating-in -that-system.
- "What Is the True Meaning of Shirk and What Are Its Types?" In *Islam: Question and Answers – Polytheism and Its Different Forms,* edited by Muhammad Saed Abdul-Rahman, 22–32. London: MSA Publication, 2003.
Islamway. "Advice to Muslims in the West." Islamway, 23 April 2014. https://en.islamway.net/article/27355/advice-to-the-muslims-in-the-west.
Islamweb. "Difficulty Fasting in Norway Due to Long Days." Islamweb, 27 February 2005. https://www.islamweb.net/en/fatwa/89463/difficulty-fasting -in-norway-due-to-long-days.
- "Services Cooling Systems for Beer, Wine, and Gays." Islamweb, 10 April 2004. https://www.islamweb.net/en/fatwa/87412/services-cooling-systems -for-beer-wine-and-gays.
- "Working as a Waiter." Islamweb, 10 June 2004. https://www.islamweb.net/ en/fatwa/87931/working-as-a-waiter.
Jackson, Sherman A. "The Second Education of the *Mufti*: Notes on Shihab al-Din al-Qarafi's Tips to the Jurisconsult." *The Muslim World* 82, nos. 3–4 (October 1992): 201–17. https://doi.org/10.1111/j.1478-1913.1992.tb03553.x.
Karam, Salam. "Dubbla Budskap i Moskén." *Svenska Dagbladet,* 23 May 2004. https://www.svd.se/a/03affb7f-e092-3f65-8088-0e74d2b6bd62/dubbla -budskap-i-mosken.
Kern, Soeren. "Europe's Fatwa Factories." Gatestone Institute, 3 February 2011. https://www.gatestoneinstitute.org/1857/europe-fatwa-factories.
Kettani, Houssain. "Muslim Population in Europe: 1950–2020." *International Journal of Environmental Science and Development* 1, no. 2 (June 2010), 154–64. https://doi.org/10.7763/ijesd.2010.v1.29.
Khaled, Amr. *Integration im Islam: Über die Rolle der Muslime in Europa.* Karlsruhe: Andalusia, 2005.
Kohlstadt, Michael. "Jeder fünfte Schüler in Dortmund ist Muslim." *Westfälische Rundschau,* 8 January 2013.
Larsen, Lena. *How Muftis Think: Manufacturing Fatwas for Muslim Women in Western Europe.* Leiden: Brill, 2018.
Laurence, Jonathan, and Justin Vaisse. *Integrating Islam: Political and Religious Challenges in Contemporary France.* Washington, DC: Brookings Institution Press, 2006.
Layton, Josh. "Mosque Leader Welcomes YouTube Crackdown on Hate Preacher Linked to London Bridge Terrorist." *Birmingham Mail,* 10 June

2017. https://www.birminghammail.co.uk/news/midlands-news/mosque
-leader-welcomes-youtube-crackdown-13167855.

Leroux, Luc. "Procédure d'expulsion engagée contre El Hadi Doudi, imam d'une mosquée salafiste marseillaise." *Le Monde*, 2 February 2018. https://www.lemonde.fr/police-justice/article/2018/02/02/procedure-d -expulsion-engagee-contre-el-hadi-doudi-imam-d-une-mosquee-salafiste -marseillaise_5251167_1653578.html.

Lewis, Mervyn, and Latifa M. Algaoud. *Islamic Banking*. Northampton, MA: E. Elgar Publishing, 2001.

Liebes, Tamar, and Elihu Katz. *The Export of Meaning: Cross-Cultural Readings of Dallas*. 2nd ed. Cambridge: Polity Press, 1993.

The Local. "Mosque Swastika Attack 'No Isolated Incident.'" *The Local Sweden*, 3 January 2014. https://www.thelocal.se/20140103/stockholm-mosque -swastika-attack-no-exception/.

Mael, Fred A., and Blake E. Ashforth. "Identification in Work, War, Sports, and Religion: Contrasting the Benefits and Risks." *Journal for the Theory of Social Behaviour* 31, no. 2 (June 2001): 197–222. https://doi.org/10.1111/1468 -5914.00154.

Malm, Fredrik. "Massmordspredikan i Svensk Moské." *Dagens Nyheter*, 21 August 2003. https://www.dn.se/arkiv/debatt/massmordspredikan -i-svensk-moske-uppmaningar-till-terrorism-mot-israeler-polisanmals -av-luf/.

Mansour, Fawaz. "The Immigration to Abyssinia: A New Interpretation." *Jami`a* 13 (2009): 57–69.

March, Andrew F. *Islam and Liberal Citizenship: The Search for an Overlapping Consensus*. New York: Oxford University Press, 2009.

March, Andrew F. "Sources of Moral Obligation to Non-Muslims in the 'Jurisprudence of Muslim Minorities' (Fiqh al-Aqalliyyat) Discourse." *Islamic Law and Society* 16, no. 1 (2009): 34–94. https://doi.org/10.1163/156851 908x413757.

Mariani, Emerte. "Cyber-Fatwas, Sermons, and Media Campaigns: Amr Khaled and Omar Bakri Muhammad in Search of New Audiences." In *Producing Islamic Knowledge: Transmission and Dissemination in Western Europe*, edited by Martin van Bruinessen and Stefano Allievi, 142–68. Abingdon: Routledge, 2011.

Masud, Muhammad Khalid. "The Significance of Istifta' in the Fatwa Discourse." *Islamic Studies* 48, no. 3 (2009): 341–66.

Masud, Muhammad Khalid, Brinkley Messick, and David S. Powers. "Muftis, Fatwas, and Islamic Legal Interpretation." In *Islamic Legal Interpretation: Muftis and Their Fatwas*, edited by Muhammad Khalid Masud, Brinkley Messick, and David S. Powers, 3–32. Cambridge, MA.: Harvard University Press, 1996.

264 Bibliography

Mawlawi, Faysal, and Jamal al-Din ʾAtiyya. "Watching Football and Playing Professionally." Muslims in Calgary, n.d. Accessed 31 December 2022. https://muslimsincalgary.ca/.

Meijer, Roel. "Politicising Al-Jarh Wa-l-Taʿdil: Rabi B. Hadi al-Madkhali and the Transnational Battle for Religious Authority." In *The Transmission and Dynamics of the Textual Sources of Islam: Essays in Honour of Harald Motzki*, edited by Nicolet Boekhoff-van der Voort, Cornelis H. M. Versteegh, and Joas Wagemakers, 375–99. Leiden: Brill, 2011.

MEMRI. "Al-Qaradhawi Speaks in Favor of Suicide Operations at an Islamic Conference in Sweden."24 July 2003. https://www.memri.org/reports/al -qaradhawi-speaks-favor-suicide-operations-islamic-conference-sweden.

Miladi, Noureddine, Saleh Karim, and Mahroof Athambawa. "Fatwa on Satellite TV and the Development of Islamic Religious Discourse." *Journal of Arab & Muslim Media Research* 10, no. 2 (November 2017): 129–52. https://doi.org/10.1386/jammr.10.2.129_1.

Mortimer, Gavin. "It's Time Europe Got Serious about Islamic Supremacists." *The Spectator*, 7 September 2017. https://www.spectator.co.uk/article/it-s -time-europe-got-serious-about-islamic-supremacists/.

Moscheesuche. "Moscheen in Dortmund." n.d. Accessed 8 November 2022. https://www.moscheesuche.de/.

Mouline, Nabil. "The Committee of Grand Ulama: An Organization in the Service of the Prince . . . and the Population." In *The Clerics of Islam*, 146–70. New Haven: Yale University Press, 2014.

Nafi, Basheer. "Fatwa and War: On the Allegiance of American Muslim Soldiers in the Aftermath of September 11." *Islamic Law and Society* 11, no. 1 (2004): 78–116. https://doi.org/10.1163/156851904772841426.

Neriya-Ben Shahar, Rivka. "The Medium Is the Danger: Discourse about Television among Amish and Ultra-Orthodox (Haredi) Women." *Journal of Media and Religion* 16, no. 1 (January 2017): 27–38. https://doi.org/10.1080/15 348423.2017.1274590.

O'Grady, Siobhán. "After Refusing a Handshake, a Muslim Couple Was Denied Swiss Citizenship." *Washington Post*, 18 August 2018. https://www .washingtonpost.com/world/2018/08/18/after-refusing-handshake-muslim -couple-was-denied-swiss-citizenship/.

Orange, Richard. "Swedish Riots Spark Surprise and Anger." *The Guardian*, 25 May 2013. https://www.theguardian.com/world/2013/may/25/sweden -europe-news.

Pall, Zoltan, and Martijn de Koning. "Being and Belonging in Transnational Salafism: Informality, Social Capital and Authority in European and Middle Eastern Salafi Networks." *Journal of Muslims in Europe* 6, no. 1 (March 2017): 76–103. https://doi.org/10.1163/22117954-12341338.

Parray, Tauseef Ahmad. "The Legal Methodology of 'Fiqh al-Aqalliyyat' and Its Critics: An Analytical Study." *Journal of Muslim Minority Affairs* 32, no. 1 (March 2012): 88–107. https://doi.org/10.1080/13602004.2012.665624.

Payton, Matt. "Nazi Swastikas Painted by Vandals inside Swedish Mosque." *Independent*, 27 November 2016. https://www.independent.co.uk/news/world/europe/swedish-mosque-nazi-swastika-hate-crime-stockholm-a7442391.html.

The Permanent Committee for Scholarly Research and Ifta'. "Fatwa 5651." Al Ifta, n.d. Accessed 23 August 2013. http://www.alifta.com/.

"The Ruling on Children's Songs." In *Islamic Fataawa Regarding the Muslim Child*, 220–1. London: Invitation to Islam Publishers, 2007.

Pinchevski, Amit, and Roy Brand. "Holocaust Perversions: The Stalags Pulp Fiction and the Eichmann Trial." *Critical Studies in Media Communication* 24, no. 5 (December 2007): 387–407. https://doi.org/10.1080/07393180701694598.

Radway, Janice A. *Reading the Romance: Women, Patriarchy, and Popular Literature*. 2nd ed. Chapel Hill: University of North Carolina Press, 1991.

Ramadan, Tariq. *What I Believe*. New York: Oxford University Press, 2010.

Rinkeby-Kista District Council. *Welcome to Rinkeby-Kista*. Stockholm: Rinkeby-Kista District Council, n.d.

Rohe, Mathias. *Muslim Minorities and the Law in Europe*. New Delhi: Global Media Publications, 2007.

Rokeach, Milton. "The Nature and Meaning of Dogmatism." *Psychological Review* 61, no. 3 (1954): 194–204. https://doi.org/10.1037/h0060752.

Saheeh International Edition. *The Quran*. London: Al-Muntada al-Islami, 2004.

Salafi Publications. *The Rise of Jihadist Extremism in the West*. Birmingham: Salafi Publications, 2010.

Saritoprak, Zeki. "Migration, Feelings of Belonging to a Land, and the Universality of Islam." In *Islam and Citizenship Education*, edited by Ednan Aslan and Marcia Hermansen, 45–56. Wiesbaden: Springer, 2015.

Sauerberg, Lars Ole. "Literature in Figures: An Essay on the Popularity of Thrillers." *Orbis Litterarum* 38, no. 2 (June 1983): 93–107. https://doi.org/10.1111/j.1600-0730.1983.tb01119.x.

Schacht, Joseph. *An Introduction to Islamic Law*. Oxford: Clarendon Press, 1982.

Schimmel, Annemarie. "Reason and Mystical Experience in Sufism." In *Intellectual Traditions in Islam*, edited by Farhad Daftary, 130–45. London: I.B. Tauris in association with the Institute of Ismaili Studies, 2000.

Schleifer, S. Abdullah. "Understanding Jihad: Definition and Methodology." *Islamic Quarterly* 27, no. 3 (1983): 117–31.

Schmoll, Thomas. "Wo landen die Koran-Bücher der verbotenen Salafisten?" *Die Welt*, 18 November 2016. https://www.welt.de/politik/deutschland/plus159595983/Wo-landen-die-Koran-Buecher-der-verbotenen-Salafisten.html.

266   Bibliography

Shadid, Wasif, and Sjoerd van Koningsveld. "Loyalty to a Non-Muslim Government: An Analysis of Islamic Normative Discussions and of the Views of Some Contemporary Islamicists." In *Political Participation and Identities of Muslims in Non-Muslim States*, edited by W.A.R. Shadid and P.S. van Koningsveld, 85–114. Kampen: Kok Pharos, 1996.

Shariff, Azim F. "Does Religion Increase Moral Behavior?" *Current Opinion in Psychology* 6 (December 2015): 108–13. https://doi.org/10.1016/j.copsyc.2015.07.009.

Shavit, Uriya. "Can Muslims Befriend Non-Muslims? Debating al-Wala' Wa-al-Bara' (Loyalty and Disavowal) in Theory and Practice." *Islam and Christian–Muslim Relations* 25, no. 1 (January 2014): 67–88. https://doi.org/10.1080/09596410.2013.851329.

– "Europe, the New Abyssinia: On the Role of the First Hijra in the Fiqh al-Aqalliyyat al-Muslima Discourse." *Islam and Christian–Muslim Relations* 29, no. 3 (July 2018): 371–91. https://doi.org/10.1080/09596410.2018.1480120.

– *Islamism and the West: From "Cultural Attack" to "Missionary Migrant."* Abingdon: Routledge, 2015.

– "Is Shura a Muslim Form of Democracy? Roots and Systemization of a Polemic." *Middle Eastern Studies* 46, no. 3 (May 2010): 349–74. https://doi.org/10.1080/00263200902917085.

– "The Muslim Brothers' Conception of Armed Insurrection against an Unjust Regime." *Middle Eastern Studies* 51, no. 4 (July 2015): 600–17. https://doi.org/10.1080/00263206.2015.1014344.

– *The New Imagined Community: Global Media and the Construction of National and Muslim Identities of Migrants*. Brighton: Sussex Academic Press, 2009.

– "The Postmodern Reconstitution of an Islamic Memory: Theory and Practice in the Case of Yusuf al-Qaradawi's Virtual Umma." In *Islamic Myths and Memories. Mediators of Globalization*, edited by Itzchak Weismann, Mark Sedgwick, Ulrika Mårtensson, 163–84. London: Routledge, 2014.

– "Raising *Salafi* Children in the West." *Islam and Christian–Muslim Relations* 28, no. 3 (July 2017): 333–54. https://doi.org/10.1080/09596410.2016.1239920.

– "Ramadan in Iceland: A Tale of Two Mosques." *Islam and Christian–Muslim Relations* 27, no. 4 (October 2016): 397–417. https://doi.org/10.1080/09596410.2016.1148392.

– *Shari'a and Muslim Minorities: The Wasati and Salafi Approaches to Fiqh al-Aqalliyyat al-Muslima*. Oxford: Oxford University Press, 2015.

– "The Wasati and Salafi Approaches to the Religious Law of Muslim Minorities." *Islamic Law and Society* 19, no. 4 (2012): 416–57. https://doi.org/10.1163/156851912X603210.

Siddiqi, Muhammad Yasin Mazhar. *The Prophet Muhammad: A Role Model for Muslim Minorities*. Translated by Abdur Raheem Kidawi. Markfield: Islamic Foundation, 2006.

Siddiqi, Muzammil. "'Necessity' That Allows Buying a House on Mortgage." On Islam, 20 October 2010. Accessed 5 July 2013. http://www.onislam.net/.

Similarweb. "Website Performance." n.d. Accessed 3 January 2023. https://www.similarweb.com/website/e-cfr.org/#overview.

Sisler, Vit. "The Internet and the Construction of Islamic Knowledge in Europe: Religious Norms in Cyberspace." *Masaryk University Journal of Law and Technology* 1, no. 2 (2007): 205–18.

Sivan, Gili. "Aliyat Ma'amado shel HaRav BeKehilot Zioniot-Datiot BaEidan HaPost-Moderni." In *Rabanut: HaEtgar,* edited by Yedidia Shtern and Shuki Fridman, 121–43. Jerusalem: The Israel Institute for Democracy, 2011.

Skovgaard-Petersen, Jakob. *Defining Islam for the Egyptian State: Muftis and Fatwas of the Dar al-Ifta*. Leiden: Brill, 1997.

Smoltczyk, Alexander. "Islam's Spiritual 'Dear Abby': The Voice of Egypt's Muslim Brotherhood." *Der Spiegel*, 15 February 2011. https://www.spiegel.de/international/world/islam-s-spiritual-dear-abby-the-voice-of-egypt-s-muslim-brotherhood-a-745526.html.

Spence, Louise. *Watching Daytime Soap Operas: The Power of Pleasure*. Middletown, CT: Wesleyan University Press, 2005.

Stockholms Stad. *Statistical Year-Book of Stockholm 2018*. Stockholm: Stockholms Stad, December 2017.

The Straits Times. "KL Mufti: Okay for Muslims to Wish Friends 'Merry Christmas.'" 22 December 2016, https://www.straitstimes.com/asia/se-asia/kl-mufti-okay-for-muslims-to-wish-friends-merry-christmas.

Strategic Research Team, Birmingham City Council. "2018 Birmingham Ward Profiles." Tableau Public, May 2018. Accessed 3 January 2023. https://public.tableau.com/views/2018BirminghamWardProfiles/2018BirminghamWardProfiles.

Stubbersfield, Joseph M., Jamshid J. Tehrani, and Emma G. Flynn. "Serial Killers, Spiders and Cybersex: Social and Survival Information Bias in the Transmission of Urban Legends." *British Journal of Psychology* 106, no. 2 (May 2015): 288–307. https://doi.org/10.1111/bjop.12073.

Tamanaha, Brian Z. *A General Jurisprudence of Law and Society*. Oxford: Oxford University Press, 2001.

Taplin, Jonathan T. *Move Fast and Break Things: How Facebook, Google, and Amazon Cornered Culture and Undermined Democracy*. New York: Little, Brown and Company, 2017.

Trope, Yaacov, and Nira Liberman. "Construal-Level Theory of Psychological Distance." *Psychological Review* 117, no. 2 (2010): 440–63. https://doi.org/10.1037/a0018963.

268 Bibliography

Trouve Ta Mosquée. "Les 59 mosquées trouvées de la ville de Marseille," n.d. Accessed 31 December 2022. https://www.trouvetamosquee.fr/mosquees/marseille-13/.

Warren, David H. *Rivals in the Gulf: Yusuf al-Qaradawi, Abdullah Bin Bayyah, and the Qatar-UAE Contest over the Arab Spring and the Gulf Crisis*. London: Routledge, 2021.

Wiedl, Nina. *The Making of German Salafiyya: The Emergence, Development, and Missionary Work of Salafi Movements in Germany*. Aarhus: Centre for Studies in Islamism and Radicalisation, 2012.

Wiktorowicz, Quintan. "Anatomy of the Salafi Movement." *Studies in Conflict & Terrorism* 29, no. 3 (May 2006): 207–39. https://doi.org/10.1080/10576100500497004.

Yaycioglu, Ali. "Ottoman Fatwa: An Essay on Legal Consultation in the Ottoman Empire." Master's thesis, Bilkent University, 1997.

Zahalka, Iyad. *Shari'a in the Modern Era: Muslim Minorities Jurisprudence*. Cambridge: Cambridge University Press, 2016.

Zweig, Stefan. *Magellan: Der Mann und seine Tat*. Wien: H. Reichner, 1938.

Index

Note: The letter *t* following a page number denotes a table.

'Abd al-Rashid, Muhammad, 45
'Abd al-Wahad, al-Hamdi, 80–1
'Abd al-Wahhab, Muhammad Ibn, 29–31, 33, 37, 95, 118
'Abduh, Muhammad, 23, 87–8, 90, 165
Abdullah as-Sueidi. *See under* Klominek, Johannes
Abu Anas, Yusuf, 118
Abu Bakr Mosque (Dortmund), 75, 77
Abu Bilal, 73
Abu Haleema, 99
Abu Khadeejah Abdul-Wahid, 95–101, 115, 117, 119, 173, 182–4, 202, 215; on Christmas, 96, 179; on European Court of Human Rights, 98; on Evolution Theory, 199; on haram in the workplace, 96; on homeschooling 182; on homosexuality, 199; on ifta', 100, 119–20; on loyalty and disavowal, 183; on migration to the West, 197–9; on mixed-gender schools, 120; on mortgages, 96, 179–80; on the Muslim Brothers, 100–1, 119; on relations with Saudi Arabia, 95–7, 184; on student loans, 96; on voting, 98
Abu Muntasir, 95–6
Abu Qatada, 98
Abyssinia, 206–8, 212
adhan, 85, 203
adultery, 36, 114, 137, 194
Afghani, Jamal al-Din al-, 23
Afghanistan War (2001–21), 45–6, 192
'Afifi, 'Abd al-Raziq, 54, 231n51
Agnarsson, Ibrahim Sverrir, 82
Agrama, Hussein 13
Al-Ansar, 31
al-Azhar University, 23, 42, 68, 83
Albani, Nasir al-Din al-, 30, 54, 72, 203
'Ali, Manwar. *See under* Abu Muntasir
Al Jazeera, 24, 112
Al-Lajna al-Da'ima lil-Buhuth al-'Ilmiyya wa-l-Ifta'. *See under* The Permanent Committee for Scholarly Research and Ifta'
Al-Majalla al-'Ilmiyya, 39, 112
Al-Manar, 87
Al-Nur Mosque (Reykjavik), 19, 110*t*, 127–8*t*, 131*t*, 140, 148*t*,

Al-Nur Mosque (*continued*)
157, 171, 176, 191, 227n31; death
of Salman Tamimi and, 92;
demographic composition of, 84;
establishment of, 82; Ramadan
fast and, 89–92; Isma'il Malik and,
89–90; rivalry with The Grand
Mosque and, 82–4
al-Qaeda, 31, 95, 98–9, 159, 203
Al-Qarawiyyin University, 85
Al-Rahman Mosque (Reykjavik),
83–4, 91
Al-Shari'a wa-l-Hayat. See under
Shari'a and Life
Al-Sharq al-Awsat, 43
Al-Sounna Mosque (Marseille),
104
al-wala' wa-l-bara'. *See under* loyalty
and disavowal
'Alwani, Taha Jabir al-, 42, 45, 191
'Anjari, Muhammad al-, 95–6
'aqida, 72, 119–20
Arab Spring, 70, 99–100, 129, 192
Asad, Talal, 5, 22
'Askari, Karim, 82–6, 90–1, 170; on
handshakes, 176
Assad, Bashar al-, 130
Association of Muslims in Iceland,
81–2

Badawi, Jamal, 49
Bakri, Zulkifli Mohamad al-,
234n124
Bamihriz, Salim, 100
Banna, Hasan al-, 23, 25
bid'a, 30, 101
Birmingham, 92, 94–5, 175, 183, 203,
207–9
bitcoin, 70
Blidi, Salim, 102–4, 115, 117;
on migration to the West, 194–5;
on mortgages, 144

Bourouba, Farid, 113, 120;
on migration to the West, 196–7;
on mortgages, 105
Burbank, Abu Talhah Dawud, 96

Caeiro, Alexandre, 108
Centre Musulman de Marseille, 105,
113
City Centre Da'wah, 94, 202, 213–5
Construal-Level Theory, 166
conversion, 47, 58, 73, 206, 208,
211–14
Council for Moroccan Mosques in the
Netherlands, 108
Council of Senior Scholars (Saudi
Arabia), 13, 30, 32, 86, 88, 128

Daesh. *See under* Islamic State in Iraq
and Syria
Dar al-Aman, 194
Dar al-Harb, 191
Dar al-Ifta' (Egypt), 13, 42, 88–9
Dar al-Islam, 39–40, 44, 53, 142, 78,
185, 191–2, 194, 198
darura: electoral participation and,
48; fasting and, 88–90; haram in the
workplace and, 52, 59; *maslaha* and,
26–8, 35, 74, 152, 155–6, 165, 182;
migration to the West and, 54–6,
202, 205; mortgages and, 43–5,
81, 103, 133–41, 158, 161, 168–9;
student loans and, 45, 140; *tarbiyya
islamiyya* and, 241–2n10
Davis, Abu Hakim Bilal, 96, 98, 179,
203, 205
da'wa, 140–2, 170, 186–203, 205,
208–15, 234n130; Christmas and,
49–50; City Centre Da'wah and, 94;
fasting and, 88–9; *fiqh al-aqalliyyat
al-Muslima* and, 9, 40–1, 55–6;
Johannes Klominek and, 73, 142,
192–3; mortgages and, 44; *salafiyya*

and, 53–6, 59, 63; service in a non-Muslim military force and, 46; The Grand Mosque of Iceland and, 83; The Salafi Mosque and, 184; *wasatiyya* and, 25–6, 40–1, 51

Dib, Khaled ʿAbd al-Hakim al-, 67–70, 112, 115–6, 155–6, 165; on *daʿwa*, 196–7; on handshakes, 176; on haram in the workplace, 162–3; on migration to the West, 195–6; on mortgages, 105, 138–40, 144–5, 162

Die Wahre Religion, 75, 78

Dortmund, 74–5, 195

Doudi, El Hadi, 104

Eid prayer, 52, 94, 101, 214

enclave, 44, 180–1

Euro Fatwa App, 113

European Council for Fatwa and Research, 15–6, 24, 58, 65–8, 70–2, 74, 104–43, 152; on Christmas, 3, 20–1, 49–50, 72, 131–2, 159; on *daʿwa*, 9, 40–1, 44, 46, 49–51, 88–9, 140–2, 197; on fasting, 88–9, 162, 164–5; on haram in the workplace, 48, 145; on inheritance, 46–7, 107–8; on loyalty and disavowal, 49–50; on marriage to a non-Muslim spouse, 46–7, 50, 107–8; on migration to the West, 3, 9, 20–1, 40–2, 197; on mortgages, 20–1, 42–5, 50–1, 78, 81, 105, 109–10, 130–42, 145, 159, 162; on student loans, 20–1, 45; on voting, 20–1, 48, 131, 196–7. *See also* Qaradawi, Yusuf al-

Facebook, 72, 94, 111

fasting: in Nordic countries, 87–91, 123, 136, 154, 160, 162, 164–5, 167, 204; practicing sports and, 156

fatwa, 3–8, 10–11, 13–15, 26–7, 38–9, 42, 55–6

Fatwa Global Center (of al-Azhar University, Cairo), 42

Faulkner, William, 7

Fawzan, ʿAbdallah b. Salih al-, 32–6, 58, 61

Federation of Islamic Organizations in Europe, 38, 65, 105

Federation of Islamic Organizations in the Netherlands, 108

fiqh, 11–15

fiqh al-aqalliyyat al-Muslima, 15–23, 113–5, 119, 127, 151, 178, 217–9; Christmas and, 3, 21, 49–50, 61–2, 72, 96, 104, 131–2, 167, 178–9, 219; *daʿwa* and, 9, 40–1, 44, 46, 49–51, 53–6, 63, 140–2, 186, 188, 190–1, 200; fasting and, 167; loyalty and disavowal and, 49–50, 62; haram in the workplace and, 48, 96, 104, 120, 145, 178; inheritance and, 46–7, 108; marriage to a non-Muslim spouse and, 46–7, 50, 108; migration to the West and, 3, 9, 21, 40–2, 53, 186, 188, 190–1, 200, 207; military service and, 45–6, 57; mortgages and, 18, 21, 42–5, 50–1, 56, 96, 103–5, 109, 131–2, 142–5, 167; student loans and, 21, 45, 96, 104; voting and, 21, 48, 131

Fiqh Council of North America, 42

fitna, 13, 28, 36, 79

Flynn, Emma, 8

Ghazali, Abu Hamid Muhammad al- (d. 1111), 27

Ghazali, Muhammad al- (d. 1996), 23, 100, 185–6, 229–30n32, 230n33

Ghudayan, ʿAbdallah al-, 95

Gibril, Mustafa, 72–3

Ginzburg, Carlo, 7

The Grand Mosque of Iceland, 16, 19, 110*t*, 117, 123, 127–8*t*,

272 Index

The Grand Mosque of Iceland
(*continued*)
131–2*t*, 140, 148*t*, 157, 170–1, 176,
226–7n30, 227n31; *adhan* and, 85;
development of, 81–6; Ramadan
fast and, 90–1; hostel and, 83,
170–1; museum and, 85; relations
with Saudi Arabia and, 82–3, 85–6
greater jihad. See under *jihad al-nafs*
Green Lane Mosque (Birmingham),
101–2, 194, 209, 214–5
Gulf Crisis (1990–1), 96, 232n69

haja: *maslaha* and, 27, 35, 41, 52, 165;
mortgages and, 43–8, 81, 137,
139–41
Halawa, Hussein, 38, 51–2
Hanafi, 44, 78–9
Hanbal, Ahmad b., 30
Hanbali, 35, 37, 44, 53
Haqq, 'Ali Jad al-, 88
haraj, 26–7, 38–40, 43–4, 51, 56, 59–60,
105
Hasan, Suhaib, 52
Hassan Blidi Mosque (Marseille), 19,
102–3, 106, 110*t*, 117, 127–8*t*, 131*t*,
144, 148*t*, 194, 227n31
Hay'at Kibar al-'Ulama' (Saudi
Arabia). *See under* Council of
Senior Scholars
hijab, 40, 103, 220–2; hijab ban and,
104, 193
Hijra, 206–7
Holland, Norman, 7
Husby Mosque (Stockholm), 19, 70–3,
110*t*, 127–8*t*, 131*t*, 141, 148*t*, 176,
193, 227n31; *salafiyya* and, 72
Husby riots, 70

Ibn Abbas Center, 70, 72–4, 116–17, 212
Ibn 'Affan, 'Uthman, 206
Ibn al-Qayyim al-Jawziyya, 30–2, 61,
142

Ibn Baz, 'Abd al-'Aziz b. 'Abdallah,
30–1, 34–5, 37, 62–3, 72, 101,
231n51, 239n68, 239n69; on loyalty
and disavowal, 60–1; on migration
to the West, 54–5
Ibn Hadi, Muqbil, 73
Ibn Sa'ud, 'Abd al-'Aziz 'Abd
al-Rahman, 29, 35
Ibn Sa'ud, Muhammad, 37
Ibn Taymiyya, Taqi al-Din, 30–1,
33–4, 36–7, 47, 50, 231–2n56
Ibn Taymiyya Brixton Mosque
(London), 101
Iceland-Palestine Association, 82
ifta', 146, 151; Abu Khadeejah Abdul-
Wahid on, 100, 119; Salim Blidi
on, 194; Bourouba, Farid on, 105;
European Council for Fatwa and
Research and, 9, 107–10, 115,
119–20, 124–7; foundations of,
11–18; Khaled al-Dib on, 69;
Johannes Klominek on, 73; Ahmad
Sadiq on, 87; *salafiyya* and, 53, 62;
The Salafi Mosque and, 177
ijtihad, 25–6, 35, 58, 121–2, 132, 141,
152, 242n10
Ikhwan. *See under* Muslim Brothers
innovation. See under *bid'a*
interest. See under *riba*
International Union of Muslim
Scholars, 24, 51
Islamic Association in Stockholm, 65
Islamic Association in Sweden, 65
Islamic banking, 21, 42–3, 137, 140,
150, 158, 162
Islamic Cultural Center of Iceland, 83
Islamic Cultural Centre of
Ireland, 38
Islamic Fiqh Council (Saudi
Arabia), 13
Islamic Foundation of Iceland, 82
Islamic State in Iraq and Syria, 31, 63,
90, 95, 98–9, 159, 192, 203

Islamic University of al-Madina, 30, 53, 73, 117
Islamization, 51, 92, 186, 190, 210, 212

Jaballah, Ahmad, 49, 52
Jabiri, ʿUbayd al-, 95
Jamaʿat al-Tabligh, 72, 98, 169–70
Jamaat-e-Islami, 175
Jamaʿiyyat Ihyaʾ Minhaj as-Sunnah, 95
Jamayki, ʿUmar, 101
Jamaʿiyyat Usul al-Din (Morocco), 85
jihad al-nafs, 72, 150
jihadi-salafiyya, 25, 31, 63, 75, 96, 98–9, 103–4
Judaism, 6, 81, 121, 150, 180
Judayʿ, ʿAbdallah b. Yusuf al-, 51–2

Katz, Elihu, 7
Kern, Soeren, 108
Khaled, Amr, 206–7
Khalfi, Mahmud, 68
Khan, Hafeezullah, 101, 194
Khayari, Muhammad, 158, 242–3n21
King ʿAbdallah (Saudi Arabia), 82
King Muhammad I University (Morocco), 78
Klominek, Johannes, 70, 73–4, 141–3, 179, 192–4, 244–5n78
kufr, 33, 46

Larsen, Lena, 5
Laurence, Jonathan, 108, 112
Liebes, Tamar, 7
London Bridge Attack, 99
loyalty and disavowal, 32–3, 49–50, 57, 60–2, 85, 181, 231n51

madhahib, 11–2, 39, 77, 79, 125; cross-*madhhab* search and, 27, 35, 41, 44, 46, 52, 78, 105
Madkhali, Rabiʿ b. Hadi al-, 63, 95–6, 101–4, 236n179

Makkawi, Muhammad al-, 70–1, 81, 193; on Christmas, 72; on mortgages, 141
Malik, Ismaʿil, 89–91
Maliki, 41, 53, 78–80, 105, 192
marjaʿiyya, 50
Markaz Imam Malik (Dortmund), 19, 80, 110*t*, 127–8*t*, 131*t*, 227n31
Marseille, 103–4
maslaha, 72, 74, 152, 242n10, 242–3n21; foundations of, 27, 35, 121–2, 165; mortgages and, 56–8; *salafiyya* and, 60; *wasatiyya* and, 41, 52
Masri, Abu Hamza al-, 98
Mawardi, Abu al-Hasan b. Habib al-, 40
Mawlawi, Faysal, 197
Mecca, 40, 50, 69, 87–9, 199, 206–7, 212
Ministry for Endowments and Religious Affairs (Qatar), 64
Ministry for Islamic Affairs, Endowments, Daʿwa, and Guidance (Saudi Arabia), 62
Ministry of Endowments (Morocco), 204
muʿamalat, 120, 142
Mubarak, Husni, 129
mufti, 4–6, 10, 12–15
Munajjid, Salih al-, 58, 64
murabaha, 43, 137, 162
Muslim Council of Sweden, 65
Muslim World League, 13, 81, 91, 187
mustafti, 4–6, 10, 13–15
Musulmans de France, 105

Najjar, ʿAbd al-Majid al-, 51, 234–5n130
Nawawi, Yahya ibn Sharaf al-, 121–2
National Fatwa Committee (Malaysia), 234n124
Nayfar, al-Shadhili al-, 41
necessity. See under *darura*
niqab, 28, 36, 86, 92, 96

274   Index

Organization of Ahl al-Sunnah Islamic Societies, 96

Progressive Party (Iceland), 92
proselytizing. See under *da'wa*

qadi, 12, 35, 139
Qaradawi, Yusuf al-, 100, 110–13, 118–19, 125, 127–41, 152; European Council for Fatwa and Research and, 38–9, 108; on Christmas, 3, 21–2, 50, 131–2, 159; on *da'wa*, 25–6, 40–1, 44, 46, 191, 197, 210; on inheritance, 46–7; on marriage to a non-Muslim spouse, 46–7, 50–1; on migration to the West, 21–2, 40–2, 191, 197, 210; on mortgages, 21–2, 42–5, 50–1, 132–42, 145, 159, 162; on student loans, 21–2, 45; on voting, 21–2; Salim Blidi and, 104; The Grand Mosque of Iceland and, 86; The Stockholm Mosque and, 66, 68–9; *wasatiyya* and, 22–9, 185, 228n3, 229n15, 229n24, 229–30n32, 230n33, 230n37. *See also* The European Council for Fatwa and Research
Qarafi, Shihab al-Din al-, 121
Qutb, Sayyid, 25, 31, 96, 191, 231n51

Radway, Janice, 8
Rafiq, Abu Iyad Amjad, 96
Ramadan, 87–92
Ramli, Shams al-Din al-, 40
Rawi, Ahmad, 38
Rayyis, 'Abd al-'Aziz al-, 62–3
Reader Response Theory, 7
Reykjavik, 81–2, 89, 91–2, 157
riba, 42–3, 158
Rida, Muhammad Rashid, 23, 87

Sadiq, Ahmad, 83–7, 123–4; on fasting, 91; on handshakes, 176; on swimming, 157
sahaba, 30, 194
Saify, Mahmoud al-, 108
Salafi Bookstore, 93–4, 102, 112
The Salafi Mosque (Birmingham), 16, 19, 110*t*, 117–20, 127–8*t*, 131–2*t*, 148*t*, 153, 171, 194, 200, 202, 205, 207, 214–15, 226–7n30, 227n31; conference and, 100; converts and, 96, 203, 214; development of, 95–6; Eid prayer and, 101, 214; ethnic composition of, 94; implications of dogmatism and, 174–81, 184; relations with Saudi Arabia and, 95–8, 100–2; schooling and, 184; The Salafi Bookstore and, 93–4, 102. *See also* City Centre Da'wah and Small Heath
Salafi Publications, 93–4, 96, 99, 111, 183, 202–3
Self-Categorization Theory, 153
Shafi'i, 40, 53, 105
shari'a 4, 9–15
Shari'a and Life (TV show), 24, 110, 112
Shaykhi, Salim al-, 45
shirk, 31–2, 37, 161
shura, 27–8, 68, 74, 103
Small Heath, 92, 104, 180, 205, 207
Stockholm, 65–6, 70, 139, 142, 144, 160, 162–4
The Stockholm Mosque, 16, 19, 110–12*t*, 116–17, 127–8*t*, 131*t*, 138, 144, 148*t*, 169, 176, 195–6, 211–12, 226–7n30, 227n31; development of, 65–7; European Council for Fatwa and Research and, 115; haram in the workplace, 163; rivalry with Husby Mosque and, 71–4

Stubbersfield, Joseph, 8
Sufism, 98
Supreme Council of ʿUlama (Morocco), 158, 242–3n21
Swedish Imam Association, 69

tabshir, 25–6, 39–40, 50
Tahrir Square, 129
tajdid, 25–6, 130
Tamimi, Salman, 81–92, 140, 171, 191; on fasting, 91; on handshakes, 176; on swimming, 157
tanfir, 26, 40, 50
taqlid, 25, 228n3
tarbiyya Islamiyya, 152
tawhid, 31–2, 37, 94
taysir, 25–7, 34, 39, 46, 56, 105, 228–9n14, 229n15, 242n10
Tehrani, Jamshid, 8
The Permanent Committee for Scholarly Research and Iftaʾ (Saudi Arabia), 30, 32, 54–5, 59, 64, 175

Umar, Abdallah b., 30, 33, 60
ʿUmar Ibn al-Khattab Mosque (Dortmund), 16, 19, 110t, 127–9t, 125, 131–2t, 195, 201, 226–7n30, 227n31; development of, 75–7;

European Council for Fatwa and Research and, 134
umrah, 213
University of Wales Trinity Saint David, 52
ʿUthaymin, Muhammad b. Salih al-, 30–1, 36; on Christmas, 61–2, 72; on *daʿwa*, 54–5; on haram in the workplace, 59; on loyalty and disavowal, 33, 60; on marriage to a non-Muslim spouse, 58; on migration to the West, 54, 59; on service in a non-Muslim military force, 57

Vaisse, Justin, 108, 112
van Esdonk, Susanne, 108
Vatican, 120
Vogel, Pierre, 78

Wah, Ibrahim al-, 158
Wahhabi, 29–31, 53
Walʿani, ʿAbd al-ʿAziz al-, 85–6; on mortgages, 141; on swimming, 157

Zahir, Yusuf, 77–8
zakat, 114
Zawahiri, Ayman al-, 31
Zweig, Stefan, 3

Milton Keynes UK
Ingram Content Group UK Ltd.
UKHW041335110124
435867UK00006B/44